Troubled Neighbours

READING UNIVERSITY STUDIES
ON CONTEMPORARY EUROPE

Troubled Neighbours

Franco-British Relations in the
Twentieth Century

Edited by
Neville Waites

Weidenfeld and Nicolson
5 Winsley Street London W1

ISBN 0 297 00433 6

Printed in Great Britain by
Cox & Wyman Ltd., London, Reading and Fakenham

Contents

Contents

Contributors

Anthony Adamthwaite was lecturer in history at University College, Cardiff, until recently. He is now lecturer in modern history with the Open University. He has written a doctoral thesis on French policy during the Munich Crisis and he is at present completing a study of French policy and the coming of the Second World War for publication.

Christopher Andrew is Director of Studies in History at Corpus Christi College, Cambridge. His publications include *Théophile Delcassé and the Making of the Entente Cordiale* (1968), *The First World War: Causes and Consequences* (1970) and articles in the *Historical Journal* and the *Journal of Contemporary History*. He is now preparing a history of French foreign policy in the nineteenth century, and a study of the French 'colonial party'.

Maurice Baumont is a member of the Institut de France. He was an attaché with the Reparations Commission from 1920 to 1927 and served on the Secretariat of the League of Nations from 1939–48. He directed the French publication of the secret archives of the Wilhelmstrasse. He is the author of many distinguished studies of diplomatic history between the two world wars.

P.M.H. Bell is senior lecturer in modern history at the University of Liverpool. His publications include *Disestablishment in England and Wales* (1969), and articles on the Second World War and its origins, notably in the *Revue d'Histoire de la Deuxième Guerre Mondiale*. He is engaged in further research into the British naval attack on France at Mers-el-Kebir in 1940.

Guy de Carmoy is Professor at the Institut d'Études Politiques in Paris, and at the European Institute of Business Administration at Fontainebleau. He has written *French Foreign Policies 1944–1968* (1970) and *The Last Year of de Gaulle's Foreign Policy* in *International Affairs* (1970). He has just completed *Le Dossier de l'Énergie en Europe* (1971).

Jean-Baptiste Duroselle is Professor at the Sorbonne (University of Paris) and has written many authoritative studies of diplomatic history in the twentieth century, notably *Histoire diplomatique de 1919 à nos jours* (5th edition, 1970).

Douglas Johnson is Professor of Modern History at University College, University of London. He has written several authoritative studies in nineteenth- and twentieth-century French history, notably *Guizot* and *France and the Dreyfus Affair*. He has been engaged in research on Sir Austen Chamberlain for some years.

Keith Sainsbury is senior lecturer in politics at the University of Reading. He has written on the Government of South Australia in *The Government of the Australian States* (ed. S. R. Davis, 1960) and *Australian Foreign Policy since 1949* (1954). He has just published a *Select Bibliography of Contemporary History 1939–70* (Historical Association, 1971). His current research is on Turkish foreign policy, and on Anglo-French relations in the Second World War.

Hugh Thomas is Professor of Modern History at the University of Reading. His books include *The Spanish Civil War* (1961), *The Suez Affair* (1967) and *Cuba* (1971).

Neville Waites is lecturer in French history at the University of Reading. His doctoral thesis is on Franco-British relations and the German problem, 1929–34, he contributed to *Contemporary History in Europe* (edited by D. C. Watt, 1969) and he is currently writing a biography of Aristide Briand.

Geoffrey Warner is Reader in Politics at the University of Reading. He has written *Pierre Laval and the Eclipse of France* (1968). His current research is on the Second World War and the origins of the Cold War.

D. R. Watson is lecturer in modern history at the University of Dundee. He has contributed to *The Right in France* (edited by D. Shapiro, 1962) and is the author of numerous articles in the *Historical Journal*, the *English Historical Review*, etc. He is writing a biography of Clemenceau, to be published in 1972.

Ann Williams is lecturer in Mediterranean History at the University of Aberdeen (seconded to the Royal University of Malta, 1969–71). She has written a number of articles on Mediterranean history and her most recent publication is *Britain and France in the Middle East and North Africa* (1969).

Introduction

Neville Waites

It may soon be unnecessary to discuss Franco-British relations as a particularly important element in European and Western politics. Yet only fifty years ago both nations commanded independent empires larger than any the world has ever known, and their recurrent rivalry was a cause for concern in all parts of the earth. Those days are gone for ever; the reasons for their passing and for recent changes in the relations between Britain and France are the subject of this book. The hub of knowledge about recent history is the main concern of the authors, 'the still point of the turning world',[1] though they also provide interconnected spokes of information and analysis which help to reveal the legacy of history to the passing present and to the imminent future. The book ends with the sombre reflection that the legacy has been more a liability than an asset; but an effort to understand recent history may help to avert unnecessary pain caused by our inescapable past.

Many aspects of recent history require a division of labour if research is to cover the evidence piled up by the typewriter and the copying machine, and scattered around the world by means of modern communications. The studies commissioned for this book have been written by specialists in their subjects who know the primary sources of evidence and the work of other historians in the same field. They seek detachment from nationalistic prejudices disturbing current world politics; and for that reason no attempt has been made to balance the number of British and French historians contributing to the book as if it were a tug-of-war contest, nor to earmark topics merely with regard to traditional Franco-British sensitivities.

The book sets out to explore the major developments in the chequered relations between British and French governments

[1] T. S. Eliot, *Four Quartets* (London, Faber 1959) p. 15.

since the beginning of the century. The intention is not to provide a linear narrative, but to highlight the points of change from bad to good relations, and *vice versa*, while distinguishing influences of national policy, personality or sheer accident. Judgements are supported as far as possible by clear evidence, and wherever the sources of evidence are either ambiguous or inadequate possible differences of interpretation have been made explicit. Both professional and amateur readers will find footnote references and bibliographies of considerable value in judging the reliability of opinions, or as a tool for their own further research. Each chapter can be read both as a self-contained study and as a contribution to the broader themes of the book. These recurrent themes are firstly, the frequently forgotten need for Britain and France to organise themselves on international lines to ensure the security and prosperity of Europe as a whole, and secondly, the importance of security in the Mediterranean area originally in the imperial interests and now in the national interests of Britain and France. Europe and the Mediterranean: two areas where British and French roles have been quite different, but where their basic needs have always proved to be remarkably similar.

Clearly, the scope of this book is broad and ambitious. But to fix a purpose requires restraint as well as ambition. Attention has been concentrated on policy rather than on public opinion. In these studies economic relations are only discussed when they influence foreign policy, for instance in the world wars, in the depression, or in moves towards European unity; regular trade and currency relations have not been given separate treatment. Restraint has also been exercised with regard to other interesting aspects of Franco-British relations, for example communications media, cultural exchanges, international political organisations, migration and tourism, inter-marriage, education in history, geography, language and literature, most of which lie inexplicably beyond the frontiers of present research.

The historians involved in this project were motivated by concern about the limitations of available published material on recent Franco-British relations, and by the need for a book that was both up-to-date in reliable detail and broad enough in scope to help readers distinguish the wood from the trees.

Nearly thirty years ago the subject was treated admirably by Wolfers,[1] and then by Jordan.[2] Despite residual merits, however, their work must be re-examined in the light of the large collections of official documents, political memoirs, and private papers made available to historians since the Second World War, much of this new evidence requiring years of painstaking research and thoughtful assimilation. This is why more recent studies, for example those by Monger,[3] Furnia[4] and Pickles,[5] have chosen a narrower focus. And for the same reason the authors of this book, while attempting a comprehensive review of Franco-British relations since the beginning of this century, were fully aware that their achievement might be limited to that of an interim study or a progress report on their research and on the work of historians in their field. The overriding determination to put pen to paper came firstly from a refusal to wait another five or ten years before improving the reading material available to those interested in the subject, and secondly, from an anxious awareness that important international decisions are being made at present on the basis of assumptions about the history of Franco-British relations which are either questionable or downright false.

Two words are used most frequently to describe the ups and downs of Franco-British relations: *entente* and perfidy. Unlike those writers on the subject who prefer to use one or the other, the authors of this book have encompassed both. They have accepted the difficult but interesting truth that both understanding and distrust, co-operation and competition, are endemic in relations between neighbouring states. Moreover, the geographical relationship is treated here more flexibly than, for example, in Sir Lewis Namier's famous rule of odd and even numbers according to which he claimed:

[1] A. Wolfers, *Britain and France Between Two Wars* (USA, Harcourt, Brace, 1940; reprinted by W. W. Norton, 1966).

[2] W. M. Jordan, *Great Britain, France, and the German Problem, 1918–1939* (Oxford University Press, for the Royal Institute of International Affairs, 1943).

[3] G. Monger, *The End of Isolation* (London, Nelson, 1963).

[4] A. H. Furnia, *The Diplomacy of Appeasement: Anglo-French Relations and the Prelude to World War II, 1931–1938* (USA, Washington DC, University of Columbia Press, 1960).

[5] D. Pickles, *The Uneasy Entente* (Oxford University Press, for the Royal Institute of International Affairs, 1966).

On the Continent the game of power politics, in whatever terms it was played, normally made a neighbour into an enemy, and therefore the neighbour's neighbour on the opposite flank into an ally. Hence the rule of odd and even numbers in international politics: if Germany was France's enemy, then Poland was France's ally, and consequently Russia the ally of Germany – numbers one and three against two and four: and even sharp ideological divisions between Germany and Russia could not prevent that rule from asserting itself in 1922 and 1939.[1]

The studies in this book make it clear that periods of intermittent rivalry between neighbouring states must be considered along with periods of co-operation, in the face of danger or when pursuing a common aim. Strength through co-operation has been appreciated by most states at one time or another in recent history, above all by Britain and France.

Specific developments in Franco-British relations must be seen in the context of a recent revolution in world politics resulting in the loss of European primacy; Britain and France have suffered a sudden fall in their importance on the world stage. Economically the fall was apparent at the beginning of the century, but it was not clear on the political level until much later. This was because there was no automatic correlation between economic potential and political ambition. In the case of the United States, for example, great wealth was accompanied by political isolationism until the Second World War. Conversely, British and French ambition for world power and responsibility long survived their loss of economic and military pre-eminence. The unpalatable realisation of their vulnerability had to be swallowed in the European conflict of 1940, but they did not fully acquire a taste for it in world politics until the frustrating Suez crisis of 1956, which was followed by a period of remarkably rapid decolonisation. The revolution in the power-structure of the world at large has frequently brought about changes in Franco-British relations and adds a further dimension to the subject.

At the beginning of the twentieth century Britain and France had a long tradition of rivalry and were competing for world power. Their imperial influence extended far beyond that of Germany, Russia or the United States, though at certain points it was limited and troubled by those powers.

[1] L. B. Namier, *Vanished Supremacies: Essays on European History* (London, Hamish Hamilton, 1958), p. 170.

The 'Entente Cordiale' in 1904 involved a division of interests primarily intended to relieve the pressure on tightly stretched imperial resources. The rise of German power was only one of several reasons for anxiety at that time, and it was only later that the Entente became a convenient basis for an alliance in war. Even so, it was mainly adapted to suit the security needs of Western Europe and the Mediterranean. When a crisis in Eastern Europe in 1914 led to the outbreak of war, the Entente narrowly avoided breakdown (see Chapter 1).

During the First World War, it became paradoxically clear that only the closest co-operation at a supra-national level could save the British and French empires and the national independence of the mother countries. Victory was ultimately achieved through an unselfish fusion of leaders and resources, after painful teething troubles, that earned the lasting admiration of the enemy; and the experience of comradeship in war left a deep impression on British and French minds which has not hitherto received its due recognition. The experiment in supra-national planning and decision-making, in particular, created a new breed of international civil servants and administrators, notably Jean Monnet and Lord Salter, who were inspired to work tirelessly for international co-operation after the war was over (see Chapter 2).

Although seriously weakened by the First World War, Britain and France remained effectively the strongest powers in the world. The embryonic strength of the revolutionary Soviet Union was very slow to materialise. American economic power did not create a sense of political responsibility for world affairs among the people and politicians of the United States; they rejected the Versailles Treaty and the League of Nations in favour of a policy of isolationism. Britain and France were to shoulder the main responsibility for the application of the peace settlement of 1919. That is why their agreements and differences in the making of the Treaty were so important. The Versailles Treaty was inevitably a mixture of severity and justice, and it required energetic support and vigilance even if it was in later years to be modified in certain details. Yet Britain and France were preoccupied with licking their own wounds and restoring their traditional imperial power along with the patched-up fabric of the pre-1914 world. This left the Versailles Treaty dangerously vulnerable to its critics in the 1920s (see Chapter 3).

An important part of the pre-war way of life had been Franco-British imperial rivalry. With no immediate threat to the security of Western Europe, this rivalry was temporarily renewed, particularly in the Middle East. The European nations, however, especially the Germans, were under no illusion that the Entente had ceased to be a basic component part of British and French foreign policies. Its influence was confirmed by the debate in Britain on the Locarno treaties; British ministers were concerned to limit their commitments to the security of Western Europe to a minimal level, not to offer Germany effective military protection in her dealings with France (see Chapter 4, and the first part of Chapter 12).

The British were rapidly losing interest in Europe as a whole. For that reason British policy was neither deliberately anti-French nor positively encouraging towards German political ambitions for a change in the European balance of power, contrary to the belief of many historians. The British simply wanted Europe to be quiet and to leave them free to concentrate on their affairs in the Commonwealth and the world at large. This was the real and original meaning of 'appeasement' and it was reinforced by the problems arising during the depression years. If Germany benefited from appeasement in the later 1930s, it had nevertheless operated in favour of France in the period up to the autumn of 1933. But the strong position France had established in that earlier period was tragically destroyed by the depression and the advent of Hitler to power in Germany (see Chapter 5).

Faced with the revival of aggressive German nationalism in the 1930s, the British and French failed to organise an effective security system for Europe. France had accepted responsibility for European security but felt that she no longer had the power to fulfil her responsibility alone. Britain, for her part, whatever her power, was almost totally devoid of a sense of responsibility for European affairs by 1936. Irrespective of the moral right of Germany to move troops into her own Rhineland, the strategic implications of the move and the stimulus it gave to German aggression were of paramount importance. The British and

French failure to check Hitler in 1936 proved fatal (see Chapter 6).

The importance of the Munich crisis in 1938 was the change it caused in British policy towards an acceptance of responsibility for the security of Europe as a whole. This change was carried further in 1939 by the offer of British guarantees to most states in Eastern Europe, so that the invasion of Poland by Hitler brought an automatic declaration of war from London in contrast to the confusion and heart-searching that arose from the Serbian crisis in 1914. Unfortunately, Britain did not have the power to protect Eastern Europe and fulfil her new responsibilities in 1938–9. France too had insufficient power and practised a complex policy of calculated irresponsibility towards Eastern Europe, apparently in order to bring about British involvement in the Munich crisis and thereby to create an adequate deterrent to dissuade Hitler from military action. Whatever the tactical successes of French diplomacy, they soon proved inadequate. Hitler was not deterred for long (see Chapter 7).

However anachronistic it may seem today, in 1940 Britain and France still occupied the central position on the world stage, though by that time the difficulty of having responsibility without real power was already painfully obvious. For that reason, the centre of gravity of the recent history of Franco-British relations lies undoubtedly in the Second World War. In 1940, the French empire was suddenly eclipsed and the British empire was narrowly saved from collapse. The painful experience of 1940, although quite different on one side of the Channel from the other, had lasting traumatic effects on both nations and their leaders (see Chapter 8).

By his courageous stand in June 1940 on what appeared likely to be the losing side, defying a death sentence in his absence from France, General de Gaulle formed a Free French movement which, in liaison with the French Resistance, gave the French people an honourable part to play in the Allied victory five years later. This was a valuable compensation for the *débâcle* of 1940 and also provided a sound basis for French national cohesion after peace was restored. Meanwhile, Churchill led Britain through the perilous summer of 1940 to ultimate victory within the Alliance. But the victory of this 'second wartime alliance' was only achieved through the total involvement of the Soviet Union and the United States. This meant that both de Gaulle and Churchill had a constant struggle to ensure recognition of their national identities and interests during and after the war; and their choice of different methods to achieve their aims, in keeping with their very different roles in the war, led to considerable friction between the two men, though never to the extent that their great mutual respect was eroded. Their protection of the British and French empires was often discouraged by their allies, and for that reason the outcome of the war in the Mediterranean was almost as important to them as victory in Europe. Hence too the importance they attached to rebuilding imperial power after 1945 (see Chapter 9, and the second part of Chapter 12).

Faced primarily with the task of reconstructing their national life after 1945, Britain and France worked independently within their quite different political traditions, co-operating occasionally in the pursuit of aims temporarily shared, for example in the distribution of Marshall Aid. But these were the years when vital decisions had to be taken on the reconstruction, political organisation and military security of Europe. France was less self-absorbed than Britain during this post-war period, partly because of her close involvement in the economic and political future of Germany. The British preference at that time for a national rather than a supra-national approach to post-war reconstruction created intractable long-term problems in their relationship with France and with other European states. Britain and France co-operated, nevertheless, when faced with a common danger, both joining NATO for defence against the Soviet Union; but that did not prevent jealousy and mutual recrimination over their status within the Western Alliance and their determination to maintain what was left of their imperial power (see Chapter 10).

Britain and France were brought together briefly in 1956 by a common danger to their imperial authority in the Middle East. Despite initial military success at Suez, their power did not match the responsibility they had assumed. The confused military and political planning of the operation, and the subsequent need to bow to the will of the United States

and the Soviet Union and to world opinion in general, led to
considerable frustration and disappointment for Britain and
France. This was their last major military operation as
independent world powers (see Chapter 11).

The failure of Britain and France to reassert their control
of the Middle East in 1956 increased the tempo of the decolonisation process which they found hard to accept. They
became reconciled to the loss of empire by the early 1960s,
but were then faced with the need to adapt this new situation
to meet the continuing requirements of national security.
The Mediterranean will always be a French frontier, and for
the foreseeable future it will be a lifeline for the supply of
vital resources, particularly oil, to Britain. Whatever the
outcome of the debate on retaining a presence 'east of Suez',
there is no retreat from 'east of Gibraltar'. Nevertheless, by
1970 Britain and France were playing a very minor role in the
Middle East. Despite many common interests, their policies
were disunited and confused regarding the future security of
the Mediterranean area (see Chapter 12).

Equally important issues for Britain and France were at
stake in the economic, political, and military organisation of
Western Europe. Franco-British rivalry in this sphere, following the loss of their empires, generated a remarkable intensity of feeling compressed as it was by the restricted
scope for activity and interest. But if there was 'a negative
balance-sheet' at the end of the 1960s, there had been at least
a decade of debate on the choices facing Britain, France and
Europe, which offered some prospect of fruitful decisions in
the 1970s (see Chapter 13).

As medium-sized powers Britain and France have sometimes appeared in recent years to be struggling for mere
prestige rather than for real responsibility. If their residual
influence were to be based on persuasion and example,
however, instead of on belief in coercion and leadership, it
could make an important contribution to international
democracy as an alternative to the sterile division of the world
into power blocs. They have an obvious opportunity to contribute to the prosperity and security of Europe and the
Mediterranean. An improvement in Franco-British relations
arising from acceptance of that opportunity would be more
profitable than merely reacting to the stimuli from the

political revival of West Germany and from the pressure
exerted by the Soviet Union and the United States. In any
event, it is hard to believe that present problems caused by
jockeying for position and influence in Europe will prevent
for long the reappearance of the generous respect and co-
operation that has formed so rich a vein running through the
history of Franco-British relations in the twentieth century.

Note on Sources

The French Government introduced a 30-year rule in the
summer of 1970. Official documents have to be catalogued,
however, before they will be available for consultation by
historians. The timetable for cataloguing varies from one
archive to another, and historians should write directly to
the archives for precise information. In the case of the Quai
d'Orsay documents will be released in two sections. Those up
to 1929 will be made available in 1973, and those up to 1945
in 1976, when the 30-year rule will be fully applied. In the
meantime, historians with specific problems relating to
Franco-British relations during the period 1918–45, may be
granted a *dérogation* by archivists at the Quai d'Orsay to
enable them to consult certain files for the purposes of
research. Such facilities may be granted immediately if the
files concerned have already been catalogued, as is the case
with most files relating to the contents of this book. Applications and enquiries should be made directly to the Quai
d'Orsay. This is the most up-to-date information on sources
at the time of going to press and supersedes information
given in the individual bibliographies.

1 The Entente Cordiale from its Origins to 1914

Christopher Andrew

There is no single satisfactory interpretation of the significance of the Entente Cordiale.[1] At different times and to different men it has meant quite different things. President Coty claimed on its fiftieth anniversary that 'the convention of 8 April 1904 embodied the agreement of our two peoples on the necessity of safeguarding the spiritual values of which we were the common trustees'. It was to something like this interpretation of the Entente that Winston Churchill appealed in 1940 when he made his famous offer to France of an Anglo-French union. There were few statesmen on either side of the Channel in 1904 who shared so romantic a view. The convention of 8 April 1904 amounted, on paper, simply to a settlement of the colonial disputes outstanding between France and England. The basis of this settlement was a transaction characteristic of the diplomacy of imperialism. 'In a word', said Paul Cambon, the French ambassador, at the beginning of negotiations, 'we give you Egypt in exchange for Morocco.'

The exchange of Egypt for Morocco did not in itself imply any change in the European alignment of either France or Britain. Paradoxically, indeed, this exchange was first proposed not by the supporters of better relations between France and England but by a group of French colonialists, the most vociferous French opponents of British foreign policy. Until almost the end of the nineteenth century no French colonialist was prepared even to consider any suggestion that Egypt become a British protectorate.[2] The strongest pressure for the decision to challenge the British presence in Egypt by sending a French expedition to Fashoda came from a powerful colonialist pressure group, the *Comité de l'Afrique Française*. Captain Marchand, the leader of the expedition, regarded the *Comité* as his only reliable supporters. And yet in 1898, at almost the moment of Marchand's arrival at Fashoda, the official journal of the *Comité* suddenly suggested French recognition for British supremacy in Egypt in return for British recognition of French supremacy in Morocco.

On the eve of the signing of the Entente Cordiale in 1904 Eugène Étienne, the leader of the French colonialist movement, claimed quite rightly that the *Comité* had been the first to discover the eventual basis for the diplomatic reconciliation of France and England. But the *Comité*'s original suggestion of an Egypt–Morocco barter in 1898 did not proceed from any feeling of friendship for England. It reflected only the reluctant recognition that France no longer had any realistic hope of preventing a British protectorate in Egypt. What influence France still retained in Egypt, Étienne believed, was useful only as a bargaining counter to secure compensation elsewhere. The *Comité*, in other words, called for an exchange of interests in Egypt and Morocco not as a way to draw closer to England but as a means to make Morocco French.

The strongest supporters of an agreement with England based on the barter of Egypt for Morocco were a small group of Moroccan enthusiasts led by Étienne. Four months before the signing of the Entente this group became the nucleus of a new *Comité du Maroc*, formed as a 'special committee' of the *Comité de l'Afrique Française*. Neither Étienne nor his followers looked on Morocco as a colony in the ordinary sense, least of all simply as another *colonie d'exploitation*. It was to be instead a future part, like Algeria, of a Greater France spanning both shores of the Mediterranean sea. 'It is not a colony', said Paul Bourde, perhaps the most influential of Étienne's followers. 'It is a part of France herself.' For almost five years, from the Fashoda crisis of 1898 to the eve of the Entente negotiations in 1903, Étienne's group continued to urge on Delcassé, the French foreign minister, their proposal for an agreement with England based on the barter of Egypt for Morocco.

Étienne's influence on Delcassé reached its peak after the elections of May 1902. In the new Chamber of Deputies Étienne was in a position of quite exceptional parliamentary power. He was leader of the colonialist pressure group in the Chamber, the *groupe colonial*, to which a third of all the deputies now belonged. And he was leader, too, of the Union

Démocratique, a republican faction on which the Combes government (in office from June 1902 to January 1905) depended for its majority. 'It is a fact', wrote Delcassé's private secretary in spring of 1903, 'that Étienne holds the fate of the cabinet in his hands.' Étienne's ability to influence Delcassé's policy was clearly demonstrated by the campaign which he conducted against a frontier treaty with Siam negotiated by Delcassé in October 1902. Colonialist opposition to this treaty was so strong that for a time Delcassé's survival as foreign minister seemed in doubt because of it. In February 1903, having weathered this opposition for four months, Delcassé gave way to it, and promised in a letter to Étienne to renegotiate the treaty. At almost the same moment Delcassé finally decided to seek an agreement with England based on the barter of Egypt and Morocco. It is reasonable to suppose that this decision reflected, at least in part, the influence of Étienne.

Delcassé's attitude towards England when he became foreign minister in 1898 was ambivalent. On the one hand he had long looked on an understanding with England as highly desirable from the point of view of France's European security. As a journalist during the 1880s he had called publicly for a Triple Entente of England, France and Russia: an idea to which he returned in his first meetings with the British ambassador in 1898. But in colonial affairs he had relished his public reputation as 'the man who insists on not giving way to John Bull'. As undersecretary and minister of colonies (from 1893 to 1895) he had shown himself far readier than the rest of the cabinet to run the risks of colonial conflict with England.

During his first year as foreign minister Delcassé showed himself anxious to reach a settlement of most of the colonial issues in dispute with England. Even had he been successful, however, no real understanding between France and England would have been achieved. For on both the major issues which separated the two countries – Egypt and Morocco – no negotiation was possible at all. Delcassé still refused to contemplate a British protectorate in Egypt; Lord Salisbury, the British Conservative prime minister, refused to consider a French protectorate in Morocco. Even the negotiations on more minor colonial problems made little progress. In August 1899 Delcassé spoke to the British ambassador, Sir Edward Monson, in what Monson considered 'a studiously impressive manner', of 'the impossibility of keeping relations with England on a friendly footing'. Salisbury himself concluded that Anglo-French relations could never rise higher than 'a mutual temper of apathetic tolerance' and that 'anything like a hearty good will between the two nations will not be possible'. Salisbury, moreover, was regarded as better disposed than most of his colleagues towards France, and in 1899 he was known to be nearing retirement. On the Continent even more than in England, the coming man was thought to be the arch-imperialist Joseph Chamberlain, probably the English statesman of whom most Frenchmen were most distrustful. Even Salisbury had said in 1898 that he could never decide whether 'war with France . . . is part of Chamberlain's object or not'.

In retrospect all French statesmen were agreed that the chastening experience of the Boer War, by ending the popularity of 'splendid isolation', marked a major turning point in British attitudes towards France. 'Without the South African War which bled Great Britain and made her wiser,' wrote Cambon, 'the Anglo-French agreement would have been impossible.' There were many British statesmen who were inclined to agree. Sir Edward Grey used the same metaphor as Cambon: 'Before the Boer War we were spoiling for a fight. . . . Now this generation has had enough excitement, and has lost a little blood and is sane and normal again.' However, when the Boer War began in October 1899 no European statesman supposed that the war would do anything but make the chances of a settlement between France and England still more remote. As a gesture of protest against French sympathy for the Boer cause, Queen Victoria cancelled her annual visit to the Riviera; instead, she 'heroically substituted a visit to Ireland', her first for many years. Cambon believed that there were a number of English statesmen (Chamberlain chief among them) who were quite capable of following the Boer War by an assault on Madagascar or some other part of the French Empire.[3] For a time the French government viewed such a possibility with utmost seriousness. At Delcassé's request the *Conseil Supérieur de la Guerre* considered a number of contingency plans for war with England: among them schemes for the invasion of England or of Egypt. As a condition of French loans to her ally, Russia, Delcassé was also able to insist that Russia construct a strategic railway from Orenburg to Tashkent to enable her to threaten India.

During the first six months of the Boer War Delcassé made two separate attempts to persuade Germany to join with the Dual Alliance (France and Russia) in demanding that England end her military occupation of Egypt. He abandoned these attempts because, as he told a friend, 'at Berlin we ran up against a brick wall'. Delcassé had always known that to bring effective pressure on Britain in Egypt France would need German support. By the spring of 1900 he knew also that he had no chance of gaining that support. That realisation marks an important stage in the origins of the Entente Cordiale, for it was an essential first step towards his adoption of the policy of an Egypt–Morocco barter urged on him by Étienne. Throughout the Boer War, however, Delcassé suspected that England might secretly be scheming to turn Morocco into a sphere of influence of her own. His suspicions were not altogether without foundation. On several occasions at the turn of the century Joseph Chamberlain discussed with German diplomats the idea of an Anglo-German division of Morocco; Nicolson, the British minister in Morocco, seems also to have supported such a scheme. In part at least, however, Delcassé's suspicions were simply a reflection of his own dreams of empire. So obsessed was he with the danger of rivals in Morocco that when he became foreign minister in 1898 he had seriously suspected even the United States of Moroccan ambitions.

Delcassé's original plan to make Morocco French, first elaborated during the early months of the Boer War, was essentially an attempt, not to purchase English consent by the offer of territorial compensation as he was urged to do by Étienne, but to override English opposition. The first stage of his plan was to obtain Italian support for French ambitions in Morocco by the offer of French support for Italian claims to Libya. The second stage was to negotiate a Franco-Spanish partition of Morocco in which the lion's share would go to France. The general framework of this plan remained unchanged until the end of 1902. Although

during the summer and autumn of 1902 Delcassé began to
envisage negotiations with England on Morocco, two things
seem certain: first, that he did not intend to begin serious
talks with England until he could present her with the *fait
accompli* of French agreements with Italy and Spain;
secondly that, as Cambon complained, he did not propose to
offer England 'any compensation except the neutrality of the
Straits [of Gibraltar] and freedom of commerce in Morocco'.[4]
At the end of June 1902 Delcassé reached final agreement with
Italy. Early in November he also reached what he believed
was a final agreement with the Spanish ambassador on the
terms of a Franco-Spanish partition of Morocco.

Delcassé's negotiations with Spain were opposed both by
Paul Cambon and by the senior permanent officials at the
Quai d'Orsay. If England and Germany simply refused to
recognise the partition agreed with Spain, they argued, it
would be 'valueless and even dangerous'. Étienne, too, called
the proposed partition 'une politique de casse-cou et
d'aventures'. He and his supporters were bitterly opposed to
the terms of the partition which they regarded as far too
generous to Spain. If the *groupe colonial* in the Chamber was
not prepared to tolerate the terms of Delcassé's frontier convention with Siam it is scarcely likely that it would have
accepted the terms of his partition with Spain.

It is hard to resist the conclusion that Delcassé was saved
from a possibly disastrous agreement with Spain, which
would have been accepted neither by Europe nor the French
Chamber, only by the cold feet of the Spanish government.
The negotiation of the partition in November was followed
by a cabinet crisis in Spain and the emergence of a new
Spanish government. By the beginning of 1903 it was clear
that the new government would refuse to sign the agreement
negotiated by its predecessor. Its motives were the same as
those of Delcassé's advisers: fear of the reaction of England,
and possibly also of Germany, to a partition concluded
without their consent.

At the very moment when his negotiations with Spain were
breaking down, Delcassé began to receive the first convincing
evidence of a general desire within the English government
for a settlement of its differences with France. During the
dozen years before the First World War French statesmen

gradually became accustomed to the gratifying spectacle of the conversion to a pro-French policy of those Englishmen whom they had formerly considered their most formidable opponents. The first of a distinguished line (which later included both Lloyd George and Winston Churchill) was Joseph Chamberlain. Chamberlain's emergence as a friend of France was a consequence of his sudden hostility towards Germany. For several years he had been a persistent advocate of alliance with Germany. When alliance negotiations broke down in 1901, however, Chamberlain came swiftly to believe that Germany had set before him the mirage of an alliance only to distract attention from the real and malevolent aims of German policy. In November 1902 Chamberlain made the first of several overtures to France. He told a French agent that he and the whole British people rejected any idea of association with Germany, and that Britain's future lay in a Triple Entente with France and Russia. The importance attached by French statesmen to Chamberlain's conversion was heightened both by his previous reputation as France's most malevolent British opponent and by the exaggerated estimate held in France of his importance in British politics. Many Frenchmen had been surprised when Balfour, and not Chamberlain, had succeeded Salisbury as prime minister in July 1902, and still regarded Chamberlain as the dominating influence in the British cabinet, especially on questions of foreign policy. 'At the present time,' wrote Cambon in the summer of 1903, 'Chamberlain is the government of England.'

Chamberlain's overtures were swiftly followed by signs of a new readiness by Lord Lansdowne, the British foreign secretary, to seek an understanding with France on Morocco. At the end of 1902 the Foreign Office, like the rest of Europe, was taken unawares by the sudden success of a rebellion in Morocco which threatened to overthrow the ruling dynasty and plunge the country into anarchy. Hitherto Lansdowne had regarded the problem of Morocco as a particularly tiresome one, and had tried to ignore it. Now, however, he was warned by his minister in Tangier that the Moroccan question might soon be opened 'in a most complicated form'. Lansdowne's immediate concern was to protect British strategic interests in the Mediterranean. If intervention in Morocco to protect European lives and property should become necessary, he wanted to limit it to as few powers as possible. At the very end of 1902, he agreed with Cambon that if intervention became necessary it should be limited to France, Spain and England, that Germany should be excluded, and that an Anglo-French understanding on Morocco was most desirable. For the moment Lansdowne had no immediate intention of giving British recognition to French ambitions in Morocco. But over the next few months, even though the rebellion itself steadily declined, he came gradually to the conclusion that Morocco was slipping into anarchy and that England was powerless to prevent the country eventually coming under French control.[5]

The breakdown of the negotiations with Spain and the almost simultaneous evidence of England's new-found friendliness for France strengthened enormously the hand of those who urged Delcassé to offer England an exchange of Egypt for Morocco. To the pressure of Étienne was added that of Cambon, now convinced that such a scheme stood a real chance of success. The moment of Delcassé's conversion can be dated almost precisely from a letter written by Cambon to his son on 3 February 1903. Delcassé, said Cambon, now saw the danger of his draft agreement with Spain. He now agreed that England would never accept French supremacy in Morocco on the terms which he had previously been prepared to offer. And he now accepted what he had always hitherto rejected: that the basis of a settlement with England must be 'territorial compensation or the parallel settlement of the Egyptian question'.

Cambon welcomed the news of Delcassé's desire for agreement with England with considerable enthusiasm. But he was not, as is often supposed, an Anglophile. Though he admired the standards of English public life, he considered the English themselves a 'slow-witted' race, 'absolutely devoid of imagination'. He was passionately opposed to the construction of the French Lycée in Kensington on the grounds that it might dissuade the French community in England from educating their children in France. French children brought up in England, said Cambon, soon learned to 'think like Englishmen', with tragic consequences.[6] But whatever his views about the English, he was convinced of the need for agreement with

England: both on the grounds of France's European security and for the furtherance of French ambitions in Morocco. Early in February 1903 he attempted on his own initiative to set negotiations going on the basis now accepted by Delcassé.

On 2 February Cambon succeeded in planting in *The Times* with the help of one of its European correspondents a report that England and France might be in the process of reaching an agreement based on the barter of Egypt for Morocco. Cambon intended that this report should be taken by the Foreign Office as a direct overture from Delcassé, and he succeeded. Monson was indignant that *The Times* should have published 'a bogus telegram' and told Lansdowne: 'There can be little doubt, I fear, that the Ministry of Foreign Affairs inspired and instigated the message.' For the moment, however, Cambon found Lansdowne unwilling to begin negotiations on the 'liquidation' of Morocco.[7] But *The Times* report did have the important effect of arousing the interest of the English pro-consul in Egypt, Lord Cromer, who soon became the most enthusiastic English supporter of an exchange of interests in Egypt and Morocco. It was partly his influence which by the summer of 1903 had persuaded Lansdowne himself of the advantages of such an arrangement.

In March 1903, a month after the report in *The Times*, Edward VII took the initiative in arranging for his own state visit to Paris at the beginning of May. Despite its popular success, the royal visit has usually been considered 'of no diplomatic importance'. To both Cambon and Delcassé, however, the visit had the very highest diplomatic importance, for they believed that Edward had it in his power to determine the direction of English foreign policy. Even Étienne, who at the end of 1902 was still complaining of Delcassé's refusal to begin serious talks with England, found that by April Delcassé could 'think of nothing but King Edward's arrival'. Edward surpassed himself during his visit to Paris. By his determined good nature and practised geniality (a quality which, in the words of his most recent biographer, he had 'developed to the pitch of a fine art') he won over almost everyone with whom he came in contact. In his meetings with French statesmen he made clear his hostility for his German nephew, William II (whom he called *à la fois fou et méchant*), expressed his sympathy with French aspirations in Morocco, and stressed his desire for an understanding between France and England. Though Lansdowne felt obliged on at least one occasion to deliver to the King a tactful lecture on his indiscretions, neither he nor any other member of the cabinet seems to have realised either the extent of those indiscretions or the construction put upon them by the French.

It was probably above all the evidence of Edward's desire for an Anglo-French Entente that persuaded Delcassé to accompany President Loubet on the state visit which he paid to London in July 1903. On 7 July Delcassé told Lansdowne that 'he was entirely in favour of a comprehensive settlement, and that the Egyptian question formed part of the larger African question which could, he felt sure, be disposed of satisfactorily if only we could come to an agreement as to the position of France and Morocco'. This was the first and crucial step in the talks which led nine months later to the signing of the Entente Cordiale. The English cabinet, Balfour told the King, were 'unanimous in their wish to proceed with negotiations' on the basis outlined by Delcassé.

On the basis of the evidence available to them, most ministers probably concluded that the exchange of interests in Egypt and Morocco was, in itself, an advantageous one. According to Lansdowne, Britain was 'powerless' whether she liked it or not, to prevent Morocco gradually falling under French control. On the other hand, Lord Cromer insisted that the concessions which France was prepared to make in Egypt were of the utmost importance and that it would be 'little short of a calamity' if her offer were not accepted.[8] But the cabinet was divided as to the European significance of the proposed agreement. For Chamberlain, as for most of the permanent officials at the Foreign Office, agreement with France would be valuable first and foremost as a check on Germany. But Chamberlain's views were not those of most of his colleagues, and in September 1903 he resigned from the cabinet over the question of tariff reform. For Balfour fear of Germany was far outweighed by fear of Russia: a fear which Delcassé, by his part in promoting the Orenburg–Tashkent railway, had done much to bring about. 'The chief military problem which this country has to face', Balfour believed, 'is that of Indian, rather than of Home, defence.' Lansdowne, though less preoccupied by the danger to India, also welcomed the fact that 'a good understanding with France would not improbably be the precursor of a better understanding with Russia'. For the cabinet as a whole, however, the agreement was essentially a settlement of past disputes with France.

Little attention was paid by most of the cabinet to Germany's likely reaction to the agreement. Even for those, like Balfour, who hoped that it might lead to a similar settlement with France's ally, Russia, there was no feeling that the Entente might be the beginning of a major diplomatic realignment. Balfour, according to a senior official in the Foreign Office, had no idea 'what may be expected from the Anglo-French understanding and would be ready to make an agreement with Germany tomorrow'.[9]

In England the decision to seek an agreement with France was a cabinet decision. In France, on the contrary, it rested on a personal decision by Delcassé. No French foreign minister in modern times has possessed so great a freedom from cabinet control. Delcassé's freedom of action was at its height during the life of the Combes ministry. On the rare occasions when a minister mentioned foreign policy Combes was accustomed to remark, 'Let us leave that subject alone, gentlemen. It is the responsibility of the president and the foreign minister.'[10] Delcassé did not trouble to communicate to his cabinet colleagues the general outline of the Anglo-French agreement until negotiations were in their final stages. The French cabinet accepted the agreement partly because it was accustomed to accept what Delcassé told it. But the success of Edward's state visit and the attitude of Étienne were also important in removing any doubts which the cabinet might have possessed on the acceptability of the Entente both to parliament and to the country at large.

The agreement concluded by France and England on 8 April 1904 was a comprehensive settlement of the colonial disputes outstanding between them, in West Africa, Siam, Madagascar, Newfoundland and New Hebrides, as well as in Egypt and Morocco. The oldest of these disputes – in Newfoundland – went back to the early eighteenth century. But the basis of the whole agreement, immediately christened the

'Entente Cordiale' by press and public opinion, was the exchange of interests in Egypt and Morocco. In April 1904 Delcassé still thought it possible that in six months' time England might regret that she had agreed to this exchange. Despite his caution in assessing the change in British policy to France, however, he attached far more potential significance to the Entente Cordiale than either Balfour or Lansdowne. He was anxious that the Entente should prove not merely a settlement of past colonial disputes but the beginning also of a lasting realignment of European forces. Potentially at least, he regarded the agreement with England as the first step towards the Triple Entente which he had advocated twenty years before as the best guarantee of French security in Europe. 'His great desire', wrote the new English ambassador in Paris, Sir Francis Bertie, early in 1905, 'is, he says, to bring about a rapprochement between England and Russia, for if those two Powers and France acted together, peace would have a long reign.'

That the transformation of the Entente desired by Delcassé did take place was due far less to his own efforts than to the inept diplomacy of Bülow and Holstein, the two architects of German foreign policy during the first Moroccan crisis. Time and time again in the years since unification German statesmen had shown that they could feel secure only in a world in which the other powers were prevented by their mutual hostility from combining against her. The sight of England and France settling differences which the German foreign office had assumed to be permanent was more than either Bülow or Holstein could stand. Germany had a good case for arguing that the Anglo-French agreement took no account of her own rights and interests in Morocco. Many of Delcassé's own advisers urged him unsuccessfully to follow his negotiations with England by negotiations with Germany. But the protection of German rights and interests in Morocco was only a secondary motive in the decision by Bülow and Holstein to provoke the first Moroccan crisis. Their main aim was the destruction of the Entente Cordiale: to prove to France that *any* agreement which she might conclude with Britain without German consent was worthless. If France could be persuaded to submit the Moroccan question to an international conference, then Germany's aims would have been achieved. For, said Bülow, 'It is out of the question the conference should result in handing Morocco ov France.' The Anglo-French agreement would thus have shown to be worthless and the possibility that the Ent Cordiale might one day become a coalition directed against Germany would have been destroyed.

The methods used by Germany ended by achieving precisely that transformation of the Entente which Bülow and Holstein were anxious to prevent. In March 1905 Germany began a war of nerves against France which culminated at the end of May and beginning of June in the threat of armed attack. This war of nerves aroused an even more hostile reaction in England than it did in France. During the closing years of the nineteenth century Lord Salisbury had several times been questioned by the German ambassador about England's attitude in the event of war between France and Germany. His answer had always been the same: 'The course of the English government in such a crisis must depend on the view taken by public opinion in this country.'[11] During the first Moroccan crisis there seemed little doubt about 'the view taken by public opinion'. Even the cool-headed Lansdowne warned the German ambassador that public pressure might force the British government to assist France against German attack.

Whatever his belief about the likely attitude of the British government if the crisis ended in war, Lansdowne was unwilling to commit Britain in advance of war to more than diplomatic support for France. The French, however, mistakenly believed that in May 1905 Lansdowne expressed the willingness of the British government to transform the Entente Cordiale into an agreement containing a binding commitment of British military support. The usual explanation of this belief is that Cambon had simply misunderstood the significance of a proposal by Lansdowne that the two countries begin 'full and confidential discussion . . . in anticipation of any complications to be apprehended during the somewhat anxious period through which we are at present passing.' This explanation is, in itself, inadequate. The famous misunderstanding was only possible because a series of private assurances from British statesmen and service chiefs had already convinced the French Foreign Office that it could count on British support in a war with Germany. 'I know well what his reply will be,' said Cambon when told to raise the question of British support with Lansdowne. Certain of the answer he would receive, he did not doubt the significance of Lansdowne's proposal. It amounted, he said, to a proposal for talks directed towards 'a general agreement which would in reality constitute an alliance'.

Cambon's interpretation of his conversation with Lansdowne was accepted without question by the French government. When the French cabinet discussed the question of British support against Germany on 6 June 1905 not a single minister expressed the slightest doubt about England's willingness to take part in a war with Germany. Some indeed suspected that the English government might actually be anxious for the crisis to end in war. The belief that England had offered France a binding commitment of armed assistance against Germany continued to colour the French interpretation of the Entente Cordiale until the First World War. Even in 1914 both the Quai d'Orsay and the French government believed a formal commitment had been freely offered in May 1905 and that only the fall of the Conservative government at the end of the year had made it impossible to obtain that commitment thereafter.[12]

Though the German war of nerves during the first Moroccan crisis ultimately defeated its own purpose, in the short term it was almost successful. Except for Delcassé, who resigned, the French cabinet decided that even with English support it dare not run the risk of war with Germany. In June 1905 it decided instead to seek a compromise settlement. Rouvier, the French prime minister, offered Germany compensation in the Congo for French supremacy in Morocco as well as co-operation in a variety of fields. Had Germany accepted these terms, the Entente Cordiale would have been destroyed and France might well have been drawn into a policy of continuing co-operation with Germany. The German government, however, found itself trapped by its own previous propaganda. Having publicly demanded an international conference and posed as the defender of Moroccan independence, it felt unable to back down and reach a separate agreement with France. By her own inflexibility Germany alienated those Frenchmen most anxious for agreement with her. Even Rouvier gradually recovered his nerve. In November he told one of his advisers: 'If Berlin thinks it can intimidate me it has made a great mistake. Henceforth, I shall make no further concessions, come what may.' A month later, he authorised the beginning of Anglo-French staff talks to discuss co-operation in a war with Germany.

Under German pressure the colonial understanding of 1904 had come to imply a European understanding also. The new significance of the Entente Cordiale as an informal, defensive coalition directed against Germany became clear as soon as the international conference on Morocco met at Algeciras in January 1906. The conference itself was a major diplomatic defeat for Germany. Contrary to Bülow's confident expectation it was not France but Germany who found herself almost isolated. Throughout the conference France depended on British support. Grey, the new Liberal foreign secretary, dared not refuse that support even when he thought the French unreasonable. 'We can't' he insisted, 'press our advice on them to the point of breaking up the Entente'.[13] If British support appeared to waver, Grey believed that France might well capitulate to Germany as she had almost done in 1905, and leave England isolated. The same fear informed his policy during the last of the Moroccan crises, that of Agadir in 1911. It was fully shared by his advisers. 'If the French get to think that we are ready to give way to Germany,' wrote Bertie, 'we shall help to throw them into the Teuton embrace.'[14]

'An entente between Russia, France and ourselves', wrote Grey during the Algeciras conference, 'would be absolutely secure. If it is necessary to check Germany it could then be done.' In April 1906 he began the negotiations which led eventually to the conclusion of the Anglo-Russian agreement of August 1907. His motive in doing so was primarily fear and suspicion of Germany. He shared the view of one of his advisers that, 'If Great Britain and Russia do not very soon come to an agreement with regard to their respective interests in Persia they may find themselves confronted there with Germany very much as France did in Morocco.' Though Grey, unlike some of his advisers, was genuinely anxious to reduce the tension between England and Germany, he remained constantly afraid of taking any initiative which might

B

endanger the understandings with France and Russia on which he believed British security depended. 'If we sacrifice the other powers to Germany', Grey believed, 'we shall eventually be attacked.'[15]

In January 1906 Cambon raised with Grey (as he had done with Lansdowne eight months before) the question of a formal British commitment of armed support against German aggression. Grey replied that though the British government could give no formal commitment, his own belief was that 'in the event of an attack upon France by Germany arising out of our Morocco Agreement, public feeling would be so strong that no British government could remain neutral'. This statement, Grey wrote later, 'defines the position that was maintained up to the outbreak of war'.[16] It also defined, though this has often been forgotten, the basic reason for French government confidence in British armed support from the Algeciras conference until the eve of the First World War.

The possibility of a European war arising out of a Balkan, rather than a Moroccan, crisis arose for the first time during the twentieth century in the Bosnian crisis of 1908–9. Until almost the end of the crisis Cambon remained uncertain whether British public opinion would take the same uncompromising attitude in a war arising out of Balkan rivalries which he did not doubt it would take in a war over Morocco. Cambon's doubts were resolved by the acceleration of the naval arms race between Britain and Germany. By the final stages of the Bosnian crisis in the spring of 1909 British public opinion appeared to Cambon (and to many others) to have been roused to a state of almost frenzied agitation by fears that for the first time for centuries British naval supremacy was in serious danger. Asquith's government, which had originally intended to build only four dreadnoughts during the next year, was assailed by the slogan 'We want eight and we won't wait' and surrendered to it. 'This new situation', wrote Cambon, 'removes my doubts about England's attitude. . . . If we are drawn into a general European conflict, English opinion will not allow the government to stand aside; this must be obvious to Berlin.'[17] From now until the eve of the First World War Cambon had no doubt about the attitude of British opinion in the event of war. And he remained confident also that in a crisis public opinion would force the British government's hand. His confidence in British opinion, like his version of Lansdowne's offer of support in 1905, was generally accepted by successive French governments.

It has been claimed for Grey by his biographer that he was always scrupulously careful not to promise France 'support which he hoped and wished to give, but which he was not certain to be able to supply when the time came'. There is no doubt that Grey was careful never to raise any hope that the Liberal cabinet might give a *formal* assurance of support. In public he took the position adopted by Salisbury and Lansdowne, that Britain's attitude in a Franco-German war 'would depend entirely on the feeling of parliament and public opinion when the trouble came'. Privately, however, he repeatedly assured Cambon that 'in a crisis public opinion would oblige whatever British government was in power to march with France'. Only a few months before the outbreak of war he told the French prime minister: 'As far as France is concerned, I give you an assurance that no British government would refuse her military and naval assistance if she were unjustly threatened and attacked. Any government which hesitated could not withstand the pressure of English opinion.'[18]

The role of British public opinion was considered so important by the French government largely because of their lack of confidence in at least a section of the Liberal cabinet. The French were well aware that some English ministers regarded the Entente, as interpreted by Grey, as the main obstacle to better relations with Germany. During the eight years before the First World War the most frequent source of French anxiety about English loyalty to the Entente sprang from the influence of the radical wing of the Liberal party and its Labour allies. The disquiet expressed by Jules Cambon (the younger brother of Paul) in 1909 was typical of the fears expressed by many French statesmen. 'I am not', he said, 'exactly *alarmed* about the Entente Cordiale, but I cannot get rid of the feeling that in certain quarters England is getting very German. I allude to a very large portion of the Liberal party and especially to the Labour party who seem to be gaining in influence and power.'[19]

The influence of radical politicians tended, as Jules
Cambon implied, to cause disquiet rather than real alarm.
When a radical statesman publicly advocated better relations
with Germany, Paul Cambon invariably reported that his
views were not those of the British people. The influence of
Edward VII was regarded as an important additional reassurance against a radical foreign policy. 'Tell us what you
want on each point', the King assured Paul Cambon during
the Algeciras conference, 'and we will support you without
restriction and reserve.' Edward's own indiscretions reinforced the vastly exaggerated belief held by French statesmen
in his control of British foreign policy. His presence on the
English throne was seen by both Cambon and the French
nation as a whole as a 'guarantee' of England's loyalty to the
Entente Cordiale. Edward's death in 1910 was regarded in
France as a considerable blow to the Entente. George V,
Cambon regretted, would never have 'the same authority' in
foreign affairs. Bertie frankly informed the Quai d'Orsay
that, like Queen Alexandra, George was rather dim: 'None
of the princes in the Danish royal family is intelligent and the
Prince of Wales is no better than his mother.'[20]

With Edward's death, Cambon gloomily concluded that
there was not a single statesman of real stature left in
England. Only Lloyd George and Winston Churchill, he
observed prophetically, really possessed the gift of leadership: but for the moment they were still *trop nouveaux venus*
and inspired too little trust. What was particularly disturbing
for the future was that both these men were widely regarded as friends of Germany and enemies of the Entente.
In December 1908 Bertie warned the Foreign Office that it
would be disastrous for Churchill to visit France: 'He would
not be believed whatever he might say.' Pichon, the French
foreign minister, strove to explain Lloyd George's friendship
for Germany to the French cabinet on the grounds that he
was 'a Celt and not an Englishman'.[21] One of the most surprising and reassuring aspects of the Agadir crisis in 1911
from the French point of view was that it suddenly revealed
both Lloyd George and Winston Churchill as firm friends of
France. Lloyd George's conversion was particularly dramatic;
Churchill later suggested that it took even Lloyd George
himself somewhat by surprise. In July 1911, at the height of

the crisis, Lloyd George, hitherto considered the most pro-German member of the Liberal government, suddenly delivered the strongest public warning to Germany so far given by a British statesman. This warning was interpreted throughout Europe as a clear promise to France of armed support against German attack. 'Messrs Lloyd George and Winston Churchill', said Cambon when the crisis was over, '. . . have been enlightened by events. They are now second to no-one in their support for the Entente Cordiale and they play a decisive role within the cabinet.'[22]

Agadir, wrote Cambon, had emphasised the truth of Grey's argument that in a crisis English opinion would force its government to stand by France.[23] But the Agadir crisis also made clearer than ever before (though not to the public) the sharply differing views within the British government on the significance of the Entente Cordiale. Lord Loreburn and Lord Morley, the two most prominent radicals in the cabinet besides Lloyd George, urged Asquith and Grey to 'make it clear that Britain had no wish to interfere between France and Germany and to undo the effect of Lloyd George's speech'. France, in their view, 'ought to be told that we cannot go beyond diplomatic support in their quarrel'.[24] The radicals' anger at the effect of Lloyd George's speech was strengthened by their discovery that Anglo-French staff talks had been taking place in secret for more than five years. But just as radical anger at the public warning to Germany was undermined by the fact that the warning was delivered by the most prominent British radical, so their wrath at the staff talks was deflated by the discovery that the talks had first been authorised in 1906 by the radicals' former hero, Sir Henry Campbell-Bannerman, soon after the Liberals took office. The radicals had possessed a complete confidence in Campbell-Bannerman. 'They were', wrote Churchill, 'quite sure he would do nothing more in matters of foreign policy and defence than was absolutely necessary, and that he would do it in the manner least calculated to give satisfaction to jingo sentiments.' It was largely because radical members of the cabinet had been prepared to take Campbell-Bannerman's policy to France on trust that British foreign policy during the first Moroccan crisis failed to receive the critical examination by the cabinet to which it was subjected in 1911. Had

Asquith, the Liberal imperialist, been prime minister in 1906, the radicals would scarcely have been so uncritical. As Churchill shrewdly observed: 'If the military conversations with France had not been authorised by Sir Henry Campbell-Bannerman, and if his political virtue could not be cited in their justification, I doubt whether they could have been begun or continued by Mr Asquith.'[25]

From the first, the staff talks started in 1906 were surrounded by a quite remarkable secrecy. For more than five years no reports of them reached either the cabinet or the Committee of Imperial Defence. But even more remarkable than the secrecy of the talks was the extraordinary lack of interest in them shown by the few statesmen who knew of their existence. Having once given his blessing to the talks, Grey scarcely took any further notice of them until the Agadir crisis over five years later. 'What they settled', he confessed to Asquith in April 1911, 'I never knew – the position being that the Government was quite free, but that the military people knew what to do, if the word was given.' Though Cambon attached the utmost importance to the existence of the staff talks, he too simply assumed that the 'military people' would know what to do 'if the word was given'. During the Agadir crisis the new French foreign minister, de Selves, wrote to Cambon to ask what arrangements had been made for Anglo-French naval co-operation. Cambon replied that he simply failed to understand the question; details had, of course, been worked out by naval experts in the staff talks. Two days later, having consulted his naval attaché, he wrote back in considerable embarrassment to report that very little had in fact been settled and to ask for his previous report to be burned. The Agadir crisis, however, gave a new impetus to the staff talks. By the spring of 1913 plans for military and naval co-operation had been worked out in remarkable detail.[26]

The content of the Entente Cordiale as it emerged from the Agadir crisis was accurately defined by the new French prime minister and foreign minister, Raymond Poincaré: 'Our Entente is not embodied in any diplomatic document; it rests only on public opinion and the talks between our general staffs.' Immediately after the Agadir crisis the French government seemed content that the Entente, even if not formally defined, had proved its strength. Hardly had the crisis been concluded, however, than fears revived of a new German attempt to undermine the Entente. The first to raise the alarm was Sir Francis Bertie. No British diplomat in modern times has had a more remarkable view of the role of an ambassador. He was, as Vansittart (who served under him in Paris) euphemistically observed, 'wholly disinclined to scrape a second fiddle or to become one of the mouthpieces which Foreign Office and Government have now made their agents'. In the spring of 1912 Bertie called at the Quai d'Orsay to put Poincaré on guard against the policy of the British government. There was, he said, a serious danger that in order to limit the naval arms race England might be persuaded by Germany to give a formal undertaking not to take part in an aggressive war against her: an undertaking phrased in such a way as to create possible obstacles to British intervention in a war forced on France by Germany. 'We are dealing', said Cambon, 'with very devious people. The German aim, remorselessly pursued for the last eight years, is to create a breach between ourselves and the English which will gradually widen, until it leads sooner or later to a complete separation.'[27]

Though all prospect of an Anglo-German agreement disappeared within a few weeks of Bertie's warning, that warning led to a new French attempt to secure a formal promise of British support against German attack. Cambon rightly believed that if the Unionists returned to power such an undertaking could be obtained. Both Balfour and Austen Chamberlain felt that the Entente had come in practice 'to have all the obligations of a formal alliance without its advantages', and urged Grey to conclude a formal alliance. Nicolson, the permanent undersecretary at the Foreign Office, privately assured Cambon that the Liberals were 'at the end of their tether' and would soon hand over power to the Unionists.[28] The survival of Asquith's cabinet had, however, one advantage which the French failed to perceive. While a liberal government was in power, radical and labour opposition to the Entente, especially in parliament, was far more restrained than it would otherwise have been. Between the Agadir crisis and the eve of the First World War there was scarcely a single full-dress Commons debate on foreign policy. Grey and Asquith had to cope with hardly more than a few 'inconvenient questions'. Had a Unionist government been in power left-wing opposition to the Entente would scarcely have been so muted.

Cambon believed that Grey himself was willing to give a formal undertaking of British support, but was prevented from doing so by his radical colleagues. The Liberal government did, however, agree to an exchange of letters in November 1912 which, though reserving the freedom of action of each government, provided for immediate consultation in a crisis. If joint action was thought necessary, it was to be on the basis of arrangements made by the general staffs.[29] Both Grey and Asquith felt convinced that if it came to war Britain would be bound to support France against German attack. But the phrasing of the exchange of letters enabled them to assure both parliament and their radical colleagues that Britain was bound by no commitment of any kind. Neither Grey nor Asquith was capable of conscious, deliberate deception. But it is difficult to avoid the conclusion that in stressing Britain's entire freedom of action they were taking refuge in a legalistic formula which disguised the moral obligation to France which both felt that Britain had incurred.

Even on the eve of war in August 1914 neither Asquith nor Grey was fully conscious of the ambiguity of his own position. Asquith wrote in his diary on 2 August: 'Happily I am quite clear in my mind as to what is right and wrong.' He then added a number of points which revealed anything but clarity of mind: '(1) We have no obligation of any kind either to France or Russia to give them military or naval help. . . . (3) We must not forget the ties created by our long-standing and intimate friendship with France.' Exactly the same contradiction is apparent in Grey's famous speech to parliament a day later on the eve of British entry into the First World War. 'This remarkable speech', wrote Lord Loreburn later, 'began with an elaborate effort to prove that the House of Commons was perfectly free to determine either for peace or war. It ended with a passionate declaration that this country would be disgraced if we did not declare war. . . .'[30]

The Foreign Office view of the significance of the Entente Cordiale during the July crisis which preceded the First

World War was summed up in a memorandum by Sir Eyre Crowe, the assistant undersecretary:

The Entente has been made, strengthened, put to the test and celebrated in a manner justifying the belief that a moral bond was being forged. The whole policy of the Entente can have no meaning if it does not signify that in a just quarrel England would stand by her friends. This honourable expectation has been raised. We cannot repudiate it without exposing our good name to grave criticism.[31]

This was the French view also of England's obligations under the Entente Cordiale. It was shared by the conservative and unionist party, and by many liberals. But it was not, as Grey and Asquith discovered, the view of a majority of their colleagues in the cabinet. Even English public opinion did not at first give France the decisive support which Grey had led the French to expect. There was a feeling, Grey believed, that if France were involved in war, 'It would . . . not be in any quarrel of her own at all; it would be because she, as Russia's ally, had the misfortune to be involved in a Russian quarrel, in which France had no direct interest and which did not arouse feeling in the French people.'[32]

The July crisis in 1914 revealed in a more acute form the divisions within the liberal cabinet over the obligations of the Entente Cordiale which had shown themselves during the Agadir crisis three years before. Until the end of July the cabinet, though deeply divided in its attitude towards France, was able to agree on a common policy of trying to avert the war. Once war became inevitable on 1 August, however, the divisions within the cabinet could no longer be concealed or reconciled. Grey and Asquith were resolved to resign unless the cabinet agreed to give France armed support. Without the German attack on Belgium there is little prospect that the cabinet would have done so. Had Germany made her attack directly across the French frontier Asquith's government would almost certainly have fallen. Whatever the action taken by the next English government there would then inevitably have followed a period of bitter recrimination not merely between France and England but also within England itself over the failure to stand by France. At the beginning of August the recrimination seemed already to have begun.

Cambon in London angrily demanded of the Foreign Office if Britain any longer knew the meaning of honour. Bertie in Paris felt 'sick at heart and ashamed'. He wrote in his diary of the French crowds cheering outside his embassy in the confident expectation of British support: 'Here today it is *"Vive l'Angleterre"*; tomorrow it may be *"Perfide Albion"*.' 'It fairly makes one gasp', wrote Neville Chamberlain a few days later, 'to think that we were within a hair's breadth of eternal disgrace. . . .'[33]

In the summer of 1914 there was a general conviction in France that Britain had acquired a moral obligation to support her against German attack. In England, however, the approach of the First World War revealed a remarkable confusion over what the Entente Cordiale really meant. Some, like Lansdowne, believed that it was actually 'stronger than an alliance', because unlike an alliance it was not limited to specific circumstances.[34] Others maintained that, on the contrary, the Entente Cordiale was no more than a phrase which carried with it no obligation of any kind. Appropriately perhaps, it was Germany who resolved the crisis in the Entente Cordiale which preceded the First World War. It was Germany who, by her hostility to the Anglo-French agreement of April 1904, had made it the beginning of a major diplomatic realignment. And it was Germany also who, by her invasion of Belgium in August 1914, succeeded in overcoming the doubts of Asquith's government and transformed the Entente Cordiale into a war alliance.

Notes

1 The phrase 'Entente Cordiale' was used on several occasions during the nineteenth century to describe periods of good relations between France and England. Since 1904, however, it has been generally used (as in this article) to refer specifically to the Anglo-French agreement of that year and the broader understanding which followed it. Except where other sources are given, the detailed evidence for the views advanced in the first half of this article is to be found in the author's *Théophile Delcassé and the Making of the Entente Cordiale* (London, 1968).

2 Britain began what she insisted was a 'temporary' military occupation of Egypt after a nationalist rebellion in 1882. Her subse-

quent failure to end that occupation did much to account for her
reputation as '*Perfide Albion*' in late nineteenth-century France.

3 *Documents diplomatiques français* (hereafter *DDF*), 3rd ser.,
vol. IX, no. 171.

4 A memorandum of July 1902 (*DDF*, 2nd ser., vol. II, no. 333) has
sometimes been taken as evidence of an earlier willingness by
Delcassé to offer England greater concessions. However, this
document states the views of the Direction Politique, which differed
in some respects from those of Delcassé himself (cf. its earlier
opposition to his negotiations with Italy). More recently, it has been
suggested that the appointment of Cogordan and Georges Louis
to senior positions in the Quai d'Orsay during the summer of
1902 may similarly have implied a new attitude by Delcassé towards negotiations with England (P. Guillen, 'Les accords franco-
anglais de 1904 et la naissance de l'Entente Cordiale', *Revue
d'Histoire Diplomatique*, 1968, p. 334). But these appointments
were part of a broader diplomatic reshuffle during 1902 which
involved the promotion of men with widely differing views (the
new ambassador in Madrid, for example, showed himself anxious
to conclude a naval agreement directed against England), and from
which it would be hazardous to draw any general conclusions about
the direction of Delcassé's foreign policy. The significance of
Cogordan's appointment is further diminished by his opposition to
Delcassé's proposed agreement with Spain.

5 G. Monger, *The End of Isolation: British Foreign Policy 1900–1907*
(London, 1963), pp. 112, 133–4.

6 *DDF*, 2nd ser., vol. XIV, nos. 94, 272. Cambon to Pichon, 16
Dec. 1909, Pichon Mss.

7 Cambon none the less suggested to Delcassé, without any justification, that a disparaging reference by Lansdowne to *The Times*
report might yet have been his way of indicating that England expected an offer of substantial compensation for French rule in
Morocco. A few months earlier he had suggested, also without
justification and probably with the same aim of trying to persuade
Delcassé to begin negotiations with England, that Lansdowne
might be hinting at an exchange of interests in Morocco and
Newfoundland.

8 French influence on the Caisse de la Dette (a board representing
holders of Egyptian bonds) had hitherto been able to frustrate all
Cromer's efforts to carry out a reform of Egyptian finances.

9 Monger, *End of Isolation*, pp. 129 ff. The growth of tension between
Russia and Japan during the later months of 1903 and the determination not to allow Britain, as Japan's ally, to become embroiled
in a Russo-Japanese War strengthened still further Balfour and
Lansdowne's desire for 'a better understanding with Russia'.
Delcassé's decision to seek an agreement with England was little
influenced by the danger of war in the Far East. Even a week before
the outbreak of war between Russia and Japan in February 1904
he was still confident that it would not take place. A number of his

Cabinet colleagues, influenced by his optimism, gambled on the Bourse in Russian securities and lost heavily as a result.

10 President Loubet was a devoted admirer of Delcassé, whom he regarded as 'a second Richelieu'. He made no attempt to influence Delcassé's policy.

11 H. Temperley and L. Penson, *Foundations of British Foreign Policy from Pitt to Salisbury* (Cambridge, 1938), pp. 519–20.

12 *DDF*, 3rd ser., vol X, no. 110. *The Memoirs of Raymond Poincaré* (London, 1926), vol. I, p. 88. For a detailed discussion of the 'misunderstanding' of May 1905 see Andrew, *Théophile Delcassé*, pp. 279–89.

13 Monger, *End of Isolation*, p. 278.

14 *British Documents on the Origins of the War, 1898–1914* (hereafter *BD*), vol. VII, no. 376.

15 Monger, *End of Isolation*, ch. 13.

16 Viscount Grey of Fallodon, *Twenty-Five Years, 1892–1916* (London, 1925), vol. I, pp. 78–82.

17 Cambon to Pichon, 20 March 1909, Pichon Mss.

18 G. M. Trevelyan, *Grey of Fallodon* (London, 1937), p. 260. *Hansard*, 27 Nov. 1911. *DDF*, 2nd ser., vol. XI, no. 558; 3rd ser., vol. IV, no. 301; 3rd ser., vol. X, no. 155. Grey did, however, always insist that for British opinion to support France, it must be clear that Germany was the aggressor. For this reason on the eve of the First World War French troops were withdrawn ten kilometres from the German frontier 'in order to show English opinion and the English government that France will in no circumstances be the aggressor' (*BD*, vol. XI, no. 338).

19 Goschen to Hardinge, 26 Nov. 1909, Hardinge Mss. vol. XV. Jules Cambon was now French ambassador in Berlin.

20 P. Cambon, *Correspondance* (Paris, 1940–6), vol. II, p. 299. *Les carnets de Georges Louis* (Paris, 1926), vol. I, p. 46.

21 Cambon, *Correspondance*, vol. II, p. 293. Bertie to Tyrrell, 18 Dec. 1908, Bertie Mss. FO 800/165. Bertie to Grey, 25 Dec. 1910, Grey Mss. FO 800/51.

22 *DDF*, 3rd ser., vol. II, no. 363. Lloyd George was to prove much more hesitant in his support of France in 1914 than in 1911. Though annoyed by his efforts to reduce the arms budget in 1914, however, the French still expected that he would once more show himself resolute in a crisis.

23 The French government shared his view: *DDF*, 3rd ser., vol. IV, no. 301; vol. X, no. 110.

24 S. R. Williamson jr, *The Politics of Grand Strategy: Britain and France Prepare for War, 1904–1914* (Cambridge, Mass., 1969), pp. 156–7.

25 Winston Churchill, *The World Crisis*, 2nd edn. (London, 1931), vol. I, pp. 36–7.

26 Grey, *Twenty-Five Years*, vol. I, p. 94. *DDF*, 2nd ser., vol. XIV nos. 175, 184. Williamson, *Politics of Grand Strategy*, ch. 13.

27 *DDF*, 3rd ser., vol. II, nos. 266, 295, 329. Lord Vansittart, *The*

Mist Procession (London, 1922), p. 53. Belief in a continuing German plot against the Entente was a recurring theme in French diplomatic correspondence.

28 *DDF*, 3rd ser., vol. II, no. 363. Memorandum by Balfour, 12 June 1912, B.M. Add. Mss. 49731: cited in M. Beloff, *Imperial Sunset*, vol. I (London, 1969), p. 172. Sir C. Petrie, *The Life and Letters of Sir Austen Chamberlain* (London, 1939), vol. I, p. 316.

29 *BD*, vol. XII, no. 416.

30 Earl of Oxford and Asquith, *Memories and Reflections* (London, 1928), vol. II, p. 9. Lord Loreburn, *How the War Came* (London, 1919), p. 225. Loreburn's summary was quite fair. Grey told the Commons that, in his own view, if Britain failed to help France, 'we should I believe, sacrifice our respect and good name and reputation before the world'.

31 *BD*, vol. XI, no. 369.

32 Grey, *Twenty-Five Years*, vol. I, p. 336.

33 Petrie, *Life and Letters of Sir Austen Chamberlain*, vol. I, pp. 375–7. *The Diary of Lord Bertie of Thame 1914–18* (London, 1924), vol. I, pp. 6–8.

34 Petrie, *Life and Letters of Sir Austen Chamberlain*, vol. I, p. 375.

Bibliography

Much more research has been done during the last decade on British than on French foreign policy for the years covered by this article. This disparity reflects, at least in part, the relative state of the British and French archives. The papers of the two main French foreign ministers during this period, Delcassé and Pichon, are far less complete than those of Salisbury, Lansdowne and Grey. There are no collections of papers of permanent officials at the Quai d'Orsay which compare with the papers of the British undersecretaries, Hardinge and Nicolson. Nor is there any equivalent in France of the summaries of cabinet discussions sent by the British prime minister to the king. For a variety of reasons the official archives of the Quai d'Orsay are also less helpful than those of the Foreign Office. The gaps in the Quai d'Orsay archives for the years from 1898 to 1905 are largely to be explained by Delcassé's passion for secrecy and his reluctance to commit important decisions to paper. Gaps for the years 1905–14 reflect the fact that important foreign policy decisions during these years were often taken outside the Quai d'Orsay, for example by Clemenceau as prime minister or Poincaré as president. To a surprising degree, omissions in the official archives of the Quai d'Orsay and the private papers of French diplomats can be made up from other sources; Delcassé, for example, sometimes revealed to a few trusted confidants information which was known neither to the cabinet nor to most of his advisers.

British foreign policy at the turn of the twentieth century has been ably covered in a number of recent works: notably J. A. S. Grenville, *Lord Salisbury and Foreign Policy* (London, 1964); Christopher Howard, *Splendid Isolation* (London, 1967); I. H. Nish, *The Anglo-Japanese Alliance* (London, 1966); C. Lowe, *The Reluctant Imperialists* (London, 1967); and George Monger, *The End of Isolation: British Foreign Policy 1900–1907* (London, 1963). A valuable new book by Zara Steiner, *The Foreign Office and Foreign Policy, 1898 to 1914* (Cambridge, 1970) appeared after this article had gone to press. Most recent research on Grey's foreign policy is still unpublished. The collaborative *Cambridge History of the Foreign Policy of Sir Edward Grey, 1905 to 1916*, at present in preparation under the editorship of Professor F. H. Hinsley will, when published, bring together the research of more than twenty historians working on various aspects of Grey's policy.

On the French side, Christopher Andrew, *Théophile Delcassé and the Making of the Entente Cordiale* (London, 1968) attempts a reappraisal of French foreign policy between 1898 and 1905. There is still no study of Stephen Pichon's years as foreign minister. Keith Eubank, *Paul Cambon, Master Diplomatist* (Norman, Oklahoma, 1960) contains comparatively little new information on Cambon's years in London, but the research at present being undertaken by Robert Weiner at Lafayette College promises to throw new light on several aspects of Cambon's career.

There have been three recent studies devoted to Anglo-French relations in the early twentieth century. P. Guillen, 'Les accords coloniaux franco-anglais de 1904 et la naissance de l'Entente Cordiale', *Revue d'Histoire Diplomatique*, 1968, provides interesting new material on English and French policy in Egypt and Morocco. In my own view, however, it overemphasises both the influence of financial interests on

British foreign policy and the extent to which France's ability to frustrate British policy in Egypt had lost its bargaining value; Cromer, who should have known, believed that it would be 'little short of a calamity' if the opportunity to buy off French opposition was not taken. P. J. V. Rolo, *Entente Cordiale* (London, 1969), though based only on published sources, combines a lucid introduction to the background of Anglo-French relations with the first detailed account of the 1903–4 negotiations. S. R. Williamson jr, *The Politics of Grand Strategy: Britain and France Prepare for War, 1904–1914* (Cambridge, Mass., 1969) is particularly valuable for its account of the development and implications of the Anglo-French staff talks. The books mentioned by Andrew and Williamson provide between them an almost complete list of available manuscript and published sources for the history of Anglo-French relations between 1898 and 1914.

Addendum: Two further relevant studies appeared shortly before the publication of this book. Christopher Andrew and A-S. Kanya-Forstner, 'The French "Colonial Party": its composition, aims, and influence, 1885–1914', *The Historical Journal*, vol. XIV (1971), No. 1, discusses, inter alia, the influence of the French colonialists on Anglo-French relations. Cameron Hazlehurst, *Politicians at War, July 1914 to May 1915* (London, 1971), begins with an analysis of British reactions to the approach of war. Finally, a new biography of Sir Edward Grey by Keith Robbins is due to appear during 1971.

2 Strategic and Economic Relations During the First World War

Jean-Baptiste Duroselle

The Entente Cordiale, signed in 1904, was gradually strengthened during the following ten years along with an increase in the danger the British and French felt Germany presented. At the end of July 1914 it was severely put to the test in the face of immediate danger and it was then that it proved its efficacy. There was in fact a curious contradiction in Franco-British relations. From one point of view there was no alliance. In an exchange of letters on 22 and 23 November 1912, the British clearly stated that 'consultation between experts is not and should not be regarded as an engagement that commits either Government to action'.[1] On the other hand, military and naval arrangements had been made with extraordinary precision, making provision for the minutest details, while no such provisions had been made between the French and Russians despite the fact that they were allies.

While the French were desperately struggling to obtain the promise of British intervention, Sir Edward Grey, disturbed by the pacifism of certain of his colleagues and unconcerned about encouraging bellicose desires, had maintained a 'suspense'. Throughout the land the Admiralty had spread confidence in a 'blue water strategy' according to which the Navy alone was sufficient for the defence of the United Kingdom. To justify entry into the war it was not the immediate danger that had to be considered (at the most a few German raids on the coast) but a long-term threat. This slowly emerged and led to the decision of 2 August, when Germany was warned that Great Britain would not tolerate German naval action off the French coast; and above all to that of 4 August when it was decided, following the violation of Belgian neutrality, to enter the war. Once these decisions had been taken, as from 4 August, the provisions laid down in the naval agreements were applied. The army was slightly slower in coming to a decision. Would they adopt the 'continental strategy', i.e. send in the British Expeditionary Force (BEF)? Such action was proposed by the war council on 5 August and on 6 August passed by the cabinet with one reservation: only four divisions out of six would be sent.[2] Thus the Entente became an alliance on the battlefield. In this chapter we shall study the essential strategic and economic aspects of this alliance.

The 'Short War': August–November 1914

Since everything had been arranged in military discussions, the transportation of the BEF and its landing at pre-selected ports, its passage through the regulating station of Amiens and its concentration in the Maubeuge region, were all carried out with wonderful precision. At the same time, with equal precision but on a much larger scale, the French covering troops, considerably reinforced by mobilisation (94 divisions) took up their positions according to Plan XVII, all to the east of the Meuse with the exception of General Sordet's cavalry corps which was concentrated at Sedan. In accordance with the doctrine of 'the offensive at all costs' adopted in 1911, General Joffre planned to attack as soon as possible, without waiting for the British. They would help to put the finishing touches to the victory, to be won in a few weeks. 'The British Army would have to hurry up if they were going to see any of the fun.'[3] It should be noted that this superb optimism of the French was largely shared by the British. A number of generals thought that, with the balance between the French and Germans what it was, the BEF 'might make the difference between a French victory and a French defeat'.[4] So thought General Sir Henry Wilson.

But all the same there was much confusion. First of all the British had never been told exactly what the French plans were. Then Joffre was absolutely certain, and was to remain so for some time to come, that the BEF was purely and simply under his command.[5]

But while Kitchener, in his instructions to Marshal French, recommended him to 'make every effort to fall in as closely as possible with the aims and wishes of our allies,' he added an unambiguous prescription: 'Your command is an entirely independent one, and you will in no case come in any sense under the orders of any Allied General.'[6]

The ordeal by fire was to show the danger of such misunderstanding and ignorance. The facts are well-known. At the very moment when Joffre's 'offensive at all costs' was failing abysmally in Lorraine, it was discovered that the Germans, not content with crossing the Meuse, had concentrated a vast number of troops on their right wing. French, 'full of hope' on the morning of 22 August,[7] learnt during the course of the day that the Germans were advancing in force, routing his troops. All that remained in their way was the French cavalry corps, the BEF and the left wing of General Lanrezac's 5th Army. On 25 August Joffre gave the general command to retreat. But on the same day, following a manoeuvre by Lanrezac not co-ordinated with the BEF, the latter just avoided being encircled in the Landrecies–Le Cateau region and lost 14,000 men. Relations between French and Lanrezac, bad from the beginning, became extremely strained to a point intolerable in a coalition. This, combined with Lanrezac's increasing nervous tension, led to the 'sacking' of the 5th Army's commander on 3 September.

The three following phases of the war were retreat, the Marne counter-offensive and the 'race to the sea'. During these operations, the British and French were largely in agreement on questions of strategy. They disagreed only on some particular aspects and on questions of timing, but never so seriously as to create an additional problem.

Conscious above all that his left wing was seriously threatened, Joffre understood, after 25 August, that he could retake the offensive only by an enormous retreating manoeuvre. French agreed. But in his interviews with Joffre on 26 and 29 August[8] he refused to begin the counter-offensive immediately and maintained that the BEF should retreat one stage in advance in order to reorganise itself. However, the creation of the 6th Army (Maunoury) on the English left, the indestructability of the German 1st Army (von Kluck) to the east of Paris, the intervention by Kitchener who had arrived in Paris on 1 September, and Lanrezac's replacement by Franchet d'Espérey, led French to inform Joffre in the evening of 3 September that he approved his plans and that the BEF would assist in carrying them out. Nevertheless it took the dramatic interview of 5 September at the chateau de Vaux-le-Pénil, near Melun, French's GHQ, for him to reach a decision: 'He murmured with emotion, "I will do everything possible." Not understanding English, I asked Wilson what the Marshal had just said. He replied, "The marshal said yes."'[9] 'British co-operation,' Spears wrote, 'was demanded in words of exalted eloquence inspired by the feeling and the truth within the man.'[10]

We know how at the battle of the Marne von Kluck's attempt to outflank the left wing of Maunoury's army created a gap exactly in front of the BEF who penetrated it and played a large part in winning the victory that would have been impossible without them. There are widely differing interpretations of this event. Spears maintains that it was the BEF 'which on the confession of the Germans themselves caused the retreat of the whole German line'.[11] A. J. P. Taylor takes exactly the opposite point of view: 'In fact the BEF did little. . . . Thirty miles separated the two (German) armies. The BEF advanced slowly into this gap. . . . It was a manoeuvre, not a battle, so far as the British were concerned.'[12] One feels that the truth lies somewhere between these two points of view.

During the phase of chase and the 'race to the sea', the two armies were once more in agreement on questions of strategy. Above all a mood of optimism reigned, 'sincere optimism' as French said.[13] Many British officers saw themselves at the Rhine within six weeks or in time for Christmas.[14] After the feeling of optimism, trench warfare showed the troops that they could bend but not break, as French put it.[15] Lastly, a mutual attempt was made to outflank the enemy's north wing. Joffre's wish to accomplish a great outflanking movement coincided with French's wish to keep the harbours of the Pas-de-Calais at all costs. 'I have always wanted,' French wrote to Joffre on 29 September 'to retake the position I first held on the left wing of the Allied armies.'[16] And Joffre replied on 30 September that 'that position could offer great advantages . . . by shortening the British lines of communication.'[17] The two men were in complete agreement about the timing and on 1 October Joffre was 'happy . . . to confirm once again that complete harmony existed between the leaders of the Allied armies.'[18] The final stage was the terrible battle of Ypres and the end of the hopes of a short war, doubly emphasised by the shortage of munitions in both armies. But the main thing had been achieved. As a German song of the time put it:

> On the coast of France stands Calais,
> And when we get there, my John Bull,
> You really will be in the soup.[19]

But John Bull and his allies had kept Calais.

If all possible provision had been made for the initial military and naval concentrations, no joint economic preparations had been made. Economic co-operation between the allies began only extremely slowly. The English and French economies were totally capitalist, based on free enterprise, the private nature of international commerce, and the private use of merchant fleets (with the exception of a few ships which were immediately requisitioned by the army and navy). On the financial level, London was the biggest market in the world and because of this the pound sterling was a world currency: 'A bill drawn up in pounds and accepted by one of the London banks specialising in this kind of business was worth its weight in gold.'[20]

But since the war was to be short, purchases were in no way increased. Countries would live on their stocks. In France, as in Germany, even the workers from the dock-yards and the armaments factories were mobilised. Advances from the Bank of France seemed sufficient to finance the war. Then in September Ribot, the Minister of Finance, launched on the general public the system of financing by short-term loans (National Defence Bonds). As the United Kingdom had about 100,000 million gold francs invested abroad and in its colonies, and France about 45,000 million, the problem of external finance seemed easily soluble. Of the 8,000 trading vessels sailing the seas of the world, Britain owned 4,000 totalling 20 million tons. France had 1·9 million tons.

So in 1914 there was no interallied economic organisation except for the International Food Commission, established on

15 August, with its headquarters in London, which was purely advisory and only dealt with army purchases in England (excluding wheat, flour, meat and sugar). There was competition for civil purchases, not only between the French and British but inside each country between the various importers. Moreover, little was imported. There was unemployment in both countries and the Americans, whose exports had temporarily dropped, had for several months been faced with a currency crisis.

Franco-British co-operation was immediately established in one sphere alone – that of economic warfare. Besides, as the British fleet was much larger than the French, France followed quite closely instructions issued from London.

As early as 6 August, President Wilson asked the belligerents to accept the terms of the Declaration of London of 26 February 1909. This Declaration, which had been ratified by neither France nor England, concerned war contraband. Designed to assist neutral countries, it reduced what was termed 'absolute contraband' to a list of eleven articles – armaments – and drew up a list of fourteen articles which constituted 'conditional contraband'. Absolute contraband going to the enemy could be seized on neutral ships even if they unloaded in a neutral port. Conditional contraband could only be seized on ships going directly to a port in enemy or enemy-occupied territory. Such restrictions would have made economic warfare almost impossible. By a British Order in Council of 20 August 1914, followed by a French decree of 25 August, the two allies succeeded in eliminating almost all distinction between absolute and conditional contraband. By the Order in Council of 6 October followed by the French decree of 30 October, many more products were added to the list of war contraband (cotton was not included, to appease the United States). But it was not easy to establish a system of supervision. A British note of 7 January 1915 shows that in November 1914 the United States exported to Denmark thirteen times more than in November 1913 and to Sweden nine times more; and that of 773 ships which left the United States between 4 August 1914 and 3 January 1915, only 45 passed through British control.[21]

1915–16 – Breakthrough, attrition or diversion

The front was stabilised and in 1915 Germany struck in the East. British forces played an increasing part in the battle. In the spring of 1915 there were 82 French divisions in action on the Western Front and 19 British. In June 1916 on the same front there were 105 French divisions and 51 British.[22] This naturally created increasingly important problems of liaison and co-ordination at different levels.

First of all in the armies. Spears, himself a liaison officer, clearly demonstrated the difference between 'horizontal' liaison – that between the BEF and the neighbouring armies – and 'vertical' liaison – officers sent by the French GHQ to the English GHQ and vice versa. The first was indispensable and worked well. The second did not please the British at all: 'British commanders resented an officer from a higher formation interviewing their own juniors. Nevertheless I am convinced that the French system was sound.'[23]

There was a French Military Mission (MMF) attached to the British GHQ, commanded by a general (Huguet in 1914, des Vallières from the end of 1914 to 7 December 1917 and de Laguiche after that) with interpreter and liaison officers. Similarly, a French liaison officer was attached to each major British unit. But liaison is not the same as co-ordination. There were important strategic decisions to be made. While, for example, Joffre and French, and from December 1915 Douglas Haig, were in general agreement that top priority should be given to the Western Front and that a breach must be made, other ideas were put forward and in particular the diversionary strategy which Churchill proposed for the Dardanelles in January 1915. Who was to take such decisions? When? And how? The problem was all the more acute since it involved a coalition in which the aims of the two members were different.

Joffre considered that Germany should be fought first and foremost on the Continent, for she was the body and soul of the enemy coalition and once she was out of action the resistance of the Axis powers would crumble. But it was Kitchener's view that the most important thing was to protect the Empire and to deploy against Germany only the smallest number of land forces possible.[24]

It could be said that from August 1914 to 1915 inter-allied

relations were still rather disorganised. The only important event was the signature in London on 5 September 1914 of a declaration by which the English, French and Russians promised not to conclude a separate peace. During this phase the general strategy was decided by the governments. Thus Turkey's entry into the war led the British Cabinet to start discussing operations in the Middle East from 25 November 1914. On 13 January, under the influence of Churchill who during both world wars advocated 'diversion' and opposed 'continental' strategy, it was decided that the navy should attack the Dardanelles. But at almost exactly the same time, on 27 December 1914, French and Joffre met at Chantilly and agreed on future offensives, in particular that of Artois. Agreed on a breakthrough strategy, the two men were not at all in favour of the Dardanelles idea, especially as it meant landing troops at Gallipoli. French voiced this opinion quite plainly as early as January 1915.[25] 'The Dardanelles plan,' Joffre wrote later, 'although sound in principle seemed, from the little I knew about it, to be based on uncertainties.'[26] And so he refused to give up a single division.

It was on tactics that Joffre and French disagreed. The problem of extending the British front, favoured by Joffre but rejected by French and his successor, began in January 1915 and was to last until the Americans came in. It was to be a lasting bone of contention between generals who agreed on questions of general strategy, and we will return to it later.

The military operations of 1915 – which are not going to be discussed here – brought many disappointments, and led Joffre to conclude that the system of co-ordination had to be improved. In June 1915, after the Russian disasters, he sent two notes to the war minister and on 7 July called a military conference at Chantilly. Since this produced some concrete results, it was decided to hold such meetings more often. 'I had no other authority,' Joffre recalled, 'than that which our Allies wished to recognise.'[27] On 2 December 1915 he received command of all the French armies – not only those on the North-East Front. But he would have liked to head the coalition and, thanks to the Battle of the Marne, he was the only general in the Entente to have won a great victory. But national feeling was against it.[28]

An important step was taken with the calling of an inter-allied conference at Chantilly on 6, 7 and 8 December 1915, with the object of adopting a plan jointly defined, prepared and executed. The idea was discussed in a memorandum of 25 November sent out by the French General Staff: 'The decision must be sought by joint offensives in the principal theatres of operation.'[29] This was the conclusion reached at the conference on 6 December. Assistance had to be given to the Serbs, and concomitant offensives on the Western, Russian and Italian Fronts to be launched. If Germany were to take the initiative, they would try to counter it without abandoning their plans. For the first time, the Entente, as a whole, displayed a common attitude towards strategy.

Preparations began immediately. The passing of the first Military Service Act by the House of Commons on 24 January seemed to be a good omen. Haig had at first hesitated to take part in a large Somme offensive in 1916, which had led Huguet, head of the French Military Mission attached to the British army, to remark: 'England wants to win with the minimum sacrifice in men, and to keep back until the end of the war an army which will carry some weight in the final settlement.'[30]

In fact, the German decision on 21 February to begin an operation in the Verdun region, not of breakthrough but of attrition, did not end Allied co-ordination, but led the British to play a much larger part, finally the largest part, in the Somme offensive. Moreover this offensive had to be delayed. From February to July, Pétain, commander of the army, later the group of armies at Verdun, was continually asking for reinforcements. Joffre tried to let him have them only 'in driblets', but even at this rate, the inferno was consuming his divisions. From 22 February Joffre used this to take up the old call to extend the British front: 'You tell me,' he wrote to Haig, 'that you are holding yourselves ready to relieve just one division. . . . You will agree, I hope, that this would be giving me *extremely limited aid*. It is the whole of the French 10th Army that needs to be relieved.'[31] Haig accepted this and the 10th Army was relieved on 14 March.

A further inter-allied military conference took place on 12 March 1916. 'It is quite true to say,' argued the French General Staff, 'that so long as the enemy concentrates his efforts against France, it will be impossible for him to undertake a large-scale offensive on another front. The French resistance gives complete cover to the other coalition armies which still have all their freedom of action.'[32] On 27 March at another conference in Paris, Joffre said: 'The fierce offensive launched by the German armies in the Verdun region must not deflect us from carrying out our jointly determined plan of action.'[33]

Finally, the Battle of Verdun had the effect of reducing the number of French troops taking part in the Somme offensive, and of increasing demands made on the English,[34] as well as of making the offensive less decisive. For the Germans Verdun was a battle of attrition. For the Entente the Somme offensive should have resulted in a breakthrough. But because of Verdun, the breakthrough never came and the Somme, like Verdun, was a battle of attrition, gory and horrific. The word 'Somme' evokes for the British the same feelings of heroism and atrocity as 'Verdun' for the French.

The years 1915–16 were not only years of great strategic conferences, but of economic conferences also. The problem with which the allies were faced was not at this stage one of tonnage, of which there was a superabundance until the end of 1916, but the problem of financing the war which was becoming more and more acute. On the one hand prices were rising – increased demand, higher freight rates, the enormous cost of marine insurance – and on the other, much had to be bought abroad and consequently currency, or credit, had to be found. France lent to Russia or Italy, but borrowed from the British. The French and British obtained credit – generally on a joint basis – from American banks,[35] and particularly from the Morgan Bank.

London was the great world financial market, and it was only natural that the United Kingdom played a leading role in this field. On 5 February 1915, England, France and Russia agreed to the principle of interdependence of financial resources for as long as the war lasted. This agreement resulted in the setting-up of a 'gold-pool' in which the British played the role of the Allies' banker. The English Treasury made advances to the French Treasury, partly for French purchases from England and partly for some of the

French purchases from the United States. England frequently arranged loans from the United States and reassigned part of them to France. In exchange, the Bank of France, which had a larger stock of gold, either sold it for a good price or, which was increasingly the case, lent it to the Bank of England as a guarantee. This system worked very well. But at the end of 1916 the Allies' credit was exhausted and loans were becoming more difficult.

With regard to food, in addition to the International Food Commission, other organisations were formed concerned with the civilian purchasing of frozen meat and wheat (the Joint Committee combined the French and Italian supply services and the British firm of Ross-Smith). As far as sugar was concerned, France decided purely and simply to use the Royal Sugar Commission, set up on 20 August 1914. The Clémentel–MacKenna agreement of 16 February 1916 laid down that the Royal Sugar Commission should be the only allied purchasing house and would supply France with 29,000 tons a month. By the Runciman–Sembat agreement of 25 May 1916, England was to supply France regularly with coal. Thus France's economic dependence upon her ally increased. Clémentel, the French minister of commerce, and his London representative, Jean Monnet, wanted to replace this heavy reliance on England with inter-allied co-operative organisations. This idea was first realised in the setting-up of the Wheat Executive in November 1916, and we shall see how it developed in the course of 1917.

As for tonnage, it was simply a question of arranging for England to help France, which was done through the Shipping Control Committee, set up on 27 January 1916. At the end of November 1916, the British were responsible for shipping 47 per cent of French imports, the remaining 53 per cent being supplied half by the French merchant fleet and half by neutral shipping. The submarine war launched on 4 February 1915 by the Germans caused no alarm until the last three months of 1916, when 350,000 tons were sunk each month. However, under the agreement of 3 December 1916 England promised to let France have what tonnage she had on 31 October (1,450,000 tons), and to send 20,000 trucks and 200 engines to help to unblock the French ports, as well as to charter ships no longer on the basis of voyage charter, but on that of time charter – for a specific length of time – which made the situation less precarious.

The Franco-British crisis of 1917

The year 1917, often called '*l'année trouble*', was notable not only for the Russian defection, a wave of pacifism, mutinies in the French and Italian armies, and widespread strikes in England. On the level of Franco-British relations, it was a period of tension, sometimes extreme, in the realm of strategy as well as in economic relations.

The month of December 1916 was marked by the formation of the Lloyd George government, supported by a War Cabinet of five who, it was hoped, would direct the war and the blockade more forcibly; and by the departure of Joffre, to be replaced by Nivelle, who on 12 December was made commander-in-chief of the north and north-east armies. One of Nivelle's first steps was to abandon the plans his predecessor had drawn up on 1 November 1916 at Chantilly with Douglas Haig.[36] The latter wished to liberate the Belgian coast by a northwards offensive. Nivelle, on the other hand, asked Haig to immobilise the enemy in the Arras–Bapaume region, and to extend his lines south of the Somme to relieve the French troops making up a main striking force of 27 divisions and earmarked for a decisive offensive.

This is how des Vallières explains the reserve shown by Haig and the English towards Nivelle. It arose from 'the fact that they do not take a large enough part in the offensive and fear lest they play only a secondary role. . . . These are distrustful people, and in the short term it is a question of convincing and involving them, but once their work has been outlined and they have committed themselves to it, their loyalty and self-respect as soldiers can be counted on to see it through.'[37] Nivelle requested the French government to intervene with the War Office.

After several preparatory meetings, the decisive conference was held at Calais on 26 and 27 February 1917, when Lloyd George backed up Nivelle's point of view. Not only was the French plan adopted but Lloyd George accepted Nivelle's suggestion that *he* (*Nivelle*) *be given, as from 1 March until the end of operations, authority over the British forces on the Western Front.* Haig could decline to comply with Nivelle's view only 'when he considered that in complying he would compromise the security of his army.' A detail worth noting is that for the first time a British Military Mission, commanded by General Sir Henry Wilson, was drafted to the French High Command (thus making it symmetrical with the MMF). Unity of command was therefore established as a result of Lloyd George's confidence in Nivelle's plans. Haig found it hard to accept such an arrangement.[38] Everything depended therefore on the outcome of the battle.

On 9 April Haig and the 3rd French Army launched the offensive followed on 16 and 17 April by two sections of French forces notably at Chemin des Dames. On 20 April it had to be admitted that the breakthrough had failed. What followed is well known: on 11 May Pétain replaced Nivelle at the head of the French army. Thus the attempt to work under a unified command came to an unhappy end. In addition, as General Wilson said, 'we have never had less contact with the Allies, and plans and offensives have never been less co-ordinated than they are at the moment.'[39] 'Today,' wrote des Vallières, 'the difference between their interests and ours is shown up very clearly.'[40] Besides, the British clearly regarded it as up to them, now that the French were exhausted, to take the direction of the war in hand.

But Nivelle's defeat was followed by that of Haig in the gory battle of Passchendaele, by which he had hoped to win the war or at least to conquer Belgium (from 31 July to the end of October). Pétain, who was waiting for 'the Americans and the tanks' and who wanted to restore the morale of an exhausted French army, undertook no important offensive. And so throughout the summer of 1917 there was no co-ordination between the British and French armies. It was only in October 'that a strong desire was detected in the British General Staff to see re-established at all levels the closeness that had existed in 1916.'[41]

The crisis between the two commands provoked by the setbacks of 1917 was redoubled by a crisis in economic relations. The German decision to launch an all-out submarine war, which meant attacking not only enemy but also neutral ships, resulted in the Americans breaking off diplomatic relations with Germany and subsequently, on 6 April 1917, entering the war. The effects of this were not really felt on the Western Front until the late spring of 1918 when American troops began to pour in. But the economic consequences of Germany's decision were much more immediate. The entry into the war of a highly prosperous nation was to provide a short-term solution to the financial problem. An American law passed in April 1917 allowed the American Treasury to help the Allies. This aid was to be granted on a monthly basis and subject to hard bargaining. But in the end, it was given. Financial worries thus lost their urgency. On the other hand, the shipping crisis became very serious, for the all-out submarine war increased losses enormously. These culminated in April when 850,000 tons were sunk.

Faced with this situation, it is not surprising that the first reaction of the United Kingdom, the major victim of torpedoing, was one of despair. She began by prohibiting the importation of luxury goods, a decision Lloyd George announced to the House of Commons on 23 February 1917. A whole series of measures had already been taken, but this ban affected the major part of normal French exports to Britain (wines, spirits, silks, etc.). And despite some concessions made by Sir Albert Stanley, President of the Board of Trade, after a trip to Paris (5–9 March 1917), the French export trade was seriously affected. France replied by passing a decree on 22 March prohibiting all imports which were not made on behalf of the State (with nevertheless a 'Derogation Committee' sitting at the Ministry of Commerce). But France imported basic essentials from England and therefore had little chance to retaliate.

The second British reaction came in April 1917 when she asked France to return 500,000 tons of shipping she had lent her by the end of June. Some officials even wanted to take back all the shipping and leave it to England to decide what cargoes would be sent to France. This demand was made at the very time that Nivelle's offensive failed.

The French reaction was naturally very strong; the press, with the censor's consent, joining in and claiming that it was simply an example of British 'egoism'. The English retorted that the French made bad use of the ships, that their ports were congested, that cargoes were unloaded several days behind schedule and that France had not requisitioned her merchant fleet.[42] To which the French replied that since they had lent an enormous amount of railway equipment to the BEF, they lacked the wherewithal to speed things up. In short, the crisis between the Allies took such a serious turn that the two governments stepped in.

The crisis was to be resolved by two successive series of negotiations in the course of which a solution based on a completely original principle was to be put forward by the young London representative of the French Ministry of Commerce, Jean Monnet.

The first negotiations took place in London between 16 and 27 August 1917 between Clémentel and several English ministers, Lord Robert Cecil, Sir Albert Stanley and Sir Joseph Maclay (shipping controller).[43] 'It brought about an agreement,' Clémentel reported, 'that to achieve military victory and construct a peace for the common good we had to bury our mutual grievances.' After the atmosphere had thus been cleared, Clémentel obtained (i) the freedom to import into England almost all French products, including luxury goods (Sir Albert Stanley was moved to say how much Great Britain appreciated France's economic difficulties and to express the admiration felt by the entire British Empire), and (ii) permission to keep under the French flag nearly all the ships Britain had lent and then reclaimed in April.

The second round of negotiations was even more important. They took place between 13 October and 3 November in London and consisted of daily meetings between Clémentel and British ministers including a member of the War Cabinet, Lord Milner, whom Lloyd George nominated.[44] The French harvest had been extremely poor and the threshing was late. Reserves of flour in Paris were down to one day, those of the army to 1–3 days. And there was also a desperate shortage of shipping. According to Clémentel, between January and September France had only been able to import 20 per cent of what she needed, Italy 21·1 per cent, Great Britain 60 per cent. He wanted to end this disparity and no longer to depend on British goodwill. To this end, he put forward a revolutionary plan formulated by Jean Monnet: *that all shipping should be pooled and apportioned not by the English government but by an inter-allied body.*

Although the British ministers accepted immediately that, as Stanley said (18 October), 'the three countries should receive the essential food supplies for their populations,' it was clear that they considered the idea of a 'shipping pool' a political sacrifice. Although Stanley agreed to increase immediate aid to France, he remained loath to accept the idea of the shipping pool right to the end. Furthermore, he wanted *first of all* to obtain the agreement of the United States. To which Clémentel replied: 'It is absolutely essential that we should be able to present a united front. . . . We will then be in a much stronger position.' 'I feel,' Clémentel telegraphed to Painlevé, the prime minister, on 26 October 'that Lord Milner and his Cabinet colleagues . . . are hesitating before a decision that seems to them . . . the most serious they have ever faced since the formation of the present government.' In a note of 30 October to the British, he stated:

We have reached a decisive turning-point in the war. Since shipping plays the most important role in the conduct of the war at the present time, it is the duty of the Allies to establish amongst themselves, for their own sakes, a unity of viewpoint and action so that they can, by means of all shipping at their disposal, deal with their most urgent needs. . . . The continuation of the current methods, with each working for the same end but completely separately, would involve the Allies in grave risks.

Between 1 and 3 November, the discussions took a dramatic turn. On the 1st, Stanley suggested to his French colleague that they should both leave for the United States the following day. Clémentel refused. On 2 November at the Ritz, Painlevé met Lord Milner, who was representing the British War Cabinet. 'It is a question of life and death for France,' Painlevé said. On 3 November, during a meeting at the Foreign Office involving numerous ministers, Balfour, Lord Robert Cecil, and eventually Lord Milner – who obtained the War Cabinet's agreement – adopted the French proposal. Stanley, 'a natural defender of British industry and commerce', tried to fight it. But finally the agreement was signed, accepting in principle the establishment of a 'shipping pool', although one limited to the transport of food supplies.

It took a long time to put the principle into practice. On 29 November 1917 at the meeting of the first 'Inter-Allied Conference' at the Quai d'Orsay (with Clemenceau, Lloyd George, Orlando and Colonel House), it was decided shortly to establish the Inter-Allied Maritime Transport Council 'to ensure the best possible use of shipping, to divide this shipping between the allies, and to adjust the plans of each in order to fit in with the shipping available.' Each country would state its needs, then periodically the Council would distribute the shipping.

'This,' said Clémentel,[45] 'marked a decisive stage in the economic history of the war.'

The year of co-operation, 1918

The winter of 1918 was both disturbing and severe. It was soon realised that after the Russian defection the Germans would be superior in strength, and it was therefore no surprise when Ludendorff launched a series of offensives before the arrival of the Americans. Moreover, because of the lack of ships, there was a grave shortage of wheat, steel, nitrate and, on the Continent, of coal. Ships for the transport of American soldiers were given priority. But 1,000 men thus took the place of 5,000 tons of merchandise. France and England were largely to supply the American army with arms.[46] But this presupposed that raw materials were freely available. In the face of these enormous strategic and economic problems an efficient system of co-ordination was essential. This was to come into being in March 1918.

Despite these difficulties and fears, a unified command was set up only under the pressure of defeat.

In September 1917, Poincaré, President of the Republic, had suggested to Lloyd George that an inter-allied General Staff be set up. But Pétain refused, and in October claimed the unified command for himself. He confided in Foch on 6 October. 'General Foch expressed the opinion that General Pétain did not know the English and was going to run into serious difficulties.'[47]

After Ludendorff had successfully brought off his first

breakthrough offensive against the Italians at Caporetto, the Entente held a meeting at Rapallo on 6 and 7 November 1917 and established an Inter-Allied War Council to 'oversee the general conduct of the war'; it was comprised of the prime minister and one member of the government of each country. There were merely 'military delegates' (Sir Henry Wilson for England, Foch then Weygand for France). Haig, who liked neither Lloyd George nor Wilson, was most discontented with this arrangement.[48] When Lloyd George asked his opinion, he maintained 'that such a body would only add to our difficulties. "The two governments, however, have decided to set it up," Lloyd George replied. I told him that under those circumstances there was nothing more to say.'[49] Thus, nothing was done about setting up a unified command.

The Supreme War Council met at Versailles on 1 December 1917, but its military role was slight. It met again on 30 January 1918. A plan drawn up by Foch and Weygand was adopted: the British would have full discretion in taking action against the Turks. On the French front they would try to fall in with the French plans. In fact, Pétain and Haig, who got on well together, were against the idea of a unified command and preferred to reach agreement between themselves. The Council set up an inter-allied general reserve under the control of a four-member executive committee presided over by Foch. But when Foch tried to set up a general reserve of thirty divisions, he came up against Haig and Pétain who announced that they had already worked out a plan together. A general reserve was therefore never created. On 14 March at a further meeting of the Supreme War Council, Lloyd George and Clemenceau recognised the impossibility of setting one up and adopted the Haig–Pétain plan. This provoked a strong, but ineffectual reaction from Foch.

However, twelve days later, at an interview at Doullens on 26 March 1918, the unified command was set up – at least the basis of it – by Clemenceau and Lord Milner, representing the British Cabinet. Furthermore, its creation was suggested by Milner and then by Douglas Haig. Foch was instructed to 'co-ordinate allied military action on the Western Front. To that end he would liaise with the Commanders-in-Chief who were invited to supply him with all the necessary information.'[50]

c

On 21 March Ludendorff had launched the first of his large-scale offensives in the Saint-Quentin region. Very suddenly the English 5th Army's situation had become extremely serious. Its fate depended on the immediate arrival of French reinforcements. But Pétain, in a state of extreme anxiety, wanted to protect Paris and to keep back the reserves in case the Germans launched a second attack in the Champagne region. Haig, on the other hand, knew that Foch wanted to hurl all the French reserves into the breach opened by the Germans in order to stop it up. 'In short,' Haig wrote on 25 March, 'everything depends on the willingness and the ability of the French to support us *immediately* with twenty high-quality divisions to the north of the Somme. The French Prime Minister must make a vitally important decision at once, so that *all* the French divisions can go to the defence of the British Front which is bearing the entire weight of the German assault alone.'[51] The following day Foch 'appeared firm and to understand the situation. Pétain, on the other hand, looked frightful and gave the impression of being scared to death and of having completely lost control of his nerves.'[52]

At the Beauvais conference on 3 April it was decided to give Foch 'the strategic direction of military operations'. 'I am in complete agreement,' Haig said, and explained that 'this new arrangement will in no way affect my attitude towards Foch.'[53] On the other hand, one section of British opinion remained hostile to such an arrangement, and the *Star* described the outcome of the Doullens meeting as 'the supreme outrage'.[54] The English maintained that 'the word generalissimo is not applicable'.[55] On 14 April Foch finally received the title of Commander-in-Chief of the Allied Armies. 'There are going to be difficulties about the Command', wrote Colonel Grant; 'Foch is the Commander-in-Chief and intends to command . . . I am convinced that we are going to fight like cat and dog.'[56]

However, the unified command worked out well. It did create tensions which led to bitter and exaggerated judgements, of which the following are just two examples: 'The English General Staff gives the impression of being totally overcome by events. The troops are in good form and their morale high, but leadership is non-existent.'[57] Exactly the opposite point of view came from Haig: 'It is urgently necessary that the French take a more active part in the fighting ... Foch talks absolute nonsense, saying that as we are engaged in battle no division should be withdrawn to rest.'[58] At the beginning of May, Haig and Foch both thought that the new German offensive would be directed against the English lines. In this they both made a monumental mistake. On 29 May it was at Chemin des Dames that Ludendorff launched his breakthrough attack, which was to take the Germans up to the Marne for the second time. Haig, in his turn, agreed under protest to send reinforcements and abandoned the idea of shortening his lines. The Paris Conference on 7 June almost completely cleared the atmosphere. 'Everything is being done to satisfy General Foch's wishes as quickly as possible,' Colonel Grant wrote.[59] While General de Laguiche wrote: 'The perfect discipline with which the Marshal as well as his Staff comply with the orders of the General Commander-in-Chief of the Armies should be noted.'[60] After the beginning of Foch's great counter-offensive of 18 July 1918, the pin-pricks and petty fights continued. But the most important point, as confirmed by all witnesses, was the spirit of comradeship and co-operation that existed between the troops of the two Allies right up to their joint victory.

A few days before the unified command was established (26 March 1918), economic co-ordination was finally achieved. The first meeting of the Inter-Allied Maritime Transport Council was held in London from 11 to 14 March. This event, which received much less attention than Foch's appointment, was no less important. It could be said that without this co-ordination 637,000 American soldiers would not have arrived in April, May and June, and 305,000 in July, etc., making a final total of two million in 1918 instead of the one million expected.

To understand clearly what actually happened, a distinction should be drawn between the Council and its Executive. The Council (in which the Americans were just observers) comprised two British ministers (Lord Robert Cecil and Sir Joseph Maclay), two French (Clémentel and Loucheur) and two Italian (Villa and Crespi). They met four times in 1918 and provided a great stimulus. But much more important, it appears, was the permanent Inter-Allied

Maritime Transport Executive which was presided over by Sir Arthur Salter, with Jean Monnet representing France, Professor Attolico representing Italy, and an American observer, Rublee.

In order to understand the important part played by this organisation, one must study its origin, its daily working and the extraordinary way its authority developed in the following months.

An organisation of genuine co-operation already existed – the Wheat Executive, set up on 27 November 1916. It was Jean Monnet who had the idea of improving and applying to shipping the methods used by the Wheat Executive.[61] Two other men helped him – Beale, the Director of the Wheat Executive who provided experience, and Sir Arthur Salter,[62] who, as Director of Shipping Requisitions, was better informed than anyone else in the world on ships, their itineraries and their cargoes.

They adopted the following procedure: (i) Each country periodically made out a list of its needs, product by product, and sent it to its representative on the Executive. (ii) The three members of the Executive met (nearly every day) and defended the interests of their own countries. (iii) But, knowing exactly what shipping was available, they had to agree on the distribution for each country. (iv) They then went back to their respective governments and defended the plan they had jointly agreed, which allotted to each country less than they had specified in (i). Although they had no supranational power by law, their *de facto* power was enormous, since they alone were in a position to divide out the shipping. And as a result of the all-out submarine war, shipping had become the bottleneck. Everything, without exception, depended upon the way it was shared out. It was only in August 1918 that the number of ships built by the Allies and their partners equalled and then exceeded the number being destroyed by the Germans. (v) In making the daily allocations they tried to make the most sensible use of ships. For example, instead of sending Indian wheat to England and Canadian wheat to Italy they reduced the distance by reversing the process. English coal for Italy was unloaded in France and transported by rail instead of going the long way round by Gibraltar, etc.

The system presupposed complete trust – the trust of the

three members of the Executive in each other. They were in fact friends (from 1919 all three were to hold administrative positions in the League of Nations and to continue working together for several years). The governments also had to trust their representatives on the Executive and there was no doubt that they did. 'It is clearly understood,' Jean Monnet wrote to Clémentel on 13 April 1918, 'that our object is to set up joint programmes with our allies. Such programmes, drawn up according to category of merchandise and fixed by the CATM in accordance with the total tonnage at the allies' disposal, should be put into effect using all the ships available, no matter what flag they sail under.'[63]

To take just one example of the size of the problems they faced: in 1913 Great Britain had imported 53 million tons of merchandise, France 45 million, Italy 18 million, making a total of 116 million tons. In April 1918, these countries, bearing the restrictions in mind, worked out their needs for the whole year to be: 30·2 million tons for Great Britain, 33·3 million tons for France, 16·5 million tons for Italy, making a total of 80 million tons. This presumed a shipping capacity of 16·3 million tons. While 22·5 million tons were available, 8 million tons had been allocated to the army and the navy, particularly for the transportation of American soldiers. That therefore left 14·5 million tons instead of 16·3 million. Consequently, further reductions had to be made.

It is extremely interesting to see how the Council developed. It was in fact the first example, in an economy hitherto based on free enterprise and national independence, of the acceptance of 'central planning' and 'internationalism'. Since shipping was the key to everything, it was necessary to subordinate to the Inter-Allied Maritime Transport Council those bodies already existing for certain products (the Wheat Executive, the Meats and Fats Executive, the Oil Seeds Executive), and above all to establish a large number of similar bodies which were to be called Executives or Programme Committees. These were formed at a great rate between April and October 1918. They then had to be regrouped into Councils. In July, there was an Inter-Allied Munitions Council, which re-grouped seven Programme Committees (nitrates, aviation, chemicals, explosives, steel, non-ferrous metals, mechanical transport), and an Inter-Allied Food Council which brought together four Executives (wheat, meats and fats, oil seeds, sugar). In August it was decided to set up a third Council for raw materials, embracing nine Programme Committees. It should be noted that Sir Albert Stanley and the Board of Trade were opposed to the idea for a long time, but gave in under pressure from the American War Industries Board on 29 August 1918.[64]

Thus under the jurisdiction of the Inter-Allied Maritime Transport Council and its Executive a vast and coherent system was set up in 1918. In October the Americans joined the system. Inter-Allied co-operation had come alive in a way hitherto unknown in world history. This is how Jean Monnet summed it up:[65] 'In setting up these consortiums we had no ideal in mind. We had no preference for any particular system; we simply complied with the requirements of the moment. Had we refused to recognise these requirements they would not have ceased to exist and would have over-whelmed us.' On 2 November he wrote, 'we have taken draconian measures, the result of which has been to sub-stitute governmental control for the natural laws of supply and demand.'

The armistice rapidly brought to an end the belated but effective measures which had been taken to co-ordinate the military strategy and the economic life of the Entente. 'Co-operation,' wrote Clémentel, 'was one of the principal in-struments of victory.'[66] But within a system of Nation-States, co-operation cannot hold out against national ambitions.

Notes

1 *British Documents on the Origins of the War, 1898–1914*, vol. X, no. 416: Grey to Paul Cambon, 22 November 1912.

2 Samuel Williamson, *The Politics of Grand Strategy. Britain and France prepare for War. 1904–1914* (Cambridge, Mass., 1969), pp. 366–67. It was decided to send a fifth division shortly after.

3 Major-General Sir Edward Spears, *Liaison 1914* (London, 1930), 2nd edn. 1968, p. 45.

4 Williamson, *The Politics of Grand Strategy*, p. 169.

5 *Archives Ministères Affaires étrangères*, Paris, Guerre 1914–18, Grande Bretagne, dossier général, vol. 2, letter from Millerand to Kitchener, 2 March 1915.

6 Marshal Lord French, *1914* (French edn.), pp. 13–14.
7 French, *1914*, p. 51.
8 Joffre, *Mémoires* (Paris, 1932), vol. 1, pp. 317–18, 340–41.
9 Joffre, *Mémoires*, p. 394. Neither Wilson (*Journal*, French edn., p. 38), nor French (*1914*, p. 100) emphasise the dramatic nature of this meeting. On the other hand, Spears (*Liaison 1914*, pp. 413–15) does.
10 Spears, *Liaison 1914*, p. 415.
11 Spears, *Liaison 1914*, p. 437.
12 A. J. P. Taylor, *English History 1914–45* (Oxford, 1965), p. 10.
13 French, *1914*, p. 129.
14 Taylor, *English History 1914–45*, p. 10; Wilson, *Journal*, p. 42.
15 French, *1914*, p. 132.
16 French, *1914*, p. 150.
17 French, *1914*, p. 151.
18 French, *1914*, p. 155.
19 Quoted in Jean Ratinaud, *La course à la mer* (Paris, 1967), p. 27.
20 Truchy, '*La Guerre et les finances françaises*' (Paris, 1926), p. 112.
21 In addition to early works on the economic war, particularly Louis Guichard, *Histoire du blocus naval* (Paris, 1929); Sir Arthur Salter, *Allied Shipping Control*, (Oxford, 1931) etc., see also Marion C. Siney, *The Allied Blockade of Germany* (Ann Arbor, 1957).
22 Cf. Marshal Fayolle, *Carnets secrets de la Grande Guerre* (Paris, 1964), pp. 98, 163.
23 Spears, *Liaison 1914*, p. 51.
24 General Koeltz, *La guerre de 1914–1918: les opérations militaires* (Paris, 1966), p. 185.
25 French, *1914*, pp. 285–86.
26 Joffre, *Mémoires*, vol. 2, p. 370.
27 Joffre, *Mémoires*, vol. 2, p. 328.
28 Cf. an important thesis by Mlle Marie-Claude Rémy, *Les problèmes de coordination de l'action chez les Alliés pendant la bataille de Verdun* (Paris, 1969), based on the archives of the French army's *service historique*.
29 GHQ 3.100 – no. 122 (quoted by Mlle Rémy, *Les problèmes de coordination*, p. 59).
30 *Archives Armée*, MMF/Brit. Son. d: EM box no. 89, 9 Feb. 1916 (quoted by Mlle Rémy, *Les problèmes de coordination*, p. 87).
31 *Archives Armée*, GHQ 3642, 22 Feb. 1916; GHQ EM Troisième Bureau, no. 15074, Joffre to Haig (quoted by Mlle Rémy, *Les problèmes de coordination*, p. 105).
32 *Archives Armée*, Dossiers Firbry, Dos. IV pce annexe no. 108: no. 7424. Introduction to the Conference of 12 March 1916 (quoted by Mlle Rémy, *Les problèmes de coordination*, p. 105).
33 *Archives Armée*, GHQ 3849 (quoted by Mlle Rémy, *Les problèmes de coordination*, p. 124).
34 According to Koeltz, *La guerre de 1914–1918*, p. 322, the number of French divisions was originally set at 46, then 34, then 30, then on 29 June when the offensive was launched, at 22. Haig engaged 25 divisions.

64 *Troubled Neighbours*

35 Cf. Pierre Renouvin, 'La politique des emprunts étrangers aux Etats-Unis de 1914 à 1917', *Annales*, 1951, pp. 289–305.

36 In what follows I have drawn to a great extent on Mlle Sylviane Pin's remarkable unpublished thesis, prepared under my supervision, *Les relations entre militaires français et militaires anglais vues par les officiers de liaison pendant la Ie Guerre mondiale*, 1968. Mlle Pin consulted in particular the MMF reports to the Deuxième Bureau (*Archives de l'Armée*), and Col Grant's Diary at the War Office.

37 *Archives Armée*, MMF/Brit. section EM, box no. 80/1, 10 Jan. 1917 (quoted by Mlle Pin, *Les relations entre militaires français et militaires anglais*, p. 85). Des Vallières goes so far as to suggest that the British were under pressure to replace Haig by Gough (*Archives Armée*, box no. 89/2, 25 Feb 1917).

38 Cf. Douglas Haig, *Carnets Secrets* (French edn.), p. 270: 'To place the British forces under French authority is sheer folly.'

39 Wilson, *Journal*, vol. 1, p. 349 (11 May 1917).

40 *Archives Armée*, MMF/Brit. section EM, box no. 89/2, 16 May 1917 (quoted by Mlle Pin, *Les relations entre militaires français et militaires anglais*, p. 97).

41 *Archives Armée*, MMF/Brit., section EM, box no. 89/3 CR de Bellaigue de Bughas, 28 Oct. 1917 (quoted by Mlle Pin, *Les relations entre militaires français et militaires anglais*, p. 105).

42 This was to be done later by the under-secretary of state for Maritime Transport, Anatole de Monzie, by a decree of 18 July 1917.

43 Account by Clémentel in the *Archives nationales françaises*, F12 7796.

44 I was able to complete the account given by Clémentel in his book, *La France et la coopération économique interalliée* (Paris, Payot, 1931), from a detailed report found in the private archives of Maurice Long, who was the French Minister of Supply at the time.

45 Clémentel, *La France et la coopération économique interalliée*, p. 285.

46 According to André Tardieu, *Devant l'obstacle, l'Amérique et nous*, France supplied the Americans with 4881 aeroplanes, 2150 75 mm. guns, 1684 other guns, 260 tanks, and all artillery ammunition.

47 *Archives Armée*, Journal de Marche, document no. 251 (quoted by Mlle Pin, *Les relations entre militaires français et militaires anglais*, p. 108).

48 *Archives Armée*, MMF/Brit., section EM, box no. 89/91. CR de Bellaigue de Bughas, 12 Nov. 1917 (quoted by Mlle Pin, *Les relations entre militaires français et militaires anglais*, p. 110).

49 Haig, *Carnets secrets*, 4 November, p. 360.

50 Cf. General Mordacq, *Le commandement unique: Comment il fut réalisé* (Paris, 1929), p. 88.

51 Haig, *Carnets Secrets*, p. 409.

52 Haig, *Carnets Secrets*, p. 410.

53 Haig, *Carnets Secrets*, p. 313.

54 Cf. *Archives Armée*, MMF/Brit., section EM, box no. 109/3

(quoted by Mlle Pin, *Les relations entre militaires français et militaires anglais*, p. 217).

55 War Office, 106/1456, Col Grant's Diary, 3 April 1918 (quoted by Mlle Pin, *Les relations entre militaires français et militaires anglais*, p. 132).

56 War Office, Col Grant's Diary, 14 April 1918.

57 *Archives Armée*, GQGA, box no. 15, C. M. de Laguiche, 11 April 1918.

58 Haig, *Carnets Secrets*, p. 417, 14 April 1918.

59 War Office 106/1456, Col Grant's Diary, 13 June 1918.

60 *Archives Armée*, GQGA, box no. 15, 10 June 1918.

61 This was confirmed to me by Lord Salter, whom I was able to interview personally. I also discussed these problems at length with Jean Monnet.

62 Lord Salter has explained the whole process remarkably well in two books: *Allied Shipping Control* (Oxford, 1921), and *Memoirs of a Public Servant* (London, 1961). Information on the subject is also to be found in Clémentel, *La France et la coopération économique interalliée*.

63 *Archives nationales*, F 12 7796, telegram no. 586 LC.

64 Clémentel's report to Clemenceau of 5 September 1918, in *Archives nationales*, F 12 7796.

65 *Archives nationales*, F 12 7796 (probably October 1918).

66 Clémentel, *La France et la coopération économique interalliée*, p. 261.

Bibliography

The most valuable primary sources for the subject of this chapter are deposited in the Archives Nationales, and the Archives Armée, Paris and in the Public Records Office, London.

Published sources used in the preparation of this study are as follows:

British Documents on the Origins of the War, 1898–1914.

Clémentel, *La France et la coopération économique interalliée* (Paris, 1931).

Maréchal Fayolle, *Carnets secrets de la Grande Guerre* (Paris, 1964).

Maréchal Foch, *Mémoires*, 2 vols. (Paris, Plon, 1931).

Marshal Lord French, *1914* (French trans.).

Guichard, *Histoire de blocus naval* (Paris, 1929).

Marshal Lord Haig, *Carnets secrets* (French trans.).

Maréchal Joffre, *Mémoires*, 2 vols. (Paris, 1932).

Koeltz, *La Guerre de 1914–1918: les opérations militaires* (Paris, 1966).

Mordacq, *Le Commandement unique: comment il fut réalisé* (Paris, 1929).

Ratinaud, *La Course à la mer* (Paris, 1967).

Renouvin, La Politique de emprunts étrangers aux Etats-Unis de 1914 à 1917, in *Annales*, 1951, pp. 289–305.

Salter, *Allied Shipping Control* (Oxford, 1921), *Memoirs of a Public Servant* (London, 1961).

Siney, *The Allied Blockade of Germany* (USA, Ann Arbor, 1957).

Spears, *Liaison 1914* (London, 1930, 2nd edn. 1968).

Tardieu, *Devant l'obstacle: l'Amérique et nous* (Paris, 1927).

Taylor, *English History 1914–1945* (Oxford, 1965).

Truchy, *La Guerre et les finances françaises* (Paris, 1926).

Williamson, *The Politics of Grand Strategy: Britain and France prepare for War, 1904–1914* (USA, Cambridge, Mass, 1969).

Wilson, *Journal* (French trans.).

For discussion of other aspects of World War I and for further bibliographical guidance see:

Renouvin, *Histoire des relations internationales: les crises du XXᵉ siecle*, Première partie, de 1914 à 1929, pp. 10–124 (Paris, 1957).

Thomson, *England in the Twentieth Century* (London, Penguin Books, 1965), pp. 15–59.

Renouvin, *La Première Guerre Mondiale* (Paris, P.U.F., collection 'Que sais-je?', 1965).

Taylor, *English History 1914–1945*, pp. 1–119 and 617–22 (Oxford, 1965).

Thomson (ed.) 'The Era of Violence, 1898–1945' in the *New Cambridge Modern History*, Vol. XII (1st edition, Cambridge, 1960), pp. 359–85.

3 The Making of the Treaty of Versailles

D. R. Watson

'We have no eternal allies, only eternal interests.' The diplomacy of 1919 provides a good illustration of this commonplace of international politics. Clemenceau repeated on several occasions the story that when he said to Lloyd George 'Within an hour after the Armistice I had the impression that you had become once again the enemies of France,' the British prime minister replied, 'Has that not always been the traditional policy of my country?'[1] Conflict between British and French policy begins as soon as the Germans request an armistice; it continues right up to the presentation of the revised terms of the treaty to the German delegation in June 1919, and, of course, afterwards.[2] Keynes was quite correct in saying that Clemenceau's overriding concern was for the security of France; equally, Lloyd George fought for British national interests. This is not to say that there was nothing but conflict between Britain and France in 1919. In both countries those in power knew well that they had one overriding concern – the potential menace of a powerful and aggressive Germany. They had a common interest in preventing a repetition of the First World War, but differed as to the means by which this end could best be achieved. We cannot make a black and white distinction between a British policy of conciliation and French insistence on guarantees, although this difference of emphasis did exist. Lloyd George and Clemenceau agreed that the treaty should combine coercion and conciliation; one of the background papers prepared by the French Foreign Office in October 1918 states 'it is better to leave the Germans with the least possible justifiable ambitions unsatisfied'.[3] If Clemenceau argued strongly for some extreme demands, such as the separation of the Rhineland from Germany, it was with the knowledge that the final settlement would be a compromise, in which it was as well to have something with which to bargain. Looking back on the settlement he disagreed with the view that the faults of the treaty were due to it being a compromise; on the contrary, he said, that made it more likely to be a just, stable and permanent solution.[4]

Basic to the policy of both statesmen was the belief that they must agree on a common policy towards Germany. Both Clemenceau and Lloyd George made concessions to the other which they personally regretted, and which brought them domestic political difficulties in order to attain this goal.[5] Neither Britain nor France could see the United States as a reliable alternative ally. There was always enough doubt about the reality of an American commitment in Europe, for geographic reasons alone, quite apart from uncertainty as to Wilson's ability to control the Senate, to ensure that for British and French alike the strongest pull was towards each other. The other theoretical alternative, a *renversement des alliances* that would have brought Germany in as the partner of either Britain or France was certainly not a real alternative in the circumstances of 1919. It was utterly inconceivable that Clemenceau, the man who had before 1914 proclaimed that Franco-German relations could never be friendly because France did not accept that the defeat of 1870 meant that she must be subordinate to Germany, should in the moment of victory accept that France should start down a road which led to German domination. For him there was no alternative to the policy of maintaining the entente with Britain. Exactly the same reasoning governed British policy-making. No matter how annoyed the British became with the French, and on some occasions between 1920 and 1924 they became very annoyed indeed, the entente with France had to remain the basis of British policy. As Eyre Crowe minuted in November 1921:

Some of the Treasury and other Downing Street tendencies are towards the substitution of an Entente with Germany in the place of that with France. This is a chimera under present conditions, and must remain so for a long time to come. What we and what the whole world wants (sic) is peace. Peace for the present must rest on the execution of the peace treaties. Those would hardly survive a breach between England and France at this moment.[6]

Although the military balance might temporarily favour France, in the long run Germany was still the stronger country, and the British government never lost sight of that truth. An entente with France remained the keystone of British policy, even if a precise and binding alliance could not be agreed on between the countries.

The sudden collapse of their enemies in the late summer of 1918 presented the Allies with the task of preparing armistice terms in a situation for which they had made little provision. Down to July a German breakthrough on the western front had seemed more likely than an immediate Allied victory. When Clemenceau came to power in November 1917, he defined his policy in the famous phrase '*Je fais la guerre*', and public discussion of peace terms was frowned on as defeatist. The earlier secret agreements with Russia and Italy had been rendered obsolete by the Russian revolution, and the publication of their terms by the Bolsheviks was proving embarrassing. It seemed wiser to avoid new commitments until the military situation became clearer.[7]

When the German government appealed to President Wilson for an armistice on the basis of his Fourteen Points,[8] it was Lloyd George who was most incensed at Wilson's unilateral negotiation, while Clemenceau acted as a restraining influence, insisting that they should do nothing to hurt Wilson's feelings. In the end the Allies agreed to the German demand for an armistice on the basis of all Wilson's declarations (not on the Fourteen Points alone), reassured by the vagueness of this commitment, and by the provisions which ensured that the Germans could not hope to continue the war.[9] There was conflict between Clemenceau and Lloyd George at this time, not about the occupation of the Rhineland, but about the armistice with Turkey, with its implications for Anglo-French rivalry in the Middle East. Lloyd George says that on this question alone there was personal unpleasantness between them, and House noted in his diary that 'they bandied words like fishwives, or at least George did.'[10]

Clemenceau at once established very good personal relations with House, Wilson's personal representative, which were of value on several crucial occasions when he deputised for Wilson, absent in America or ill, but in the last resort House could not commit Wilson further than he wished to go in a pro-French direction. In the two months between the armistice and the opening of the peace conference the French statesman attempted to establish a special relationship with both British and Americans, promising each that he would work with them against the other.[11] From the French point of view there was a real danger of an Anglo-Saxon front which would deprive France of her minimum requirements. Clemenceau was bound to take every opportunity to avoid this. Certainly he was not honest in telling House that nothing of importance was to be discussed in the Anglo-French talks of 1–3 December.

By far the most important question for the French was the Franco-German border, and the possible detachment of the Rhineland from Germany. Whatever his own views Clemenceau had to deal with a strong party which regarded the maintenance of the French army on the Rhine as *the* essential basis of the peace settlement. Foch was the spokesman for this group but behind him were his chief of staff Weygand, President Poincaré, and an influential group of journalists and literary men. Foch opened the campaign for the separation of the Rhineland from Germany by insisting on its occupation under the armistice; a letter to Clemenceau on 16 October revealed his views about the long-term implications of this occupation, and the first of his three memoranda on the subject was sent to the Prime Minister on 27 November.[12] In this, the most extreme of the three, Foch demanded the incorporation of the Rhinelanders in the armies of the western alliance, as the only way to even the demographic imbalance between France and Germany. His paper talked of the Rhineland being made into one or more autonomous states, but the scheme was in fact a thinly disguised annexation; this proposal was never endorsed by the French government.

On 1 December 1918 Clemenceau and Foch arrived in

London, and Foch presented his scheme to the British at an informal meeting from which Clemenceau was absent.[13] Lloyd George interpreted this as a cunning move on Clemenceau's part with the idea that Foch, full of the prestige of a victorious commander, would be more persuasive than he himself could be. In fact Foch was notoriously a bad negotiator.

It is more likely that this was the first of Clemenceau's attempts to demonstrate to Foch that the French could not dictate peace terms when the war had been won by an alliance. By remaining absent he allowed Foch to sound out the British without committing himself either for or against Foch's proposals. Lloyd George and Bonar Law revealed their doubts about Foch's ideas; Foch was equally reluctant to commit himself when Lloyd George questioned him about a temporary occupation of the industrial area of the Ruhr in order to enforce payment of reparations. It is ironical that this idea, which was to cause the British government so much annoyance when put into practice by the French, should have been first suggested by Lloyd George.

It has often been said that at these meetings Clemenceau and Lloyd George arrived at an informal agreement that in return for an adjustment of French claims in the Middle East Lloyd George would support the French demands on the Rhine. This supposed bargain is particularly appealing to those who like to see statesmen as the puppets of mysterious economic interests, and to whom the mere whisper of the oil-fields of Mosul is enough to explain and condemn the policy of both. It is not surprising that no record of any bargain of this kind is to be found in the official minutes of the discussions. Lloyd George and Clemenceau both believed in private and informal methods of doing business, and they met privately several times during the three days, apart from the official discussions. There is no doubt that an agreement was reached about spheres of influence in the Middle East. Lloyd George tells us so in his memoirs.[14] The question is – was this in return for a promise to support France in European questions? This seems unlikely. The agreement about the Middle East was by no means one-sided; the French were given something in return for what they surrendered, in the form of a right to a share in the oil of the British sphere and confirmation of the French position in Syria – a bargain which Lloyd George later honoured, however reluctantly. The most that can be said is that French concessions in the Middle East, which Clemenceau quite rightly regarded as of secondary importance to France, were made 'in an effort to secure British support for France in her demands against Germany'.[15] That Lloyd George did not give a definite promise of such support is suggested by all that we know about later negotiations, and by the unanimity with which French accounts talk of Clemenceau's disappointment with the results of the London meetings.[16]

The preparation of the peace treaties began in earnest on 12 January 1919. It would be impossible in the space available to attempt to cover all the negotiations stage by stage. I shall only attempt to outline the main features of French and British policy, and to discuss specifically the Rhineland and the treaties of guarantee, the Saar, Germany's frontiers with Poland and Czechoslovakia, and Reparations. These questions were crucial for Anglo-French relations. Whole areas such as the question of relations with the various contending parties in Russia, the settlement in the Middle East and with regard to the successor states to Austria–Hungary, have been ignored. It must be remembered that this principle of selection will tend to give an exaggerated impression of conflict, and that there were many topics on which Britain and France found it easy to work in harmony.

In some respects the negotiations at Paris in 1919 are among the best documented events in history. Most of the informal discussions among the leading figures, were minuted in English by Hankey and in French by Mantoux, and both of these records have been published. But, although we know how the Allies presented their cases to each other, we are less well served when seeking to discover the internal arguments on each side. A good deal is known about the making of British policy, and more will be revealed now that the British official records have been opened for research. But the French archives remain closed.[17] Even when they are opened there will be no equivalent of British cabinet minutes:

as in Britain before 1916 the convention was that no record was made of cabinet discussions. In any case Clemenceau dominated his government to such an extent that it is doubtful whether issues were often seriously discussed by the full cabinet. Clemenceau worked with a few intimates: two of the most important, Mandel, who managed internal affairs, and Tardieu, who was concerned with the diplomatic negotiations, were not even ministers.

What, then, were his views about the problem of Germany, and the policy which he ought to follow in the making of the peace settlement? It may well be that the story of his summing up his views on the Germans in the lapidary expression '*ils sont trop*' is apocryphal, but it is a good epitome of his views. The imbalance between France and Germany in population and economic resources, already serious enough before the war, had been made much worse by the fighting. Added to this was the fact that Russia, the essential counterweight to Germany before 1914 was, for some time at least, removed from the diplomatic chessboard. The conclusion was that the balance of power resulting from the allied victory was precarious. Germany would seek to challenge the settlement, and every precaution must be taken to make this impossible. The essential requirement was the maintenance of the unity of the three powers, Britain, France and the USA, that had won the war; but much else was needed, a strong strategic position along the Rhine and an economic settlement which would allow France to restore her devastated territory at the expense of Germany.

Talking to Martet in 1929 Clemenceau revealed his lack of sympathy for the Germans, 'There has been too much bloodshed. In twenty years, or in forty years time ... perhaps ... when memories are dimmed.' Nevertheless the Germans had a right to exist, and Franco-German relations could be perfectly correct provided that Germany abided by her treaty engagements: 'Perhaps I hate Germany; but I do not wish her to disappear. Providing that she leaves us alone.' But when Martet asked him whether he thought that Germany would act in such a way as to allow correct relations on these terms, he replied '*Non*'.[18]

Many in France found Clemenceau's policy too weak towards Germany. For it allowed Germany to survive as a nation-state with a strong central government. There was a period between November 1918 and January 1919 when it seemed possible that Germany might spontaneously disintegrate. No doubt if this had happened the French government would have welcomed it, but by February it was clear that the forces making for national unity were too strong. From that time French policy assumed that Germany would survive as a unified state, and the French generals who compromised themselves by fostering the pathetic attempts at a separatist coup in the Rhineland were firmly admonished, whatever encouragement they may have had earlier.[19] Evidence about the basic good sense of Clemenceau's government on the question of German unity comes from one of its bitterest opponents, Jacques Bainville, who tells us that not once, but ten times during the negotiations, Clemenceau's collaborators told him that war and defeat had strengthened German unity, and that the particularist forces were unrepresentative minorities.[20]

All the documentary evidence available about French policy confirms that this was the view of the French government throughout.[21]

It was not by civilian politicians, but by the military leaders that the battle for the extreme programme of dismembering Germany, at least to the extent of separating the Rhineland, was fought. It was no easy task for Clemenceau to be sure of maintaining his control over policy in the face of Foch's attempts to use his immense prestige to influence political decisions. Wilson and Lloyd George showed little understanding of French politics when they told Clemenceau that he should dismiss Foch for insubordination.[22] The fact that the French army did not intervene directly in internal politics between 1851–1958 has obscured the fact that the possibility of intervention was never entirely absent. Ever since 1870 the army had had tremendous emotional importance, and the heroic struggle of 1914–18, at last crowned with victory, had brought immense prestige to the army and its leaders. In contrast the civilian politicians had allowed their prestige to sink very low. Indeed, to attempt a slight essay in counter factual analysis, it is hard to imagine any other issue in 1917 than some form of military dictatorship if Clemenceau had not existed. This danger still existed, and it was an important factor in Clemenceau's calculations.[23]

These, then were the main aims of Clemenceau's policy in 1919. Firstly, to maintain the alliance with Britain, and if possible reinforce it by a firm American guarantee. Secondly to improve the Franco-German frontier in the Saar, if possible by annexing the whole area with its mineral resources. Thirdly, to ensure that the left bank of the Rhine was strategically in Allied control, both as a defensive measure to prevent a lightning invasion as in 1914, and to leave Germany, in her turn, open to the threat of invasion of the vital industrial area of the Ruhr; this was particularly necessary in view of the need for some means of putting pressure on Germany in the event of her taking action against the new states on her eastern border. Fourthly, to provide an economic settlement that would allow France to recoup her wartime losses at German expense. The motives behind these policies were military and strategic security in the narrow sense, financial and economic recovery as the essential concomitant of the maintenance of France as a great power, and in the widest sense, the need to restore national self-confidence after the terrible struggle which had so nearly brought France to her knees. Clemenceau never lost sight of this psychological factor in the settlement; as he told Wilson and Lloyd George on more than one occasion, it was vital that France got certain safeguards. For otherwise there was a danger that '*le ressort vital de notre peuple*' would be broken.[24]

Lloyd George, who had more than European affairs to contend with, had a more complicated balance sheet to draw up. A brief sketch of his policy as it concerned France and Germany would include the following elements. Firstly the need to associate the USA with Britain in the maintenance of the European balance of power. Secondly, as far as possible to conciliate Germany by making a moderate peace settlement. Thirdly to use the reparations provisions as a lever by which the USA could be persuaded to make concessions on war debts, which otherwise would impose a crushing financial burden on Britain. Britain had few territorial demands to make of Germany on her own behalf, but the dominions demanded annexation of German colonies, and British security dictated severe limitation of German armaments on land and sea. Lloyd George, with his country seemingly at the apogee of its imperial power and with no parallel to the mutinies which had almost broken the French army in 1917, was not worried, as were the French, by the danger of a failure of national willpower. In fact, as future developments were to show, Britain, just as much as France, was to be stretched beyond her resources in the attempt to maintain the settlement of 1919. Even in the short term, with rebellious populations to control in Egypt, Ireland and India, and immense responsibilities in Europe, the Middle East and the Far East, Sir Henry Wilson was very worried about the gap between British power and British responsibilities.[25] But Lloyd George was only gradually to show awareness of these limitations.

On 10 January 1919 Foch presented a revised version of his proposals to the Government. In this memorandum he abandoned the idea of incorporating the Rhinelanders into his armies, and contented himself with demanding the creation of an autonomous state, or states, a permanent Allied occupation, and an economic union with France.[26] Clemenceau told Tardieu to adopt this proposal as the basis of a note to be presented to Britain and America. Doubtless this was a bargaining position from which he could retreat in return for concessions. He said so explicitly in 1929.[27] As the bargaining eventually produced not only the abortive treaties of guarantee, but Lloyd George's reluctant consent to a 15 year occupation of the Rhineland by the Allied armies, these bargaining tactics can be said to have been extremely successful.

Tardieu's note was presented on 25 February 1919. It stressed the joint Allied interest in containing Germany, and drew the analogy with the control of the seas on which Britain and the United States insisted for their security. It pointed out the importance of control of the Rhineland if the Allied powers wished to intervene in Germany to support the Poles or Czechs. Discussion of this scheme by a committee of experts, Tardieu, Mezes (for the USA) and Kerr (for Britain) produced deadlock by 12 March. Lloyd George then introduced the idea of a joint Anglo-American guarantee against German invasion, as an alternative to the French plan. The moment Wilson returned to Paris on 14 March, Lloyd George put this proposal to him. Wilson agreed, and that afternoon the two saw Clemenceau at an informal meeting with neither secretary nor interpreter present. Clemenceau demanded time for consideration. Having discussed the matter with Pichon, Loucheur and Tardieu, he replied that, in return for the guarantee France would drop her demand for the autonomy of the Rhineland, but he maintained his insistence on an Allied military occupation.[28] The British and Americans could not agree to this.

It was at this point that Lloyd George withdrew to Fontainebleau with his closest advisors for two days of concentrated thinking. Their deliberations produced the Fontainebleau memorandum, which argued for a moderate peace as the only alternative to plunging Germany and the greater part of Europe into Bolshevism. Clemenceau replied with a bitter comment to the effect that Britain had first secured her own requirements (the German fleet and colonies) and was now seeking to appease Germany at the expense of France. By this time the French were in conflict with the British and Americans on at least four important questions, the Rhineland, the Saar, the Polish frontier and reparations.

In view of the deadlock, and of the fact that he was one against two (the Italians were at no stage important except in relation to their own claims) it is remarkable how much of the French position Clemenceau managed to save. On the Rhineland it was Wilson who gave way first. The essence of the compromise was that the French abandoned their demand for an indefinite, and then, for a 30 year period of occupation. In return, first Wilson and then a reluctant Lloyd George, agreed that the temporary occupation which they had always accepted, might be stretched to mean up to 15 years, and perhaps longer. They saw this as little more than a form of words designed to allow Clemenceau to clear himself with French opinion, and stressed the clauses which allowed for an earlier withdrawal if the Germans fulfilled their obligations under the treaty. The French argued the other way, pointing out to critics at home that they had secured clauses allowing for extension of the occupation beyond 15 years. Clemenceau and Tardieu could thus claim that they had secured the essentials of Foch's demand. In fact, perhaps unconsciously, they misrepresented the extent to which the form of words eventually agreed on, gave France a unilateral right (by clause 429 of the treaty) to continue the occupation if the promised treaties of guarantee did not materialise.[29]

Foch, who had already argued his case before the Council of Four, made a last effort to sabotage the bargain which Clemenceau had fought so hard to achieve. On 25 April he was allowed to present his arguments to a meeting of the French cabinet. In the subsequent discussion we are told that Clemenceau cast doubt on the military arguments for the occupation; with modern methods of warfare it was an out-of-date conception. President Poincaré, well known as a supporter of Foch, took no part in the debate, and the cabinet gave its unanimous support to Clemenceau's policy.[30]

Why did Lloyd George offer the treaty of guarantee? In the first place it was a form of words which helped Clemenceau over his domestic political difficulties. Lloyd George was well aware that the circumstances in which the treaty would operate – an outright attack on France by Germany –. were most unlikely to occur in the foreseeable future; and, in such circumstances, as the French pointed out in the later nego-tiations for a new treaty, Britain would be forced in her own interests, to intervene, as she had in 1914. To be of real value to France the treaty would have to be worded to cover a much wider range of possible German action, and to be given teeth in the form of a military convention. Thus Lloyd George could say to British critics that the treaty bound us to nothing that we were not already obliged to do under the Covenant of the League of Nations and in our own interests following our traditional policy of preventing European domination by any one power. However, Professor Nelson has argued cogently that the real interest of the treaty for Lloyd George was else-where. It lay in the fact that the joint treaties of guarantee were a way of ensuring a precise American commitment to intervene in Europe to help maintain the balance of power achieved in 1918. It was 'a fulcrum on which to lever Wilson and his colleagues into acceptance of a precise political and military commitment by the United States in Western Europe.'[31]

Turning to the French side, why did Clemenceau accept the offer of the treaties of guarantee? Doubtless the fact that they were a good card to play against the annexationist lobby was important. In any case Clemenceau could argue that he had not given up very much in return for the treaties. He had abandoned the French demand for political separation of the Rhineland from Germany, but he had never regarded this as feasible, and it was only the military and the right wing who argued strongly for this. He had also given up the French demand for a permanent Allied occupation of the area. But although, under the terms of the treaty, the occupation of the whole area between the French frontier and the Rhine was only to last for five years, there were provisions for its prolongation if Germany did not execute all the clauses of the treaty. The reparations provisions would ensure that France could make use of these clauses if she felt strong enough.[32] Clemenceau visualised the occupation not in terms of a new war with a strong Germany, which was ruled out by the disarmament clauses, but as a means of putting pressure on a weak Germany. The circumstances in which this might be needed included German failure to pay reparations, or German aggression in eastern Europe. In the last resort it was in terms of the psychological needs of the French people, of the need to restore French morale, that Clemenceau demanded the occupation. When Lloyd George argued for a moderate peace to prevent Germany lapsing into Bolshevism, Clemenceau replied that if the French people were not given a modicum of security, then there was danger of Bolshevism in France rather than in Germany. 'Bolshevism' should not be taken too literally; it certainly did not then have the meaning with which it has been filled by the development of a powerful totalitarian state-machine. Rather it was a shorthand for the collapse of legal and constitutional order, a chaos in political and economic life, out of which the most likely outcome then seemed to be an old-fashioned military dictatorship. The psychological importance of the occupation of the Rhineland emerges clearly in Tardieu's account of Clemenceau's arguments against Lloyd George's attempt in June 1919 to win French agreement to a reduction in the period of the occupation. Against Lloyd George's argument that German disarmament, and the treaties of guarantee made the occupation unnecessary as a strategic safeguard, Tardieu reports that Clemenceau said:

In the years to come, we need a barrier behind which our people can work in security and rebuild their ruins: that barrier is the Rhine. I must reckon with the national feeling. Not that I am afraid of being overthrown: that is of no concern to me at all. But I do not wish, in giving up the occupation, to do something that would break the vital will of our people.[33]

These arguments refuted those who said that the occupation was silly, because it provided France with security while Germany was helpless and would be ended when Germany grew stronger.

Before the peace conference opened there are indications that the French government hoped for British support on the question of the Rhineland, while expecting opposition from them to plans for annexing the Saar. In the event the positions were reversed. It was Wilson who first agreed to demands for a long occupation of the Rhineland, and this dragged a reluctant Lloyd George along so as to maintain his overall aim of an American commitment. In the Saar question the basic conflict was between Wilson and Clemenceau with Lloyd George playing the role of conciliator.

The afternoon meeting of the Council of Four on 9 April was the decisive one for the Saar. Wilson was in a weak position, facing an almost solid Anglo-French front, and having already conceded the case for a special economic status for the French. His own advisers insisted that this meant a special political relationship as well. But he stood firm on the basic position that the special regime in the Saar should not be merely a façade covering French annexation, and that at the end of 15 years the Saarlanders should have the chance to express their own views in a genuine plebiscite.[34] Doubtless the primary French interest in the Saar was economic, although the strategic position was also a factor in their calculations. It was not simply a temporary shortage of coal that worried them. That could have been provided for by a German obligation to deliver set quantities of coal for a few years, as Wilson suggested. It was the need to provide for the permanent linking up of the Saar coal and the Lorraine iron ore. Finally the French never accepted that it was only economic arguments that mattered in the Saar. The first French memorandum argued that historically the Saar was French, and that a substantial part of its population was still French speaking. Here, as in the Rhineland question, the psychological factor was important.[35]

Of the territorial changes imposed by the Treaty of Versailles only the German–Polish frontier produced the same degree of controversy among the Allies as did the Rhineland and the Saar. It is not surprising that the small rectifications to the Belgian frontier and the partitioning of Slesvig led to little argument. It is more surprising that the creation of Czechoslovakia, out of the territory of Austria–Hungary, did not lead to serious consideration being given to drawing a new frontier in Bohemia and Moravia so that three million Germans should not be included in the new state. Here was certainly a potential Alsace-Lorraine in reverse, and in view of the difficulties that were to result for Britain in 1938, it is ironical that no effort was made to rectify the situation in 1919. It is clear that Lloyd George was as favourably disposed towards the Czechs, whom he regarded as a practical, cultured and modern people, as he was prejudiced against the Poles.

The French were also able to insist on the banning of the union of Austria and Germany without meeting any opposition from Lloyd George, and very little from Wilson. To some extent this may have been due to vague ideas about Austria taking part in a Danubian federation that would give economic unity to the old territories of the Habsburg Empire. It was this possibility, and its implication of German economic domination of the whole area, that had been used as an argument in the French memorandum of November 1918 in favour of allowing Austria to join Germany.[36] Presumably the French had now changed their minds because they realised that there was no danger of the successor states agreeing to any such economic union.

The question of the Polish–German frontier caused very much more disagreement between the Allies than these other territorial questions.[37] It was here that Lloyd George was most consistent in his attempts to achieve a moderate settlement, which could, he hoped, win German acceptance. In the end, with little support from Wilson, he achieved very

considerable modifications of the original tough French proposals. The problem of the German–Polish frontier was a
very difficult one. In the first place national self-determination
could provide no simple solution in an area where language-
groups were inextricably intermingled, and where the Poles
could claim that much of the German population was of
recent origin, installed there as part of a deliberate anti-
Polish colonisation policy by the pre-war German government. Secondly the Polish demand for access to the sea,
authorised by one of Wilson's Fourteen Points, was in
inevitable conflict with the German demand for a land-link
between east Prussia and the rest of Germany. Compromise
could be reached on Danzig in the 'free-city' formula, but
there could be no squaring of the circle where the Polish
Corridor was concerned.

With very little support from Wilson, and in the face of
French opposition, Lloyd George forced through the decision to organise a plebiscite in Upper Silesia, as a result of
which a considerable area that had been awarded to Poland
remained German. This was the most important change made
to the treaty in response to German objections. It remained
true, however, that even moderate German opinion objected
more strongly to the Polish frontier than to any other of the
territorial changes. As Clemenceau said, no solution that
would seem just to the Allies, would be acceptable to the
Germans. But, if the main consideration were the strategic
and economic viability of Poland, the concessions on which
Lloyd George insisted did little to weaken the new state. His
feeling was that, in any case, Poland would be too weak to
defend herself against Germany. The important thing was, if
possible, to create a Poland that Germany would not wish to
attack, and, in any case, not to create a Polish state that
would be condemned by the opinion of Britain and the
dominions.

The French had exaggerated hopes of the long-run military
potentialities of Poland.[38] Clemenceau insisted that if
Germany were allowed to dominate eastern Europe, the war
would be as good as lost. This was the danger against which a
strong Poland was needed.[39] The famous *cordon sanitaire*
between Germany and Russia was as much designed to
prevent the Germans taking the opportunity provided by

Bolshevik chaos, to penetrate and dominate Russia as she had at the time of Brest-Litovsk, as it was intended to prevent the Bolshevik virus from infecting western European society.

Reparations were one of the issues on which Lloyd George, defending British interests and with his freedom of manoeuvre limited by public opinion, contributed most to ensuring that the treaty would be repugnant to Germany. The basis of Lloyd George's policy was that although Britain had not suffered actual physical destruction as had Belgium and northern France, the costs of the war had imposed an enormous financial burden on her. Our overseas assets had been diminished, and we had incurred vast short-term debts in the United States. These debts were partly on our own behalf, and partly on behalf of France and the other Allies to whom we had lent on a great scale, and whom we were still supporting financially in 1919. The ideal solution from the British point of view would have been an all-round cancellation of these war debts. But the Americans refused to regard the loans they had made as their contribution to a common war effort: they were ordinary commercial liabilities. The armistice agreement, expounding German liability to restore the invaded territories, and to make reparation for damage done to civilian property, allowed France and Belgium to hope for large sums, but did not offer much to Britain. Hence the casuistical interpretation of these clauses, so that the reparations section of the peace treaty bore little relation to the armistice agreement. The most complete study of reparations argues that if the French had made common cause with the Americans to resist British attempts to stretch the reparations clauses, they would, in the end, have received more.[40] The British attempted first to argue the case for German payment of an indemnity to cover the full cost of the war, or rather as much of it as could in practice be wrung out of them. When this was vetoed by the Americans, the specious reasoning of including the cost of pensions to wounded soldiers and dependants of those killed, in the bill for civilian damages achieved much the same result. This greatly increased the total bill presented to Germany, but as the limiting factor was her capacity to pay, the net effect was to increase the proportion of reparations going to Britain and to reduce that going to France.

Although Lloyd George took up the idea of including pensions in March 1919, it was the French who had first introduced it.[41] They were just as eager as the British to get the Germans to admit liability for the full costs of the war. At governmental level it was the French, much more than the British, who seem really to have expected to be able to extort astronomical sums from the Germans. There seem to be three main reasons for the French attitude. In the first place there was the pressure of public opinion. '*Le Boche paiera*' was an essential safety valve in the disturbed social and economic conditions of 1919. Secondly, the French government seems to have had very poor advice from its financial and economic experts about the feasibility of transferring huge sums of money from Germany to the Allies. Loucheur was more realistic, but Klotz who was in charge of French finances, seems to have had no understanding of the difficulties.[42] It was Klotz, as minister of finance, who was responsible for the reckless methods which allowed the French unfunded debt to snowball in 1919, thus creating the formidable problems that were only solved when the franc was stabilised in 1926 at one fifth of its pre-war value. But Clemenceau, who remarked that the way to stop inflation was to hang a few speculators, shares the heavy responsibility for this *débâcle*. The only explanation of this policy is that Germany would pay huge sums in reparations, although even they were prepared to admit that what was actually received would be far less than the public expected. Finally there can be no doubt that Keynes was right when he said that in the last resort Clemenceau wanted an impossible sum to be imposed so that the French would have a perfect excuse for interfering in German affairs.[43] The occupation could be prolonged if Germany did not execute all the clauses of the treaty, and if the reparations clauses were impossible to execute then France could demand the right to remain in the Rhineland for as long as she liked.

Lloyd George's policy on reparations fluctuated wildly in response to the contradictory pressure of British public

opinion, the immediate and narrowly financial interpretation of British interests, fears that Germany would not
sign, and long-term considerations of making a durable
peace. Thus at the time of the armistice he was cautious, fearing that the Germans would not sign. When they had signed
he allowed himself to be carried away by the emotions aroused
during the election campaign, and pressed for reparation and
indemnity. By March he was personally cautious in private
discussion, but was forced to take a tough line by the pressure
of public opinion. There is no doubt that what he was looking
for, and thought he had found in the clauses adopted, was a
form of words that would satisfy public opinion for the
moment, and allow the actual sum demanded to be scaled
down later. This was the great advantage to be derived from
leaving the calculations to the Reparations Commission. At
the same time he was determined not to agree to a settlement
that would allow the French to collect large sums in reparations while not giving Britain anything to set against her
war debts. Once again, as in the diplomacy of the treaties of
guarantee, Lloyd George kept one eye fixed on America.

It would be impossible in a short space to sum up an essay
which has already been compressed. By way of conclusion, I
end with a few reflections on the role of Lloyd George and
Clemenceau in the peace negotiations. Both had a dominant
position in their respective countries, and within quite a wide
degree of latitude British and French policy was what they
chose to make it. They both liked to work informally and with
a small group of intimate advisers and associates. They both
tended to look on their respective Foreign Offices as primarily
executive in function, and both had foreign ministers who
were prepared to accept a subordinate role. There was little
danger of either being defeated in parliament, although both
frequently used this non-existent danger in their diplomatic
bargaining. Lloyd George was probably more vulnerable in
this way than Clemenceau. For he lacked a firm party base.
So did Clemenceau, but this was normal in French politics.
The real constraints on both were not in their cabinets and
parliaments, but in their assessment of the total political

situation. In the French case this meant the views of the military leaders, and the inchoate popular feelings expressed in the mounting wave of social discontent, largely the result of inflation, but taking the form of revolutionary talk under the impact of the Bolshevik example.

Granted that the key to an understanding of Anglo-French relations in 1919 is to be found in the characters of these two men, what can we say about this? Neither has yet been made the object of a satisfactory biography, but a few observations can be offered. Lloyd George, the mysterious enchanter, the Welsh magician, as Keynes pictured him, is the more difficult case.[44] His political genius, like that of F. D. Roosevelt, lay in intuitive grasp of a situation, rather than in clarity of expression and consistency in the details of policy. His undoubtedly great achievements in 1919 have been obscured by the miscalculations of 1922, and by the fact that the American repudiation of the treaty kicked away what he regarded as its major prop; this was no fault of Lloyd George's who had done everything he could to associate the United States with the European settlement. As a result, his full stature as a statesman has not yet emerged; at least there is no consensus of opinion on it. Compared to Clemenceau, Lloyd George was much more flexible in policy. His sensitive antennae responded to the pressures of the environment in a way that at times infuriated those with whom he had to deal. Nevertheless in no sense at all was he a weak man, and when he was determined on something he could fight for it with grim tenacity. Beneath all his shifts and turns in 1919 was a grasp of the underlying reality of the situation. The two essentials of his policy were to produce a treaty that would conciliate Germany as far as possible, while at the same time giving the victors strategic security, and to associate the USA with the European settlement in a permanent and practical way, not merely in the high-flown rhetoric of the Covenant.

Clemenceau is less of a problem than Lloyd George. After the French manner he was much more given to expounding principles and arguing from them. His basic principle was not that might is right: Keynes was quite wrong when he said that 'his theory of politics was Bismarck's'.[45] But he did believe that right had to be defended by might, in a world where 'Covenants without the sword are but words', as Hobbes once said. He argued as strongly as Wilson that the peace should be a just peace. He differed from Wilson in his estimate of what the terms of a just peace would be, and even more profoundly by his insistence that it would have to be maintained by force against the Germans who would never voluntarily agree with their victors on a definition of justice. However moderate the peace, it was the fact of defeat that Germany would not forgive. Thus the allies would have to defend their settlement, and force Germany to abide by the treaty; it was axiomatic that she would try to overthrow it. In the parliamentary debate about the ratification of the treaty, he offered his country, not relaxation after her heroic effort but a continuation of the struggle.[46]

Clemenceau showed great skill as a negotiator in 1919; his tact in dealing with Wilson, Lloyd George and even Orlando, was in striking contrast to his brutal methods with the plenary sessions of the conference and with his subordinates, up to and including the foreign minister Pichon,[47] but this flexibility in negotiation was designed to achieve a goal that he adhered to rigidly throughout. In some ways, the character of Clemenceau had more in common with that of President Wilson, than it had with the flexible nature of Lloyd George.[48] The parallel was at its closest in their common attitude towards German reaction to the settlement. Whereas this was always an important factor for Lloyd George, Wilson's policy of '*Fiat justitia, ruat caelum*', produced practical results that were identical with Clemenceau's hostility to Germany. When Wilson had made up his mind that a certain provision of the treaty was just, he was not prepared to alter it because the Germans objected. This tallied with Clemenceau's view that however many concessions were made, the Germans would never pardon the Allies for defeating them.

Looking back, Clemenceau's attitude to the settlement seems more consistent than that either of Wilson or of Lloyd George. Wilson could not see that a peace that was 'harsh and just',[49] would require to be defended in the age old ways of balance of power politics. While Lloyd George for his part would have had to achieve a settlement far more favourable to the Germans if they were ever to accept it willingly and permanently. In fact it is quite inconceivable, in the circumstances of 1919, that the Allies and Germany could have agreed on a peace settlement satisfactory to both. The time for a compromise peace was before Germany had been defeated, and then the Germans themselves had not been prepared to offer satisfactory terms. On the reparations clauses, one of the parts of the treaty that offended the Germans most, Lloyd George did not exercise a moderating influence, even if he might have wished to do so. Instead he helped to insert this bone of contention into the treaty with disastrous results, both on the development of German politics, and in that it provided a fertile field for Anglo-French quarrels. The Fontainebleau memorandum began 'It is comparatively easy to patch up a peace which will last for thirty years,' and went on to argue that they must aim higher and longer than that. In setting his sights so high Lloyd George was trying to achieve more than could be expected in this imperfect world. Clemenceau never gave way to the illusion that the German signature on a treaty in 1919 could by itself preserve the *status quo* for an indefinite future. If the settlement were to endure, it would be because the balance of forces which it expressed had also been preserved.[50]

Chronology

1918

4 October	Germany and Austria-Hungary demand armistice
5 October	Inter-Allied meetings in Paris commence
31 October	Second series of inter-allied meetings in Paris commence
11 November	Armistice with Germany
26 November	Foch's memorandum on Rhineland
1–3 December	Anglo-French conference in London
14 December	British general election

1919

10 January	Second Foch memorandum on Rhineland
12 January	Peace conference opens
13 January	First meeting of Council of Ten
8 February	Lloyd George returns to London
15 February	Wilson returns to USA
19 February	Clemenceau wounded
25 February	Tardieu memorandum on Rhineland

1 March	Return of Clemenceau
5 March	Return of Lloyd George
10 March	Meeting of Clemenceau, Lloyd George and House to set up ad hoc committees to consider Germany's western frontier and reparations
14 March	Wilson returns to Paris: offer of treaties and guarantee to France
22–24 March	Lloyd George at Fontainebleau
24 March	First meeting of Council of Four
28 March	Crisis in Council of Four over Saar, Rhineland and reparations
9 April	Wilson concedes special regime for Saar
13 April	German delegation invited to Versailles
14 April	Wilson accepts 15 year occupation of Rhineland.
16 April	Lloyd George returns to London to ward off attacks in parliament
22 April	French cabinet overrules Foch's objections to proposed terms of treaty
7 May	Text of treaty presented to German delegation
29 May	German delegation presents counter-proposals
4 June	Committee appointed to revise German-Polish frontier
16 June	Allied reply handed to German delegation
23 June	Germany accepts treaty
28 June	Treaty signed: last meeting of Council of Four

Notes

1 J. Martet, *Le Tigre* (Paris, 1930), p. 59.
2 A Chronology for the guidance of readers is at the end of this Chapter, pp. 88-9.
3 *L'Allemagne de Demain et les Allemands d'Autriche, Klotz papers*, dossier 19.
4 G. Clemenceau, *Grandeurs et Misères d'une Victoire* (Paris, 1929), p. 220.
5 P. Mantoux, *Les Délibérations du Conseil des Quatre* (Paris, 1955), vol. II, p. 271.
6 *British Documents on Foreign Policy, First Series*, vol. XVI, p. 828.
7 P. Renouvin, 'Les Buts de Guerre du Gouvernement Français, 1914–1918', *Revue Historique* (1966), CCXXV, pp. 1–38.
Clemenceau took care to make no public comment on Wilson's Fourteen Points. See A. J. Mayer, *Wilson vs Lenin, Political Origins of the New Diplomacy 1917–1918* (paperback edition, New York, 1964), p. 384.

D

8 For the specific dates of negotiations at this time and during the following months, the reader should refer to the chronology at the end of this Chapter.

9 The crucial point was when House said that Wilson 'had insisted on Germany accepting all his speeches, and from there you could establish almost any point that anyone wished against Germany', Lloyd George, *Truth About the Peace Treaties* (London 1938), vol. I, p. 80. Lloyd George used this argument when the Imperial War Cabinet discussed the armistice on 5 November. H. I. Nelson, *Land and Power, British and Allied Policy on Germany's Frontiers, 1916–1919* (London, 1963), p. 87.

10 Lloyd George, *War Memoirs* (2 volume edition, London, 1938), vol. II, p. 1974. House Diary, 30 October 1918, quoted by J. Nevakivi, *Britain, France and the Arab Middle East, 1914–20* (London, 1969), p. 70.
 Minutes of the Supreme War Council, conference held at the Quai d'Orsay on 30 October 1918, CAB 28/5, 84:
 'The British had captured 3 or 4 Turkish armies, and had incurred hundreds of thousands of casualties in the war with Turkey. The other governments had only put in a few nigger policemen to see that we did not steal the Holy Sepulchre.'

11 Nelson, *Land and Power*, pp. 134–5.
 Mordacq writes that the purpose of the London meetings was to present Wilson with a united British-French front. *Le Ministère Clemenceau* (Paris, 1931) vol. III, p. 6.

12 Foch's letter of 16 October is given by R. M. L'Hopital, *Foch, l'Armistice et la Paix* (Paris, 1938) pp. 33–6. There is an English translation in F .Maurice, *The Armistices of 1918*, pp. 34–5. The texts of his three memoranda have been printed many times; the most convenient source is Mermeix, *Le Combat des Trois* (Paris 1922), pp. 205–22, and *Papers Respecting Negotiations for an Anglo-French Pact*, Cmd. 2169 (London, 1924).

13 Most authorities, even the usually reliable F. S. Marston, *The Peace Conference of 1919, organisation and procedure* (London, 1944) p. 44 and chronology p. 235, have been misled by Lloyd George's mistake in *The Truth about the Peace Treaties* vol. I, pp. 131–2, and place this meeting on the evening of 30 November. In fact the French party left Paris at 10.30 p.m. on 30 November, only arriving in London at 2 p.m. on 1 December, so that the conversations with Foch took place on the evening of 1 December, the date given by Hankey's minutes, cf. Mordacq, *Le Ministère Clemenceau*, Vol. III, pp. 24–5 and *The Times*, 2 December 1918. Another inaccuracy in Lloyd George's account is that the other British politician present was in fact Bonar Law, not Balfour. More serious is the way Lloyd George begins his extract from the minutes of the conversation in the middle of one of Foch's sentences; the part omitted referred back to the discussion, totally ignored in Lloyd George's account, in which he had been asking Foch about the feasibility of occupying the industrial region of the Ruhr in order

to secure Reparations payments. It is often said that Lloyd George's Memoirs, although tendentious in interpretation, are reliable in their factual and documentary parts. It seems however that, in detail, this is not so.

14 Lloyd George, *The Truth about the Peace Treaties*, vol. II, p. 1038. Mordacq tells us about the frequent unofficial conversations, *Le Ministère Clemenceau*, vol. III, p. 26.

15 M. S. Anderson, *The Eastern Question* (London, 1966), p. 377.

16 Mordacq, *Le Ministère Clemenceau*, vol. III, p. 72.

J. Laroche, *Au Quai d'Orsay avec Briand et Poincaré* (Paris, 1957), p. 64.

Nelson, *Land and Power*, p. 220 and Nevakivi, *Britain, France and the Arab Middle East*, p. 92, state that Clemenceau complained in March and April 1919 that Lloyd George 'had broken his word over the Rhineland, Syria and the division of Reparations', but it is not obvious that the passages they quote refer to a bargain arrived at at the December meeting.

17 This Chapter went to press before the French government decided to open the archives up to 1940 under a new 'thirty-year rule'.

18 J. Martet, *Le Tigre*, pp. 71–2.

19 This question has been studied by J. C. King, *Foch Versus Clemenceau, France and German Dismemberment, 1918–1919* (Harvard, 1960). This valuable analysis cannot be regarded as definitive, as King had no access to the French archives. The official archives remain closed but some light is shed by the private papers of General Mangin, which I intend to use as the basis of a study on this subject.

20 J. Bainville, *Les Conséquences Politiques de la Paix* (Paris, 1920), p. 65.

21 Bibliothèque de Documentation Internationale Contemporaine, Klotz Papers, Dossiers 18 and 19. Nelson has commented on these sources, *Land and Power*, pp. 112–18. There is another document in the Klotz collection, signed by Hanotaux, advocating the dismemberment of Germany, which Nelson treats as if it might be regarded as evidence for French official policy. Hanotaux, however, had no official position, and was in contact only with Foch. The document analysed by Nelson is printed, along with other memoranda drafted by Hanotaux for Foch, in G. Hanotaux, *Le Traité de Versailles de 28 Juin 1919* (Paris, 1919). He states that they were later forwarded to the Foreign ministry 'à titre personnel', *Le Traité de Versailles du 28 Juin 1919*, p. xvii.

22 Clemenceau, on 13 June 1919, 'Vous m'avez dit, M. Bonar Law, qu'en Angleterre vous n'auriez pas supporté pendant dix minutes qu'un général prît cette attitude. . . . Si j'agissais comme vous l'auriez fait peut-être je créerais, vous le savez, une situation dangereuse.' Mantoux, *Les Délibérations du Conseil des Quatre*, vol. II, p. 410. Weygand states that he and Foch knew very well that Clemenceau could not dismiss Foch. M. Weygand, *Mémoires* (Paris, 1950), vol. II, p. 48.

23 A perceptive analysis of the unspoken assumptions governing the relations of Foch and Clemenceau is to be found in P. C. F.

Bankwitz, *Weygand and Civil–Military Relations in Modern France* (London, 1968), pp. 31.

24 A. Tardieu, *La Paix* (Paris, 1921), p. 219. For further analysis of this passage see below p. 79-80.

25 Wilson was Chief of the Imperial General Staff. See his letter of April 1919 to Admiral Cowan, printed by C. E. Callwell, *Field Marshal Sir Henry Wilson, his Life and Letters* (London, 1927), vol. II, p. 182. 'My whole energies are now bent to getting our troops out of Europe and Russia and concentrating all our strength in our coming storm centres viz England, Ireland, Egypt and India.'

26 Mermeix, *Le Combat des Trois*, pp. 210–19 gives the text.
Comment in Nelson, *Land and Power*, p. 199 and King, *Foch Versus Clemenceau*, p. 24. Nelson blurs the distinction between Foch's proposals here and in the November memorandum.

27 Nelson, *Land and Power*, p. 208 states that in his talks with Martet, Clemenceau denied adopting this proposal as a bargaining counter. He gives the English translation as his source. In fact in the French text Martet says that Clemenceau did say explicitly that it was a bargaining position:
'La thèse de Foch et de Poincaré est une thèse mauvaise en soi. C'est une thèse qu'un Français . . . républicain ne peut faire sienne, un instant, que dans l'espoir d'obtenir par ailleurs d'autres garanties d'autres avantages.'
J. Martet, *Le Silence de M. Clemenceau*, p. 248.

28 L. Loucheur, *Carnets Secrets 1908–1932* (Bruxelles, 1962), pp. 71–2.

29 J. Martet, *Le Silence de M. Clemenceau*, p. 249, cf. A. Wolfers, *Britain and France between Two Wars* (New York, 1940), pp. 38-9.

30 Mermeix, *Le Combat des Trois*, pp. 229–30.

31 Nelson, *Land and Power*, pp. 219–20.
This interpretation would be contradicted by the assertion in L. A. R. Yates, *United States and French Security, 1917–1921* (New York, 1957), p. 80, that 'the British had determined to give France a guarantee against a German attack even if the United States did not'. Yates gives no source reference for this strange view, which is contradicted by all Lloyd George's diplomacy at this time, but it seems to be derived from a remark by House, who added, when he told White about Wilson's agreement to the guarantee: 'England was resolved to give this guarantee whether the United States did or not.' *Foreign Relations of the United States, Paris Peace Conference*, XI, p. 133. House was notoriously ill-informed and inaccurate at this stage.

32 The arguments used by the French government in reply to the Chamber's committee on the treaty which asked for a justification of the abandoning of the policy outlined in the memorandum of 25 February are printed in L. Barthou, *Le Traité de Paix* (1919), pp. 233–49.

33 A Tardieu, *La Paix*, p. 219. Although placed within quotation marks by Tardieu, this is part of a factitious compilation in which Tardieu gives the essence of Clemenceau's arguments against the

revision of the treaty between 23 May and 13 June. Some of the phrases he uses can be found in Mantoux's minutes. I have not been able to find the ones quoted here, but Tardieu, writing in 1921 and close to Clemenceau, can be accepted as a good witness: even if the actual words were never spoken, such were Clemenceau's profoundest feelings about the settlement; several other passages in Mantoux's minutes reveal the same outlook.

34 P. Mantoux, *Les Délibérations du Conseil des Quatre*, vol. I, pp. 203-7.

35 When Lloyd George said that what mattered for France was to have the Saar coal, Clemenceau replied: 'Cela dépend du public auquel vous pensez: pour les industriels français, évidemment. Mais le reste de la France attache à la région de la Sarre une autre importance.' Mantoux, *Les Délibérations du Conseil des Quatre*, vol. I, p. 204. A. Tardieu, *La Paix*, gives texts of French memoranda, pp. 279-89 and 294-6. Discussion of the Saar problem in Nelson, *Land and Power*, pp. 249-91, and S. P. Tillmann, *Anglo-American Relations at the Paris Peace Conference of 1919* (Princeton, 1961), pp. 184-9.

36 *L'Allemagne de Demain et les Allemands d'Autriche*, Klotz Papers, Dossier 19.

37 Nelson, *Land and Power*, pp. 145-97, and P. S. Wandycz, *France and her eastern allies, 1919-25* (Minneapolis, 1962), pp. 29-48.

38 Clemenceau implied (*Grandeurset Misères* pp. 160-1) that the new states of eastern Europe would be a better balance to German strength than Russia had been because they would be free.

39 Mantoux, *Les Délibérations du Conseil des Quatre*, vol. II, p. 319. 'L'Allemagne, écrasée à l'ouest, n'a plus qu'une idée, celle de jouer sa partie à l'est. Si elle la gagne, si elle s'empare politiquement et surtout économiquement de la Russie, elle a gagné la guerre.'

40 E. Weill-Raynal *Les Réparations Allemandes et la France* (Paris, 1948), vol. I, p. 128.

41 French proposals for a preliminary peace with Germany (Nov. 1918), document in Fonds Clemenceau, printed in *Foreign Relations of the United States, Paris Peace Conference*, vol. I, p. 372.

42 L. Loucheur, *Carnets Secrets*, pp. 74-5.

43 P. M. Burnett *Reparation at the Paris Peace Conference*, vol. I, p. 436 (New York, 1940): 'Keynes suggested that in his opinion the French demand for a big indemnity was a basis for continued occupation and ultimate acquisition of the Rhine provinces.' Keynes developed this theme, of course, in his famous tract *The Economic Consequences of the Peace* (London, 1919).

44 J. M. Keynes *Essays in Biography* (London, 2nd edn., 1951), p. 36. 'Prince Wilson sailing out from the west in his barque George Washington sets foot in the enchanted castle of Paris to free from chains and oppression, and an ancient curse, the maid Europe of eternal youth and beauty, his mother and his bride in one. There in the castle is the King with yellow parchment face, a million years old, and with him an enchantress with a harp singing the Prince's own words to a magical tune.' In this fairytale Clemenceau, of

course, was the King, and Lloyd George the enchantress. Keynes wrote this in 1919, but decided not to publish it in *The Economic Consequences of the Peace*.

45 J. M. Keynes *The Economic Consequences of the Peace*, p. 29.

46 See his reply to Louis Marin: 'Oui, il nous faut de la vigilance. . . .' Chambre des Députés: Deuxième Séance du 25 Septembre 1919, printed in G. Clemenceau, *Discours de Paix* (Paris, 1938), pp. 216–17.

47 R. Lansing, *The Big Four* (London, 1922), p. 25.

48 The common factors in the outlook of Wilson and Clemenceau have been pointed out by Professor J. B. Duroselle in an article 'Wilson and Clemenceau', published in *Centenaire Woodrow Wilson* (Geneva, 1956), the proceedings of a conference held at the Carnegie Institute, Geneva. Professor Duroselle, I think, exaggerates the degree to which these common factors, at a very abstract level, led to agreement on policy.

49 Wilson to Smuts, 16 May 1919, quoted by Nelson, *Land and Power*, p. 325.

50 My obligations are far too numerous to list here, but I feel that I must take this opportunity to thank Professor Renouvin, and my colleagues Dr C. J. Bartlett, and Mr A. Turner, with whom I have discussed the problems dealt with in this essay. I have an especial debt to Mr Turner who read and commented on an earlier draft.

Bibliography

The bibliography of the peace conference is immense, and any attempt at a comprehensive survey would take more space than is available for the whole essay. The following note tries only to state the present position on access to source material, and to provide an introduction to recent secondary accounts. I make no attempt to be comprehensive in listing secondary works, but merely list those that I have found most useful. A guide to the older material can be found in the following:

1 B. C. Binkley, 'Ten Years of Peace Conference History', *Journal of Modern History* I (1929).

2 P. Birdsall, 'The Second Decade of Peace Conference History', *Journal of Modern History* XI (1939).

3 F. S. Marston, *The Peace Conference of 1919, organisation and procedure* (London, 1944) has a bibliography which provides a useful checklist of original sources and secondary works published up to that time.

I. SOURCE MATERIAL

(A) *Unpublished*

The present position is that the American official archives have been open for some time and have been extensively consulted. Even more valuable have been the immense collections of private papers which various American participants in the peace negotiations took home with them, in many cases containing duplicate copies of official material. Writing before 1941, P. Birdsall was able to make some use of these private collections, and more recently they have provided the material for detailed studies by H. I. Nelson and S. P. Tillman.

The British archives have only recently been opened, and as yet there has been little time for publication of work based on them. The first detailed study based on British official archives of this period is R. Ullman, *Britain and the Russian Civil War* (London, 1968), an illuminating study but one which does not bear directly on the problems considered in this essay. Ullman's bibliography provides a useful list of the British collections of private papers which he was able to consult.

In France the *Archives Nationales* allow access to materials up to the fall of the Clemenceau ministry in January 1920. Unfortunately neither the Foreign Office, nor the Ministry of War hand over their records to the Archives Nationales; in both cases the limit for consultation is 11 November 1918. J. Bradley was allowed to consult material of a later date for his study *Allied Intervention in Russia* (London, 1968), but his case seems to be exceptional. To all intents and purposes then French archives remain closed for the indefinite future.[1] Some important French official memoranda, and a certain amount of correspondence is available in the Klotz papers in the Bibliothèque de Documentation Internationale Contemporaine in Paris, but coverage is haphazard. The papers of the foreign minister, Pichon, are available in the Bibliothèque de l'Institut de France, but they consist mainly of letters received by him, and are not very helpful. With these exceptions, there are no French private papers of any con-

---

[1] This Chapter went to press before the French government decided to open the archives up to 1940 under a new 'thirty year rule'.

sequence as yet available to scholars. Poincaré was prevented by death from completing his memoirs, which provided a valuable record up to the end of 1918: his papers have now become available. The unpublished material in the Musée Clemenceau is jealously guarded from prying eyes.

(B) *Published*

A large amount of material has already been published. Important documents were published as early as 1921 in A. Tardieu, *La Paix* (Paris, 1921). Mermeix, *Le Combat des Trois* (Paris, 1922), L. L. Klotz, *De la Guerre à la Paix* (Paris, 1924), and R. S. Baker, *Woodrow Wilson and World Settlement* (London, 1922). The most comprehensive of the early publications was D. H. Miller, *My Diary at the Paris Peace Conference*, 22 vols. (New York, 1928) of which only forty copies were printed. The American collections have been superseded by the opening of the archives, and by the publication of United States, Department of State, *Papers Relating to the Foreign Relations of the United States: the Paris Peace Conference, 1919*, 13 vols. (Washington, 1942–7). *British Documents on Foreign Policy 1919–1939, First Series* (London, 1947 and after) begins at the point where this essay stops, with the signing of the Treaty of Versailles. However, some earlier documents are included on occasions. A few documents were published in *Papers Respecting Negotiations for an Anglo-French Pact, Cmd 2169* (London, 1924). The story from the French side is in *Documents Relatifs aux Négociations Concernant les Garanties de Sécurité Contre une Agression de l'Allemagne* (*10 Janvier 1917–7 Décembre 1923*) (Paris, 1924). The early French publications have not been superseded, and often provide the only access to French memoranda. The most valuable material for the study of the negotiations is to be found in the minutes of the Council of Ten, the Council of Four and the Council of Foreign Ministers, published in vols. 3–6 of the *Paris Peace Conference 1919*. A French version printed from the notes of the interpreter is to be found in P. Mantoux, *Les Délibérations du Conseil des Quatre* (24 Mars–28 Juin 1919) 2 vols. (Paris, 1955). This includes some material not to be found in the English version, which has been translated in P. Mantoux,

Paris Peace Conference 1919, Proceedings of the Council of Four (24 March–18 April), Publications de l'Institut Universitaire de Hautes Études Internationales, 43 (Geneva, 1964). Background material on the French side is to be found in the various studies produced by the Comité d'Études; these are very rare, and to the best of my knowledge, no copies exist in this country.

D. Lloyd George gives a very full account with extensive quotations from official documents, in his *War Memoirs* (London, 6 vols., 1933–6, 2 vols., ed. 1938) and in *The Truth about the Peace Treaties*, 2 vols. (London, 1938). G. Clemenceau, *Grandeurs et Misères d'une Victoire* (Paris, 1930) is more of a polemic against Foch than memoirs, and is not at all helpful in detail. More useful are the accounts of his conversations with his private secretary in 1927, 1928 and 1929. The latter published them as J. Martet, *Le Silence de M. Clemenceau, M. Clemenceau Peint par lui-même*, and *Le Tigre* (Paris, 1929–30). An English version, *Clemenceau* (London, 1930) was issued. General J. J. H. Mordacq, Clemenceau's personal military adviser, has left a detailed account *Le Ministère Clemenceau, Journal d'un Témoin* (Paris, 1930–31) as well as several books on the making of the armistice. Although valuable as an almost day to day account Mordacq was not well informed except on technical military matters, and his evidence on general political questions is neither reliable, nor usually very illuminating. It would be quite impossible to list all the material published by, or on, the secondary figures, and I make no attempt to do so. Good lists are available in the studies of H. I. Nelson and S. P. Tillmann (see below), to which should be added a few scraps from Loucheur's diary published by J. de Launay, *Secrets Diplomatiques 1914–1918* (Bruxelles, 1963), and *Carnets Secrets 1908–1932* (Bruxelles, 1962).

II. SECONDARY ACCOUNTS

This is in no sense intended to provide a full bibliography: it is merely a list of these works which I have found most useful. If a recent work has superseded earlier accounts they are excluded; where they have not been superseded older works are listed. There has been no scholarly survey of the peace settlement as a whole since P. Birdsall wrote in 1941. In spite of its title, A. J. Mayer, *Politics and Diplomacy of Peacemaking, Containment and Counter-Revolution at Versailles 1918–1919* (London, 1968), does not do this, and is not directly relevant to the problems considered here. Mayer set himself the task of relating governmental policy to public opinion, and to evolution of the domestic political situation in the different countries. The result is a book from which we learn little about the making of policy, and which is vitiated by an exaggerated view of the impact of the Russian revolution on the peace settlement.

P. C. F. Banckwitz, *Weygand and Civil-Military Relations in Modern France* (London, 1968).

E. Beau de Lomenie, *Le Débat de Ratification du Traité de Versailles* (Paris, 1945).

P. Birdsall, *Versailles, Twenty Years After* (London 1941).

P. M. Burnett, *Reparation at the Paris Peace Conference from the standpoint of the American delegation*, 2 vols. (New York, 1940).

L. G. Cowan, *France and the Saar 1680–1948* (New York, 1950).

J. B. Duroselle, 'Wilson et Clemenceau' in *Centenaire Woodrow Wilson* (Geneva, 1955).

J. C. King, *Foch versus Clemenceau, France and German dismemberment 1918–1919* (Cambridge, Mass., 1960).

T. Komarnicki, *The rebirth of the Polish republic, a study in the diplomatic history of Europe 1914–1920* (London, 1957).

M. Lambert, *The Saar* (London, 1934).

A. S. Link, *Wilson, the diplomatist* (Baltimore, 1957).

A. M. Luckau, *The German delegation at the Paris Peace Conference* (New York, 1941).

V. S. Mamatey, *The United States and East Central Europe 1914–1918* (Princeton, 1957).

A. J. Mayer, *Political origins of the new diplomacy 1917–1918* (Yale, 1959).

H. I. Nelson, *Land and Power, British and Allied Policy on Germany's Frontiers, 1916–1919* (London, 1963).

J. Nevakivi, *Britain, France and the Arab Middle East, 1914–1920* (London, 1969).

D. Perman, *The Shaping of the Czechoslovak State, Diplomatic History of the Boundaries of Czechoslovakia, 1914–1920* (Leiden, 1962).

P. Renouvin, *L'Armistice de Rethondes* (Paris, 1918).

P. Renouvin, *Le Traité de Versailles* (Paris, 1969).

S. P. Tillmann, *Anglo-American Relations at the Paris Peace Conference of 1919* (Princeton, 1961).

P. S. Wandycz, *France and her Eastern Allies 1919–25* (Minneapolis, 1962).

E. Weill-Raynal, *Les Réparations Allemandes et la France*, 3 vols. (Paris, 1938–1948).

L. A. R. Yates, *United States and French Security, 1917–1921* (New York, 1957).

4 The Locarno Treaties[1]

Douglas Johnson

All historians are agreed that in the period after the peace conference, French dissatisfaction with the treaty arrangements was one of the dominant factors in the European situation. Once the demand for a separate Rhineland had faded and the idea of an Anglo-American guarantee of assistance had been dropped, then successive French governments showed a constant insistence on the need to reinsure against future German aggression. Sometimes this took the form of attempts to persuade the British to join in coercion of Germany; sometimes it sought to secure from the British a pledge of military assistance should German aggression recur. There was the maintenance of heavy French armaments and the formation of alliances with Poland and with the states of the little Entente (Czechoslovakia, Yugoslavia and Roumania). The problem of reparations was, for the French, directly linked to the nature of Franco-German relations and French security. In all these aspects of policy British governments disagreed with the French. They saw no reason to coerce Germany; they thought that any commitment to France would be both impracticable and unwise; they regretted French involvement with the states of eastern Europe and were not willing to get mixed up in the problems of this area; they thought that French policy made it more difficult to reach any general disarmament agreement; they believed that the problem of reparations was quite distinct from the problem of European security. With such differences it is hardly surprising that the many attempts of the two governments to find agreement failed. In August 1922 there was an open breach between England and France on the question of reparations and in January 1923 when France (and Belgium) occupied the Ruhr it appeared that the Entente was in ruins. But a solution seemed to be found to the reparations question when, in August 1924, an inter-allied conference accepted the report of the Dawes committee which put the emphasis on the need for German economic strength. A new attempt was made to find a solution to the security question when Ramsay MacDonald, who became Prime Minister in January 1924, and Édouard Herriot, who became French prime minister in June, co-operated in trying to devise a means whereby the League of Nations could provide the machinery to prevent future aggression. But the experts in both Britain and France were agreed that this progress was largely illusory. All the elements which had caused trouble still remained.

When Stanley Baldwin formed his second government on 5 November 1924, the two appointments which aroused most interest were those of Winston Churchill as chancellor of the exchequer and Austen Chamberlain as secretary of state for foreign affairs. The latter appointment in particular was seen as ending the split in the Conservative party which had existed since the break-up of the coalition (1915–22) and which had been accompanied by frequent misunderstandings and disagreements between Baldwin and Chamberlain. When the first Baldwin government had been formed after the resignation of Bonar Law in May 1923, Baldwin had explained to Austen Chamberlain that had Curzon refused the Foreign Office, then he would have been offered this post. Since Curzon had accepted Baldwin then offered Chamberlain the Washington embassy, which the latter refused, privately considering it to be an insult. Later in the same year approaches seem to have been made to him, suggesting that he should replace Curzon. Although Chamberlain felt no obligations towards Curzon, nevertheless he thought that this move resembled an intrigue and he made no attempt to encourage it. The political situation was then very complex and relations between Chamberlain and Baldwin were far from cordial. Although after the formation of the first Labour government Chamberlain agreed to return to the Opposition front bench, he was still expressing his distrust of Baldwin, a distrust which was emphasised by the Conservative leader's complaint to *The People* on 18 May 1924 that intrigues were being concocted against him.[2]

It was in October 1924 that Baldwin, anticipating another election and a possible Unionist government, raised with Austen Chamberlain the question of what post he would choose. Chamberlain at first thought of a post with few departmental responsibilities but which would be suitable for someone of his eminence. He mentioned becoming the Lord President of the Council or the Lord Privy Seal, possibly with or, as he said, preferably without, the leadership of the House of Commons. Baldwin however replied that it would not be possible for Curzon to return to the Foreign Office since this would have a deplorable effect on France. Here we have the first suggestion of what Baldwin was later to explain to Curzon, that it would be necessary to make a fresh start in foreign affairs and have the minister responsible for it in the Commons. He explained to Chamberlain that he was thinking of offering the Lord Presidency of the Council to Curzon. At the same time there was a difficulty over Lord Birkenhead, who was then Austen Chamberlain's closest associate. Birkenhead recognised that Lord Cave would be Lord Chancellor in the Unionist government, and therefore he chose to be Lord Privy Seal. This meant that of the two first choices made by Chamberlain, the one was wanted by Curzon and it looked as if the other was wanted for Birkenhead. Therefore Baldwin suggested that Chamberlain should go either to the Foreign Office or to the India Office, and on 10 October Chamberlain wrote to his wife, who was then in Aix-les-Bains, asking her opinion.

Which shall it be? Both are confronted with the most difficult problems. In either one might find oneself in the twinkling of an eye involved in some great row in which one might lose one's reputation more easily than make it. The India Office I know something of; in the Foreign Office I have everything to begin afresh. The India Office leaves a little leisure; the Foreign Office is one of the most exacting offices that there is. I think that I should be welcomed at either office, but the Foreign Office involves, I think more entertainment and therefore expense. The Foreign Office is the highest office in the public estimation and one that, as you know, I have in past times thought I should have enjoyed. Now I dread a little the undertaking of such a very exacting office – I would sooner be Prime Minister! . . . Assuming that we succeed, shall I face the immediate crises in Irak and in Egypt, the problems of the League of Nations and of disarmament, of Russia and the like, or the equally difficult and dangerous, though more restricted problems of India?[3]

Mrs Chamberlain advised him to accept the Foreign Office.

This arrangement was not communicated to Curzon until the beginning of November, by which time, Austen told his wife, 'The papers are beginning to talk of me as possible Foreign Secretary, which George Nathaniel will not like.'[4]

Chamberlain did not enjoy the process of government making. He found that Baldwin had been a good deal stiffened by his electoral victory and not disposed to accept advice or suggestions unless they chimed in with his own ideas. The appointment of Churchill he found amazing (although he had advised Baldwin to give him office), that of Steel-Maitland to the ministry of labour he found 'shocking' and he was deeply distressed that Sir Robert Horne had not been invited to an important post. He was not happy with two of the ministers with whom he would have to deal as foreign secretary. He had permitted himself 'a slight hesitation' when he had heard that Amery was to have the colonies, and he had positively objected to Lord Robert Cecil being given a special position at the League of Nations. It was with words like 'I should like to throw up the whole business' and 'S.B. is mad' that he told his wife of the government's completion.[5]

But he had never had any doubts as to his own position. And it is interesting to see that with the exception of Baldwin's remarks concerning Curzon and France, there had been no mention of the principle by which foreign affairs would be directed. During his first few weeks of office he was at pains to point out that he did not go to the Foreign Office with any ready-made policy. He emphasised that he needed time to form 'at any rate some first impressions of the many new problems with which I have now to deal' and he often confessed to 'some bewilderment' about the conflicting reports which he received from abroad.[6] In any case he was immediately flung into a number of urgent and particular affairs which were unconnected with the formulation of general policy. He was made chairman of a Cabinet committee to consider the authenticity of the Zinoviev letter; and the murder of Sir Lee Stack, Governor-General of the Sudan, on 19 November, caused a number of emergency Cabinet and Foreign Office meetings.

However there were indications of what sort of a policy Chamberlain would follow. For one thing he was determined that there should be a policy and that no one should have any doubt as to who was foreign secretary. He had earlier expressed contempt for the way in which Curzon had allowed his policy to be overruled and determined by Lloyd George.[7] And he quickly asserted his own position within the Cabinet. He was worried that certain of his colleagues would not respect his own control of foreign affairs and would seek to interfere. In November he warned Cecil that he should not make statements about matters of foreign affairs until they had been discussed in Cabinet, and he expressed the fear that because Cecil had played such as important role in the formation of the League of Nations, there was a danger that in all that affected the League he might be regarded as foreign minister. 'I must make it clear,' wrote Chamberlain, 'that there is only one foreign policy and only one authorised exponent of it.'[8] He refused to send Foreign Office papers to Cecil and in the months that followed there are examples of how Cecil's interference in foreign affairs was a frequent source of irritation to him.[9] He also had to watch Churchill carefully, since in addition to his determination to break off relations with Soviet Russia, the chancellor of the exchequer claimed that in his position it was necessary for him to have a general knowledge of world affairs and there were occasions when they disagreed over the dividing line between foreign policy and financial policy.[10] There were times too when Foreign Office officials felt some alarm at Churchill travelling abroad and the Paris embassy was worried in case he would go beyond 'the rather arid region' of financial conversations in Paris, particularly as he was a friend of the French statesman Loucheur.[11] Chamberlain also felt that Curzon (who died suddenly in March 1925) had been trying to trip him up and oust him from his place, whilst he was frequently in dispute with Amery (who was at the Dominions and Colonial Office and of whom he had no high opinion) over the procedure of consulting the Dominions.[12] But fortunately for Chamberlain, the prime minister showed no disposition to interfere in foreign affairs. As he later explained to his stepmother (who had become Mrs Carnegie) 'I presume that he has some confidence in my handling of my own job and I suspect that he feels he knows less than nothing about foreign affairs and he has no opinion to offer.'[13]

In this way therefore Chamberlain established his position at the Foreign Office, so that there were later those who thought that he was over-dominant and that he took too much upon himself.[14] It was also natural that someone with Chamberlain's experience (he had been in parliament since 1892 and the first appointment which he had held, civil lord of the Admiralty, dated from 1895) should establish a departmental ascendancy. He worked well with his permanent officials but he was in no way in their hands. Ambassadors soon noted that their communications were being carefully read, that the foreign secretary was well-informed and anxious that his instructions and speeches should be noted and understood. Chamberlain was a great believer in personal contact and consultation. Sometimes it was his officials who urged him to travel and to meet people, as Sir Eyre Crowe advised him to meet Mussolini in December 1924.[15] Undoubtedly too he was assiduous in his attendance at League meetings because otherwise he feared that Lord Robert Cecil would play too prominent a role in his absence. But Chamberlain's intense diplomatic activity also sprang from his experience in domestic affairs, when he had often believed that he could, by direct contact, find the real qualities of his interlocutor and establish cordial relations of a personal nature which would be important for the evolution of affairs. Chamberlain's affability was to become legendary and he was to acquire considerable influence in foreign capitals.

But there had been another indication of what Chamberlain's view of policy was to be. He had criticised the British government's reactions to the French occupation of the Ruhr and he had found Ramsay MacDonald's speeches at Geneva 'verbose and meaningless' for all that they met with general applause.[16] When in the House of Commons during July 1924 he recommended to the consideration of the Labour government some principles of foreign policy, he had declared 'we should make the maintenance of the Entente with France the cardinal object of our policy.'[17] His affection for France was well-known and shortly after taking office he was reported as saying that he knew no French ministers, he knew only France.[18] He made a point of receiving the retiring French ambassador, Saint-Aulaire (whom Curzon had described as 'a man so perfidious and base' and 'so venomous as a snake'[19]) in order to demonstrate what a good friend he was to France. In a conversation 'd'ami à ami' he showed how, in the past and especially in 1914, he had been loyal to French interests.[20] This singling out of Anglo-French relations as a key point (though not, of course, a unique point) in British diplomacy, was to be at the centre of Chamberlain's diplomacy. It became a commonplace to accuse him of being too pro-French. Thomas Jones was to note that it was a national tragedy that Austen spoke French[21] and addressing a private meeting of the Labour party in 1926, Ramsay MacDonald was reported as saying that 'Sir Austen spoke French and like an actor wished to show off,' so that if one examined Chamberlain's attitude from the day he took office, 'the way was plastered with concessions to the French'.[22]

The new government had to face up to two particular and immediate problems, both of which arose from the general problem of European security and both of which were central to Anglo-French relations. The first was the evacuation of Cologne. By the Treaty of Versailles the evacuation of this zone fell due on 10 January 1925 provided that the conditions of the treaty had been properly carried out. The French had been claiming that there were good reasons for saying that this was not the case, and that there was legal justification for a prolongation of the French occupation, but it was obvious that such a prolongation would lead to a further deterioration of Franco-German relations and to a worsening of the general situation. It was equally obvious that no amelioration was likely and that the French government would not permit evacuation until they had received satisfaction concerning security. There might not have been a '*rapport juridique*' between evacuation and security, but there was as the then French prime minister, Édouard Herriot, was to put it, a '*rapport de causalité*' between the two. The second immediate problem for the new government was that a decision had to be taken on the MacDonald–Herriot plan which had been formulated during the Fifth Assembly of the League of Nations in September 1924. This ambitious scheme which was known as the Geneva Protocol, sought to close a gap in the Covenant of the League and to meet French and Belgian security fears by making arbitration compulsory for all disputes, by stigmatising war as an international crime, by providing for the reduction of armaments to the lowest point consistent with national safety and for the enforcement of international obligations by common action.

Chamberlain saw Herriot in Paris on his way to the Rome meeting of the League Council in December 1924. He had no policy to put forward, but he discussed both the question of Cologne and that of the Protocol and he did everything he could to win French confidence. He was favourably impressed by Herriot. He found him 'more businesslike and less verbose and declamatory than I had expected . . . rather oppressed by his internal difficulties and obsessed in every question by his fear of Germany.' To his wife he said that 'he was not only a good man to do business with but also genuinely anxious to act cordially with us.'[23] The result of these conversations was that Chamberlain decided to make a careful examination of the French allegations against the Germans and to try to assess how important the German violations of the treaty were. He explained to the Cabinet that he found it difficult to get exact information on these points. To the British ambassador in Berlin he explained that he wanted to separate and eliminate the small matters and then get the French to concentrate on the big issues. His idea was to hasten the evacuation, but he thought he would have to make some concessions to the French. He was already showing signs of impatience with the Germans. 'It must have been a German,' he wrote, 'who, in the story of my boyhood, fell into a pond and exclaimed, "I *will* be drowned and nobody *shall* save me." '[24]

Discussions about the Protocol were slow at getting started. On 21 November 1924 Chamberlain told Lord Burnham that the Cabinet had not yet begun to consider the Protocol. It could be accepted, rejected or amended. A little later he told the ambassador in Brussels that 'conversations amongst ourselves' had only just begun.[25] It was on the 25 November that he had suggested to Baldwin that all the implications of the Protocol should be surveyed by a political sub-committee of the Cabinet as well as by the Committee of Imperial Defence. No one doubted the difficulties which the Protocol created and it was said that even Ramsay MacDonald had doubted whether he could persuade either the Dominions,

parliament or British public opinion to accept an arrangement which could involve giving up to an international body
the power of deciding about peace or war, and which would
immeasurably have increased British liabilities. Furthermore,
as Chamberlain saw, the acceptance by the British government of an increase in their international obligations, would
not necessarily mean that the French would abandon their
desire to supplement the Protocol by a tripartite treaty between England, France and Belgium.[26] Herriot had, in a
memorandum of 11 August 1924, spoken of an Anglo-French
pact as an essential factor in the maintenance of peace in
Europe. When Chamberlain saw Herriot on 5 December 1924
he had put a very direct question on this matter, but Herriot
had confined himself to saying that France would like the
greatest measure of security possible, thus leaving the impression that the question of a pact would still arise even
if England signed the Protocol.[27]

Early in January 1925 Chamberlain told Fleuriau, the new
and soft-spoken French ambassador who had a special
mission from his government, that he thought it unlikely that
the British government would be able to ratify the Protocol as
it stood, and he spoke of the possibility of presenting amend-
ments which would render it acceptable to the governments
of the Empire. It was not until later that he learned from the
British ambassador in Washington that the American
secretary of state hoped to see the Protocol die a natural
death, and it was later still that the committees recommended
that the Protocol could not be accepted.[28] But on the
4 January 1925 Chamberlain had prepared a memorandum
stating that the rejection of the Protocol was unavoidable.
He went on to state that rejection settled nothing. Rejection
pure et simple, he pointed out, made matters much worse, as
every unsuccessful attempt to settle a political problem
always does. 'It is time, therefore, that we at the Foreign
Office should attempt to develop a constructive policy.'

Chamberlain regretted that there would be no conference
with the Dominions on the question of the Protocol and he
regretted that the British had failed to convey to the
Dominions, 'the urgency, the difficulty, the complexity and
the absolutely vital character of the problem which remains
for solution.' He believed that the question of security domi-

nated the policy of all continental actions, possibly even in the Far East and the Pacific.

Taking the European problem alone I see no prospect of the continuance of cordial relations with France in Europe or else-where, unless we can somehow give her a sense of security. Looking at Germany I see no chance of her settling down to make the best of new conditions unless she is convinced that she cannot hope to divide the Allies or to challenge them with any success for as long a time as any man can look ahead. As long as security is absent, Germany is tempted to prepare for the '*Revanche*'. 'The Day' will still be the national toast and with far more reason whilst French fears, goading France to every kind of irritating folly, will keep alive German hatred and lead us inevitably, sooner or later to a new catastrophe.

And what will be our own position? We shall lose all influence over French policy. Do what we may, we shall win no gratitude from Germany. We shall be dragged along, unwilling, impotent, protesting, in the wake of France towards this new Armageddon. For we cannot afford to see France crushed, to have Germany or an eventual Russo-German combination supreme on the Con-tinent, or to allow any great military power to dominate the Low Countries.

On the other hand it is idle even for the warmest supporter of an alliance with France to deny that such a proposal would meet with far more opposition at home and in the Dominions than would have been the case in 1919, and that such an alliance has been rendered far more difficult by the steps which France has taken to replace the former Franco-Russian alliance by her treaty with Poland.

Therefore Chamberlain invited his officials to proceed to a complete reappraisal of British foreign policy. Amongst other things he asked for a survey of Britain's historical commit-ments to Europe. But what would the Foreign Office propose?

I am frankly at a loss. Can we propose an Anglo-French-Belgian pact of guarantee to be followed by a Quadruple Pact embracing Germany? Or ought we to propose a unilateral declaration of British interests and what we should regard as a *casus belli*? Or again, is there a third course? And in any case, are we going to defend our vital interests in the West whilst safeguarding our-selves against being dragged into a quarrel over Lithuania, or Latvia, or Poland or Bessarabia?[29]

It is doubtless this sort of approach which has caused Mr A. J. P. Taylor to speak of Chamberlain's 'puzzled way'.[30] But he gave a more pointed indication of his own views when he told the ambassador in Paris of his desire 'to find some means of giving a sense of security to France, for without it I should despair of getting such an improvement in her relations with Germany as must be the basis of any appeasement of European animosities.' A day or so later he warned the ambassador in Berlin to be more discreet, since in the negotiations with the French it was absolutely essential that they should be convinced of how he was honestly striving to meet the French point of view and to secure their safety. They had not to fear that he had come under any conflicting obligation towards the Germans.[31] And it is interesting to reflect that this desire to convince the French of his sympathy for them coincided with the existence of a considerable anti-French sentiment. In the Cabinet Cecil had early complained that 'though we hear a great deal about the necessity for French security, the necessity for security for some other nations in Europe seems no less essential to peace.'[32] The treasury experts reported that the French economy was strong and that financial trouble was only budgetary and was caused by under-taxation; the following month, a note by the commercial councillor of the British embassy in Paris on the 'Present Economic Power of France', aroused some envious comment by British officials.[33] Churchill had written contemptuously about the French alliance system as 'a pack of small nations in leash to France'.[34] Foreign Office officials had frequently shown themselves suspicious of French intentions. They commented in hostile fashion on the French interpretation of the Protocol and on how 'they had turned their ingenious minds' to making use of the League of Nations.[35] The British representatives in Paris continually emphasised the confusions and uncertainties of French politics, and even reported on the disorganisation and disorder of the Quai d'Orsay. Eric Phipps, of the Paris embassy, commented on the latter subject that 'it would be a case of the tail wagging the dog were it not for the fact that the dog itself is practically non-existent'. The greatest suspicion was expressed of certain French personalities, Poincaré obviously, but more surprisingly Berthelot, Briand's close

associate.[36] The British ambassador in Berlin was not alone
in pointing out that the former German military predominance had passed to France, and that this was not the
military predominance of Germany in 1914, but one of a far
more pronounced and indisputable character.[37]

But Chamberlain pressed on, encouraged doubtless by the
reports that the fall of MacDonald had been welcomed by
some French politicians.[38] A Note by Mr Ronald McNeill,
parliamentary under-secretary of state, urged that since
England would have to support France and Belgium if ever
they were invaded by Germany, then why should not England
simply say this? Stressing the chronic nature of German untrustworthiness he believed that such a British commitment to
France 'would allay the fear in France which is the most disturbing element in Europe today.'[39] As the Foreign Office
officials prepared their assessment of British policy,
Chamberlain's comments urged them to be more positive.
On 26 January Mr Harold Nicolson, then of the Foreign
Office, noted 'we have not the faintest idea of who our future
enemy may be. She may of course be Germany. But with
equal likeliness she may be Russia, Japan or even France.'
'Why Japan?' asked Chamberlain and on the possibility of
the enemy being France he commented, 'only if there were no
Germany.' Nicolson continued his ruminations with the
question 'by founding our future policy predominantly on the
entente with France, would we not be committing ourselves
to a more rigid attitude than is desirable?' Chamberlain
commented that he feared Mr Nicolson wanted 'isolation
and drift.'[40] The upshot of all this discussion was the
memorandum written by Harold Nicolson in which he
analysed French fears and stressed the need for Great Britain
to look to her defences. The conclusion was that the first hope
of stability in Europe lay in a new *entente* between the British
Empire and France.[41] This was presented by Chamberlain
with a note stressing the fact that this memorandum represented the personal view of the secretary of state and of the
Foreign Office as a whole. About the same time he expressed
his views on Mr Headlam-Morley's memorandum on the
historical aspects of Britain's relations with Europe. 'I would
say broadly,' he wrote, 'that in Western Europe we are a
partner; that comparatively speaking in Eastern Europe our

role should be that of a disinterested *amicus curiae*. Our safety in certain circumstances, is bound up with that of France or Belgium or Holland. If this be secured I do not believe that it is bound up with Roumania for example.'[42]

It was during the formulation of this policy that the German government had approached the British government with the suggestion of a mutual security pact. It was on the 20 January 1925 that Lord D'Abernon, British ambassador in Berlin, who had for some time been using the phrase 'iron curtain' to indicate a means of removing danger areas from Europe, transmitted the German memorandum. He stressed the secrecy of this move, reported that it had not been discussed in the German Cabinet, and explained that Stresemann wanted things to move quickly. He was obviously disconcerted not to have had any immediate reply and after a little more than a week had gone by he was talking of the possibility of Stresemann withdrawing his offer.[43] It has been suggested that Chamberlain did not appreciate the significance of the German move;[44] on the other hand, as it has been pointed out, the German offer could not be viewed in isolation, and Chamberlain did not make this mistake.[45] He realised that the German proposal had to be considered alongside all the other subjects of discussion and he could not easily accept a German proposal which was secret and not to be communicated to the French. Had he done so then all possibility of exerting any influence in Paris would have been destroyed. As it was there had been a leak of information and the French ambassador had already been pressing Sir Eyre Crowe with inquiries as to what was afoot. Chamberlain had had to speak in the most general terms and to suggest that certain proposals had been put forward in conversation only, carefully avoiding any suggestion that there had been a memorandum. Chamberlain believed that 'at some later time' France would be willing to consider some such proposals as had been made, but not until the attitude of Great Britain to the question of French security had been more clearly defined. A violent speech made by Herriot on 28 January (called by the Germans 'the reverse road to Damascus') had greatly disturbed Chamberlain. But he considered that it had been addressed to England as much as to Germany and whilst suggesting to Herriot that such a speech was not helpful, he clearly thought that it emphasised the need to reassure the French. This was all the more necessary since Chamberlain's one positive suggestion for Germany was his statement that they should join the League.[46] Nevertheless, in conditions of great secrecy, on 9 February the Germans presented the same suggestion to Herriot, who was reported ten days later as having kept the German note in his pocket book and as having kept it from his usual advisers.[47]

It has been often said that Stresemann originally made these proposals because he was disturbed at the prospect of an Anglo-French pact. If this is so, he need hardly have worried since Harold Nicolson's memorandum and Chamberlain's eagerness to have such a pact aroused considerable opposition. Churchill, for example, wrote a vigorous memorandum in which he refused to accept as an axiom that England's fate was involved in that of France, and in which he suggested that it was only by standing aloof that Britain could test her value to France and exercise any real influence on France.[48] There was a general disapproval of the proposal on the grounds that it was unacceptable both to public opinion at home and in the Dominions, and there was a general feeling that, as Hankey had earlier put it, 'astute French politicians' had used the Protocol as a lever with which Great Britain was being forced into a pact.[49] Amongst the diplomats, the ambassador in Brussels wrote to his colleague in Berlin (after twice seeing Chamberlain) 'there seems to be a good deal of mushy stuff talked about our frontiers being on the Rhine,' whilst a memorandum from D'Abernon expressed doubt whether the future attitude of France would be less 'domineering' when assured of English support and said since aggression was more likely to proceed from the strong side rather than from the weak, then in the actual state of affairs it was more likely to come from France and the Petite Entente than from Germany.[50]

It should be emphasised that Chamberlain was not thinking exclusively of an Anglo-French pact. He was thinking of a pact with which Germany was to be associated, although he thought it important that arrangements should first be made with France and Belgium. Therefore, although there is some difficulty in establishing the details of what happened in the course of March and although Chamberlain's memory may well have been at fault, it does seem that he was obliged to change his procedure rather than his policy. His main insistence was that Britain had to have a positive policy and if he had to go to Geneva and announce rejection of the Protocol, he would resign if he could not propose any alternative policy. And for the detail of that policy, what he particularly wanted was to be able to deal with the essence of the problem as he saw it, namely the fear of Germany with which France was obsessed. On both points he was presented with great difficulties when he confronted the Cabinet, on 2 and 4 March. As Chamberlain later remembered it, at the first meeting only Cecil and Lord Eustace Percy seemed to give him any positive support. The Protocol was buried but it was with the greatest difficulty that the idea of a quadrilateral pact (Britain, France, Germany, Italy) was accepted as the basis for discussion, the idea of a direct Anglo-French-Belgian pact being ruled out. At a second Cabinet meeting on 4 March, presided over by Chamberlain in the absence of Baldwin, an attack against this had been organised and Chamberlain was finally only authorised to explore the possibilities of the Stresemann proposal. When he spoke in the House of Commons on the eve of his conversations with the French prime minister, whom he was meeting on his way to Geneva, he could do little more than emphasise this country's involvement in Continental affairs.[51]

On 6 March 1925 Herriot and Chamberlain had dinner together at the British embassy in Paris. All accounts show that it was a gay affair. Herriot was witty and amusing. Chamberlain told many anecdotes, including the story of Sir Daniel Stevenson, who hoped to be appointed simultaneously British ambassador to Paris and Berlin since then he would be able to reach a perfect settlement of all international questions. But Herriot was deeply shocked when Chamberlain told him that there was no possibility of an Anglo-French-Belgian pact and when he explained the limits of British commitment. Chamberlain describes him as suddenly looking 'a sick man', whilst Phipps commented that he had presumably been gingered up before dinner by Poincaré, the Poles, and the permanent officials, 'and his fear of them is probably even greater than of *Germania mendax*'. The next day Chamberlain thought that Herriot still looked very ill and when he left lunch and went off to continue discussions Phipps thought that he gave 'an indefinable impression of a patient going to the operating room.' Phipps noticed that he had carefully roped Briand into the photograph which was taken of Chamberlain and himself, so as to saddle Briand with some of the responsibility for any new setbacks. There was the suggestion too that Herriot would have liked to bring Briand into the talks, but 'the wily Aristide walked away, humming and puffing a big cigar.' Whilst Phipps pressed on Herriot's entourage the idea that it was essential to take advantage of Chamberlain's ('so sincere a well-wisher to France') presence at the Foreign Office, Chamberlain decided that he ought to seek authorisation to go further in his discussions with Herriot. He feared that the French would insist upon occupying Cologne well beyond the stipulated period and he foresaw the ending of understanding with France. He noted how Herriot was very difficult on the question of occupation and how earlier, he had become 'much more rhetorical' and said that 'he looked forward with terror to Germany making war upon us again in ten years.'[52] The need to reassure France had never been so great.

The upshot of all this was that Chamberlain cabled Baldwin, Sir Eyre Crowe suggested to Baldwin that Chamberlain should be authorised to say that the British government might take part in a series of separate but linked pacts, and Baldwin called together a number of colleagues to discuss these matters. The meeting again showed the strength of hostility to France and to Chamberlain's policy. As reported by Crowe, Churchill was all for letting France 'stew in her own juice' and saw no reason why Great Britain should take action or make any decision. Other ministers were equally vehement and only Cecil gave any support to Chamberlain. That it was the Foreign Office's policy as much as Chamberlain's is clear from the bitterness with which Crowe describes the scene ('I have never heard even Mr Ramsay MacDonald, in his most woolly-headed pronouncements, talk such utter rubbish as Mr Amery poured forth') and Chamberlain felt that he would have to resign.[53] But in fact Baldwin asserted himself, and whilst deterring Chamberlain from taking any precipitate action, he gave him full and effective support. On 19 March Chamberlain and

Fleuriau established the points on which they were agreed: that Germany should enter the League, and there should be no reduction in the occupation on the left bank of the Rhine, that the Allies should agree amongst themselves before entering into formal negotiations with Germany, and that Great Britain should undertake no obligations concerning frontiers other than those of France and Germany (together with Belgium), although she would not weaken any provisions of the existing treaties concerning them.[54] On 20 March the Cabinet approved Chamberlain's policy and on 24 March, in the House of Commons Chamberlain explained his views, emphasising the importance of the British mediatory role.[55]

In this way the negotiations which led to Locarno got under way. It is true that Chamberlain still found himself opposed by Dominions opinion. Amery admitted that it was difficult to continue opposing from the Dominions' point of view every suggestion that the Foreign Office had to make on European security, but he explained that he had only acquiesced in Chamberlain's policy because he thought it committed Great Britain and the Empire to something 'so remote and contingent that we are not likely in fact ever to be called on to intervene'. He passed on to Chamberlain the Dominions' objections.[56] It is true too that Chamberlain continued to be criticised for being, allegedly, too ready to make concessions to the French.

But it seems likely that once the crisis of March had been overcome Chamberlain's difficulties were relatively slight and were amply compensated by Briand becoming foreign minister after Herriot's parliamentary defeat on 10 April 1925.[57] Chamberlain had met Briand during March and he had been struck by his 'spirit of sweet reasonableness' and by his anxiety 'to make the best of what, from his point of view, may be a bad business'. He particularly noted his determination to restrain both the Germans and the Poles. For his part Briand had been reported as being delighted with these conversations and he was optimistic about the success of negotiations.[58] The co-operation between Briand and Chamberlain was to become one of the most striking features of the negotiation. Chamberlain never tired of repeating his admiration for Briand, and he saw the Germans in a most unfavourable light. Briand, for him, was a man with 'a European mind'; he felt he could count on his 'good sense, suppleness, liberality and courage' and when he told D'Abernon 'you would greatly reassure me if you could with equal confidence predicate the same qualities in the Germans', D'Abernon found himself noting his disbelief that Chamberlain could be so pro-French and so suspicious of the Germans.[59] But on the eve of Locarno, Chamberlain was writing from his country house where he was resting before going 'to fight with the Germans at Ephesus or some other Swiss town' and recording that 'Briand has almost taken my breath away by his liberality, his conciliatoriness, his strong and manifest desire to promote peace. At every stage' concluded Chamberlain, 'Briand disproves the common assertion that the difficulty is now with France'.[60]

Of course, it is possible to give another emphasis to Briand's policy. Once Chamberlain had successfully asserted his policy within the Cabinet, and for as long as he could prevent someone accidentally ruining things as they proceeded, then his chief anxiety was to limit French commitments to Czechoslovakia and Poland. He always made it clear that Great Britain would not take part in any guarantee of the eastern frontiers and his remark that no British government would ever risk the bones of a British grenadier for the Polish Corridor has often been recalled. He insisted that he could not count on the durability of the eastern frontiers as he could on those of the west. Briand attempted, for a time, to devise some means of associating the eastern frontiers with those of the west; but eventually he ceased his insistence. It has been said that he virtually abandoned the policy of French alliances with eastern Europe.[61] There can be no doubt that Chamberlain succeeded in limiting British obligations and in keeping British hands free.[62] If he was scathing about the Germans in his private correspondence, he was firm with the French in negotiation.

The different agreements which are associated with Locarno were already well advanced when the conference began on 5 October 1925. They were initialled on 16 October and signed in London on 1 December. The words of the Final Protocol state the aims of the seven countries which took part in the conference. 'The representatives . . . seek by common agreement means for preserving their respective nations from the scourge of war and for providing for the peaceful settlement of disputes of every nature which might eventually arise between them.' Essential to the whole agreement was the treaty of guarantee which bound Britain, France, Germany, Belgium and Italy, to uphold the territorial *status quo* of the Belgian-German and Franco-German frontiers established at Versailles, as well as the demilitarisation of the Rhineland which had also been stipulated at Versailles. Germany and Belgium, and Germany and France, mutually undertook that they would not make war on each other, except in self-defence or in the event of a flagrant breach of the relevant article of the Versailles treaty. Britain and Italy were guarantors of the convention signed by the other three powers and would be obliged to take action in the event of a flagrant breach of the agreement.

Obviously it was hoped that these agreements would usher in a new era of reconciliation. Whilst Chamberlain hoped that he had brought Germany firmly into Western Europe and had prevented any German agreement with Soviet Russia and whilst he thought that the chances of agreement between Britain and Italy over Mediterranean affairs were enhanced, the main expectations were directed towards France and Germany. Of course, Chamberlain had said to the Germans at Locarno that there were no promises, the pact was not to be bought by promises which were not part of it. But there was, in fact, much talk about concessions in the occupation arrangements and Chamberlain emphasised the need for such reassurance.[63] And since such promises and expectations were necessarily imprecise, there were bound to be disappointments and recriminations. Although Cologne was evacuated at the end of January 1926, there were immediate suggestions that French troops in the Rhineland had actually increased in number; even without this specific belief, there were many who claimed that there was an anomaly in the very existence of a large Rhineland garrison after Locarno.[64]

Chamberlain's response to these criticisms was to place all his confidence in Briand. He was convinced that Briand intended to terminate the occupation as rapidly as possible. 'Every sign I get of the workings of his mind shows me that he is desirous of interpreting our agreement in the largest and broadest spirit. No other French minister could do as much as he can do.'[65] It was true that Chamberlain sometimes grew impatient, as in 1928, when whilst welcoming Briand's statement that he could carry out the complete evacuation of the Rhineland, he urged Tyrrell (then ambassador in Paris) to take every opportunity of impressing on Briand, Berthelot 'and even on Poincaré' how impatient British public opinion was becoming about the evacuation. And yet he added, 'but if we press the French, it is not less necessary that we should press the Germans. They are . . . the most difficult nation to help in the world.'[66]

This attachment to Briand inevitably caused Chamberlain to watch French politics with an unusual concern. The possibility of Briand becoming prime minister and of Tardieu going to the Quai d'Orsay was the sort of rumour that alarmed him greatly. He regretted when, in 1926, a ministerial crisis removed Briand from Geneva, since it meant that he had to deal with Paul-Boncour who, though a pacifist, was a pacifist *à la mode française*, that is to say, presupposing that France would have her way. It is little wonder that Tyrrell, when he was still the permanent head of the Foreign Office, tactfully suggested that Chamberlain should try to win over Poincaré, adding, 'I should feel happier about our future relations with France which at present depend a little too much on Briand'.[67] The British foreign secretary was only too ready to be assured that French foreign policy was firmly set in lines laid down by Briand (as when Pierre Laval, 'with a significant and reassuring smile', told Phipps that Poincaré, 'no longer had any influence over Parliamentary opinion in the field of foreign affairs').[68]

Some of the annotations made by the officials of the Foreign Office suggest that they did not always accept these views. One finds comments to the effect that after eighteen months the French had made no attempt to carry out the promises made at Locarno. One finds regrets that Poincaré should make the speeches he did. And the Briand–Stresemann meeting at Thoiry in 1926 was greeted with more than a little alarm. It is perhaps significant that in 1929 Chamberlain was writing to Rumbold in Berlin that he never really understood what had happened at Thoiry and he had been unable to reconcile the differing accounts of what took place there and what happened afterwards. A direct Franco-German *rapprochement* was open to many Foreign Office interpretations, few of them favourable.[69]

The crisis and unpleasantness which accompanied Germany's admission to the League in 1926, and the Anglo-French Compromise on armaments in 1928 are two examples which are sometimes given of how Chamberlain made mistakes in his diplomacy because he was too anxious to please Briand and to co-operate with the French.[70] With failing health, Chamberlain tended to look back rather than forward; he never forgot 'the sunshine of Locarno'. Perhaps the greatest drawback of the Locarno agreements was the manner in which they dominated European diplomacy. Up to Locarno Chamberlain saw the entente with France as something which had to be created and consolidated. Thanks to his patience, skill and affability he succeeded. But after Locarno it is as if he were not sure what to do next. Having been the protagonist of the entente it was almost as if he had become its prisoner.

Notes

1 A version of this article first apeared in the *Birmingham Historical Journal*, VIII 1961, pp. 60–91. Many of the quotations from the Austen Chamberlain papers have been reproduced in Chapter 14 of *Baldwin* by Keith Middlemas and John Barnes (London, 1969) where the reference to my article is incorrect.
2 P. J. Hannon to Chamberlain 31 October 1923 and Chamberlain's reply on the same date; Sir Philip Lloyd-Graeme to Chamberlain 3 November 1923. These letters are in the *Austen Chamberlain Papers* in the University of Birmingham Library. I am grateful to the Librarian and Trustee of the Chamberlain Papers, Dr K. W. Humphreys, for permission to quote from this collection. Where not otherwise stated letters to and from Chamberlain are in the *Chamberlain Papers*.
3 Chamberlain to Mrs Ivy Chamberlain, 10 October 1924.
4 Chamberlain to Mrs Ivy Chamberlain, 2 November 1924.
5 Chamberlain to Mrs Ivy Chamberlain, 5 November, midnight 5 November and 6 November 1924. Lord Robert Cecil became Lord Privy Seal with special responsibility for League affairs.
6 Chamberlain to Lord d'Abernon (British ambassador in Berlin), 11 November 1924 and to F. D. Lugard, 1 December 1924.

7 See Lord Derby's Diary 15 March and 23 November 1922, in Randolph S. Churchill, *Lord Derby 'King of Lancashire'* (1959) pp. 428–9, 488.

8 Chamberlain to Cecil, 11 November 1924 and to Lord Salisbury, 2 January 1925.

9 Chamberlain to Baldwin, 20 November 1924 and various letters to Cecil in June 1925.

10 Letters from Churchill to Chamberlain, 14, 21, 22 November and 1 December 1924. In a carefully worded letter to Churchill, Chamberlain predicted that he would 'greatly enhance your reputation in this new post, which will give you an opportunity of showing to the country your possession of just those powers which perhaps hitherto have been recognised only by your personal friends'. 15 December 1924.

11 The Marquess of Crewe (British ambassador in Paris) to Austen Chamberlain, 4 January 1925.

12 Chamberlain to Mrs Ivy Chamberlain, 27 March 1925.

13 Chamberlain to Mrs Carnegie, 30 September 1925.

14 Thomas Jones, *A Whitehall Diary* vol. II (London, 1969), suggests this. See p. 144.

15 I am grateful to Mr P. G. Edwards of Nuffield College, Oxford for this information.

16 Chamberlain to Mrs Carnegie, 11 September 1924.

17 *House of Commons Debates*, 5th series, 14 July 1924, CLXXXVI, col. 109–10.

18 The *New Statesman*, 15 November 1924.

19 The Marchioness Curzon of Kedleston, *Reminiscences* (1955), pp. 185–6.

20 Chamberlain to Mrs Ivy Chamberlain, 5 November 1924.

21 Thomas Jones *A Whitehall Diary*, vol. II, p. 161.

22 A security officer sent Chamberlain a report of this meeting, 9 April 1926, which is kept in the *Chamberlain Papers*.

23 Chamberlain to Sir Eyre Crowe and to Mrs Ivy Chamberlain, both written on 6 December 1924.

24 Chamberlain to Lord D'Abernon, 9 January 1925, *D'Abernon Papers*, BM Add. Mss. 48928.

25 Chamberlain to Lord Burnham, 21 November 1924, to Sir George Grahame, 1 December 1924.

26 Chamberlain to Cecil, 19 November 1924.

27 These matters were surveyed in the Marquis of Crewe's *Annual Report on France for 1924*, 29 January 1925. Public Record Office (PRO) FO 371/11050.

28 Chamberlain to Crewe, 6 January 1925, FO 371/11064; Sir Esmé Howard to Chamberlain, 9 January 1925.

29 Memorandum by Chamberlain, 4 January 1925, FO 371/11064.

30 A. J. P. Taylor, *The Origins of the Second World War* (1961), p. 53.

31 Chamberlain to Crewe, 6 January 1925, to D'Abernon, 9 and 12 January 1925.

32 Cecil to Chamberlain, 17 November 1925.

E

33 Memorandum by Sir Warren Fisher, 22 January 1925 in the Chamberlain Papers; *Note on the Present Economic Power of France*, 15 February 1925 in FO 371/11045.

34 Churchill to Chamberlain, 1 December 1924.

35 See the annotations which accompanied the report of the presentation of the Protocol to the Chamber on 28 November 1924 in FO 371/11064. Sir George Grahame to Lord D'Abernon, 18 December 1924 in *D'Abernon Papers*.

36 See Phipps to Crowe, 16 February 1925. Berthelot had been forced to leave the Quai d'Orsay in March 1922 and on hearing that he might return a Foreign Office official minuted, that wherever M. Berthelot went it must be hoped that he would not return to the Quai d'Orsay 'where his *cassant* manner did nothing to smooth the path of Anglo-French relations' (23 February 1925). FO 371/11045. Briand recalled Berthelot to the Quai d'Orsay in 1925.

37 Memorandum by D'Abernon, January 1925. *D'Abernon Papers*.

38 Phipps to Crowe, 10 January 1925, FO 371/11045.

39 Note by Mr Ronald McNeill on a substitute for the Geneva Protocol, 16 January 1925, FO 371/11064.

40 FO 371/11065.

41 Memorandum by Mr Harold Nicolson. British policy considered in relation to the European situation, 20 February 1925, FO 371/11064.

42 Note by Chamberlain, 21 February 1925, FO 371/11064.

43 D'Abernon to Chamberlain, 20, 23, 29 January 1925. *D'Abernon Papers*.

44 L. S. Amery, *My Political Life*, vol. II (1953), p. 302. The question is complicated by Chamberlain's inability to get on with the German ambassador in London, Sthamer, about whom he frequently complained. He might have been less than just towards him. See *Historische Zeitschrift*, CLXXI (1956), p. 324.

45 See George A. Grün, 'Locarno: Idea and Reality', *International Affairs*, XXXI, 1955, p. 483.

46 Chamberlain to D'Abernon, 3 February 1925, D'Abernon to Chamberlain, 31 January 1925. *D'Abernon Papers*.

47 D'Abernon to Chamberlain, 19 February 1925. *D'Abernon Papers*.

48 Memorandum by W. S. Churchill, 23 February 1925. *Chamberlain Papers*.

49 Note by Sir Maurice Hankey, 23 January 1925. *Chamberlain Papers*.

50 Sir George Grahame to D'Abernon, 4 March 1925. Memorandum by D'Abernon, 28 February 1925. *D'Abernon Papers*.

51 See the comment in Middlemas and Barnes, *Baldwin*, p. 353. See Chamberlain to D'Abernon, 11 September 1930, and Chamberlain to Harold Nicolson, 28 May 1934. This last letter was à propos of Harold Nicolson's statement that Lord Curzon was one of the authors of the Locarno policy. See Harold Nicolson, *Curzon: The Last Phase* (1934). In his reply Nicolson offered to cut out this passage in succeeding editions. See also Lord Eustace Percy to Chamberlain, 5 March 1925.

52 Chamberlain to Mrs Ivy Chamberlain, 8 March 1925; Chamberlain to Sir Eyre Crowe, 7 March 1925, (two letters) FO 371/11065. Chamberlain to Sir Eyre Crowe, 8 March 1925; Phipps to Crowe, 7 March 1925, FO 371/11050.

53 For a fuller account of this meeting see Douglas Johnson, *Austen Chamberlain and the Locarno agreements op. cit.*, pp. 74–6, and Middlemas and Barnes, *Baldwin*, pp. 353–6.

54 Chamberlain to Crewe, 19 March 1925.

55 *House of Commons Debates*, 5th series, 24 March 1925, CLXXXII, col. 317–18. This idea of Britain as the mediating force between France and Germany was seen by some as the main attraction to the British. See Saint Aulaire, *La mythologie de le paix* (Paris, 1929), p. 212. For Chamberlain's later remarks about Britain's mediatory role see FO 371/13351.

56 Amery to Chamberlain, 15 June 1925; prime minister of Australia to Amery, 6 May 1925.

57 It is surely only proper to emphasise that Herriot did not die in April 1925 as is stated in Middlemas and Barnes, *Baldwin*, p. 359. He lived until 1957. He had been expecting his defeat and in March he had told the British ambassador that Poincaré's silence made him uneasy.

58 Memorandum by Chamberlain, 9 March 1925, FO 371/11065. Phipps to Crowe, 19 March 1925, FO 371/11045.

59 Chamberlain to Tyrrell (permanent head of the foreign office), 8 June 1925, FO 371/11070; Chamberlain to D'Abernon, 15 September 1925, *D'Abernon Papers*; D'Abernon, *An Ambassador of Peace* (1929–30), vol. III, pp. 194–5.

60 Chamberlain to D'Abernon, 30 September 1925, *D'Abernon Papers*, BM Add. Mss. 48929.

61 See Piotr S. Wandycz, *France and her Eastern Allies 1919–1925* (Minneapolis, 1962).

62 See the discussion in F. S. Northedge, *The Troubled Giant* (1966).

63 Chamberlain to Crewe, 14 July 1925, to Tyrrell, 14 October 1925, to Crewe, 17 October 1925, to Lord Kilmarnock, 17 October 1925.

64 Crewe to Chamberlain, 31 January 1926.

65 Chamberlain to D'Abernon, 2 February 1926, *D'Abernon Papers*.

66 Chamberlain to Tyrrell, 18 December 1928, FO 371/12906.

67 Note by Chamberlain on letter from Phipps, 30 June 1927, FO 371/12624; Chamberlain to Tyrrell, 9 March 1926 and Tyrrell to Chamberlain, 6 December 1926.

68 Phipps to Chamberlain, 3 May 1927, FO 371/12126.

69 Chamberlain to Rumbold, FO 371/12906. See an interesting note by Mr M. H. Huxley, 10 August 1927, FO 371/12126.

70 There are two articles dealing with these matters, both of which are sharply critical of Chamberlain. See David Carlton, 'Great Britain and the League Council crisis of 1926', *Historical Journal*, XI (1968), pp. 354–64; David Carlton, 'The Ango-French Compromise on Arms Limitation, 1928', *The Journal of British Studies* VIII (1969), pp. 141–62.

Bibliography

The standard authority on Austen Chamberlain remains Sir Charles Petrie's *The Life and Letters of the Right Hon. Sir Austen Chamberlain*, 2 vols. (1940). A different version of the origins of the negotiations which led to Locarno is presented in L. S. Amery, *My Political Life*, vol. II (1953) and Chamberlain's memory is corrected in one instance by Keith Middlemas and John Barnes, *Baldwin* (1969). Viscount D'Abernon's role in the negotiations is discussed by F. G. Stambrook, 'Das Kind' – Lord D'Abernon and the Locarno Pact, *Central European History* I, 3, September 1968, pp. 233 *ff*. For Briand the standard authority remains Georges Suarez, *Briand, sa vie et son oeuvre*, 6 vols. (Paris 1938–1952) but see also the collection of speeches and writing edited by Achille Elisha, *Aristide Briand* (Paris, 1965). Many of the issues that arose between Britain and France are discussed in A. Wolfers, *Britain and France between Two Wars* (1940) and in F. S. Northedge, *The Troubled Giant* (1966). A more specific discussion of the Locarno agreements is by George A. Grün, 'Locarno: Idea and Reality', *International Affairs*, XXX, 1 October 1955, pp. 477 *ff*. Three volumes of documents concerned with the Locarno agreements are *Documents on British Foreign Policy, 1919–1939*, Series 1a, vol. I (1966), vol. II (1968), vol. III (1970). They are all concerned with reactions to the agreements.

5 The Depression Years

Neville Waites

French foreign policy in the 1920s provoked more lively political controversy than for many years. Frenchmen debated whether their peace and security should depend principally on the power and vigilance of France and her allies, or on a search for eventual reconciliation with enemies defeated in the First World War. A tough intransigent policy from 1919 to 1924 had some success, but its drawback, shown clearly by the Franco-Belgian military occupation of the Ruhr, was that it alienated former allies and involved unlimited military expenditure. The danger of isolation and a shaky economic and financial position persuaded French leaders to give priority to international reconciliation, particularly with Germany, and this approach was given popular encouragement by the *Cartel des gauches* success in the 1924 elections. The man who became personally identified with this policy was Aristide Briand, Foreign Minister for an almost unbroken spell from April 1925 until his retirement and subsequent death early in 1932. Briand helped restore Franco-German relations to a peaceful footing with the Treaty of Locarno in 1925, and further kindled the 'Locarno spirit' by welcoming Germany in 1926 to become a member of the League of Nations. He had a flair for persuasive idealistic oratory, a cello-like voice befitting his plea for international harmony, and became identified as 'the apostle of peace' after his co-authorship in 1928 of the Briand–Kellogg Pact to outlaw war as an instrument of national policy.[1]

Yet in his foreign policy Briand always remained a Frenchman and a shrewd political realist. Realism in the long term involved recognising Germany as the largest nation in western Europe, and as a neighbouring power that France would have to live and work with; but a more immediate reality in the 1920s was French control of European affairs.

In comfortable awareness of this, Briand and his compatriots could not bring themselves to sacrifice their position of authority after 1930, when the allied occupation ended and Germany recovered economic and territorial independence. Briand no longer used the nationalistic terminology of his pre-Locarno days, when he had regarded France as 'the defender no only of her own frontiers but of all frontiers, of all peoples' and had described the League of Nations as 'a general alliance'.[2] Nevertheless, his plan for European federal union, put forward in May 1930, was suspected by many observers, as well as by the Germans, of being designed above all to preserve French hegemony in Europe. This plan was destroyed by the depression, which intensified nationalistic suspicions; but Briand's success in defending French interests can be illustrated by a Quai d'Orsay memorandum on international problems, written in 1932 after his death, which could still refer to France as *'maîtresse de la paix'*. It was unjust that Briand should have been charged by nationalistic critics, as for instance in the scurrilous press attacks by Léon Daudet of *Action Française*, with wanting to put France in the German pocket. On the contrary, continuing French mastery of the peace at the time of his death only revealed the failure of his policy from a very different point of view – that of the pursuit of eventual Franco-German reconciliation.[3]

In 1930 Germans rejoiced as the last foreign troops left their soil, but they were still subject to many international restrictions. The Rhineland, containing many important towns including Bonn, at present the capital city of West Germany, had to remain permanently without military protection. Not until 1935 would the Saarlanders have the plebiscite, whose result could be predicted, enabling them to return to Germany. In military terms, Germany was confined to having a navy smaller than that of France, and similarly to having an army restricted to 100,000 men without the support of tanks or heavy artillery or an air force. In 1930 these restrictions appeared to be permanent. Other nations were worried about considerable expenditure on arms that the Germans were allowed to possess, but the French in particular hoped that German commitments to pay reparations, under the Young Plan, until 1988, would restrict their financial freedom indefinitely. It could not have been foreseen in 1930 that within six years the combined effects of world depression and Nazi dictatorship would sweep away all these restrictions on German freedom, and on German irresponsibility. In 1930 it was not yet clear that the world was entering a period of manic depression, and Europe was still dancing to a French tune. But perhaps the most remarkable feature of the situation is that the British were content to keep in step.

Historians have long argued that in the inter-war period peace was unstable, France was fragile, and Britain exacerbated French vulnerability by appeasing Germany.[4] Such a view is held in the light of the Second World War and may well be an accurate interpretation of the late nineteen-thirties. But a very different perspective is needed to understand the problems and policies of 1930. The belief in a durable peace, and the relative strength and security of France at that time, have both been made clear in the first part of this chapter. The intention now is to show in rather more detail that British policy was not deliberately anti-French, and certainly not pro-German, in the years before 1934. Having established a new interpretation of the early 1930s, it will then be necessary to account for the transition in British policy towards appeasement from late 1933 which bedevilled the relations between Britain and France in the years before the Second World War.

Britain was always a world power, never merely a European power. And British attention was drawn away from Europe particularly during the inter-war years for two reasons. Firstly, the First World War had demonstrated the importance of imperial resources, and victory brought increased imperial responsibilities in the form of Mandated Territories. Secondly, the war sapped British strength while increasing the power of Japan and the United States to challenge British naval supremacy and to threaten the security of the Empire. Maintaining world prestige and responsibility without an equivalent world power forced the British post-war governments to reduce commitments in Europe to an absolute minimum. This could be done quite safely after 1919, when the German battle fleet was scuttled at Scapa Flow, but in later years it required good relations with the French who had become the strongest European power.

In 1930 the British government was as anxious as ever about developments overseas. The danger of an arms race with America and Japan was narrowly averted by an agreement reached at a Naval Disarmament Conference held in London.[5] At the same time the intractable problems of India were examined by a Statutary Commission whose report provoked a heated debate in Parliament the intensity of which can be clearly gauged by its effect on the igneous career of Winston Churchill, a respected Chancellor of the Exchequer until 1929 but confined to the back-benches throughout the 1930s partly due to his advocating strong British rule in India. The Indian controversy also coincided with negotiations for the conversion of the Empire into a Commonwealth which was established by the Statute of Westminster in 1931; and parallel economic negotiations culminated in the Ottawa Agreements of 1932 which elaborated a trading system of imperial preference.

The importance of these British preoccupations was explained in November 1930 to a Belgian colleague by Lord Tyrrell, then British ambassador in Paris and formerly Permanent Under-Secretary at the Foreign Office:

> Britain, France must understand, is taking less and less interest in the Continent. Since 1914, a new factor has profoundly affected British policy: that is the interdependence of the mother-country and the Dominions. The latter . . . suffered too much during the Great War . . . to allow the mother-country to increase her international obligations and to involve herself where Commonwealth interests are not directly at stake.

Tyrrell's Belgian interlocutor drew the conclusion that Britain would only intervene in a European conflict if she were under a direct threat, and he believed that this was a fact of considerable importance.[6] Isolationism was infectious: it was at this time that Belgium began withdrawing from her alliance with France, finally declaring her neutrality in 1936.

For the British to keep out of European affairs and yet to retain a sense of security they needed to be on good terms with France, their nearest neighbour and the strongest European power. This was made possible by a lasting fund of confidence inherited from their wartime alliance. Not only had leading politicians such as Sir Austen Chamberlain and Arthur Henderson served in war cabinets; a significant number of influential diplomats such as Tyrrell, Vansittart, Sargent and Craigie, to name but a few, had served their apprenticeship at the Foreign Office during the years of the Entente Cordiale. Certainly the confidence in France shared by these men was severely shaken by episodes like the Ruhr crisis of 1923, but if at times the British were irritated by high-handed French activities in Europe they lacked the power and the determination to do much about them.

The complexity of British policy towards France can best be illustrated by looking at the issue of disarmament which was reaching an interesting and hopeful stage in 1930. At that time, Sir George Milne, the Chief of the Imperial General Staff, was complaining to a cabinet sub-committee on disarmament that the French were 'heavily over-insured' against any conceivable threat. He believed that, if one left aside mobilisation problems, the French army was stronger on the new conscription period of twelve months, through an increase in auxiliary manpower, than under the former eighteen-month system. Milne's criticism, however, had a blunt edge. He went on to tell the sub-committee that in exchanges of confidential military information, as in 1914, 'on a reciprocal basis we still treated the French in a different manner from other countries'. Although this did not involve any regular staff talks it was a clear sign of a continuing special relationship.[7]

This relationship had, for instance, given rise to the Anglo-French Compromise of July 1928, when France gave support to the British in their dispute with America over naval disarmament, while in return Britain agreed that reserve strength should not be included in any future reduction of land forces so that the short-service French army would enjoy a great advantage over the long-service German Reichswehr in debates on disarmament. The existence of this secret agreement was denied in the face of strong international protest, particularly from across the Atlantic, and British naval proposals were subsequently modified; but the agreement on reserves survived the storm. The British interest in this was not so much to hide what arms they had as to hide what they did not have.[8] The old entente evidently died hard and would continue to influence disarmament negotiations in the 1930s.

Nevertheless, the entente was severely strained by economic problems during the depression. The British had been fighting an uphill struggle for economic health since 1919. Free trade, the British ideal, was imprisoned by preferential treaties and cartels, and at the same time exploited by subsidisation and dumping; while free monetary exchange on the gold standard was restricted by the burden of international reparations and war debts and obligations inherited from the First World War. The well-known British prescription for world financial health was the Balfour Note of 1922, which called for the simultaneous reduction and ultimate cancellation of war debts from ex-allies and of reparations from ex-enemies. What has *not* received due attention from historians hitherto is the extent to which the British resigned themselves to the continuation of these inter-governmental payments in view of American insistence that war debts must be repaid in full with interest like any other commercial debts, and also French insistence on their sacred right to full reparation of war damage by Germany. It was America more than France, however, who effectively frustrated the British desire for surgery on this financial cancer, for Britain needed to cover war debts, until Washington changed its policy, by keeping up reparations receipts from Germany. Hence the unedifying spectacle in 1929 of the Chancellor of the Exchequer, Snowden, haggling for the largest possible share of reparations for Britain. In the process he insulted his French opposite number, but it is also worth noting that his wrath was mainly directed against the Italians, and that the Germans found him anything but congenial. The importance placed on reparations by the British, however reluctantly, accounts for the abrupt reply given to the Germans by Henderson, as Foreign Secretary, when asked whether he would support a possible appeal for a moratorium on reparations to alleviate German economic difficulties. He was categorical in saying that 'if the German Government should decide to adopt such a course, they must expect no support or help from this country in the inevitable difficulties which they will bring upon themselves'. He then expressed the hope that 'we may hear no more of the proposal'.[9]

This was in the autumn of 1930, but it proved impossible to turn a blind eye as the depression deepened in 1931, a year to which the British historian Arnold Toynbee gave the epitaph '*annus terribilis*'.[10] On 5 March MacDonald, the British Prime Minister, wrote to Washington suggesting a 'big international move to try and straighten out the present deplorable economic conditions of the world', but he did not receive any encouragement.[11] Impending financial collapse in central Europe, however, and particularly in Germany where both America and Britain had large economic interests, impelled President Hoover to action on 20 June 1931 in the form of a proposed moratorium on all inter-governmental debts, including reparations and war debts, for a period of one year.

The Hoover moratorium proposal brought to the cloudy British horizons a brilliant ray of hope that the policy of scrapping both reparations and war debts, shelved since 1922, might suddenly be on the point of fulfilment. The euphoria was, however, that of the sick man who inherits a fortune and dreams of recovering to enjoy it. Britain was soon to feel the full impact of the depression, which would bring about the formation of a National Government and then the devaluation of the pound. Nevertheless, during that brief summer, the British summoned up reserves of diplomatic energy to make the most of their unexpected opportunity. Filled with optimism by Hoover's proposal, Sir Robert Vansittart, permanent head of the Foreign Office, brushed aside French fears that reparations and war debts would never be the same again by asserting:

[He] did not believe that any really intelligent man had considered that the present system could endure for a couple of generations. Most observers had probably estimated that the present system would continue for some time only because no change of heart or attitude was to be expected on the part of the United States. All that had happened was that that change . . . had come and come with astonishing rapidity, and we could all only welcome it, especially if people would remember the widespread and freely vented criticism of the United States in the past.[12]

There was a vast difference, however, between a moratorium for one year and complete cancellation. It would take long months of hard bargaining and bitter misunderstanding before the Balfour Note could be finally deposited in the Foreign Office archives.

To France the Hoover proposal came as a brutal shock. The American President had originally intended to follow up prior soundings among political leaders at home by having discussions with governments abroad, possibly taking until the end of June before presenting his plan to the world. It was a press leakage that precipitated the announcement on 20 June. There was some justification, nevertheless, for the French belief that they had been deliberately kept in the dark. Although it was understandable that Hoover should give priority to seeking support from Congress leaders for such an important policy decision, it had not prevented him from sounding out the British at the same time. But when he heard on 15 June that if France held out on reparations Italy and Britain could not co-operate with his plan, Hoover, with the concurrence of his Secretary of State, Stimson, decided to wait until France was ready to play her part, and 'as the evidence was growing and increasing that France was getting increasingly scared [i.e. about the German financial crisis] it might be as well to get her even a little more scared before she gained any idea that we might act'. So the British were given the impression that the Americans were anxious to consult the French themselves, while Stimson cabled his ambassador in Paris, Walter Edge, urging him *not* to consult the French government.[13]

In the event, French annoyance that the proposal came as a *fait accompli* intensified their resistance to the moratorium, which was only accepted a fortnight later on 6 July, along with French reservations to keep the reparations system operating in principle. French indignation that a sacred right to reparation for their suffering in the First World War should be treated on the same level as the repayment of inter-allied loans was merely exacerbated by American attempts after 20 June to argue that their sacrifice in war debts exceeded the French sacrifice in reparations. Such arguments were treated as hypocritical for it was assumed, with reason, that the American motive was self-interest in seeking protection for credits and investments in Germany. It was not until later in the summer that a standstill agreement on commercial debts followed the Hoover moratorium on inter-governmental payments.[14]

British commercial interests in Germany were such that American motives were shared in London; and in all fairness these motives were both self-interested and magnanimous. The moratorium on inter-governmental debts was intended to start a healthy chain reaction. Firstly, it might create confidence in Germany's ability to raise money to meet commercial obligations. Secondly, investors might be encouraged to keep their money in Germany. Thirdly, German trade and industry might then recover. Fourthly, Germany might then form an economic dam in central Europe to stem the tide of world depression. Nevertheless, British support for the Hoover moratorium subjected their relations with France to considerable strain during the financial crisis of 1931.

The moratorium was not the first point of friction between Britain and France in that troubled year; though there was no actual break with French policy on the part of Britain. Trouble had arisen in March when an Austro-German plan for a customs union was announced. The French immediately smelt an *Anschluss* and their hackles were up; protestations from Berlin and Vienna that the plan was purely economic, and could even include other nations, were quite unavailing. The British view was that the customs union would not be objectionable as such, but they realised that 'in the present circumstances, the political considerations involved dominated the whole problem'. They hoped some alternative scheme could be devised to satisfy the French as well as the Austrians and Germans. But this ostensibly neutral position was in fact biased in favour of France. Acceptance of any alternative scheme was impossible without an implied confession by Austria and Germany that their own plan was at fault; hence their rejection of a French offer of trading privileges to Austria and loans to Germany, which was made on condition that the customs union was dropped. By July, however, Austria's economic decline forced her to seek French financial support on French terms. The French victory was a little delayed when loans were made to Austria

by the Bank of England, which was trying to play its traditional role as international creditor; but the pound was too
weak to give sole support to Austria for long, and the French
had to be called in. It had not been the policy of the British
government to indulge in financial competition with France;
the Bank of England was independent at that time and its
wilful Governor, Montague Norman, was the key figure in
the advance to Austria. He was always advocating highly
personal ideas to solve the economic problems of central
Europe. The British Government confined itself to privately
condemning the French handling of Austria as blackmail.
Even Vansittart, who normally sympathised with French
views, complained that the French attitude was like that of
'the stronger man making conditions with the weaker one
while the house was on fire'. France eventually managed to
sabotage the customs union, but international distaste for
the methods used accounted largely for the general lack of
sympathy for the French when their rights to reparations
were jeopardised by the Hoover moratorium.[15]

By the summer of 1931, all the major powers had come to
realise the need for co-operation with France. The fortnight
of delay before implementation of the moratorium further
weakened Germany's financial position to a point where she
had to seek loans from France; and the German crisis
in turn aggravated British and American problems. France
was now the strongest financial power in the world and had
not yet been stricken by the depression.[16]

This situation generated emotions in Britain ranging
from desperation to envy, which found expression in suspicions that French withdrawals of credits from London
during August and September were deliberate sabotage of
the pound for the purpose of making Paris the financial
capital of Europe. Such withdrawals, however, which were
not only made by the French, were simply due to a loss
of economic confidence. The British Government found,
for example, that it had to submit to the most stringent
terms to raise a loan at that time from the sympathetic
J. P. Morgan Company of New York. There is no firm
evidence that French financial transactions were deliberately
anti-British; in fact there were many remaining French
credits in London which suffered from the devaluation of the

pound in September, and the French were among those who gave help to stabilise sterling at its new level.[17]

Domestic political and economic problems left Britain too weak to sustain pressure on the French and Americans to accept a permanent and drastic revision of reparations and war debts, which was essential to any improvement in British prospects. It was from the sidelines, therefore, that the British watched with interest the visit to Washington in October 1931 undertaken by Pierre Laval, French Prime Minister from January 1931 to February 1932. After Laval's conversations with Hoover, the official communiqué referred to inter-governmental obligations merely to the extent that 'some agreement regarding them may be necessary covering the period of business depression, as to the terms of which the two governments make all reservations. The initiative in this matter should be taken at an early date by the European powers principally concerned within the framework of the agreements existing prior to 1 July 1931.' This did little to satisfy British hopes on the face of it, for Hoover had recognised the sanctity of the Young Plan and had subordinated war debts revision to a reparations settlement satisfactory to France. The impression in London, however, was that Hoover 'would like to embark on a policy of revision based on some system of revised capacity to pay', but that he could not state this in public without a French concession, in disarmament for example, to satisfy American public opinion. This glimmer of hope was encouraged by reports from Paris. Jacques Rueff, a financial adviser who had accompanied Laval to Washington, had said that 'President Hoover was apparently prepared to contemplate a reduction of the annuities which might be permanent and not limited to the period of the depression. . . . It was understood that it would be possible to discuss the revision of war debts simultaneously with the discussion on reparations . . . through diplomatic channels'. Most American financial opinion favoured revision, but Hoover had to consider the political difficulties that such action involved.[18]

The Americans had given Laval a free hand in Europe, and the British realised that they were too weak to force the pace. Consequently, apart from persistent trading rivalry, there was a slackening of the tension that had troubled

Franco-British relations during the summer. On 15 December, for example, the British cabinet agreed that 'the Chancellor of the Exchequer should follow up indications he had received of French willingness to go rather far in rendering us financial assistance if they could get an all-round settlement including reparations and disarmament'. Plans went ahead smoothly for a conference on reparations to be held in January 1932, to be followed probably by one on war debts. But then the French lost control of the situation through two developments. Firstly, Hoover's political difficulties were underlined in December when Congress ratified the moratorium along with a resolution opposing any suggestion that the indebtedness of foreign countries to the United States should be in any way cancelled or reduced. Secondly, just when the European nations were feeling that a further moratorium was inevitable, much to the chagrin of the Germans who wanted the Young Plan revised, there was a press leakage of a conversation in Berlin early in January in which the Chancellor was reported as saying to the British ambassador that Germany could not pay any reparations either now or at any foreseeable time in the future. The Germans were indeed putting their case strongly, but they were horrified by this press version which, without the usual diplomatic reservations, was interpreted by the French as an ultimatum making a conference impossible. To make matters worse, the British appeared at first to be implicated in the ultimatum. A warlike atmosphere developed and some national leaders compared the press leakage with the Ems telegram of 1870. Angrily, the French Government ordered a concentration of troops and equipment near to the German frontier. It was some time before negotiations could be resumed, and then the most that could be agreed was to postpone the reparations conference from January to June 1932, the very end of the Hoover moratorium period.[19]

The crisis of January 1932 was the only occasion between 1923 and 1936 when France might have used military sanctions against Germany. It therefore deserves closer attention than historians have so far paid to it. The German ambassador reported from Paris on 22 January his conviction that French right-wing advocates of a preventive war would probably be outweighed by the deep love of peace shared by most French people. He believed that preparations for military sanctions would not lead to offensive action without the case being taken first to the Court of International Justice at The Hague. The Germans heard similar reassurances on likely French policy from the new British Foreign Secretary, Sir John Simon. This confidence in French respect for international law, and in governmental control over the military, is a measure of the stabilisation of peace since 1923, through the development of the League of Nations and the Court at The Hague, and through the influence on France exerted by Aristide Briand and his supporters. The same outlook was reaffirmed in September 1932 when Édouard Herriot, as Prime Minister, was asked to authorise military preparations to counter any future German remilitarisation of the Rhineland, and replied that France would consult the League of Nations before taking any independent action. The same policy was in fact adopted in the crisis of March 1936.[20]

Of course, both France and Germany underwent deep material and psychological changes between 1932 and 1936. Unlike March 1936, when the French government was advised that military action was impossible without total mobilisation, in 1932 France had both the power and the will to take military action against Germany. The Germans were under no illusion that France was restricted to a defensive posture by the Maginot Line. Similarly the British believed that Germany was incapable of successful resistance to a French and Belgian attack in 1932, which was given serious consideration by the War Office as the most likely source of conflict at that time rather than the perennial Polish problem.[21]

Calm was restored by June 1932, and the British shared German hopes that the slate might be wiped clean of reparations at the postponed Lausanne conference, as a prelude to a subsequent cancellation of war debts. They were somewhat disappointed, for it was agreed that after a further moratorium to allow for economic recovery Germany should make a final payment of three thousand million Reichsmarks. It may seem surprising, therefore, that the Lausanne agreement was accompanied by an Anglo-French Declaration that they would exchange views and information on 'any questions . . . similar in origin to that now so happily settled at Lausanne', and that they would work for a disarmament agreement 'beneficial and equitable for all the powers concerned'. The bilateral character of this Declaration was changed when it was signed by other delegations; but there was also a secret Anglo-French interpretation of the Declaration whose terms were of considerable importance:

> On all points raised by Germany and arising, now and in the future, in connection with the liberation of Germany from her obligations under the Treaty of Versailles, His Majesty's Government would return no definite answer to the German Government until they had first talked the matter over with the French Government. It would be understood that the French Government would act in a similar manner. . . .

The interpretation was drawn up by MacDonald on behalf of the National Government, and his opposite number, Herriot, agreed to it for France in a spirit of 'firm friendship'.[22]

Why were the British anxious to co-operate so closely with the French at that time? The answer given by MacDonald to the British cabinet on 12 July was that it arose from the German habit of approaching His Majesty's Government separately: 'If we adopted a sympathetic attitude German advances went further', so candour was necessary if Britain was to get French co-operation. But MacDonald made no mention of his main concern which was to prevent German piecemeal advances to the French.[23]

Activities behind the scenes at the Lausanne conference had made MacDonald extremely anxious about German policy. He heard on 27 June that the new Chancellor, von Papen, had proposed privately to Herriot an agreement involving German freedom from some of their disarmament restrictions under the Versailles Treaty, in return for supervision of German forces by the French General Staff and French freedom from German demands that they disarm to the Versailles Treaty levels. There were additional political proposals for a Franco-German alliance against the Soviet Union, and for a consultative pact by which frontier disputes, with Poland for example, would not be raised by Germany without prior consultation with France. Private conversations on these points broke down, however, when von Papen made over-confident press statements about his having political authority to make concessions to France to secure a favourable reparations settlement; this frightened his colleagues in Berlin who promptly clipped his wings and forced him to retract his far-reaching proposals. Herriot had evidently taken the proposals seriously. He and other French delegates at Lausanne discussed them with the Germans for ten days before von Papen beat a sudden retreat. It was only then that Herriot informed MacDonald, presumably having decided that the German Government was too unstable to carry on any worthwhile negotiations.[24]

'Any such idea would upset everything', protested MacDonald when told about the German proposal for an alliance with France. British policy was transformed overnight. Instead of pressing France to wipe the slate clean of reparations, MacDonald now supported Herriot in seeking a further moratorium until the German economy had recovered sufficiently to allow a final lump-sum reparations payment to be made. The Germans were driven by heavy Franco-British pressure to agree to this, and the conference ended with an unexpected success for France.[25]

During the final stages of the conference MacDonald kept a close check on all discussions, and the Anglo-French Declaration with its secret interpretation was clearly intended to prevent a recurrence of bilateral Franco-German negotiations. His feelings were probably mixed. He may have feared the emergence of a monolithic power in Europe, or simply a militaristic agreement that would sabotage disarmament; but he must have been particularly aware of the furious reaction likely to come from the Americans if they saw that reductions in reparations coincided with a deal on armaments among the Europeans. In fact all eyes were now focused on Washington, for the Lausanne agreement could not be ratified until there was a similar agreement to revise war debts.

Even the disarmament conference, which had opened at Geneva in February 1932 and had been marking time during the French and German election campaigns in the spring, was unlikely to make any real progress until after the American presidential election in November. Meanwhile, Simon, the British Foreign Secretary, had to work hard to bring about provisional disarmament agreements so that the

Geneva conference could be tided over the summer by an optimistic resolution. Simon wrote to MacDonald on 18 July expressing his hope that the resolution 'may be born tomorrow, and duly baptised the next day; then it can be buried for six months and dug up again after the American elections'.[26]

In this situation, there was little British sympathy for German attempts to draw international attention to their demand for equal rights in disarmament negotiations, which would involve either rapid world disarmament to the Versailles levels imposed on Germany, or German freedom from those impositions so that they could achieve the security through rearmament that was enjoyed by other nations. Simon's resolution in July did not provide for equal rights, and when the Germans threatened to leave the conference, insisting that their demands be discussed immediately, he was provoked to remark irritably that he 'regarded the present as a very inopportune moment to raise a discussion on the German claim. . . . The great immediate need of Europe was economic recovery, and economic considerations must take precedence of everything else. . . . The Lausanne settlement was only provisional, and nothing could be more prejudicial to its confirmed success than an upset of confidence in Europe.'[27]

All the care taken not to offend American susceptibilities was to no avail. Even after the presidential election in the autumn, which brought Roosevelt to the White House, it proved politically impossible for America to relinquish war debts. Britain made a token payment in December, but the French Chamber of Deputies prevented Herriot from following suit. It was ironic that the tearing up of agreements between the ex-allies during the crises arising from the depression did irreparable damage to international confidence before Adolf Hitler even entered the stage of world politics. Hopes of reconciliation centered for a while on the World Economic Conference of June 1933. But the United States was fast retreating into economic isolation, firstly devaluing the dollar and leaving the gold standard, then rejecting even the token war debts payments made by Britain on the grounds that they were tantamount to covert default.

By then, in any case, the British had been forced to pay

more attention to problems in Europe, particularly the rise to power of Hitler in Germany and the declining prospects of disarmament. There had been profound changes in Germany during 1932. Increasing National Socialist influence in the country was reflected by a spirit of ambitious nationalism: increasing military influence in the government brought a concentration on disarmament problems in German foreign policy.[28]

The British had always realised that no German government would be resigned to abject disarmament in a suspicious world where other nations were fully armed; but they hoped that disarmament could be made internationally effective in time to prevent German impatience hardening into a grudge. Meanwhile, periodical reports on German secret rearmament were received in London which expressed anxiety about future German potential but generally concluded that at present Germany was not a danger to any neighbouring power. In any case, most information came from secret sources that could not be used to support an open charge that Germany was breaking the Versailles Treaty. After thirteen years of peace, the British military attaché in Berlin, Marshall-Cornwall, drew up a memorandum in which he questioned the advisability of continuing with a restrictive policy towards Germany by the use of 'methods which ultimately rest on the deployment of superior strength. . . . The time must be nearly ripe for the replacement of these really ineffective restrictions by a more broad-minded settlement based on mutual acceptance and obligations.'[29]

This advice was given at the end of 1931. By the following autumn, as a result of Germany's threat to leave the Disarmament Conference, the problem was not merely known to the British government but was acknowledged for the first time. Simon, backed by his Foreign Office advisers, wanted to take a strong line against German claims to equal rights; this was partly because such claims might jeopardise war debts negotiations by creating unrest, but also because the German case was legally flimsy and acceptance of equality in principle might be used later, for instance, to disrupt the machinery of the League of Nations. French observers welcomed Simon's line but feared that it might be overruled by MacDonald, who was more amenable to practical compromise than to legal principle.[30]

MacDonald wrote privately to Simon about the German problem on 22 September 1932, commenting bluntly that 'unsettlement and suspicion have taken the place of growing trust and co-operation, and for that Germany is solely to blame'. But the British Prime Minister was still cautiously optimistic for reasons that he confided to Édouard Herriot in a letter written on 10 October:

> We must all meet and face up to the problems which fate has given us to deal with. . . . Metaphorically we have now to face a bow drawn to the utmost stretch. . . . I do not believe that any of us can rigidly resist the German claim that the Treaty of Versailles must in some respects be reconsidered. . . . My own feeling is that Germany wants to rearm, but it has put its request in such a way as to delude many people on both sides of the Atlantic, and the attitude of 'we will not listen' has swung a great many more people into sympathy with Germany. . . . I just want . . . an understanding to allow ordinary Geneva machinery to work. . . . Is it possible to get the four big European Powers . . . to understand each other? You may shake your shaggy head at this, but it is the idealism which has carried us thus far.

By mid-November British policy was aiming to draw Germany back into the disarmament conference, Simon publicly accepting equality of rights but only on condition that there was no increase in German power to carry out military aggression.[31]

The French too were becoming more flexible, for Herriot believed that other powers must make disarmament attempts to prevent Germany from rearming. By presenting a new French plan to the disarmament conference in November 1932, he hoped to make clear French willingness to disarm, if only to ensure Anglo-American support in the event of an open clash with Germany. Thus he rejected on the one hand the advice of the armaments manufacturers, which was to allow Germany to rearm while increasing French arms, and on the other hand the view of influential advisers at the Quai d'Orsay that France could remain militarily strong while rejecting German demands and rely on international moral pressure to stop Germany rearming. Herriot believed that both these policies would lead to an arms race and then to war. His chosen policy was to achieve disarmament by converting all national armies into short-service militias which the

French Left had always considered more defensive and controllable than professional armies; Herriot condemned the latter for 'creating policies around them. . . . If we mean to have a democratic State there must be a democratic army.' He believed that the Germans would have a militia anyway, through the exploitation of existing para-military forces, but instead of this being added to the Reichswehr, Herriot's plan would *destroy* the Reichswehr and thus give France the security to reduce her own arms within a League of Nations system of mutual assistance in the event of aggression. His plan was intended to work whether Germany joined it or not, for a German refusal to co-operate would facilitate the creation of an effective French alliance system.[32]

In the autumn of 1932 Germany was generally isolated and faced the danger of international hostility towards her ambitions. On the other hand, Franco-British relations were closer than for many months. Herriot was confident that the French disarmament plan would also persuade the Americans to agree to a consultative pact on security problems; and MacDonald underlined the importance of that with a general assurance that 'if it were possible to obtain a consultative pact with the co-operation of the United States, His Majesty's Government could go further than had previously been the case'. This was, however, on 2 December, and the hopeful situation was ruined by subsequent deadlock over the war debts issue, so that opposition to Germany was in disarray when Hitler came to power in January.[33]

International pressure, combined with a willingness to negotiate on all sides, brought about a German return to the Geneva disarmament conference on 11 December 1932, by agreement on an ambiguous formula granting 'equality of rights in a system which would provide security for all nations'. This gave support on paper to both German and French theses, and the real issue remained for the conference to settle. But men acquainted with the living context of those abstract words were sure of one thing, that the original Versailles disarmament restrictions on Germany were beyond resuscitation.[34]

Sir Austen Chamberlain, now an influential elder statesman, felt that rather than accept the return of Germany on those terms it would have been better for Britain to urge the conference to press on with a convention which could then have been handed to Germany for acceptance, or for rejection 'at her peril'. But what peril could be threatened so long as Britain was not active in Europe? There were still woolly assumptions in the most unlikely circles that Europe was a kind of club from which Britain could resign in pique. Churchill, for example, suggested to the House of Commons on 23 November 1932, that Britain could promote the redress of grievances in Europe 'by merely threatening, if our counsels are not attended to, to withdraw ourselves ... from our present close entanglement in European affairs'. And earlier that year, Vansittart had asserted that 'beyond a certain point the quarrels of Europe are not our quarrels, and the point may now be reached, when, failing agreement on our contribution, we must say so. This has been the consistent attitude both of our statesmen and of our people.' Influence in Europe was impossible without power and the will to use it. Even when the British launched a rearmament drive in 1934 their naval priorities were not suited to security in Europe. Yet escape from Europe was equally impossible; Britain was in a geological trap which on the human timescale had the dreadful permanence of heaven or hell.[35]

Hitler's advent to power in Germany at the end of January 1933 came as no great surprise. The first stage in his rise came in the elections of September 1930 when his party won 107 seats; and the second stage began with the July 1932 elections when the Nazis became the largest party in the Reichstag with 230 seats. Early moves were anticipated to bring the party into the Government, and prominent civil servants were already reconciled to working with Hitler. But his intransigent, and surprisingly ambitious demands for the Chancellor's post and senior ministries had delayed his entry into a coalition government for six more months.[36]

'It's a nuisance, of course, having a lunatic asylum next door', remarked Flandin, the former French Finance Minister, 'but we are not unduly worried; the people of France are keeping almost surprisingly calm. Our war material is in good order, and for the present, at any rate, we have still a certain military superiority over Germany.'[37] This kind of detachment in Paris accounts for the apparent lack of official French consideration for the idea of a preventive war. A new, more menacing government had been formed in Germany, whether transient or lasting it was hard to foresee; but there had been no infringement of international law that would justify an appeal to the League of Nations, and non-interference in the domestic politics of other nations was a convention respected until more recent times. Everyone was appalled by the violent developments in Germany; but Tyrrell, the British ambassador, reported from Paris in May that French opinion had been 'extraordinarily calm'. His explanation for this was that 'for the first time in twelve years perhaps, France finds that her feelings and fears are shared by Great Britain and the United States of America. She is no longer isolated.'[38] But sympathy was a very long way from a united course of action.

Some men hoped that Hitler would be restrained by the weight of governmental responsibility. Sir Austen Chamberlain, for example, when told in November 1933 by Sir Horace Rumbold, the former British ambassador in Berlin, that Hitler was certainly the driving force in the Nazi party and the brains behind its anti-Communist and anti-Jewish campaigns, replied that this might still afford a glimmer of encouragement because 'the bigger he is and the more dominating the more chance there seems to me of his gradually becoming more reasonable'.[39] Chamberlain was one among many at that time who admired Mussolini and hoped that Hitler might develop along similar lines. This was a catastrophic mistake. While democratic politicians associate government primarily with responsibility, dictators see it in terms of power, which is essentially irresponsibility. With responsibility one is mellowed: with power one is corrupted.

For several months after coming to power Hitler was, nevertheless, so preoccupied with internal politics that he left foreign policy, and disarmament problems in particular, to his experts; his disarmament representative at Geneva, for example, received no instructions at all between March and May 1933.[40] But increasing international suspicion of Germany was shown by the insistence at Geneva that any military changes made under a disarmament convention must be subject to inspection by international observers. Thus a British Disarmament Plan in March, which went further than the abortive French Plan of the previous

November by including proposed detailed figures for each country, was divided later into a probationary period during which Germany would reorganise the Reichswehr *without rearming*, followed by a second period in which other powers would reduce armaments while Germany acquired some hitherto forbidden weapons in order to arrive at a position of effective equality by the end of the life of the convention. Although effective equality within a few years was an advance on previous offers to Germany, the initial period of probation would have involved her in submission to closer international control than at any time since the Inter-Allied Disarmament Control Commission left German soil in 1927.

The discussions dragged on until the autumn of 1933. Then the British, after consultation with the French and Italians, pressed the disarmament conference to conclude a convention. Sir John Simon explained to the cabinet in London that he would ask the Germans point blank to agree to 'a period of trial and waiting before the complete scheme came into operation', a period in which there must be no rearmament. He argued that this course 'would bring the Germans out into the open'.[41] It did. They left the disarmament conference and the League of Nations for good.

British firmness at this point was very brittle. Simon was not convinced that his *démarche* would have complete success; but understandably he though it better than 'to sit tight and see nothing turn up'. Even if it were successful, he did not believe that a supervised disarmament convention would prevent the growth of German aggressiveness; but it would 'provide some check, and (most important of all) if Germany flagrantly disregarded her signature, would unite the moral condemnation of the world against her'. Simon's colleagues supported his strong line, advising him that British opinion was united in opposition to any immediate German rearmament.[42]

The British Government was much more confused when it came to discussing what action should be taken if Germany broke off disarmament negotiations. One suggestion was that Britain should denounce the Treaty of Locarno to avoid involvement in European disputes; but Simon explained that the terms of the Treaty made such action legally impossible.

In the face of similar expressions of anxiety from other colleagues he did concede that 'the Cabinet could not possibly
decide in favour of any further commitment'. In his view 'it
would be fatal to give some vain encouragement to the
French'. Anthony Eden, the leader of the British delegation
at Geneva, reported that in answer to French questions as to
likely British reactions if Germany rearmed illegally he had
spoken in vague terms of possible economic sanctions. In
this cautious atmosphere the most remarkable comments
came from Walter Elliot, then Minister for Agriculture and
Fisheries, who argued that it was important to give the
French a positive reply to their queries 'to avoid giving the
impression that we were already disinteresting ourselves in
the affairs of Europe and that if we could not obtain a measure
of disarmament we should disinterest ourselves further'.
He felt that British public opinion should be warned of the
dangers, and that 'if the Germans started to re-arm in a
flagrant manner, it would appear to afford a *casus belli*'.
The ministers mainly responsible for foreign policy, Simon,
Eden, and MacDonald, were agreed however that the French
would expect no answer beyond the understanding that all
powers would resume their freedom of action in the event of
flagrant German rearmament.[43]

In view of this attitude adopted by the British Government
Simon had no alternative to a resumption of negotiations
with Berlin to seek some minimal agreement on disarmament
in 1934, but these efforts too were in vain. In October 1933
MacDonald felt able to refer to 'our admirable existing
relations with the French', and Simon's firm line at the
disarmament conference at that time was welcomed in
Paris.[44] It soon became clear, however, that there was no
substance in British expressions of sympathy; so the French
Government turned its energies to the creation of a new
alliance system involving the Soviet Union.[45] The British
discouraged these moves, fearing a division of Europe into
two irreconcilable armed camps. But this policy, for all its
faults, had served France well in 1914; and a really effective
Franco-Soviet alliance in the 1930s might have allowed
Britain to remain a sheltered off-shore island. It was not
possible, however, for history to simply repeat itself. The deep
and insidious ideological divisions in Europe during the

1930s destroyed firstly the Franco-Soviet alliance, then France herself, and finally brought Britain to the brink of defeat in 1940.

British disinterest in Europe in the years before 1932 had allowed France to hold the dominant position, and the French hoped that the basic mutual confidence between Britain and France might be turned into an active partnership when real trouble arose. British determination to uphold their world role, however, meant that to prevent the development of a threat to Britain from the European continent it was necessary for her to come to terms with Germany, now the most restlessly ambitious power. As Britain thus inadvertently undermined French security, a new period of strain and misunderstanding in Franco-British relations began.

Notes

1 Apart from G. Suarez, *Briand* (Paris, Plon, 1938–52), the most useful work on Briand's foreign policy is Achille Elisha, *Aristide Briand* (Paris, Plon, 1967), which is a selection of his speeches with a short introduction. On the Briand–Kellogg Pact consult L. E. Ellis, *Frank B. Kellogg and American foreign relations, 1925–9* (Rutgers University Press, New Jersey, 1961), Chapter 7. The present writer is at work on a biography of Briand, based on sources recently made available, to be published by Macmillan and Co., New York, in 1972.
2 These remarks are quoted in A. Wolfers, *Britain and France Between Two Wars* (originally published in 1940, then reprinted by W. W. Norton and Co. Ltd, USA, 1966), pp. 18 and 158.
3 Details and contemporary discussion of Briand's plan for European union can be found in A. Toynbee (ed.), *Survey of International Affairs, 1930* (RIIA, 1931), and in L. Woodward and R. Butler (eds.), *Documents on British Foreign Policy* (HMSO), ser. 2, vol. I.; the Quai d'Orsay memorandum referred to above is in *Documents diplomatiques français, 1932–9*, ser. 1, vol. I, p. 232.
4 Note, for example, the title as well as the argument in E. H. Carr, *The Twenty Years' Crisis* (1939); the view is also expounded in Wolfers, *Britain and France Between Two Wars*, pp. 248–9, and is corroborated on the British side in M. Gilbert and R. Gott, *The Appeasers* (Weidenfeld & Nicolson, 1963).
5 For a detailed study of naval disarmament problems at this time consult R. G. O'Connor *Perilous Equilibrium* (Kansas University Press, Lawrence, 1962).

6 An extract, translated by the present writer, taken from long and interesting reports in *Documents diplomatiques belges, 1919–39*, vol. II, nos. 216 and 218.

7 Copies of the minutes of these sub-committee meetings are in the private papers of one of the members, Lord Lothian, deposited at the Scottish Record Office, GD40/17/95, File 1.

8 Milne dropped the interesting remark that if the Germans had known how little ammunition British troops had in 1914 they would have broken through, *Lothian Papers*. On the Compromise consult *O'Connor*, pp. 21–2, and David Carlton, 'The Anglo-French Compromise on Arms Limitation, 1928' in *Journal of British Studies*, VIII, 1969, pp. 141–62.

9 *Documents on British Foreign Policy* (cited hereafter as *DBFP*), ser. 2, I, 535–9; also private papers of Sir Horace Rumbold, in private possession, letter from Henderson 11 Nov., 1930 File.

10 For details on 1931 consult Toynbee (ed.), *Survey of International Affairs, 1931*; more recent studies are E. W. Bennett, *Germany and the Diplomacy of the Financial Crisis, 1931* (Harvard U.P., 1962); and G. Warner, *Pierre Laval and the Eclipse of France* (London, Eyre and Spottiswoode, 1968), Chapter I.

11 *Foreign Relations of United States (FRUS)*, 1931, I, 611.

12 *DBFP*, 2, II, 95–7.

13 Unpublished *Diary of Henry Stimson*, entry for 15 June 1931 (Yale University Library, USA); see also Bennett, *Germany*, p. 133, for evidence of Hoover's anti-French prejudices.

14 Bennett, *Germany*, pp. 169–70.

15 Details of the customs union crisis are in Bennett, *Germany*, pp. 40–81; references above to British views are in *DBFP*, 2, II, 42 and 95–6, and in *FRUS*, 1931, I, 25.

16 An explanation for the peculiarly strong position of the French economy at this time is in G. Wright, *France in Modern Times* (London, John Murray, 1962), pp. 464–8, and with more detail in A Sauvy, *Histoire économique de la France entre les deux guerres* (Paris, Fayard, 1965–7), vol. I, pp. 114–28, and vol. II, 15–27.

17 Bennett, *Germany*, p. 248 and note 6; there is penetrating criticism of 'reckless over-lending' by British bankers as a major cause of the crisis in H. Dalton, *Memoirs: Call Back Yesterday* (London, Muller, 1953), pp. 283–4; for contemporary criticism of France see P. Einzig, *Behind the Scenes in International Finance* (London, 1931), p. 50; but see also his revised opinion in *World Finance* (London, 1935), pp. 225–6.

18 Details of Laval's visit to Washington are in Warner, *Pierre Laval*, pp. 45–51; documentary evidence of British impressions of the visit can be found in official government archives at the Public Records Office, FO 371/15198/C8348, FO 371/15197/C7906, FO 371/15198/C8385.

19 Warner, *Pierre Laval*, pp. 50–3; B. H. Liddell-Hart, *Memoirs*, vol. I (London, Cassell, 1966), pp. 190–1; the British cabinet agreement 15 Dec. 1931 is in the archives at the PRO, Cab. 23/69/260.

20 The German ambassador's report is in the *German Foreign Ministry Records* (*GFMR*), on photostats, available at the British Foreign Office Library, K936/K241027–31; Simon's view is in *DBFP*, 2, iii, 80–82; Herriot's policy statement is in *Documents diplomatiques français* (*DDF*), ser. 1, vol. I, pp. 207–8.

21 Memorandum from War Office to FO, 2 March 1932, *DBFP*, 2, III, appendix iv, pp. 602–5.

22 For details of the Lausanne negotiations see *DBFP*, 2, III, particularly the important developments on pp. 344, 368–9, 423 and 438; for the French view consult M. Soulié, *La Vie politique d'Édouard Herriot* (Paris, Colin, 1962), pp. 370–1.

23 Cabinet conclusions of 12 July, in archives at PRO, Cab. 23/72/44 (32), pp. 76–106 and appendices 1 and 2.

24 É. Herriot, *Jadis* (Paris, Flammarion, 1952), vol. II, pp. 322, 338–9, and 342–5; his biographer, Soulié, *La vie politique*, pp. 363–4, contrives to say less on all this than Herriot himself; Von Papen, *Memoirs* (Eng. trans., London, Deutsch, 1952), pp. 175–6, is interesting but shaky on dates.

25 *DBFP*, 2, III, 271–2, 274–81, 284, 344, 423.

26 Simon's letter is in the archives at the PRO, FO 371/16431/ W. 8178G.

27 *DBFP*, 2, IV, 109.

28 Details of developments in Germany are in A. Bullock, *Hitler: a study in tyranny* (London, Penguin, 1962), and F. L. Carsten, *The Reichswehr in Politics* (OUP, 1966).

29 *DBFP*, 2, I, app. ii, pp. 598–603; II, app. iv, pp. 515–24; III, app. iv, pp. 602–5; these are some of the British views on German military strength; see also Carsten, *Reichswehr*, for a sceptical view of the effectiveness of German secret rearmament.

30 *DDF*, ser. 1, vol. I, pp. 188–9.

31 These letters are in the private papers of Lord Simon, which I have been able to consult owing to the kind permission of his son.

32 See particularly the French views expressed in *DDF*, 1, I, 568–9; other useful references are documents 250, 268, 272, 273; also *DBFP*, 2, 258; the best study of French defence policy during this period is R. D. Challener, *The French Theory of the Nation in Arms, 1866–1939* (New York, Columbia UP, 1955).

33 Archives at PRO, FO 371/16469/W. 13393.

34 *DBFP*, 2, IV, 377, 241–2 and 287–95; these documents mark the important stages leading to the return of Germany to negotiations early in December 1932. These negotiations can then be followed on pp. 308–78. The text of the agreement by which Germany rejoined the disarmament conference is on pp. 377–8.

35 Chamberlain's comments are in a letter of 17 May 1933, in his private papers, Box 40, deposited at Birmingham University Library, and I am grateful to the librarian for permission to consult them; references to Churchill and Vansittart are from M. Gilbert, *The Roots of Appeasement* (London, Weidenfeld & Nicolson, 1966), pp. 133 and 136–7; conflicting claims on British policy in 1933–4

are discussed in detail in D. C. Watt, *Personalities and Policies* (London, Longmans, 1965), pp. 83–116.

36 *DDF*, I, 28–9 and 106.

37 A. Werth, *France in Ferment* (Jarrolds, 1934), p. 23.

38 *DBFP*, 2, V, 267.

39 *Austen Chamberlain Papers*, Box 40.

40 Evidence of Hitler's preoccupation is in *DDF*, 1, III, 189–91; and in *DBFP*, 2, V, 189–90.

41 Minutes of Cabinet meeting 9 Oct. 1933, in archives at PRO, CP 52 (33).

42 Note by Simon annexed to minutes of conversation at 10 Downing Street, 4 Oct. 1933, also attended by MacDonald, Baldwin, Eden and Hankey, CP 228 (33).

43 Minutes of Cabinet meeting on 20 Sept. 1933, 51 (33), Cab. 23/77; although this meeting was some time before Germany left the disarmament conference it is of great value to the historian because the prime minister asked the secretary to circulate fuller minutes than usual for the benefit of absent ministers, including the chancellor of the exchequer, Neville Chamberlain.

44 Cabinet meeting, 9 Oct. 1933, CP 52 (33).

45 The remarkable story of the Franco-Soviet Alliance of 1935 can be followed in W. E. Scott, *Alliance Against Hitler* (Duke UP, North Carolina, 1962).

Bibliography

Sir Llewellyn Woodward, one of the historians who compiled *Documents on British Foreign Policy, 1919–1939*, once remarked that if the official archives were opened to the public, historians would not find anything not already available in the newspapers of the time. It may be true that the change from a fifty to a thirty year rule has not brought many documentary revelations that would excite the man in the street. But it is important to the historian to be able, in any case, to dispel suspicions that sensational documents exist. Furthermore, it is only by consulting the papers of ministers and government departments involved in the decision-making process that the historian can assess the contemporary opinions and values behind decisions, which very often official dispatches and statements leave obscure.

The published French series *Documents diplomatiques français, 1932–1939* has been difficult to compile owing to the losses in 1940, as well as to the departmentalised nature of

French government under the Third Republic. But this has resulted in a collection of documents from various sources which is of remarkable interest to the historian. Now that France too has changed to a thirty year rule the processes of decision-making in French foreign policy should become even more clear.

Apart from the official archives, collections of private papers and interviews with survivors of the period in question provide the best means of understanding the living context of official policy statements. For my work on this chapter, I have benefited from the kind permission of the present Lord Simon to consult the papers of his father, who was British secretary of state for foreign affairs from 1931 to 1935; of the chief librarian at Birmingham University to consult the papers of Sir Austen Chamberlain; of the son of Sir Horace Rumbold to consult the Rumbold papers; of the curators of the Stirling Library at Yale University to consult the diaries and papers of Henry Stimson.

I am also very grateful for the permission to interview the heirs of Aristide Briand, M. and Mme Billiau; also M. René Massigli, the colleague of Briand at one time; and Sir Arthur Willert, the press officer at the Foreign Office in the years up to 1935.

In addition to particular sources of information for this chapter one must single out the invaluable pioneering studies which provide the most useful introduction to the subject:

W. M. Jordan, *Britain, France, and the German Problem, 1919– 1939* (Oxford University Press for the Royal Institute of International Affairs, 1943).

A. Wolfers, *Britain and France Between Two Wars* (New York, Harcourt, Brace, 1940, reprinted by W. W. Norton, 1966).

PRIMARY SOURCES

British archives are available at the Public Records Office, London; and at the Scottish Records Office, Edinburgh, one can consult the papers of Lord Lothian, an influential Liberal who served briefly in the National Government in 1931–2.

French archives were recently made available under the new thirty year rule and are deposited at the Archives Nationales, Paris.

German archives were captured, apart from some that were destroyed, at the end of World War II, and large sections were microfilmed. Photostats taken from the films are available for consultation in the three capitals of the victorious western powers. The British collection is housed in the Foreign Office Library, London.

American archives are available, partly on microfilm, at the US National Archives, Washington DC.

Apart from the published series of British and French diplomatic documents already mentioned, there are:

Documents diplomatiques belges, 1919–1939.
Documents on German Foreign Policy, 1919–1945.
Foreign Relations of the United States, (1919– still continuing).
Documents on International Affairs (1919– still continuing), a series of speeches, statements, and published material, compiled by the Royal Institute of International Affairs, a private organisation, to supplement the annual *Survey of International Affairs.*

MEMOIRS

Lord Avon, *The Eden Memoirs: Facing the Dictators* (London, Cassell, 1962).

H. Dalton, *Memoirs: Call Back Yesterday, 1887–1931* (London, Muller, 1953).

A. François-Poncet, *Souvenirs d'une ambassade à Berlin, 1931– 1938* (Paris, Flammarion, 1946).

É. Herriot, *Jadis*, vol. II (Paris, Flammarion, 1952).

H. Hoover, *Memoirs of Herbert Hoover*, vol. ii, 1929–33 (New York, 1952).

C. Hull, *Memoirs of Cordell Hull* (New York, 1948).

B. H. Liddell-Hart, *Memoirs*, 2 vols. (London, Cassell, 1966).

F. von Papen, *Memoirs* (translated, London, Deutsch, 1952).

J. Paul-Boncour, *Entre deux guerres*, vol. II, 1919–1934 (Paris, Plon, 1945).

Lord Simon, *Retrospect* (London, Hutchinson, 1952).

Lord Snowden. *An Autobiography* (London, Nicholson and Watson, Ltd, 1934), 2 vols.

H. L. Stimson and M. Bundy, *On Active Service in Peace and War* (New York, 1947).

A. C. Temperley, *The Whispering Gallery of Europe* (London, Collins, 1938), written by a leading military member of the British delegation to the disarmament conference at Geneva, 1932–4.

F

Lord Templewood, *Nine Troubled Years* (London, Collins, 1954), written by the former Sir Samual Hoare who was influential on India and disarmament in the early 1930s before becoming foreign secretary in 1935.

Lord Vansittart, *The Mist Procession* (Lord, Hutchinson, 1958).

SECONDARY SOURCES

BIOGRAPHIES

R. Binion, *Defeated Leaders: the Political Fate of Caillaux, Jouvenel, Tardieu* (New York, 1900).

A. Bréal, *Philippe Berthelot* (Paris, Gallimard, 1937).

A. Bullock, *Hitler: a Study in Tyranny* (2nd edition, London, Penguin, 1962).

J. Chastenet, *Raymond Poincaré* (Paris, Julliard, 1948).

G. Craig and F. Gilbert, *The Diplomats, 1919–1939* (Princeton U.P., 1953, reprinted by Atheneum, New York, 1965), including useful brief studies of Austen Chamberlain, Berthelot, Henderson, Léger, Neurath, Rumbold, François-Poncet and others.

A. Elisha, *Aristide Briand: discours et écrits sur sa politique étrangère* (Paris, Plon, 1967), more a collection of documents with an introduction than a biography.

L. E. Ellis, *Frank B. Kellogg and American Foreign Relations, 1925–1929* (New Jersey, Rutgers University Press, 1961).

R. H. Ferrell, *The American Secretaries of State and their Diplomacy: Kellogg and Stimson*, vol. XI in the series (New York, 1963).

M. A. A. Hamilton, *Arthur Henderson* (London, Heinemann, 1938).

P. Miquel, *Poincaré* (Paris, Fayard, 1961).

M. Soulié, *La Vie politique d'Édouard Herriot* (Paris, Colin, 1962).

G. Suarez, *Briand*, 6 vols. (Paris, Plon, 1938–45), vol. VI deals with the years 1923–32 and is very thin and disjointed for two reasons. Firstly, it was published posthumously. Secondly, Briand's heirs prevented Suarez continuing to have access to the family papers when he began to collaborate with the Germans.

G. Warner, *Pierre Laval and the Eclipse of France* (London, Eyre and Spottiswoode, 1968).

On the British side, there is a need for biographical studies of Ramsay MacDonald, Arthur Henderson, Sir John, later Lord Simon. On the French side, there is a need for biographical studies of Briand (a gap the present writer is about to fill), Paul-Boncour, Tardieu, and Daladier.

OTHER WORKS

N. H. Baynes, *The Speeches of Adolf Hitler, April 1922–August 1939* (London, 1942).

E. W. Bennett, *Germany and the Diplomacy of the Financial Crisis, 1931* (Harvard University Press, 1962).

É. Bonnefous, *Histoire politique de la Troisième République: la République en danger*, vol. V of a series of 7 vols. (Paris, Presses Universitaires de France, 1962), written to give details of political debates and governmental changes and policies, to cover a period when there was no *L'Année politique*.

D. Carlton, *MacDonald Versus Henderson: the Foreign Policy of the Second Labour Government, 1929–1931* (London, Macmillan, 1969).
'The Ango-French Compromise on Arms Limitation, 1928' in *Journal of British Studies*, **VIII**, 1969, 141–62.

E. H. Carr, *The Twenty Years Crisis* (London, 1939), written by a historian who had worked on the Foreign Office staff in the early 1930s.

F. L. Carsten, *The Reichswehr in Politics, 1919–1933* (Oxford University Press, 1966), which argues that secret German rearmament was not very advanced or dangerous before 1933, based on German archives, which are most likely to reveal the truth.

G. Castellan, *Le Réarmement clandestin du Reich, 1930–1935* (Paris, Plon, 1954), which presents French secret service documents to show that German rearmament was dangerous by 1930.

R. D. Challener, *The French Theory of the Nation in Arms, 1866–1939* (New York, Columbia University Press, 1955), which is the best study of French defence policy between the wars. A very thoughtful general discussion is supported by a wealth of source references to facilitate further study.

J. Chastenet, *Histoire de la Troisième République*, vol. V of a series (Paris, Hachette, 1955–62), written by the former editor of *Le Temps*, a journalist turned historian with a wealth of inside information at his disposal.

B. Collier, *The Defence of the United Kingdom*, part of the military series edited by J. R. M. Butler entitled: 'History of the Second World War' (London, HMSO, 1957), Chapters 1, 2, and 3.

J. B. Duroselle, *Histoire diplomatique de 1919 à nos jours* (Paris, Dalloz, 5th edn. 1970).

156 *Troubled Neighbours*

P. Einzig, *Behind the Scenes in International Finance* (London, Macmillan, 1931).
—*France's Crisis* (London, Macmillan, 1934).
—*World Finance* (London, Macmillan, 1935).
M. Gilbert, *The Roots of Appeasement* (London, Weidenfeld and Nicolson, 1966), which is more useful on public opinion than on government policy and blurs the difference between appeasing Europe, i.e. wanting Europe to be quiet, and appeasing Germany, i.e. making concessions to satisfy Hitler's appetite.
—and R. Gott, *The Appeasers* (London, Weidenfeld and Nicolson, 1960).
B. Granzow, *A Mirror of Nazism: British Opinion and the Emergence of Hitler, 1929–1933* (London, Gollancz, 1964), the best available introduction to the British press opinion of that period, though requiring further reference to press sources for the reader to have a balanced picture.
A. Grosser, *Hitler, la presse et la naissance d'une dictature* (Paris, Colin, 1959), a very useful study of selections from the international press in 1932–3, usually allowing the extracts to speak for themselves.
K. H. Jarausch, *The Four Power Pact, 1933* (Madison, University of Wisconsin Press, 1966).
W. N. Medlicott, *British Foreign Policy Since Versailles* (London, Methuen, 1969).
C. A. Micaud, *The French Right and Nazi Germany, 1933–1939* (Durham North Carolina, Duke University Press, 1943).
J. Minart, *Le Drame du désarmement français, 1918–1939* (La Nef de Paris Éditions, 1960), written by a soldier who sat on government committees handling the disarmament conference problems in 1932–3. He tends to support Weygand without taking into account Herriot's wider economic and diplomatic problems. His book should be read with frequent reference to *Documents diplomatiques français*, ser. 1, vols. I–III.
J. Néré, *La Troisième République, 1914–1940* (Paris, Colin, 1967).
R. G. O'Connor, *Perilous Equilibrium* (Lawrence, Kansas University Press, 1962), a concise and effective introduction to naval disarmament.
G. Peel, *The Economic Policy of France* (London, 1937).
P. Renouvin, *Histoire des relations internationales: Les Crises du XXe siècle, 1914–1945*, vol. VIII of a series, itself in 2 parts (Paris, Hachette, 1957–8).
E. M. Robertson, *Hitler's Prewar Policy and Military Plans, 1933–1939* (London, Longmans, 1963).
A. Sauvy, *Histoire économique de la France entre les deux guerres*

in 2 vols. with a 3rd yet to appear (Paris, Fayard, 1965–), combines an exciting discussion with weighty statistics, unfortunately often blurring the distinction between them.

W. E. Scott, *Alliance Against Hitler: the Origins of the Franco-Soviet Pact of 1935* (Durham North Carolina, Duke University Press, 1962), which is the most penetrating study of the diplomacy of the early 'thirties, ranging more widely than the title would suggest.

D. C. Watt, *Personalities and Policies* (London, Longmans, 1965), containing some fascinating studies of British foreign policy in the making, notably essays 4 and 5 dealing with the rival claims of Europe and the Far East to have priority in British policy.

E. Weill-Raynal, *Les Réparations allemandes et la France*, in 3 vols. (Paris, Nouvelles Éditions Latines, 1948), essential study.

A. Werth, *France in Ferment* (London, Jarrolds, 1934), written by a contemporary eye-witness, the Paris correspondent of the *Manchester Guardian*, containing much primary source material presented in a very readable account.

J. W. Wheeler-Bennett, *Hindenburg, the Wooden Titan* (London, Macmillan, 1938).

—*The Nemesis of Power: the German Army in Politics, 1918–1945* (London, Macmillan, 1953).

—*The Pipe Dream of Peace: the Story of the Collapse of Disarmament* (New York, W. Morrow and Co., 1935), still the most useful introduction to issues at the disarmament conference of 1932–4.

G. Wright, *France in Modern Times* (London, John Murray, 1962), a historical survey from 1760 to 1960, with a good introduction to the inter-war years for the general reader and the young student.

6 The Rhineland Crisis: 7 March 1936

Maurice Baumont

With the hindsight of more than thirty years and in the light of the catastrophic events of the Second World War, it is generally felt that the Rhineland crisis of 1936 marked the decisive moment when Hitler should have been checked. It is now agreed, Eden states in his memoirs, 'that Hitler should at that point have been called to order, if necessary by force'.[1] This was the last opportunity of halting the dictator.

What effect did the crisis of March 1936 have on Anglo-French relations?

Although the two countries appeared to be on generally friendly terms, relations between them had often been strained since the victory that the armistice of November 1918 had confirmed. Their attitudes differed very greatly at a time when they were the leading powers, since the United States had returned to isolationism, Russia was in the throes of civil war, Austria–Hungary had collapsed and Germany had been defeated. There is no doubt that these diverging attitudes largely contributed to the collapse of the state of affairs created in 1919.

Tension had been particularly acute in 1922 when Lloyd George and Poincaré had come face to face in Europe as well as in the Middle East, and in 1923 when Poincaré, after much hesitation and despite London's attitude, had decided to occupy the Ruhr. In any argument between France and Germany England had nearly always upheld German claims. Tension had been eased, however, after Poincaré, winning a victory over the Reich in September 1923, had, in November, reluctantly allowed a team of experts to study the possibilities of German payments in order to avoid a complete break with England. From 1924 on, with the Dawes plan followed by the evacuation of the Ruhr, there had been a move towards appeasement.

With Aristide Briand, foreign minister from April 1925, and Sir Austen Chamberlain, who headed the Foreign Office in Baldwin's Conservative government from October 1924 to May 1929, we come to the euphoric days of Locarno. During this period these two men worked together most amicably on the whole.

With England once more under a Labour government, it was not long before Anglo-French relations underwent a radical change. At The Hague conference of August 1929, Snowden, the chancellor of the exchequer, described the views expressed by Henri Chéron, his French opposite number, as 'grotesque and ridiculous'.

From the summer of 1931 the Coalition government was in power under Ramsay MacDonald with Sir John Simon as foreign secretary. At the disarmament conference which opened in Geneva in February 1932, Britain was strongly in favour of France disarming while at the same time recognising the right of Germany, who had been disarmed under the Treaty of Versailles, to rearm. It seemed that Britain regarded France as the only aggressive power, and in principle, British opinion coincided with the relatively widely-held German view. It was contended that Germany would not allow herself to be treated as a second-class nation, that with the passage of time it was impossible to keep Germany alone theoretically disarmed, and that Germany must be allowed some re-armament within the context of disarmament by other powers. On 11 December 1932 at Geneva, Herriot, morally isolated, ended up by agreeing to a joint declaration by Great Britain, the United States, Italy and Germany, recognising the principle of equal rights to armaments within a system of equal security for all nations.

In 1932 world opinion was mobilised to force France to disarm. But with Hitler's rise to power in January 1933 Germany's expansionist strength upset the hoped-for balance. It was an incontestable fact that since autumn 1932 the Reich had openly violated the Versailles Treaty, and the activities of organised military groups were blatantly obvious.

Nevertheless, the British government continued to press for arms limitation, hoping that an agreement with Germany could be reached on the basis of international co-operation whereby Germany would agree to limit her arms. It was Britain's opinion that if France were disarmed Germany would stop rearming.

On 14 October 1933 Hitler left the League of Nations and the disarmament conference. It was decided to continue the conference, and meanwhile the British sought outside the League to see what agreements Hitler would undertake.

The French note of 17 April 1934 rejected the British proposals: 'German re-armament has rendered all negotiations useless. France will henceforward assure its security by its own means.'[2] This note caused a scandal in London where it was considered that the disarmament conference had failed thanks to the French.

The Franco-Soviet pact of May 1935 did not please the British; and the Anglo-German naval pact of 18 June aroused the indignation of the French.

Clear-cut differences emerged between the British and French in the complications arising over Ethiopia. The Italo-Ethiopian affair became Italo-British. Now Britain reversed her policy of refusing to accept any risks and liabilities other than those inherent in the League of Nations pact and the Locarno treaties. She had previously had no desire to accept any collective or automatic obligations. From now on she called for full enforcement of the pact, whereby if a state attacked a member of the League it would be declaring war on all member countries.

Paris, however, which had been the champion of collective security since 1919, suddenly changed its line when it became a matter of confronting Rome. The French government was naturally forced to condemn fascist aggression against Ethiopia, but it wanted to be persuaded that this was simply a question of colonial aggression as traditionally practised by the great powers, and not to use the League's powers other than in a situation of its own choice. Eden pointed out to Laval that if the Geneva sanctions were not effective against Mussolini they would never be effective against any other country. If the League of Nations did not work then, it could not be relied on in the future.[3]

The Italian campaign in Ethiopia was a trial of strength between England and Italy. England, wanting to drive Italy out of Africa by force, demanded sanctions, while France advocated conciliation. The British held that Laval's contortions and vacillations indicated that he was prepared to sacrifice the League of Nations to Rome, while the French maintained that the British wanted to use the League of Nations to defeat Italy.

On 9 December 1935 Sir Samuel Hoare and Laval drew up a compromise plan, to get the Negus of Abyssinia to accept 'an area reserved for Italian settlement and economic expansion'. The publication of this 'secret plan' in the French press brought about Hoare's fall from office on 18 December, and his replacement at the Foreign Office by Anthony Eden. Laval did not continue long in office either and, abandoned by Radical ministers like Herriot, he fell on 22 January 1936.[4]

The Ethiopian affair brought about a strong reaction against France in England, weakening support for an alliance and swelling the number of isolationists and those who wanted to come to some agreement with the German Führer.

For Hitler, whose power had increased remarkably since 1933, France became a choice target. After Laval's fall in January, Sarraut formed an interim ministry pending a general election due to take place in April. The election campaign had virtually started. Meanwhile, the French were wondering what Hitler was planning to do next. There was no doubt that he was up to something. But what?

From the summer of 1935 talk of the imminent occupation of the demilitarised Rhineland was on everyone's lips. Awaiting his moment, Hitler was getting ready to wipe out unilaterally the whole of part five of the Treaty of Versailles which laid down Germany's military status. Alerted by its consuls, military attachés and the Berlin embassy, the Quai d'Orsay could not be under any illusion. It was rumoured almost everywhere that Hitler was going to abrogate the status of the Rhineland to regain 'the watch on the Rhine'.[5]

In the autumn and winter of 1935 military preparations in the Rhineland were very obvious and a show of force was increasingly expected. In Germany the impression gained from the British press was that London would not object to the installation of German garrisons in the demilitarised zone, an opinion which was reflected in the German press. The French for their part reacted against this trend of opinion with strong words. On 13 January 1936, ambassador François-Poncet told secretary of state von Bülow that any violation of the status of the Rhineland would at once result in 'an extremely grave situation' and that it was important that they should have no illusions on this score.[6]

On 22 February, Flandin, the Foreign Minister, invited his diplomatic representatives, in a circular, to indicate clearly in their conversation that 'the French Government will not allow its interests to be undermined by a unilateral repudiation of treaty stipulations'.[7]

No-one believed that Hitler would act with the violence he was to show. On 17 February, General Maurin, the minister of national defence, wrote to the foreign minister:

> You have asked me what I feel about the possibility of France's supporting a more liberal interpretation of the treaty clauses, in the event of the Germans taking the initiative of opening negotiations on the Rhineland. It seems to me such negotiations should be avoided . . . If they cannot be avoided, they should stick strictly to the provisions of the Peace Treaty and the Locarno Pact.[8]

France, completely on the defensive, never dreamt of launching an attack on the Reich if it were to make a move. On 14 February, Lieutenant-Colonel Beaumont-Nesbitt, the British military attaché, asked Commander Petitbon of the General Staff: 'What do you plan to do, either on your own or together with us, if the Germans occupy the left bank of the Rhine?'[9] At a meeting of the chiefs of the General Staff on 19 February, General Gamelin refused to entertain the idea that 'France could occupy the demilitarised zone on its own' and declared that 'England does not seem prepared to take the necessary steps in the time desired'.[10] 'There was no plan' Eden wrote later, 'to seize, say, the zone's strategic points.'[11] Coercive measures that could be applied without resorting to force were what was wanted.

At the end of January 1936 at the time of George v's funeral in London, Flandin asked leading British ministers what attitude the United Kingdom would adopt if the left bank of the Rhine were reoccupied. Prime minister Baldwin answered by asking what the French government would do.[12] On 27 February the Council of Ministers debated the question. General Maurin considered that they could only adopt a strictly defensive position, unless they were to call up the reserves (three classes) and the frontier guards of all classes which would enable them to take up defensive positions from which they could then advance. Thus France would only undertake any action by force previously ratified by the Locarno signatories and by the League of Nations Council.

On 27 February Flandin told the Belgian ambassador that if Germany violated the clauses concerning the demilitarised Rhineland, 'the French government would not take any independent action; it would only act in agreement with the Locarno co-signatories'. On 5 March Flandin told Eden the same thing.[13]

On 22 February, Mussolini was informed by Ambassador von Hassell of the actions which the Führer was about to take. He declared that he would stay 'apart from the Locarno powers if they decided to act'.

On 27 February, the Franco-Soviet pact was ratified by the Chamber of Deputies with a huge majority. Hitler took this as a pretext to occupy the demilitarised zone. The instructions to carry out the occupation were given on Saturday, 7 March. On the morning of that day the German foreign minister, Neurath, delivered successively to the ambassadors of Great Britain, France and Italy, a memorandum, copies of which were delivered simultaneously in the three foreign capitals. It denounced the Locarno Pact and offered negotiations for a new pact based on equal rights.[14]

This show of force hit France like a thunder-clap, heralding worse outrages: the time had come finally to curb Hitler's activities. 'I find it difficult to believe,' wrote ambassador François-Poncet, 'that the French Government, faced with a *fait accompli*, will not react vigorously.'[15] Later it was thought that it ought to have countered German provocation with military action since it had the power, in such a clear-cut case as this, to take a strong initiative and inform its guarantors, England, Belgium, and Italy, each of whom was justified in intervening without waiting for the decision of the League of Nations Council. It could have regarded its action as one of legitimate self-defence in the face of 'a hostile act'. While referring the matter to the League of Nations Council, it had the right to take immediate military action in a spontaneous show of strength.

The Council of Ministers met on the morning of Sunday, 8 March and declared that Germany had committed an act of hostility. In the evening, Sarraut, the prime minister, delivered a vigorous and scathing speech on the radio. It was impossible to negotiate with a country which had broken its word, and 'international relations will come to an end if this becomes common practice.' He proclaimed, 'We are not prepared to let Strasbourg once again come under the fire of German guns'. Putting the procedure laid down at Locarno into practice, the government decided to refer to the League of Nations Council and to warn the Locarno signatories. Few ministers – Sarraut, Paul-Boncour and Georges Mandel – were in favour of action. Flandin was completely confused. All the same, the possibility of military action by France, even completely on her own, was not ruled out.[16]

But at the military conference which took place on 10 March, Generals Maurin and Gamelin argued for delay. At a time of depleted ranks in the army they were wary of telling Sarraut the prime minister to go ahead. And as Piétri, the minister for the navy, remarked, any military action could lead to total war. If they were to pledge themselves to action, general mobilisation would be necessary. General mobilisation – with the elections six weeks away. As far as the minister for aviation, Marcel Déat, was concerned, the most important thing was that France should not appear the aggressor.[17]

When, instead of acting alone, the stunned French turned to their allies, there was a unanimous desire for peace. Czechoslovakia and Yugoslavia declared themselves ready to agree with whatever France decided, and in Poland Colonel Beck made it known that he was 'ready to take part in any discussion with the French government concerning the situation created by Germany's action'.[18]

But on March 7 Eden lost no time in telling the French ambassador that 'in view of the gravity of the situation it was desirable that no action likely to compromise the future irreparably be taken before the governments concerned had had the chance to consult with each other'. On March 9, while denouncing the violation of an international treaty, he told the House of Commons that it was necessary to keep calm: 'There is no reason to suppose that the German action constitutes a hostile threat.' Ambassador Corbin remarked that Eden was in no way moved by the denunciation of the treaty, but rather appeared to be inwardly relieved at the lifting of a long-dreaded evil. His attitude was that of a man wondering what advantages could be derived from a new situation rather than what barriers should be erected against the threat. And in his *Memoirs* he was to write: 'There was not one man in a thousand in England ready to put his life in danger by joining France in action against the reoccupation of the Rhineland. No one in England was prepared to do this, literally no one.'[19]

On 10 March the Locarno signatories met at the Quai d'Orsay. Flandin tried to get their support for a joint plan of action, including the possibility of resorting to military force – support which was refused him by the Belgian Premier, van Zeeland, who advocated above all that Hitler's adversaries should stick together. They were implying their acceptance of the *fait accompli*. 'No course of action must be taken against Germany which could lead to war.'[20]

Flandin went to London in order to 'act in France's best interests'. According to Georges Bonnet who was a member of the Sarraut Cabinet, Baldwin declared categorically that 'Britain cannot accept the risk of war'. Flandin stated that 'we could be heading for a break with Great Britain if we insist on having our own way'. The French ministers had been struck by the categorical attitude shown by London which at that point in time wanted to avoid any trouble with Germany.

Under the Locarno Treaty England, as well as Belgium and Italy was bound to oppose the occupation of the de-militarised zone. But, without mentioning Italy who was totally disinterested in all that Locarno represented, it was clear that the British would not think of fighting to prevent the stationing of German troops in Cologne, Mainz and Saarbrücken. The Treaty mentioned sanctions. England, who in 1935 had taken the lead in imposing sanctions against

Italy, was the first in 1936 to advise against imposing them on Germany. In her eyes, the violation of the Locarno Pact was not as serious as the aggression against Ethiopia. Even those who condemned Germany's action began to wonder optimistically whether if the past were wiped out the foundations of a new Europe might not be laid. *The Times* welcomed 'a chance to rebuild' the Continent. It was clear in advance that Britain was not going to agree to a literal interpretation of the Locarno Treaty. But Hitler had been cunning enough to offer all kinds of attractive bait. Two hours after the Western powers had been told of his decision to reoccupy the Rhineland, the Führer started pressing in the Reichstag for a European agreement. Germany, who had no further territorial claims in Europe, would never break the peace. In a torrential outburst, he repeatedly confirmed his desire for peace with France.[21]

British opinion on the whole considered that Germany was quite justified, from a moral point of view, in rejecting France's presumptuous claims. Ambassador von Hoesch revealed that 'even in the highest circles there was violent reaction against France's "blackmail"'. Everyone was trying to convince themselves that things would sort themselves out. According to Lord Lothian, the Germans were only reoccupying their own land. It was quite natural that Germany should be able to do what she wished in her own territory. The zone her troops were reoccupying was unquestionably under her full sovereignty; it could not remain demilitarised indefinitely. It was not French territory which had been violated, only the Treaty of Versailles in which nobody any longer believed.

Was the way now open for a change in the balance of British alliances? French cartoonists were already depicting Albion as a large bony female nestling in the arms of the Führer. Englishmen in high places accused France of supporting Mussolini and being ready to accept his control of the Mediterranean, a cry which eclipsed that of German hegemony. Full responsibility for the failure in Ethiopia was laid at her feet. Britain, increasingly impatient, paid only very slight attention to French opinion, and turned her efforts towards bringing about a reconciliation with Germany.

If France had taken action despite London's reluctance to

do so, would it not have been almost impossible for the United Kingdom to leave her to go ahead on her own? Paul-Boncour thought so, and it is a question which has often been asked.[22] 'I doubt,' Eden was to write 'whether world opinion in 1936 would have approved of such action by France.[23] He was right, it would not have met with much sympathy. It would have been attacked as a repetition of the 1923 invasion of the Ruhr, which had been denounced by Pope Pius XI. But times had changed; Hitler posed a grave threat to European civilisation. The same Pius XI, on 16 March 1936, confided to the French ambassador, Charles-Roux:

'If you had immediately marched 200,000 men into the area occupied by the Germans, you would have done everyone a great service.' I replied that it was in the interests of peace that we did not do so. 'Yes,' he answered, 'and that was very commendable; and then you had doubtless reckoned on getting no support from the English, and even less so from the Italians. But I repeat, if you had taken such action, you would have rendered everyone a great service. There now, isn't that a most unexpected statement from someone Maurras dubbed a Germanophile?'[24]

French military action would have been deplored in March 1936. Eden believed later that there would probably have been some fighting; but would that have exposed France to the deadly risk of a full-scale war? Faced with the enormity of the danger, most Frenchmen, believing in effortless peace, did not see any virtue in taking a risk. 'This essentially peaceful country,' Eden continued, 'realised that in this situation pacifism was not enough and it sought a path of action which would win public approval without incurring the risk of war: there was no such path.'[25]

Faced with the shock of Saturday, 7 March, the French hesitated and were lost.

Notes

1 Anthony Eden, Earl of Avon, *Memoirs: Facing the Dictators*, (London, Cassell, 1962), p. 367.
2 *Documents on British Foreign Policy, 1919–1939*, ser. 2, vol. vi,

pp. 631–3; for comment on circumstances see Eden *Memoirs*, pp. 89–90, and André François-Poncet, '*Souvenirs d'une ambassade à Berlin*' (Paris, Flammarion, 1946), p. 17.

3 Eden, *Memoirs*, pp. 257–8.

4 For details on the French role in the Abyssinian crisis see Geoffrey Warner '*Pierre Laval and the Eclipse of France*' (London, Eyre and Spottiswoode, 1968), pp. 94–129; see also Eden *Memoirs*, pp. 300–301.

5 French information on these rumours can be found in *Documents diplomatiques français, 1932–1939* ser. 2, vol. I, Docs. 25, 27, 29, 30, 36, 37. Cited hereafter as *DDF*.

6 *DDF*, Doc. 49.

7 *DDF*, Doc. 217.

8 *DDF*, Doc. 196.

9 *DDF*, Doc. 187.

10 *DDF*, Doc. 203.

11 Eden, *Memoirs*, p. 353.

12 *DDF*, Doc. 184, Annexe; see also Pierre-Étienne Flandin, *Politique française, 1919–1940* (Paris, Éditions Nouvelles, 1948).

13 *DDF*, Doc. 241; Flandin, *Politique française*.

14 *Documents on German Foreign Policy, 1918–1945*, Series C, vol. V, Doc. 3.

15 *DDF*, Doc. 299.

16 *DDF*, Doc. 337, Note 2; Flandin, *Politique française*, p. 201; for the detailed circumstances see J-B. Duroselle, 'Les Incertitudes de notre politique militaire: la France et la crise de mars 1936', in Édouard Bonnefous, *Histoire politique de la Troisième République* (Paris, 1965), vol. VI, pp. 387–92.

17 General Gamelin, *Servir* (Paris, Plon, 1946), vol. II, pp. 204 *ff.*; see also Bonnefous, *Histoire politique*, pp. 390–92.

18 *DDF*, Docs. 303, 343, 360.

19 *DDF*, Docs. 301, 316, 339; Eden, *Memoirs*, p. 338.

20 *DDF*, Doc. 380; Flandin, *Politique française*.

21 Hitler's speech of 7 March is quoted in extracts in Norman H. Baynes (Ed.) *The Speeches of Adolf Hitler, April 1922–August 1939.* (London, 1942), vol. II, pp. 1271–1302.

22 Joseph Paul-Boncour, *Entre deux guerres*, vol. III, pp. 36–7. (Paris, Plon, 1946.)

23 Eden, *Memoirs*, p. 367.

24 *DDF*, Doc. 447.

25 Eden, *Memoirs*, pp. 360, 367.

Bibliography

N. H. Baynes, *The Speeches of Adolf Hitler, April 1922–August 1939* (London, 1942).

É. Bonnefous, *Histoire politique de la Troisième République* (Paris, Presses Universitaires de France), vol. V, 1962, vol. VI, 1965.

Documents on British Foreign Policy, 1919–1939 (HMSO).

Documents diplomatiques français, 1932–1939 (Paris, Imprimerie Nationale), series 2, beginning Jan. 1936.

Documents on German Foreign Policy, 1918–1945 (HMSO).

R. A. Eden, the Earl of Avon, *Memoirs: Facing the Dictators* (London, Cassell, 1962).

P.-É. Flandin, *Politique française, 1919–1940* (Paris, Éditions Nouvelles, 1948).

A. François-Poncet, *Souvenirs d'une ambassade à Berlin* (Paris, Flammarion, 1946).

General Gamelin, *Servir* (Paris, Plon, 1946), 3 vols.

J. Joll (Ed.), *The Decline of the Third Republic*, St Antony's Papers, no. 5 (London, Chatto and Windus, 1959), containing an article by W. F. Knapp 'The Rhineland Crisis of March 1936', pp. 67–85.

J. Paul-Boncour, *Entre deux guerres* (Paris, Plon, 1945–6), 3 vols.

E. M. Robertson, *Hitler's Prewar Policy and Military Plans, 1933–1939* (London, Longmans, 1963).

G. Warner, *Pierre Laval and the Eclipse of France* (London, Eyre and Spottiswoode, 1968).

D. C. Watt, 'German Plans for the Reoccupation of the Rhineland: a note', in *Journal of Contemporary History*, I, 4, Oct. 1966, pp. 193–9.

7 Reactions to the Munich Crisis

Anthony Adamthwaite

The continuing controversy

'It was Munich which saw our victory destroyed', wrote
Georges Bernanos, 'not Bordeaux or Rethondes'.[1] At Munich,
on 29 September 1938 France joined with Great Britain,
Germany and Italy in destroying the independence of
Czechoslovakia. For twenty years Czechoslovakia had been
the ally of France and the friendship of the two countries
was sealed in an alliance of 1925. With the surrender of the
Bohemian bastion German predominance in central Europe
was assured. Not only had France's military and political influence collapsed but her cultural line of defence – what Georges
Duhamel called the Descartes Line[2] – had been swept away.

The French looked for a scapegoat and found one in
perfidious Albion. 'The Munich Agreement', recorded André
François-Poncet, French ambassador in Berlin in 1938, 'was
the logical consequence of the policy practised by Britain and
France, but principally inspired by Britain.'[3] The polemic
continues. In January 1968 M. Pompidou, then French
prime minister, suggested that Britain was solely responsible
for not evicting Hitler from the Rhineland in 1936 and for
abandoning Czechoslovakia in 1938.[4] On the British side
the former prime minister, Mr Harold Macmillan, writes:
'still more discreditable than even the British government's
weakness' was 'the much less pardonable story of France's
collapse'.[5]

Of the four men who determined British and French policy
in 1938, only two survive – Édouard Daladier, French prime
minister,* and Georges Bonnet, foreign minister. Unlike the
British prime minister, Neville Chamberlain, and foreign
secretary, Lord Halifax, the French ministers have, as yet,
escaped the anatomisings of historians. The international

* This chapter went to press before the death of Daladier in October 1970.

history of the inter-war years has been a blindspot for French historians.[6] The tradition of French historiography is partly to blame. Biography has been almost completely neglected in France. Moreover the fact that both Daladier and Bonnet are alive and continued their political careers under the Fourth and Fifth Republics has deterred biographers. In addition, the French have tended to be academic purists, holding that proper historical research could not be undertaken without access to documents. The fifty year rule and the paucity of published French documents have therefore acted as powerful deterrents. A major reason for the neglect of French policy in 1938 lies in the assumption that because France seems to have played a secondary, supporting role in the approach to Munich her contribution does not deserve the detailed investigation devoted to the moves of the other great powers. 'The key to French policy', it is affirmed, 'lay in the final analysis in London.'[8] But in agreeing with Alice that London was the capital of Paris, historians have left important questions unanswered. Why did France allow her partner to take the initiative in the Czech crisis? But for British pressure, would France have fought for Czechoslovakia? What was the significance of Munich for France and for Anglo-French relations?

In his memoirs,[9] Bonnet laboured to thrust the whole burden of Munich upon Chamberlain and Halifax. He argued that in defence of Czechoslovakia he had tried to build up a military alliance to stop Hitler. In particular, he sought a firm British commitment. By early September 1938 the efforts to enlist the support of France's allies – Great Britain, Poland, Romania, the Soviet Union – were all to no avail. Only France was 'faithful found among the faithless'. Alas, without a British promise of help, France could not stand alone. Nevertheless, in London, her leaders fought a strong rearguard action in order to save what they could of their ally. In the end France had no choice but to submit to Britain's guidance.

The apologia presented by Bonnet and seconded by Daladier,[10] though not without its adherents,[11] does not square with the evidence, and a new appraisal of French policy is needed. Scholars who insist on waiting until they possess all the evidence will have to wait for ever because many gaps in the French record will never be filled.[12] In the light of the evidence now available it is possible to construct a consistent interpretation of France's role in the Munich crisis. The Anglo-French partnership was founded on self-interest, both countries needed each other. By 1938 Britain had the upper hand and France saw in this development a solution to her predicament. France was in a quandary, in Bonnet's words, she did not want 'to be placed before the dreadful alternative' of breaking her pledge to Czechoslovakia 'or of beginning another world war'.[13] Bonnet therefore wanted Britain 'to put as much pressure as possible' on Czechoslovakia 'to reach a settlement with the Sudeten Deutsch in order to save France from the cruel dilemma of dishonouring her agreements or becoming involved in war'.[14] By encouraging and exploiting British leadership France furnished herself with an excellent reason for not fighting. Fundamentally the British and French were at one in seeking a peaceful settlement of the Sudeten dispute and in seeing in its solution an opportunity of reaching an understanding with Germany. Much of the discord of Anglo-French relations stemmed not from a disunity of purpose but from the fact that both governments tried to shuffle off on to each other the responsibility for the sacrifice of Czechoslovakia.

In the view of Robert Coulondre, French ambassador at Moscow in 1938, Chamberlain's announcement in the Commons on 24 March 1938 that Britain could not give a guarantee to France in the event of the latter going to the help of her ally, marked the point at which the British prime minister 'took over the reins of the Franco-British team and guided it to war'.[15] However, the crucial period for the shaping of British and French policies towards Czechoslovakia lay in the six months from October 1937 to March 1938. And Chamberlain took over the reins of the Franco-British team in November 1937. At the Anglo-French conversations in London on 29–30 November the French prime minister, Chautemps, and his foreign minister, Delbos, agreed, in response to British suggestions, that France should urge Czechoslovakia to make concessions to the Sudeten German minority. As for Germany, the British idea, accepted by the French, was that the initiative in making an approach should rest with London. All, however, was not plain sailing.

Chamberlain told the cabinet that 'at one time it looked as though the French were going to press for some more forthcoming attitude on Central Europe' but 'no encouragement had been given them ... finally they had agreed that appropriate concessions might be made by Czechoslovakia and that an attempt should be made to reach a general settlement with Germany'.[16]

In advocating conciliation in Central Europe the British were preaching to the converted. Since Hitler's Rhineland *coup* it had been clear that the French were not prepared to resist an extension of German influence over Austria and Czechoslovakia. On 22 April 1937 the American ambassador at Paris, William C. Bullitt, found 'general agreement' in government circles that 'recent developments' were closing the door to French influence in central and eastern Europe.[17] Belgium had abandoned her military alliance with France in 1936 and returned to the neutrality of 1914. Thus France lost a major element in her security. France's alliance obligations were reaffirmed but the tone was muted. When the congress of the Radical party met at Lille in October 1937 the reaffirmation of alliance pledges given by the foreign minister, Delbos, neither mentioned Czechoslovakia by name nor stated unequivocally what France would consider as a *casus foederis*. In early November Hitler's emissary, Franz von Papen, took soundings in Paris. After conferring with the 'rather weak' prime minister, Chautemps, who seemed to be 'pushed forward' by his 'aggressive' minister of finance, Bonnet, von Papen concluded that the French would do their 'utmost to effect a general settlement with Germany' and would raise no objection 'to an evolutionary extension of German influence either in Austria ... or in Czechoslovakia'.[18] After acquiescing in British leadership in November Chautemps and Delbos resigned themselves to the inevitable. In February 1938 Chautemps thought it 'probable' that 'central and eastern Europe would slip into the hands of Germany without war'.[19] In the same month a major parliamentary debate on foreign affairs – the only one in 1938 – drew from Delbos another general reaffirmation of French pledges – so fainthearted as to be almost valueless. According to the Czech minister at Paris, Stefan Ossuky, the foreign minister, before making his speech had wanted 'to run away' but had been 'propped-up' by his permanent officials.[20]

A change of government on 13 March 1938 did not alter the course charted by Chautemps and Delbos. The evolutionary extension of German influence in central Europe might be acceptable but Hitler's annexation of Austria on 12 March shocked France into the realisation that her power and prestige were disappearing overnight. After Austria, Czechoslovakia. For the first time France was aware that she might suddenly be called upon to honour her treaty with Czechoslovakia. In less than a month the Socialist prime minister, Léon Blum, and foreign minister, Paul-Boncour, issued four reassertions of loyalty to French commitments. But the strong declarations were a sign of weakness, not of strength, aimed at restoring national self-esteem, severely shaken by the *Anschluss*.

Chamberlain did not have the 'slightest confidence'[21] in Blum and his Popular Front government and would not allow the French ministers to come to London for consultations.[22] However, the French were offered advice. On 24 March Halifax told them that Britain could not add to her obligations by giving an undertaking to come to the help of Czechoslovakia. In any event, a guarantee would have no value because as a result of the *Anschluss* 'the heart of Czechoslovakia' lay 'open to attack'.[23] And even if Britain entered a war, she could offer no more than the 'economic pressure' of blockade. On the same day in the Commons Chamberlain publicly confirmed the refusal to give a guarantee but closed on an equivocal note: 'Where peace and war are concerned, legal obligations are not alone involved. . . .'[24] The British attitude influenced but did not determine French policy. Before receiving Halifax's broadside France's military and political leadership had already examined the possibilities of helping Prague and concluded that German action could not be prevented. At a meeting of the Committee of National Defence on 15 March,[25] Daladier, then minister of war and national defence, declared that France could only help indirectly by manning the Maginot Line and diverting a proportion of the German forces. In this discussion and in the discussions which followed between London and Paris, it was, as the German ambassador at Paris, Count Welczeck, shrewdly saw, 'not so much a question of seeking possibilities of really giving help to Czechoslovakia as of seeking difficulties which would make help appear hopeless'.[26] French opinion showed no enthusiasm for the Czech cause and the *Anschluss* marked the beginning of a powerful press campaign against the idea of fighting for Prague. The French Left wanted to save Czechoslovakia in Spain and much of the discussion at the meeting on 15 March concerned the possibilities of French intervention in the Spanish Civil War. All parties, with the exception of the Communists, were agreed on the importance of recommending caution and conciliation in Prague. On 10 April 1938 the Senate drove Blum out of office for a second time. The British were highly gratified. On 17 March the Foreign Office had decided 'that anything we can do to weaken the present French government and precipitate its fall would be in the British interest'.[27] One of Paul-Boncour's last acts as foreign minister was to reply on 9 April to Halifax's memorandum of 24 March. Without attempting to challenge the political and military arguments marshalled by Halifax, the French minister agreed that 'nothing should be left undone to eliminate occasions of friction or conflict' in Czechoslovakia, and France was 'ready unreservedly' to co-operate to this end.[28]

On 10 April 1938 Daladier formed a predominantly Radical administration which, with minor changes, survived until March 1940. His foreign minister was Bonnet. Bonnet has had to share with Chamberlain much of the opprobrium for Munich. He has been called 'appeasement personified'.[29] By contrast Daladier has been given the benefit of the doubt and treated as an appeaser in spite of himself. He was 'convinced that a firm policy could alone stop Hitler. But he was at a loss how to do it'.[30] Daladier, however, had much more faith in conciliation than has been realised. His choice of Bonnet as foreign minister was a pointer to his outlook. Paul-Boncour's story of how on 10 April after hearing his defence of French commitments in eastern Europe Daladier decided not to keep him on at the Quai d'Orsay is well-known.[31] Less well-known, though rumoured at the time, was the intervention of the British ambassador at Paris, Sir Eric Phipps, who reported:

We were nearly cursed by having Paul-Boncour again at the

Quai d'Orsay. I therefore had Daladier and Reynaud informed
indirectly that it would be most unfortunate if Paul-Boncour were
to remain. . . . Daladier himself was in full agreement. . . . Finally
after an interview of over an hour with Paul-Boncour he did the
right thing. . . . I felt it was my duty to take a certain risk, though
it was a very small one as my messages were quite indirect and I
can always disavow them.[32]

But the choice of Bonnet was Daladier's own – the British
would have preferred the former prime minister, Chautemps.
The appointment of Bonnet threw light on the new government's foreign policy. It was predicted that the foreign
minister would 'put French relations with Italy on a sensible
basis as soon as possible' and would 'welcome any opportunity' of coming to 'a reasonable understanding with
Germany'.[33]

The Actors and Their Stage

Daladier, born in 1884, was a few years older than his foreign
minister. The son of a baker of Carpentras, Vaucluse, his
was a more plebeian origin than Bonnet's. Unlike the men of
his native Midi, he was a man of few words, and silence lent
him an air of wisdom. Unfriendly observers were quick to
point out that he was silent because he had nothing to say.
A widower, he lived simply with his two sons and a sister. In
Paris a taciturn nature and a Napoleonic cast of feature were
distinct assets. In London the French leader was not judged
over-impressive. 'Compared to our own ministers who were
resplendent in stars and ribbons,' noted Harold Nicolson in
April 1937, 'he looked like some Iberian merchant visiting
the Roman Senate.'[34] In the early 1930s Daladier was seen as
a strong man who would reinvigorate the Republic and the
Young Turks of the Radical party looked to him for dynamic
leadership. His mismanagement of the anti-parliamentary
riots of 6 February 1934 spoilt the image, which he had culti-
vated, of the strong, silent leader. He was not in fact the man
of destiny so many had believed him to be, on the contrary
those who knew him well considered him to have an irresolute
personality with an inherent self-distrust.[35] After meeting him
at the Anglo-French talks in April 1938 Chamberlain did not
think him 'so strong as his reputation'.[36] Moods of self-doubt

fettered his powers of initiative and decision; after being talked into making up his mind he would go back upon it or he would make himself inaccessible to advisers like Gamelin, chief of the general staff, who demanded a ruling from him.

Bonnet was born in 1889 into a well-to-do legal family of the Dordogne. As the foreign minister who led France first to Munich and then into the Second World War he has not had a good press. Chamberlain thought him 'clever, but ambitious and an intriguer'. 'The French', he concluded, 'are not very fortunate in their foreign secretaries.'[37] Villain or no villain, Bonnet was not without friends. In *Les Hommes de bonne volonté* Jules Romains supplies a sympathetic sketch of the minister.[38] His predecessor at the Quai d'Orsay, Paul-Boncour, a stern critic of France's Munich policy, pays tribute to the 'kindness and help' of Bonnet when the latter served under him in 1932.[39] Even Halifax, who like his master tended to be contemptuous of the French, commented in April 1939 on reports that Bonnet would shortly lose his post: 'we have got on well together, although I know that he is not everybody's cup of tea'.[40] Both Bonnet's policy and personality have been unjustly maligned. 'You know Daladier is easier to influence than I am', he remarked to Phipps.[41] This was no idle boast. His colleague Anatole de Monzie, minister of public works, summed him up as follows:

Whilst very courageous in the long run, he is much less so in the heat of the moment. . . . Because he is reticent, he is accused of lying or of deceit. False accusation . . . Bonnet is discreet so that his policy may be successful. . . . Now I note that having adopted the peace party, he is sticking to it with the foresight of a statesman. . . .[42]

Though the foreign minister's main aim in the Czech crisis was to avoid fighting for Czechoslovakia and to put the blame for a retreat on others, his long-term goals were Franco-German reconciliation and a European settlement. The ends and the means chosen may be questioned yet it should be recognised that the minister did pursue an ideal, even if misguidedly.

It has been said that whereas appeasement in Britain was a doctrine, in France it was a confession of weakness.[43] Such a view over-simplifies the issues to the point of distortion. Undoubtedly the character of French foreign policy owed much to domestic pressures. The France of 1938 was a nation at war with itself, torn by social strife and overwhelmed by the economic effects of the Great Depression. While the British economy was making a slow recovery, the French economy was in the doldrums. Socially, France was much more divided than Britain. The legislation of Léon Blum's Popular Front government of 1936 fanned the flames of class conflict. The inability of successive governments to deal effectively with economic and social problems helped to nurture a mood of national self-doubt and pessimism in which appeasement could flourish.[44] However, too much has been made of political divisions; too little of the stability of the Daladier government of 1938. France, according to Chamberlain had 'two faults' which destroyed 'half her value'. She could never keep a secret 'for more than half an hour, nor a government for more than nine months'.[45] Daladier's ministry lasted not nine months but nearly two years, an achievement which in the inter-war years was only surpassed by Poincaré's governments of 1922 and 1926. Far from weakening the administration, the German threat consolidated it.[46] Fortified by full powers Daladier governed almost without parliament.

The franc was the Achilles heel of French policy. While sterling was relatively strong, the franc was under constant attack. The task of defending the currency and stemming the gold rush from France dissipated the energies of governments. Daladier's Radical cabinet was too conservative-minded to impose exchange controls. On 4 May the franc was devalued for the third time in three years. Speedy efforts to get on better terms with Berlin and Rome restored somewhat the confidence of the bankers,[47] but in August a major financial crisis erupted and Daladier was said to be on the verge of resignation. Chamberlain refused a personal plea for help from the French Prime Minister – 'material assistance' was 'not possible'.[48] Daladier and his colleagues upheld the dogma of the balanced budget. An extremely modest re-armament programme had been launched in 1936 but it was thought that any major increase in expenditure would bankrupt the country.[49] In August 1938 Bonnet, who had won his spurs as a minister of finance, expressed his fear that 'if France should have to continue to arm at the present rate it would be necessary to regiment the entire country placing the civilian population on soldiers' wages and soldiers' rations. In no other way could the present level of the franc be maintained and the essential military expenditures made'.[50]

If domestic trials and tribulations dictated the broad goals of French policy – a conciliatory approach to the Czech problem paving the way to a general European settlement – much of the driving force of appeasement sprang from a variety of considerations, military, moral and political, several of which were shared by British policy-makers. Militarily, France was still the strongest land power but with the building of the Maginot Line from 1930 she gradually became a prisoner of her concrete and steel defences. She possessed neither the will nor the means to effect a swift offensive against Germany. The assumption of French policy was that no action would be undertaken without British assistance and in the Munich crisis the French promised not to take any offensive measures without previous consultation and agreement with London. The occupation of the Ruhr in 1923 taught France that unilateral action against Germany was too risky an enterprise. Thenceforward she tried to keep in step with Britain. Hence her acquiescence in Hitler's Rhineland *coup* in 1936. What weighed heavily on French decision-making was not a sense of military inferiority or unpreparedness but the apprehension that even with British help a war over Czechoslovakia would be a repetition of 1914–18, 'a modernised battle of the Somme', as Gamelin warned Daladier.[51] Although alarmist reports of the weaknesses of the French air force influenced British and French leaders in September 1938, air power did not play a decisive role in long-term French planning because, in the view of the general staff, the air force was 'accessory to the army'.[52]

Like Chamberlain and Halifax, Daladier and Bonnet were men of peace. The Great War in which both the prime minister and foreign minister had seen active service left them with an enduring horror of war. They shrank from a holocaust which might destroy not only France but Europe. In a broadcast of 21 August 1938 Daladier announced his resolve 'to do everything to spare Europe the annihilation of its civilisation'.[53]

War was dreaded not for its own sake alone but as a

harbinger of social revolution. France might survive another conflagration but not the 'wisely-built' Republic, endowed with liberal institutions affording security, dignity and independence to its citizens.[54] Thus spoke the Republic of Passy. The French ministers represented a governing elite, panicking at the prospect of losing its privileged position. Joseph Caillaux, the man of Agadir, who as chairman of the Senate finance committee was still an influential figure, voiced his fears that 'heavy air bombardments of factories round Paris might 'well cause another Commune'.[55] The shadow of Stalin darkened the horizon in the east. On the weekend of 19–21 May reports of German troop movements on the Czechoslovak border triggered off an international crisis. On 22 May Daladier 'had a secret and quite private meeting'[56] with the German ambassador at Paris. Speaking 'as one ex-Service man to another' the French prime minister described his vision of Armageddon: 'the catastrophic frightfulness of modern war would surpass all that humanity had ever seen. . . . Into the battle zones . . . Cossack and Mongol hordes would pour'.[57]

The outlook of the French statesmen was motivated by a deep-seated dislike of Versailles. 'Both are convinced', wired the American ambassador, Bullitt on 15 September 1938, 'that the treaty must be revised and at bottom regard an alteration in the Czechoslovak state as a necessary revision – the necessity for which they pointed out nearly twenty years ago'.[58] Reinforcing this distaste for the Versailles structure was the conviction that France could no longer maintain her presence in central and eastern Europe. Hitler's reoccupation of the Rhineland in March 1936 confirmed the feeling that the eastern allies were dangerous liabilities.[59] France had no offensive plans to help Czechoslovakia or Poland[60] but while the Rhineland had been demilitarised there remained some incentive for the French army to strike out from the cover of its fortifications. In May 1937 the Radical leader, Édouard Herriot, president of the Chamber of Deputies, pointed out that 'France with only 40 million inhabitants could no longer regard herself as a Great Power of sufficient military strength . . . to maintain her position in central and eastern Europe'.[61]

French appeasement was propelled by a consciousness that the country's survival as a Great Power was at stake. Daladier warned his countrymen that France was in danger of becoming a second-rank power, 'a kind of museum'.[62] It seemed that if nothing was done France and Germany would drift into war. With the Czech dispute settled, Daladier and Bonnet looked forward to 'negotiations . . . to bring together Germany and France in genuine friendship'.[63] Daladier's desire for Franco-German *rapprochement* was no panic reaction to the Czech crisis but sprang directly from the trenches. At Marseilles in October 1938 he told the congress of the Radical party:

> When at Munich I heard the heart of the German people beating, I could not prevent myself thinking, as I had done at Verdun . . . that between the French and German peoples . . . there are strong ties of mutual respect which should lead to loyal co-operation.[64]

Indeed, Daladier's outlook in 1938 was largely inspired by earlier essays in conciliation. As prime minister in 1933 he had not only agreed to join in Mussolini's Four Power Pact – as had Paul-Boncour, his foreign minister – but had also made unofficial contact with Hitler through the journalist, Count Fernand de Brinon, president of the *Comité France-Allemagne*, and later Vichy ambassador to the German occupation authorities. Plans for a secret Daladier–Hitler meeting and a subsequent Franco-German declaration seem to have been mooted.[65] Nothing came of it all because of the fall of the government in October 1933. Even before that event, however, he was characteristically beginning to have misgivings, fearing the reactions of Paul-Boncour and of the Chamber. The attempts of 1933 were not forgotten. On his return from Munich he defended the agreement with the words: 'It's my policy, it's the Four Power Pact.'[66]

While Chamberlain and Halifax were on the whole close and loyal partners, little love was lost between Daladier and Bonnet. In January 1938 the foreign minister had narrowly failed to form a government of his own and in the months ahead his eye was on the premiership. On 25 September before leaving for London with Daladier he was said to have threatened to resign.[67] Two days later at a cabinet meeting there was an angry clash between the two men.[68] Though much the same emotions and motives operated in the case of both men, Bonnet was the more extreme in his views. In April he was reported to be 'even keener than Daladier on steering clear of France's obligations to fight for Czechoslovakia'.[69] In the consistency and persistency of their pursuit of peace Chamberlain and Bonnet had much in common. Halifax did not go all the way with Chamberlain. In Paris at the height of the crisis in September Bonnet sought to persuade Daladier into accepting a settlement at any price. In London Halifax acted as a brake. Chamberlain was prepared to accept Hitler's Godesberg demands but Halifax, after some soul-searching, plumped for refusal.[70] Between Chamberlain and Daladier there were important differences. The Frenchman was more of a realist than the Englishman. Daladier's apprehensions that Hitler was bent on destroying Czechoslovakia and dominating Europe were fully expressed in the three Anglo-French conferences which took place during the Czech crisis. The British prime minister disagreed and 'doubted very much' whether Hitler 'really desired to destroy' Czechoslovakia.[71] Although Daladier was, for negotiating purposes, deliberately putting as strong a case as he could against Hitler, it is clear that he genuinely did not share Chamberlain's faith in Hitler as a man of his word.[72] His first and last encounter with the Führer was at Munich. On his return he told the American ambassador that Chamberlain 'had been taken in a bit by Hitler'. He 'was an admirable old gentleman, like a high-minded Quaker who had fallen among bandits' and his 'last conversations with Hitler had not been helpful'.[73] Sour grapes maybe. Daladier was annoyed that Chamberlain had stolen a march on him by concluding with Hitler the Anglo-German agreement. In practice there was no sharp contrast between French realism and British idealism. With Chamberlain, Daladier deluded himself that some settlement could be reached with Germany, if only a *modus vivendi*. Jean Zay, minister of education, records him telling the cabinet on 30 September of his conviction that contacts with Hitler and Goering would be fruitful.[74] The essential difference between the two prime ministers was one of temperament – having adopted an idea or principle Chamberlain pursued it ruthlessly and fanatically, by contrast Daladier was very English in his pragmatic and sceptical outlook. Language was another barrier to understanding. Chamberlain's command of French and Daladier's knowledge of English were far from perfect.[75]

The Crisis

On 27 April Daladier and Bonnet flew to London for a two-day conference with the British. The guidelines of their policy were already established, if not predetermined. London knew in advance the standpoint of the French ministers. In Paris on 24–25 April Leslie Hore-Belisha, secretary of state for war, had talked to Daladier and Gamelin. The British minister noted that Daladier 'seems to be ready to fall into line with us' and Gamelin thought 'it was impossible for France to give military assistance to Czechoslovakia'.[76] Bonnet, too, wasted no time in expressing his readiness to bring pressure to bear on President Benes of Czechoslovakia.[77] Further evidence of the state of mind in which the French approached the Anglo-French talks comes from the German record. The German embassy in London received two reports from a journalist informant who claimed to have had a private talk with Daladier on 28 April and also to have spoken to Fernand de Brinon who was in London with the French ministers.[78] The pith of these reports was 'Daladier's hope that Chamberlain and Halifax would themselves suggest that pressure should be put on Prague' so that the French 'could acquiesce without seeming to have taken the initiative'.[79] In London the French, by asking for a firm pledge of British support for Czechoslovakia, almost brought proceedings to breaking point. Daladier, in particular, spoke as an opponent of German expansionism. 'War could only be avoided if Great Britain and France made their determination quite clear to maintain the peace of Europe. . . .'[80] However, after a luncheon adjournment, it was quickly agreed that Britain and France would jointly urge concessions in Prague. The April talks set a pattern for Anglo-French conversations in September. The French at first resisted and then gave way, conveying the impression of bowing to British pressure. They acted in this way for a number of reasons. Uppermost was Daladier's desire to preserve French honour – hence resistance was for the record. At least France would seem to have resisted British designs. Daladier was a victim of his own temperament. With his natural irresolution the French prime minister was in two minds about appeasement. He favoured conciliation but suspected that Hitler was not to be trusted. Finally it was a matter of strategy and tactics. Bonnet's 'whole policy', as he confided to Bullitt, 'was based on allowing the British full latitude to work out the dispute'.[81] In making great play of their suspicions of Germany the French sought to bluff the British into thinking that France would fight for her ally. Chamberlain and Halifax might believe that if the worse came to the worst France would do no more than mobilise in the shelter of the Maginot Line but French declarations were sufficiently strong to leave a doubt about her intentions. Daladier and Bonnet assumed that in order to guard against the risk of being dragged into war by France Chamberlain would readily take the initiative in Berlin and in Prague. Also, the French hoped that if the British spoke strongly enough in Berlin Hitler might not attack Czechoslovakia. And even if the warning went unheeded Britain would be fully committed to France. By asking a high price for their co-operation – a firm pledge of support – the French won important gains. Chamberlain secured Daladier's agreement to joint pressure in Prague but in return he had to promise action in Berlin. Should concessions fail to produce a settlement, Britain would warn Germany that she might have to support France.

On 19–20 May a German invasion of Czechoslovakia appeared imminent. The chance of involving the British more deeply was too good to be missed and Bonnet urged Halifax to make the warning agreed upon in the London talks. The warning was duly delivered. The British saw in the crisis an opportunity of breaking the Franco-Czech alliance. Believing Bonnet to be 'only too anxious to follow any lead we may give at Prague', Phipps suggested the Czechs be told that 'by mobilising two classes' they 'had in effect broken their treaty with the French'.[82] But Bonnet was too slippery to be caught so easily. He needed more evidence that Britain did not want to fight. Halifax obliged. On 22 May he warned the French not to 'assume' that because the British had warned Germany they would 'at once take joint military action' in defence of Czechoslovakia.[83] Bonnet took down 'copious notes' and having 'thoroughly understood' the British position he was ready to appear accommodating. 'If Czechoslovakia were really unreasonable', he promised, 'the French Government might well declare that France considered herself released from her bond.'[84]

While the British busied themselves in Berlin and in Prague, the French marked time. Bonnet did not put the strong pressure on Prague which he led London to believe he was exercising. Officially until September France trod lightly in Prague, privately a number of different emissaries were employed to undermine Czech confidence in the French alliance.[85] On 1 June Bonnet agreed to Halifax's suggestion of a joint *démarche* to put the 'greatest possible pressure' on Benes.[86] In fact the representations were made separately and the French *démarche* was exploratory, not minatory.[87] By July Czech-Sudeten negotiations had reached deadlock and the British decided to send a mediator, Lord Runciman. Runciman was a godsend to the French. And in order to secure acceptance of the British proposal the French for the first time showed their teeth in Prague. Bonnet and Alexis Léger, secretary general of the Quai d'Orsay, both advised immediate and unconditional acceptance of a mediator.[88] Bonnet explained to Bullitt his thinking. 'If the Czechs should refuse British mediation the British would then make it clear that they were not prepared to go to war . . . it would then be possible for France to take a similar attitude.'[89]

In the approach to Munich Anglo-French relations turned largely on procedure, not principle. In September the crisis came to a head. The Sudeten leaders broke off negotiations with the Czechs and on 12 September at the Nazi party rally at Nuremberg Hitler publicly demanded self-determination for the Sudeten Germans. Three days later Chamberlain flew to meet Hitler at Berchtesgaden. Halifax stressed to the cabinet how 'very important' it was 'that we should avoid allowing the French to say that they came to London and found that we had decided to give the show away'.[90] Both partners endeavoured to keep each other guessing about their ultimate intentions. In vain the French attempted to obtain a plain statement of British policy. On 10 September 'desperately anxious'[91] for a way out of France's predicament Bonnet sent a private letter to Halifax in which he asked: 'we are going to march, will you march with us?'[92] Halifax, in reply, preserved the ambiguity of earlier utterances but his answer was negative enough to please Bonnet. He now had the ammunition to fire off at colleagues, like Mandel and Reynaud, who criticised his lack of firmness towards Germany. The French continued to say that in the event of a German attack on Czechoslovakia they would fulfil their obligations. On 8 September Daladier declared 'most positively' that France would march 'to a man'.[93] Five days later the French front collapsed. The combination of Hitler's Nuremberg speech and the outbreak of a Sudeten revolt on 13 September pricked the French bubble. All Bonnet could say was that peace must be saved at any price. Of calmer calibre, Daladier kept his nerve but he was not the man of 8 September. Asked 'point-blank' whether he adhered to the opinions he had expressed on 8 September, he replied 'with evident lack of enthusiasm' that if Germany used force France would have to follow suit.[94] Phipps concluded that the French had been bluffing. As if to confirm his diagnosis, Paris produced peace proposals. On 12 September Léger, who is usually singled out as the guardian of France's traditional interests, suggested the summoning of a Four Power conference. Next day Bonnet repeated the suggestion and on the same day Daladier proposed a Three Power meeting. He tried to telephone Chamberlain but the British prime minister would not speak to him.[95] Without consulting Paris, Chamberlain arranged to see Hitler at Berchtesgaden.

The meeting at Berchtesgaden, cabled Bullitt, was a 'personal triumph' for the French foreign minister since the 'chief aim' of his diplomacy had been to engage British intervention.[96] In the Anglo-French discussions in London on 18 September after the Berchtesgaden visit the pattern of the April talks was repeated. The darkest hour was before lunch. Daladier put on a brave front. 'Germany's real aim was the disintegration of Czechoslovakia . . . in a very short time Germany would be master of Europe'.[97] During lunch the two Prime Ministers had a private talk and when the conference was resumed the French readily accepted a British suggestion that some arrangement for the cession of the Sudetenland to Germany might be acceptable to Hitler. There was a price to pay for French agreement. The French asked for and received a British promise of a guarantee for

Czechoslovakia. Daladier, it is argued, had 'built better than he knew. He had committed Great Britain to opposing Hitler's advance in the east'.[98] This is to read too much into a guarantee which never in fact materialised. What Daladier won was a British promise of participation in a general, international guarantee, conditional upon Czechoslovakia's acceptance of an Anglo-French plan of cession and upon the neutralisation of her foreign policy. It cost Chamberlain little to promise participation in a guarantee which could only come into force with the agreement of all the guarantors. 'A British guarantee for Czechoslovakia', explained Daladier, 'would therefore help France in the sense that it would help to stop the German march to the East'.[99] More candid was Bonnet's reasoning that France 'would be making a very big concession in agreeing to the cession of Sudeten territory . . . French public opinion would only be prepared to accept such sacrifices if in return . . . Britain would guarantee the neutrality of Czechoslovakia'.[100] In other words, the French wanted a guarantee in order to tranquillise France, not eastern Europe. After the conference, Sir Samuel Hoare, home secretary, complimented Chamberlain on his success in ensuring that the decisions taken were joint ones 'for which we could not be saddled with the major share of responsibility'.[101]

From his second meeting with Hitler at Godesberg (22–24 September) Chamberlain returned with a demand for the occupation of the Sudetenland by 1 October. The Anglo-French discussions of 25–26 September revealed for the first time a divergence of principle. Hitherto both partners had been agreed on the necessity of Czechoslovakia making concessions and France's main aim had been to ensure that the major share of responsibility for imposing a settlement rested with Britain. Hitler's new demands touched the raw nerve of French policy – the fear of having to choose between war and surrender. Chamberlain accepted the Godesberg terms, seeing in them 'a wonderful opportunity to put an end to the horrible nightmare of the present armament race'.[102] For the French, however, Hitler's demands were a matter of life and death. In accepting Germany's ultimatum they would be inflicting on themselves a humiliation almost as grievous as war itself. On 25 September, before Daladier and Bonnet left for London, the French government rejected the German demands. 'A complete swing-over of opinion' against further concessions to Germany had taken place.[103] Nevertheless Daladier was not resigned to war and in the Anglo-French conference he made the first move towards a compromise, proposing that 'an international commission should be set up with a definite time-limit . . . so that within a week the German districts might be evacuated. . . .'[104] The British then cross-examined the French upon their military plans – matters which could have been dealt with in staff talks during the spring and summer but which Chamberlain preferred to save to the last moment in order to bring the greatest possible pressure to bear on the French. Again, the crucial decisions were reached away from the conference table. At midnight the conference was adjourned and early in the morning of 26 September Chamberlain saw Daladier alone[105] and told him that he was sending his adviser, Sir Horace Wilson, as the bearer of a written message to Hitler. If Hitler's response was unfavourable Wilson would warn him that in the event of a German attack on Czechoslovakia France would fulfil her obligations and Britain would support her. Gamelin, chief of the French general staff, who had been called to London, then joined Chamberlain and Daladier for a private discussion. He gave a good account of Czech strength and French intentions. In his memoirs Lord Templewood (Sir Samuel Hoare) claimed that Daladier was given the 'specific pledge of a British expeditionary force'.[106] This was not the case. The oral warning, entrusted to Wilson, was couched in vague and general terms. A written copy was given to Daladier but that was all. No British expeditionary force existed in 1938. In April the French had been told that Britain would not even equip two divisions 'specifically for war on the Continent'.[107] In practical terms, as the French well knew, the British pledge of support was worth little. On their return to Paris on the 26 September the French quickly put the new pledge to the test. Bonnet asked Halifax for 'very early replies' to the following questions. If France became involved in war with Germany, would Great Britain mobilise at the same time as France, introduce conscription and pool the economic and financial resources of the two countries?[108] Before replying Halifax took the French firmly in tow. He requested and obtained the agreement of the French not to take any offensive measures (including a declaration of war) without previous consultation and agreement with London. Then in the evening of 28 September he replied to Bonnet's questions. Assistance to France, he reminded Paris, would be mainly by sea and in the air and the most that could be sent to France, if it were decided to send any at all, would be two divisions, perhaps not fully equipped. Conscription and the pooling of resources raised constitutional issues on which parliament would have to decide. By then the British replies were of no consequence. In the afternoon of 28 September Chamberlain and Daladier had accepted invitations from Hitler to attend a conference in Munich on the following day.

At the Munich conference (29–30 September) Mussolini produced a working draft which was accepted by Chamberlain and Daladier as 'a basis for discussion'.[109] The text of the agreement which finally emerged differed little from the Italian draft, which was itself based largely on a British timetable, proposed by Chamberlain on 27 September and seconded by Daladier. By all accounts, including his own,[110] Daladier said little. The French received two luncheon invitations – one from the British delegation and one from Goering. Moody and morose, Daladier refused the Reichsmarschall and failed to turn up for the British. In the evening of 29 September the atmosphere became more relaxed, the French prime minister settled on a sofa and ordered Munich beer – rumour-mongers embroidered the event and spread stories of drunkenness. At 2.15 am on 30 September the agreement was signed, providing for the evacuation and occupation of the Sudetenland by successive stages between 1 October and 10 October. The whole operation was to be supervised by an international commission, composed of representatives of the Four Powers and of Czechoslovakia. Daladier had little taste for English humour and 'declined' Chamberlain's suggestion that 'he should take the Agreement to Prague'.[111]

The Effects of Munich

British and French opinion greeted the Agreement with almost hysterical relief. But if more had been known about the manner in which peace had been preserved there would have been less pleasure at the fact of its preservation. Small

wonder that returning from Munich Daladier felt grave misgivings as to the reception awaiting him in Paris. The secrecy
of British and French policy did not go unobserved. Jay
Pierrepoint Moffat, chief of the division of European affairs in
the state department, noted that 'through all this crisis what
has surprised me is that the governments of the democracies
have not taken their people or their parliaments into their
confidence'.[112] The major decisions were made without
reference to cabinet or to parliament. Daladier sent the
Chambers on holiday in June and did not recall them until
3 October. In the night of 20–21 September in order to secure
Czech acceptance of the Anglo-French plan of cession Prague
was warned that refusal would mean the loss of French
support. The decision to present this ultimatum was made by
Daladier and Bonnet alone, though Lebrun, president of the
Republic, was consulted by telephone.

Chamberlain, it is said, 'while steadily resisting any commitment to Prague, tightened his links with Paris'.[113] In fact
far from strengthening Anglo-French ties Chamberlain
loosened them. His confidence in the French was never strong
and in September it grew less and less. No high-level staff
contacts took place until Gamelin visited London on 26
September and the exchanges on that occasion were of a very
general kind.[114] The pledge which Chamberlain gave to
Daladier on 25–26 September was given not with the intention of cementing Anglo-French unity but as a sop in order to
win French support for a last appeal to Hitler. Anglo-French
solidarity might be the 'kernel'[115] of Chamberlain's foreign
policy but the policy itself was focused on Anglo-German
understanding. Chamberlain saw in the Anglo-German naval
agreement of 1935, which had caused so much heartburning
in France, a model of the type of agreement he wanted to
reach with Germany. Having achieved a settlement of the
Czech dispute, he lost interest in the French and concentrated
on his main objective. He concluded with Hitler the Anglo-
German agreement and 'saw no reason whatever for saying
anything to the French'.[116]

Munich did not make for closer Anglo-French relations. Of
necessity both partners had worked in close harness, but
without enthusiasm. British leadership strengthened the anti-
pathies which had bedevilled the entente since the end of the

Great War. What caused resentment was not so much British
guidance as the high-handed way it was exercised. In turn the
French were ignored and then browbeaten. They 'felt themselves very badly used by Downing Street'[117] and the French
Communists were reported to be 'passionately anti-British'.[118]
Daladier and Bonnet were 'furious',[119] at being cross-examined
in the Anglo-French talks on 25–26 September.

French foreign policy in 1938 had a more independent
character than has hitherto been conceded. The French role
was an active one, encouraging as well as supporting British
initiatives. When war seemed imminent on 27 September the
French not only supported a British timetable for the transfer
of the Sudetenland but offered Hitler 'a rather more extended
occupation'[120] of Czech territory. On occasion France took
the initiative. In early June François-Poncet broached to the
Germans the idea of informal British, French and German
discussions on the neutralisation of Czechoslovakia under a
three power guarantee. While accepting the surprises which
the British sprang on them – the Berchtesgaden meeting and
Anglo-German Agreement – the French had some of their
own in store. They encouraged the British to believe that they
were exerting strong pressure on Prague; in fact until
September the French line was cautious and moderate. When
in the night of 20–21 September a French ultimatum was sent
to Prague Britain was made to bear the burden of responsibility. President Benes was warned that in refusing the Anglo-
French plan he would break 'Anglo-French solidarity' and so
'deprive French assistance of any practical value'.[121] But for
British pressure, would France have stood by her ally? It was
most unlikely. In Churchill's metaphor Britain and France
'represented a front of two over-ripe melons crushed together'.[122] France had no plans for a major offensive against
Germany[123] and the indications were that she would have
avoided a formal declaration of war and asked the council of
the League of Nations for a finding of aggression.[124] Much
would then have depended on the duration of Czech resistance
and the temper of French opinion.

For France, despite some tactical successes in diplomacy,
Munich was a bloodless Sedan. In less than three years she
had suffered three major blows – the Rhineland *coup*, the
Anschluss and then Munich. Implicit in French appeasement

was the assumption that German expansion in the east would
be both gradual and peaceful, giving France the opportunity
to make a graceful exit. Instead of a process of peaceful compromise Hitler had snatched what he wanted at gunpoint.
Mingled with the relief which greeted Munich were feelings
of shame and humiliation. In the pre-Munich discussions
France had tried to avoid a choice between war and abdica-
tion. And, but for Hitler, the ideal of peaceful bargaining
might have been attainable. France would then have had a
much less painful adjustment to the position of a second-class
power. Apart from the blow to prestige and the loss of a
valuable ally, Munich was harmful to French morale because
it set a dangerous precedent. Nearly a million men had been
mobilised and then stood down. When mobilisation was
ordered a second time in 1939 and no major offensive occurred many Frenchmen again expected to be demobilised. Thus
Munich contributed to the demoralisation which accompanied the *débâcle* of 1940.

Notes

1 G. Bernanos, *Lettre aux Anglais* (Rio de Janeiro, 1943), p. 6.
2 G. Duhamel, *Mémorial de la Guerre blanche 1938* (Paris, 1939),
p. 74.
3 Quoted in Gilbert Fergusson, 'Munich: the French and British
roles', *International Affairs*, October, 1968, p. 649.
4 Fergusson, *International Affairs*, p. 649.
5 H. Macmillan, *Winds of Change* (London, 1966), p. 562.
6 See Neville Waites 'The State of Contemporary History in France'
in *Contemporary History in Europe: Problems and Perspectives*,
ed. D. C. Watt (London, 1969), pp. 89–96.
8 J. W. Wheeler-Bennett, *Munich, Prologue to Tragedy* (London,
1963), p. 33.
9 G. Bonnet, *La Défense de la Paix*, I, *De Washington au Quai
d'Orsay* (Geneva, 1946).
10 See Daladier's testimony in *Les Événements survenus en France de
1933 à 1945, Témoignages et Documents*, I, pp. 1–82 (Paris, ND).
11 Gilbert Fergusson, *International Affairs*, accepts much of Bonnet's
defence. Arthur H. Furnia, *The Diplomacy of Appeasement*
(Washington, 1960), follows Daladier closely.
12 See Bibliography.

13 *Documents on British Foreign Policy, 1919–1939*, ser. 3 (London, 1949), (hereafter *DBFP*), I, 286.

14 *DBFP*, ser. 3, I, 219, n. 2.

15 Quoted in Fergusson, *International Affairs*, p. 649.

16 *Public Record Office* (hereafter *PRO*), Cab. 23/90.

17 *Foreign Relations of the United States: Diplomatic Papers 1937* (hereafter *FRUS*), I, (Washington, 1954), p. 78.

18 *Documents on German Foreign Policy, 1918–1945*, Series D, London, 1950 (hereafter *DGFP*), I, nos. 22 and 63.

19 *FRUS*, 1938, I, p. 27.

20 *Documents and Materials relating to the Eve of the Second World War*, I (Moscow, 1948), no. 4.

21 Keith Feiling, *The Life of Neville Chamberlain* (London, 1946), p. 347.

22 *Papers of Sir Eric Phipps* (hereafter *Phipps Papers*), Foreign Office minute, 17 March 1938.

23 *DBFP*, I, 106.

24 *DBFP*, I, 114.

25 General Gamelin, *Servir*, II, *Le Prologue du Drame* (Paris, 1946), pp. 322–8.

26 *DGFP*, II, no. 120.

27 Blum's first government had been in 1936–7. *Phipps Papers*, Foreign Office minute, 17 March 1938 (approved by Halifax).

28 *DBFP*, I, 136.

29 A. J. P. Taylor, *The Origins of the Second World War* (London, 1963), p. 197.

30 Taylor, *Origins of the Second World War*.

31 J. Paul-Boncour, *Entre Deux Guerres*, III (Paris, 1946), pp. 97–101.

32 *Phipps Papers*, Phipps to Halifax, 11 April 1938.

33 *FRUS*, 1938, I, p. 177.

34 H. Nicolson, *Diaries and Letters 1930–1939* (London, 1966), pp. 298–9.

35 See Robert Coulondre, *De Staline à Hitler* (Paris, 1950), pp. 143–5; Gamelin, *Servir*, I, p. 61; Jean Zay, *Souvenirs et Solitude* (Paris, 1946), p. 249.

36 Feiling, *Life of Neville Chamberlain*, p. 353.

37 Feiling, *Life of Neville Chamberlain*, p. 353.

38 J. Romains, *Les Hommes de bonne volonté*, vol. XXV, *Le Tapis Magique* (Paris, 1946), p. 254.

39 Paul-Boncour, *Entre Deux Guerres*, vol. III, p. 101.

40 *Phipps Papers*, Halifax to Phipps, 6 April 1939.

41 *DBFP*, V, p. 800.

42 A. de Monzie, *Ci-devant* (Paris, 1941), pp. 54–5.

43 J.-B. Duroselle, *L'Europe de 1915 à nos jours: vie politique et relations internationales* (Paris, 1964), p. 316.

44 Jules Romains captures this mood in *Les Hommes de bonne volonté*, vol. XXVII, *Le 7 Octobre* (Paris, 1946), pp. 221–6.

45 Feiling, *Life of Neville Chamberlain*, p. 323.

46 For Daladier's skilful exploitation of the international situation

in order to strengthen his government see Léon Blum's articles in *Le Populaire*, in *L'Oeuvre de Léon Blum*, IV, ii (Paris, 1965), pp. 203–12.

47 See John Morton Blum, *From the Morgenthau Diaries*, I (Boston, 1959), pp. 501–2.

48 *PRO*, Records of the Prime Minister's Office, Premier I/267, Chamberlain to Daladier, 17 August 1938.

49 However, in August 1938, the British embassy at Paris estimated that in 1936–37 only one fifth of the total of government borrowing had gone to rearmament (*PRO*, FO 371/21595/C7986).

50 *FRUS*, 1038, I, p. 65.

51 Gamelin, *Servir*, II, p. 345.

52 *Phipps Papers*, Phipps to Halifax, 4 September 1938.

53 Édouard Daladier, *Défense du Pays* (Paris, 1939), p. 20.

54 Bonnet, *Défense de la Paix*, I, p. 345.

55 *DBFP*, II, no. 1083.

56 *DBFP*, I, no. 286.

57 *DGFP*, II, no. 194.

58 *FRUS*, 1938, I, p. 601.

59 See *Documents diplomatiques français 1932–1939*, ser. 2, 1936–1939 II, (Paris, 1964), no. 372.

60 See Général P.-É. Tournoux, *Défense des Frontières, Haut Commandemant, Gouvernement et défense des frontières du nord et de l'est, 1919–1939* (Paris, 1960), pp. 333–41.

61 *FRUS*, 1937, I, p. 97.

62 Daladier, *Défense du Pays*, pp. 103–4.

63 *FRUS*, 1938, I, pp. 601–2.

64 Quoted in *L'Homme Libre*, 28 October 1938.

65 See F. de Brinon, *Mémoires* (Paris, 1949), p. 28; *Les Procès de Collaboration: Fernand de Brinon, Joseph Darnand, Jean Luchaire*, (Paris, 1948), pp. 200–7; Georges Bonnet, *Le Quai d'Orsay sous Trois Républiques* (Paris, 1961), p. 128. According to de Brinon, the contacts were in August–September 1933. The French documents for this period have not yet been published. But since Daladier did not tell the Quai d'Orsay, the documents are unlikely to add to our knowledge.

66 Paul Reynaud, *Mémoires*, II, *Envers et Contre Tous* (Paris, 1963), p. 219.

67 See Gamelin, *Servir*, II, p. 350. Bonnet denies that he threatened to resign but says he sent Daladier a letter setting out his opposition to war (M. Bonnet to the author). However, on 19 September there were rumours of Bonnet having threatened to resign, *The Papers of Hugh Dalton* (hereafter *Dalton Papers*), 19 Sept. 1938.

68 *Carnets Secrets de Jean Zay* (Paris, 1942), pp. 19–20.

69 *DGFP*, II, 147.

70 See William R. Rock, *Appeasement on Trial* (1966), p. 127.

71 *DBFP*, I, 164.

72 *PRO*, Cab. 23/95, cabinet of 24 September 1938.

73 *FRUS*, 1938, I, p. 712.

74 J. Zay, *Carnets Secrets*, pp. 25–6.
75 See *FRUS*, 1938, I, p. 601.
76 R. J. Minney, *The Private Papers of Hore-Belisha* (London, 1960), pp. 120–1.
77 See *DBFP*, I, 147.
78 *DGFP*, II, 143, 147.
79 *DGFP, Ibid.*, 149.
80 *DBFP*, I, 164.
81 *FRUS*, 1938, I, p. 501.
82 *DBFP*, I, 256–257.
83 *DBFP*, I, 271.
84 *DBFP*, I, 286.
85 For example, the French ambassador at Warsaw, Léon Noël, and the novelist Jules Romains were sent to Prague (Léon Noël, *L'Agression allemande contre la Pologne* (Paris, 1946), pp. 198–203; Jules Romains, *Seven Mysteries of Europe* (London, 1941), p. 23).
86 *DBFP*, 354.
87 *DBFP*, I, 389.
88 *New Documents on the History of Munich*, edited by V. F. Klochko (Prague, 1958), 21, 22.
89 *FRUS*, 1938, I, p. 536.
90 Cabinet of 17 September 1938, *PRO*, Cab. 23/95.
91 *DBFP*, II, 814, n.i.
92 *DBFP*, II, 814.
93 *DBFP*, II, 807.
94 *DBFP*, II, 857. At a second interview with Daladier on 13 September Phipps reported the French Prime Minister as saying that 'at all costs Germany must be prevented from invading Czechoslovakia because in that case France would be faced with her obligations'. On 14th Chamberlain reported this statement to the cabinet and added that the 'language' was 'significant' (*PRO*, Cab 23/95).
95 See cabinet of 14 September, *PRO*, Cab 23/95. Also Sir David Kelly, *The Ruling Few* (London, 1952), pp. 258–9.
96 *FRUS*, 1938, I, p. 600.
97 *DBFP*, II, 928.
98 A. J. P. Taylor, *Origins of the Second World War*, p. 220.
99 *DBFP*, II, 928.
100 *DBFP*.
101 Cabinet of 19 September, *PRO*, Cab. 23/95.
102 *PRO*, Cab. 23/95 (cabinet of 24 September).
103 *DBFP*, II, 1106.
104 *DBFP*, II, 1093.
105 *PRO* Cab. 23/95. Corbin was present as interpreter. See also Daladier, 'Munich', in *Candide*, 1961 (four weekly articles 7–28 September).
106 Lord Templewood, *Nine Troubled Years*, (London, 1954), p. 315.
107 *DBFP*, I, 164.
108 *DBFP*, II, 1120.
109 *DGFP*, II, 670.

110 Daladier, 'Munich'.
111 *DBFP.*
112 J. P. Moffat, *The Moffat Papers* (Cambridge, Mass., 1956), p. 214.
113 W. N. Medlicott, *The Coming of War in 1939* (London, 1963), p. 20.
114 Marshal of the Royal Air Force Sir John Slessor writes: 'it is horrifying to recall the extent of our ignorance about the military policy and the forces of the French'. *The Central Blue: Recollections and Reflections* (London, 1956), p. 146.
115 'I regard Franco-British solidarity as the kernel of our foreign policy . . .', letter of Chamberlain to Daladier, 8 July 1938, *PRO*, FO 371/21591–21592.
116 Lord Strang, *Home and Abroad* (London, 1956), p. 147.
117 *Dalton*, 19 September 1938 (reports from Paris to National Council of Labour).
118 *Dalton*, 19 September 1938.
119 *Private Papers of Hore-Belisha*, p. 148.
120 *DBFP*, II, 1151.
121 Quoted in F. Vnuk, 'Munich and the Soviet Union', *Journal of Central European Affairs*, October 1961, p. 304.
122 W. S. Churchill, *The Second World War*, I, *The Gathering Storm* (London, 1964), p. 266.
123 On 26 September 1938, General Lelong, French military attaché in London, told Captain Sir Basil Liddell Hart that 'perhaps by next Spring or Summer they would be ready for a major offensive', *Liddell Hart Papers*,
124 See *DBFP*, II, 914, 1106.

Bibliography

1 UNPUBLISHED SOURCES

OFFICIAL PAPERS

Under the thirty-year rule British government papers can be consulted. I have used the foreign office and cabinet papers for 1937 and 1938.

In France a fifty-year rule is still in force and, save to a privileged few, the papers are closed for this period. There are in any case major gaps in the French record which will never be filled. The cabinets of the Third Republic did not keep official minutes of their proceedings. Further, many important foreign ministry files were destroyed in 1940–1944. For 1938 the losses include the following: the foreign minister's memoranda of his talks, departmental minutes to the minister, 'private letters', confidential and secret papers.[1] As foreign minister, Bonnet kept his own

[1] For further details see *Documents Diplomatiques Français 1932–1939*. Ser 2 (1939–1936), I, Paris, 1963, vii–xi.,

copies of important documents. In order to replace files which had been destroyed the Vichy government arranged to have copies made of Bonnet's papers, but in 1951 the French foreign ministry informed a parliamentary commission of enquiry that it could give no assurance that these copies were authentic and complete.[2]

PRIVATE PAPERS

I am grateful to Lady Francis Phipps for allowing me to consult the papers of Sir Eric Phipps and also to the late Captain Sir Basil Liddell Hart for permission to use his papers. My thanks are due also to the Keeper of Manuscripts of the British Library of Political and Economic Science for permission to use the Hugh Dalton Papers.

2 PUBLISHED DOCUMENTS

Documents on British Foreign Policy, 1919–1939 (HMSO, 1946) ser. 3, vols. I–II.

Documents on German Foreign Policy, 1918–1945 (HMSO, 1948 on), ser. D, vols. I–II.

Documents Diplomatiques Français 1932–1939 (Paris, 1963) ser. 1 (1932–1936), ser. 2 (1936–1939). Six volumes have so far appeared. There is nothing, as yet, for 1938.

Foreign Relations of the United States: Diplomatic Papers (USGPO 1943). I have used: 1937, vol. I (Washington, 1954); 1938, vol. I (Washington, 1955).

New Documents on the History of Munich (Prague, 1958).

Documents and Materials Relating to the Eve of the Second World War (Moscow, 1948), 2 vols.

Documents Diplomatiques Belges 1920–1940 (Brussels, 1964), vol. V, 1938–1940 (Brussels, 1966).

Les Événements Survenus en France de 1933 à 1945. Rapport de M. Charles Serre, Député, au nom de la Commission d'Enquête Parlementaire, 2 vols.; *Témoignages et Documents Receuillis par la Commission d'Enquête Parlementaire*, 9 vols. (Paris, ND).

3 MEMOIRS AND DIARIES

Léon Blum, *L'Oeuvre de Léon Blum*, IV, ii, 1937–1940 (Paris, 1965).

John Morton Blum, *From the Morgenthau Diaries*, I (Boston, 1959).

Georges Bonnet, *La Défense de la Paix*, I, *De Washington au Quai d'Orsay*, II, *Fin d'Une Europe* (Geneva, 1946–48).

[2] See *Les Événements Survenus en France de 1933 à 1945: Témoignages et Documents* (Paris, ND). IX, p. 2692.

Le Quai d'Orsay Sous Trois Républiques (Paris, 1961).
De Munich à la Guerre (new and enlarged edition of *Défense de la Paix*). (Paris, 1967).
Fernand de Brinon, *Mémoires* (Paris, 1949).
Winston S. Churchill, *The Second World War*, I, *The Gathering Storm* (London, 1964 edition).
Robert Coulondre, *De Staline à Hitler* (Paris, 1950).
Édouard Daladier, *Défense du Pays*, (Paris, 1939).
Réponse aux Chefs Communistes, discours prononcé à l'Assemblée Nationale le 18 Juillet 1946 (Paris, 1946).
'Munich' in *Candide*, 1961 (four weekly articles 7–28 September).
André François-Poncet, *Souvenirs d'une Ambassade à Berlin* (Paris, 1946).
Keith Feiling, *The Life of Neville Chamberlain* (London, 1946).
Maurice Gustave Gamelin, *Servir*, 3 vols. (Paris, 1946–7).
Harold Macmillan, *Winds of Change* (London, 1966).
R. J. Minney, *The Private Papers of Hore-Belisha* (London, 1960).
Anatole de Monzie, *Ci-devant* (Paris, 1941).
Harold Nicolson, *Diaries and Letters*, 1930–1939 (London, 1966).
Léon Noël, *L'Agression Allemande contre la Pologne* (Paris, 1946).
J. Paul-Boncour, *Entre Deux Guerres*, 3 vols. (Paris, 1945–7).
Paul Reynaud, *Mémoires*, 2 vols. (Paris, 1960–3).
Jules Romains, *The Seven Mysteries of Europe* (London, 1941).
Sir John Slessor, *The Central Blue: Recollections and Reflections* (London, 1956).
Lord Strang, *Home and Abroad* (London, 1956).
Lord Templewood, *Nine Troubled Years* (London, 1954).
Jean Zay, *Carnets Secrets de Jean Zay*, publiés et commentés par Philippe Henriot (Paris, 1942).
Souvenirs et Solitude (Paris, 1946).

4 SECONDARY WORKS

Georges Bernanos, *Lettre aux Anglais* (Rio de Janeiro, 1943).
Georges Duhamel, *Memorial de la Guerre Blanche 1938* (Paris, 1939).
Jean-Baptiste Duroselle, *L'Europe de 1815 à nos jours: vie politique et relations internationales* (Paris, 1964).
Arthur J. Furnia, *The Diplomacy of Appeasement* (Washington, 1960).
Sir David Kelly, *The Ruling Few* (London, 1952).
A. J. P. Taylor, *The Origins of the Second World War* (London, 1963).
W. N. Medlicott, *The Coming of War in 1939* (London, 1963).

William R. Rock, *Appeasement on Trial* (Archon Books, 1966).

J. W. Wheeler-Bennett, *Munich: Prologue to Tragedy* (London, 1963).

D. C. Watt, *Contemporary History in Europe: Problems and Perspectives* (London, 1969).

5 ARTICLES

Gilbert Fergusson, 'Munich: the French and British roles', *International Affairs*, October 1968, pp. 649–65.

F. Vnuk, 'Munich and the Soviet Union', *Journal of Central European Affairs*, October 1961, pp. 284–304.

6 NEWSPAPERS

L'Homme Libre (Paris).

8 The Breakdown of the Alliance in 1940

P. M. H. Bell

In May and June 1940 Britain and France suffered a stagger-ing defeat at the hands of Germany, with disastrous effects on Anglo-French relations. At the beginning of May the two countries were allies. They had beaten Germany before and looked forward to doing so again. Within two months they were separated, first by differences arising out of the military situation, later by the French decision to ask for an armistice and so to abandon a war which the British were determined to continue. After the armistice, Britain and France were in effect enemies. British shells crippled the French squadron at Mers-el-Kebir; French bombs fell on Gibraltar. The British government supported the Free French movement led by General de Gaulle, a rebel against his own state; the French government collaborated with Germany. The interests of the two states, which had been so close as to form the basis of an alliance, first diverged and then came into conflict. In this dramatic and revealing crisis, Anglo-French relations passed through three phases: alliance, separation, and enmity.

Alliance

In 1939 the British and French took up the threads of their alliance where they had been laid down in 1918. The Supreme War Council, to co-ordinate the policies of the two govern-ments, was re-created, and met frequently. A joint economic planning committee, with Jean Monnet as chairman, was set up in December 1939. A British expeditionary force went again to north-east France, where its commander, Lord Gort, was placed under the orders of the French commander of the north-east theatre, General Georges – though with a right of appeal to London if a French order should appear to endanger the safety of his forces.

On 28 March 1940 the two governments published a joint declaration:

> The Government of the French Republic and His Majesty's Government in the United Kingdom of Great Britain and Northern Ireland mutually undertake that during the present war they will neither negotiate nor conclude an armistice or treaty of peace except by mutual agreement.
>
> They undertake not to discuss peace terms before reaching agreement on the conditions necessary to ensure to each of them an effective and lasting guarantee of their security.
>
> Finally, they undertake to maintain, after the conclusion of peace, a community of action in all spheres for so long as may be necessary to safeguard their security and to effect the reconstruction, with the assistance of other nations, of an international order which will ensure the liberty of peoples, respect for law, and the maintenance of peace in Europe.[1]

At the time it was made, this declaration was seen in the context of a future Allied victory, and the need to avoid the conflicts of policy which had plagued Britain and France between the wars. The undertaking not to negotiate separately for an armistice or for peace was regarded as a formality. Reynaud (who became prime minister of France on 22 March 1940) commented to the Chamber of Deputies that this was a matter of honour – *'en réalité il n'y a pas de question'*.[2] Within three months of the declaration, a separate armistice was to become the most urgent of questions.

The Germans opened their offensive in the west on 10 May 1940 and won swift and overwhelming victory. By 14 May they had broken through in the Ardennes. On 20 May they reached the sea at Abbeville, at the mouth of the Somme, encircling the Belgian, British and French forces in Flanders. On 27 May the Belgian army capitulated. By 4 June the evacuation of British and French troops from Dunkirk ended, and the French rearguard surrendered. On 5 June the Germans resumed their offensive against the remaining French armies on the Somme. On the 9th they attacked along the Aisne. By 11 June it was clear that these battles had been won and lost: the French armies were no longer capable of organised resistance.

Up to 4 June it was possible to say that the British and French tried to face the defeat as allies, though already events were forcing them apart. The problems of the alliance in this phase were twofold. Firstly, there were the immediate problems arising out of the fighting itself; and secondly there was the deeper problem posed by the possibility of total French defeat.

Difficulties were inevitable when turmoil and uncertainty prevailed on the field of battle, communications were slow or non-existent, and most people had a natural desire to blame someone else for the disasters around them.[3] Two episodes have attracted much attention. One was the retreat of the British forces commanded by General Franklyn from Arras, ordered by Gort at Franklyn's request on the evening of 23 May. The force involved was not large – two divisions, each a brigade under strength. The immediate reasons for the retreat were pressing – Franklyn's men were at the tip of a narrow salient, in imminent danger of being cut off. It was a time when more than one formation, British and French alike, were in retreat. Yet of this incident, M. Henri Michel, in an account of the campaign which is sage, balanced and wholly free from polemic, writes: 'he [Gort] had moved a pawn on the chessboard, in the hope of saving it; but the whole game of chess was to be affected by it. He had made the first scissors cut in the delicate fabric of the Allied coalition. . . .'[4] The apparent discrepancy between cause and effect is explained by the circumstances in which the retreat was ordered.

On 19 May General Weygand replaced General Gamelin as commander-in-chief of the French armies. He formed a plan for the armies cut off in Flanders to attack southwards, while a new army hastily forming along the Somme moved northwards to meet them. On 22 May, at a meeting in Paris, he expounded this plan to the British and French prime ministers, Churchill and Reynaud, who endorsed it. The retreat from Arras, therefore, was ordered only a day after the Allied prime ministers had agreed, not on retreat, but on attack. Weygand heard about the retreat on the morning of 24 May. He asserted that it had not been enforced by German pressure, and told Reynaud that it was impossible to command an army which remained dependent on London, whence the order for retreat must have come. This was not so: the initiative had come from Franklyn at Arras, while in London on 25 May General Ironside, the chief of the imperial general staff, wrote in his diary: 'Gort has withdrawn from Arras. . . . Why Gort has done this I don't know. He has never told us that he was going to do it or even when he had done it. He has used his discretion. . . '.[5] But this was unimportant. The damage, more psychological than military, had been done. Militarily, it is unlikely that the Weygand Plan was ever more than a forlorn hope. Psychologically, the British retreat pushed Weygand towards abandoning the counter-offensive, and it marked for him, only five days after taking over command, the unreliability of the British.

After the retreat from Arras came the retreat to Dunkirk and the evacuation to England. At the start of this operation, there was a dangerous lack of co-ordination between the British and the French. On 20 May the British began preparations at Dover in case an evacuation by sea became necessary. On 26 May, the British government sent orders to Gort to retreat to the coast and attempt evacuation. Churchill informed Reynaud, and asked that corresponding orders be issued to the French forces in Flanders. In fact, no such orders reached General Blanchard, commanding the First Army Group, until 29 May. Meanwhile, on 28 May, there was a meeting between Gort and Blanchard, at which Gort insisted on following his orders to withdraw to the coast, while Blanchard insisted on holding his positions. The consequence was that far more British than French troops were evacuated in the early days. On 30 May the figures were 114,000 British and only 6,000 French. By 31 May they stood at 150,000 British and 15,000 French. The final total was 224,320 British and 141,842 Allied, nearly all French. It is true that after 29 May, when the order was given that the two nationalities were to be brought off in equal numbers, equality was achieved.[6] But the last British troops left on 2 June. The last French embarked in the early hours of 4 June, leaving between 30,000 and 40,000 men to surrender to the Germans. The French protected the evacuation of the British, and paid the price: which was scarcely equality of treatment in any sense of the words. The vital role of the French rearguard is recognised in all responsible British accounts of Dunkirk, without somehow sinking into the national consciousness.

Dunkirk has remained an emotional issue, meaning quite different things on each side of the Channel. Its immediate military significance, however, was simple. The BEF was home, but it was not an organised force, and it had lost all its equipment. The British had left the continent, and were in no position to return. In the battle which resumed in France on 5 June, only two British divisions and three squadrons of the RAF were engaged. The Anglo-French military alliance was at an end. It had survived under the strain of the German offensive for just over three weeks.

Even while it was still in existence, while a substantial (though inadequate) British army was in France, the very basis of the alliance was in question. Beneath the immediate problems of military co-operation there lay the deeper problem posed by the possibility of the total defeat of France. The realisation of this possibility came early. Reynaud telephoned Churchill at 7.30 am on 15 May and told him: 'We are beaten; we have lost the battle.'[7] This alarm, and the confusion and disarray which seized Paris that day and the next, were the reaction to the news of the German breakthrough in the Ardennes. These fears subsided when the Germans were seen to be heading for the Channel, not Paris, but at the *Comité de Guerre* on 25 May the possibility of defeat was clearly and formally considered. Weygand said that if the northern armies were destroyed, the line of the Somme and the Aisne would be defended but might be broken. If it were broken, the armies could then fight only for the honour of the country. The possibility of Germany offering reasonable terms was raised by President Lebrun; Weygand and Reynaud both said that the ending of hostilities was a matter for both the allies. It was agreed that Reynaud should explain the gravity of the military situation to the British, and discuss with them the possibility of a separate peace.[8] On 28 May Weygand prepared a memorandum for Reynaud, saying that the defence of the Somme-Aisne line was crucial; that the British should be asked for all possible help; and that they should be told that the definitive rupture of the French line would mean that French resistance was effectively at an end.[9]

Reynaud passed on the substance of Weygand's note to the British ambassador. Earlier, on 26 May, the French prime minister had been to London, where according to Churchill he 'dwelt not obscurely upon the possible French withdrawal from the war'.[10] But the French did not at this stage force an open examination between the Allies of the issues raised by a possible French armistice. (It may be that Reynaud should have done so after the *Comité de Guerre* of 25 May, but it appears that he did not.) What they did was to appeal to the British to save the day, to throw everything into the decisive battle of France and hold the Germans there. These appeals were principally for fighter squadrons and the direct intervention of bomber command in the land battles; though after Dunkirk they asked too that the evacuated troops should be sent back to France with the greatest speed, even before they were fully reorganised. How to reply to such appeals raised crucial questions for the British.

The British were early aware of the possibility of the defeat of France. Churchill was deeply impressed by his visit to Paris on 16 May. He telegraphed to the Cabinet that the situation was 'grave in the last degree', and that 'the French resistance may be broken up as rapidly as that of Poland unless this battle of the Bulge is won.' His first recommendation was the despatch of six further fighter squadrons to France.[11] But on his return to London he began to prepare for the contingency of a French defeat. On 17 May he instructed Chamberlain to examine the consequences of the fall of Paris and the withdrawal of the BEF from France. The next day he asked the chiefs of staff to consider sending only half of the 1st Armoured Division to France – 'One must always be prepared for the fact that the French may be offered very advantageous terms of peace, and the whole weight be thrown upon us.'[12] On 19 May the chiefs of staff had before them a draft memorandum on 'British strategy in a certain eventuality', meaning the fall of France and a separate peace between France and Germany. This memorandum in its final form was discussed by the Cabinet on 27 May, along with the reply of the chiefs of staff to a formal question from Churchill on Britain's ability to carry on the war alone. Both papers argued that everything depended on the air: 'the crux of the matter is air superiority'. Given this, invasion could be prevented, industrial production kept up, and Germany ultimately defeated.[13] These conclusions set out at length what

Air Chief Marshal Dowding, the head of fighter command, had already written on 16 May:

I believe that, if an adequate fighter force is kept in this country, if the fleet remains in being, and if home forces are suitably organised to meet invasion, we should be able to carry on the war single-handed for some time, if not indefinitely. But if the Home Defence Force is drained away in desperate attempts to remedy the situation in France, defeat in France will involve the final, complete, and irremediable defeat of this country.[14]

The French and British thus drew wholly contrary conclusions from the same premiss: that the battle engaged in France was one which, if lost, would lead to the total collapse of the front in France and perhaps to a separate peace. The French concluded that the British should commit all their resources (which amounted in effect to the RAF) to save the front in France. The British concluded that they must not commit all their resources, lest they be left naked at home in the event of the collapse of the front in France. Both countries could claim good arguments, based both on national self-interest and on the ultimate interests of the alliance itself.

While there was still some hope of turning the tide in France, the French could advance the classical military principle of concentration at the decisive point. As late as 11 June, during a meeting of the Supreme War Council at Briare, Weygand told Churchill: 'Here is the decisive point. Now is the decisive moment. It is therefore wrong to keep *any* squadrons back in England.'[15] At an earlier stage, Ironside, CIGS until 27 May, had felt the same, writing in his diary on 17 May: 'What we want now is fighting. Fighting for our lives. The struggle is now. There is no use holding anything up for a problematical continuance of the war if France collapses.'[16] Some writers looking back have taken the same view. Eddy Bauer, the Swiss military historian, argues that fighter command should have been committed to the battle in France, in support of the Weygand Plan. By shooting down Stukas in France, the RAF could have diminished the power of the German armour; and even a later air attack on Britain would have been weakened by German losses in France.[17]

Against this, the British held that this application of classical principles was mistaken, and that ultimately it was even in France's own interest that fighter command should be preserved. Churchill replied to Weygand's assertion on 11 June: 'This is not the decisive point and this is not the decisive moment. That moment will come when Hitler hurls his Luftwaffe against Great Britain. If we can keep command of the air, and if we can keep the seas open, as we certainly shall keep them open, we will win it all back for you.'[18] Dowding did not believe that his fighter squadrons would turn the battle in France. As early as 14 May he said that to meet Reynaud's request for ten more squadrons would be 'like pouring water into the desert'. He produced a graph for the Cabinet on 15 May, showing that at the current rate of losses in France the supply of Hurricanes would be exhausted by the end of May. The conditions which later made for success in the Battle of Britain were absent in France, where there were no radar stations or operations rooms, and where airfields were open to ground attack. Looking back, Dowding's biographer reaches the opposite conclusion from Bauer: 'Today it is obvious that, if every one of Dowding's squadrons had been sent across the Channel when the Germans aimed their first blow, they could have done nothing to save France from defeat.' They could have supplemented a stronger and better organised defence on the ground, but they could not have been a substitute for it.[19]

Thus both sides had good arguments, which historians can still support. But the British government had control of its own air force. After early hesitation, in which Churchill's sense of history and personal generosity towards the French played some part,[20] the strength of fighter command was not committed except over Dunkirk. Its strength was husbanded for the battle of Britain. On 5 June, when the German offensive opened along the Somme, Weygand handed Reynaud the following note:

The commander-in-chief is obliged to take note that appeals to the British goverment have been in vain. We bear the weight of the German attack without the benefit of any further help from Britain, either in fighters or in extra divisions.[21]

Separation

From 5 June, the British role in the battle of France was confined to exhortation, with very little help. The two British divisions already in France were swallowed up in the collapse which followed the first few days of stern fighting.[22] Another division, and parts of a Canadian division, were sent to Cherbourg and Brest, but eventually withdrawn from French command on 15 June. Churchill, notably at the Supreme War Council at Briare on 11 June, urged the French to fight on, invoking the desperate days of March 1918 and throwing out suggestions for defending Paris, or fighting a war of columns and guerrillas if co-ordinated defence broke down. But, as Pétain pointed out, in March 1918 the British had had sixty divisions in the line. Without the divisions, the exhortations carried no weight.[23]

The French, thus left in effect alone, had to grapple with the problems raised by their defeat. Two possible courses were open. One was to acknowledge defeat and ask for an armistice, which would in all likelihood lead to a peace. The other was to acknowledge defeat in the main battle, but to carry on the war, perhaps in Brittany, more likely from French North Africa. The choice began to be forced upon the government from 9 June onwards, though there had been discussions earlier. On 9 June Pétain (whom Reynaud had brought into his government on 18 May) read out at a meeting of the *ad hoc* war committee, which met most mornings during the crisis, a note arguing that it was necessary to ask for an armistice. On the same day, Weygand prepared a note which he handed to Reynaud on the 10 June, warning him that the front might be broken at any moment, and the co-ordinated defence of the country become impossible. On 12 June, Weygand decided that this moment had come. That evening he told the Cabinet, meeting at the Château de Cangé, near Tours, that only the ending of hostilities could save the armies from collapse. He therefore asked the government to seek an armistice. There ensued a period of confused debate, within the French government and between the French and the British, carried on in the stress and muddle of the movement of the French government from Tours to Bordeaux, and under the pressure of the advancing German armies.

Within the French government, the chief advocates of an armistice were Pétain and Weygand, with support from a number of ministers which increased as the days went by, but did not become a clear majority even by 16 June.[24] Among the reasons which led Pétain and Weygand to demand an armistice, the overriding consideration was their belief that not just the battle of France but the war itself was lost. Resistance in Brittany or North Africa was impossible, and to attempt it would only worsen the situation; the defeat or surrender of Britain would not be long delayed. From this basic premise, subsidiary motives followed automatically. First, all hesitation in reaching a decision to ask for an armistice meant a useless sacrifice of French lives – and it must be remembered to Pétain's honour that a great part of his prestige in the war of 1914–18 arose from his care for the lives of his men. Second, it was important to secure an armistice while there were still enough disciplined units in existence to maintain order in France and avert revolution or anarchy. Third, Pétain at least was convinced that Britain would make peace after only a token resistance, having sacrificed France; it was therefore right for France to move first. Fourth, Pétain and Weygand were determined not to leave the soil of France, which would be an act of desertion in face of the enemy. Finally, there was the wish to rebuild, even re-create, France: to save her from the political and spiritual morass of the Third Republic. In such a context, defeat could be almost welcomed as the refiner's fire to purify the soul of France.

Reynaud opposed these arguments principally by denying the basic premise. The war was not lost, but could be carried on by the French fleet and empire, in alliance with the British, who would continue the fight. He also held that it was simply impossible to come to terms with Nazi Germany – '*Hitler, c'est Gengis-Khan*'. Moreover, France must not separate herself from Britain and the United States: '*il est impossible de concevoir l'avenir de la France sans l'amitié et l'appui du monde anglo-saxon.*'[25] Reynaud and his supporters formed a majority in the Cabinet, but did not possess the prestige and moral authority of Pétain and Weygand. Reynaud himself had summoned both these aged and distinguished soldiers to his aid, and he never felt strong enough to dismiss them and face the consequences.

These two sets of arguments and beliefs about the present and future of France carried quite different implications for Anglo-French relations, the course of which would turn on the French decision. Meanwhile, as allies the British had the right to be consulted about an armistice, and under the declaration of 28 March they had a technical right of veto. Consultation took place during Churchill's last visit to France on 13 June. He had been hastily invited by Reynaud after Weygand requested an armistice on the 12 June, and the prime ministers met in the prefecture at Tours. Reynaud put the question: supposing a French government (which would not include himself) were to say that they must come to terms with Germany, would Britain acknowledge that '. . . France, after having sacrified the best and finest flower of her youth, would deserve to continue to benefit from Franco-British solidarity, while having authority from Britain to conclude a separate peace?'

The British record of the meeting goes on:

Mr Churchill said that in no case would Britain waste time and energy in reproaches and recriminations. That did not mean that she would consent to action contrary to the recent agreement. The first step ought to be M. Reynaud's further message putting the present position squarely to President Roosevelt. Let them await the answer before considering anything else. If England won the war France would be restored in her dignity and in her greatness.[26]

This, of course, was technically only the answer to a hypothetical question, but in fact there was no doubt of the immediacy of the issue. Churchill was sympathetic, but British consent was clearly withheld, and further consideration of the question postponed until an attempt had been made to secure American help.

Consultation between the governments should have been taken a step further at this point, for Reynaud had been charged to invite Churchill to meet the French Cabinet. Reynaud, however, did not deliver this invitation, and an opportunity for contact and explanation was lost.

The French government continued its peregrinations and discussions, divided and floundering. Eventually, on 15 June, Reynaud reluctantly accepted a proposal made by Frossard and taken up and elaborated by Chautemps. This was that the French people would only understand and accept a move to North Africa to carry on the war if they were convinced that German terms would be unacceptable; therefore they should ask British permission to seek the terms of an armistice.[27] Reynaud did so in a telegram despatched on the evening of the 15th, assuring the British that the Cabinet did not doubt that the terms would be unacceptable. The approach would be made through the USA, and it was explicitly stated that the surrender of the French fleet to Germany would be considered an unacceptable condition. Reynaud added that he would probably have to resign if the British government refused its consent.[28] This was no longer consultation with the British: they were now formally asked to release France from the declaration of 28 March. The British reply was sent in a telegram despatched at 12.35 pm on 16 June:

Our agreement forbidding separate negotiations, whether for armistice or peace, was made with the French Republic, and not with any particular French Administration or statesman. It therefore involves the honour of France. Nevertheless, *provided, but only provided, that the French Fleet is sailed forthwith for British harbours pending negotiations*, His Majesty's Government give their full consent to an inquiry by the French Government to ascertain the terms of an armistice for France. His Majesty's Government, being resolved to continue the war, wholly exclude themselves from all part in the above-mentioned inquiry concerning an armistice.[29]

This was followed by a second telegram, amplifying certain points in the first. It is important that even at this stage the British government did not accept as sufficient Reynaud's assurance that the fleet would not be surrendered, but instead insisted on its despatch to British waters.

The British thus sought absolute security in the matter of the French fleet. But on a French approach for armistice terms they were less intransigent than they might have been. They gave their consent subject to one clear condition. But at that point everything was clouded by the spectacular irrelevancy of the offer of union between Britain and France, made by the British Cabinet on the afternoon of 16 June. The British, and the small group of Frenchmen in London who helped to produce the proposal, hoped to prevent France from asking for an armistice by making this dramatic gesture. In order to allow the proposal to be considered by the French government under favourable conditions, instructions were sent to the British ambassador in Bordeaux, Sir Ronald Campbell, to suspend action on the two telegrams about an armistice and the French fleet. In fact, Campbell and General Spears, Churchill's personal representative in France, were convinced that the offer of union superseded the telegrams. It appears that they told Reynaud that the telegrams had been cancelled. Reynaud said two days later that they had actually been taken away from him.[30] The British government's intention of *suspending* action on the two telegrams was thus lost at Bordeaux, and a confusion was created from which Anglo-French discussions of the fate of the French fleet never wholly recovered.

The offer of union was a damp squib. When Reynaud read it to the French Cabinet, which met about 5 pm on 16 June, it was scarcely discussed. Resentment against the British was high among those who wanted an armistice, and the offer made little appeal even to those who did not. It was useless to propose union to a country where opinion at that time was profoundly anti-British, and where even those who wished to fight would fight only for France. The only consequence of the proposal was that Reynaud did not read out or give the sense of the British telegrams to the French Cabinet, which therefore did not on 16 June hear either of the British consent to a French approach for an armistice, or of the stipulation about the fleet.

At this point the French consultation with Britain and the attempt to secure British consent to armistice negotiations came to an abrupt end. During the evening of 16 June, Reynaud resigned and Pétain became prime minister of France, with Weygand, Darlan and Baudouin as ministers of defence, marine and foreign affairs respectively. Without further ado the new government opened negotiations with Germany. At 12.30 am on 17 June Baudouin asked the Spanish ambassador to transmit a request for terms for an armistice and for peace. At 1 am he told the British ambassador what had been done. At 12.30 pm on 17 June, Pétain broadcast to the French people: '. . . I tell you today that we must end the fighting.' For the press this was changed to 'we must seek to end the fighting': but the original version represented the truth.[31]

The separation had come about. There was no effective link between a British government determined to fight on and a French government determined to come to terms with

Germany. Indeed, in the desperate circumstances of the time, there was almost bound to be hostility.

Enmity

The French armistice with Germany was signed on 22 June; that with Italy on 24 June. The agreement with Germany was the key document. It placed about three-fifths of the territory of metropolitan France under German occupation, including Paris and the Channel and Atlantic coasts. The French armed forces were to be reduced to 100,000 men, with armaments decided on by Germany. The cost of the occupying forces was to be borne by France. German prisoners of war were to be released at once, but French prisoners of war were to remain until the conclusion of peace – an important means of pressure on the French government. These terms were severe, but there were important limitations to the German demands. The fleet was not to be handed over, but to be disarmed under conditions which will be discussed later; and there were no demands on the empire. These limitations were imposed by Hitler, who did not want to see the British gain the French fleet, nor the French take up the war from London and North Africa. The French belief that the fleet and the empire were their best bargaining counters in negotiation with Germany was thus justified, and this is of vital importance in relations between France and Britain, for the British were also much concerned with the French fleet and empire.

Compared with the situations of the other countries defeated and occupied by Germany (Poland, Denmark, Norway, Holland, Belgium), France had escaped fairly lightly. Given that Germany had definitively won the war, and that France would have to go on living in a Europe dominated by Germany, the best available policy was to make the armistice terms work and hope for eventual peace terms which would not be wholly disastrous. This was the reasoning of the principal members of the French government, notably Pétain himself, Weygand and Darlan. The need to co-operate with Germany, to an extent not yet determined, thus became the prime element in French foreign policy as soon as the armistice was signed. This in itself was bound to bring about difficulties with Britain. But there was a deeper influence at work, poisoning French relations with Britain. It seems clear that throughout France at the time of the armistice there was bitter resentment against Britain. M. Henri Michel has written: 'The defeat gave rise to an outburst of antipathy that the collapse had released from the national subconscious.'[32] M. Lamouroux writes in similar terms 'The nation today [he is writing of 16 June 1940] is temporarily, but profoundly, anti-British among its leaders as well as among the mass of its people.'[33] This resentment arose partly from the Dunkirk evacuation, partly from the small forces which Britain had contributed to the whole campaign.[34] It showed itself publicly in speeches by members of the French government. More important, it was prominent in the minds of the leaders of that government. On 25 May Pétain had doubted, at the *Comité de Guerre*, whether France had a duty to an ally who had helped her so little; on 4 June he had told Bullitt, the American ambassador, that England would fight to the last Frenchman. Darlan made plain his feelings against the British on 1 July – before Mers-el-Kebir.[35] The French government thus felt no particular responsibility towards its former ally.

Across the Channel, the British government adopted, from a date well before the conclusion of the armistice, a policy hostile to Pétain's government. On 17 June, General Lord Dillon (British liaison officer at the headquarters of General Noguès, the French commander in North Africa) presented a message asking Noguès to continue the war. On June 18, the British consuls-general at Tunis, Algiers and Rabat made similar appeals to the French authorities there. In Syria, the British representative at Beirut offered the French high commissioner assistance if he would fight on, and the British commanders at Cairo visited Beirut on the 20th.[36] Similar approaches were made to the French authorities in West and Equatorial Africa, Somaliland and the West Indies. These were attempts to subvert the French empire from its obedience to the government in France, and to persuade its leaders to continue the war.

At the same time, the British government welcomed General de Gaulle to Britain, and allowed him to use the BBC to make his now famous broadcast of 18 June, summoning the French people to fight on.[37] He broadcast again on 19 June:

Faced with the confusion in French hearts, faced with the collapse of a government which is in bondage to the enemy, faced with the breakdown of our institutions, I, General de Gaulle, French soldier and leader, am conscious that I speak for France.[38]

This was before the terms of an armistice were agreed. On 23 June, after the armistice with Germany had been signed, the BBC broadcast two declarations by the British government, the first stating that it could not consider the Bordeaux government as that of an independent country, the second stating that Britain would recognise a French national committee representing independent French elements determined to continue the war and fulfil France's international obligations. On 28 June, the British government recognised de Gaulle as 'leader of all Free Frenchmen, wherever they may be, who rally to him in support of the Allied cause'.[39] This was the first step towards the recognition of a provisional French authority in opposition to the legitimate government of France.

These movements to subvert the French empire and to encourage a dissident French organisation began immediately after the French government asked for an armistice. The armistice itself only confirmed the British government in a stance which it had already taken up. Churchill said on 23 June that his government had learned 'with grief and amazement' that the German terms had been accepted. Such terms could not have been submitted to 'by any French Government which possessed freedom, independence and constitutional authority'. They meant that 'the whole resources of the French Empire and the French Navy would speedily pass into the hands of the adversary for the fulfilment of his purpose.'[40] This declaration, and others on the same and following days, proclaimed British distrust of Pétain's government, and expressed a strong (though disputable) view of the nature of the armistice terms. Holding such views, and in the circumstances of June 1940, Churchill's government was not likely to wait and see how the situation worked out.

For both the British and the French, the most vital and pressing problem was that of the French fleet. This powerful instrument of war included two new battleships nearing completion, the *Richelieu* and the *Jean Bart*; two modern battle-cruisers, the *Dunkerque* and the *Strasbourg*; five old battleships; an aircraft-carrier; and a large number of modern cruisers, destroyers, and submarines. The withdrawal of this force from active operations put a great strain on the Royal Navy. If it were to be taken over by the Germans and Italians, it might tip the balance of sea power against Britain, and even lead to a successful invasion of the British Isles. For France, the fleet was no less important. It had great psychological significance as the one force remaining intact after the disasters of the battle of France. It was vital as a bargaining counter in negotiations with Germany; for the defence of the French empire; and, in all calculation, for the future of France.

Article 8 of the armistice with Germany, dealing with the fleet, ran as follows:

The French war fleet, with the exception of the part permitted to the French Government for the protection of French interests in its colonial empire, is to be assembled in ports to be specified and is to be demobilised and disarmed under German or Italian supervision. The choice of these ports will be determined by the peacetime stations of the ships. The German government solemnly declares to the French Government that it does not intend to use for its own purposes in the war the French fleet which is in ports under German supervision, with the exception of those units needed for coastal patrol and for mine sweeping. Furthermore, they solemnly and expressly declare that they have no intention of raising any claim to the French war fleet at the time of the conclusion of peace. With the exception of that part of the French war fleet, still to be determined, which is to represent French interests in the colonial empire, all war vessels which are outside French territorial waters are to be recalled to France.[41]

The peacetime stations (*ports d'attache*) for two-thirds of the French navy were Lorient, Brest, Cherbourg and Dunkirk, all within the German zone of occupation.

The French government and Admiral Darlan thought it likely that the Germans would try to seize the fleet, and were determined to prevent this. They took two separate courses to this end. On the one hand, they tried to amend the terms of the armistice to allow the warships to go to North Africa after being demilitarised. The Germans refused to change the text of the armistice, but negotiations went on with the German and Italian Armistice Commissions, which resulted by 1 July in a concession whose significance is not wholly clear, but which would apparently have allowed warships then in the Mediterranean to be stationed in unoccupied ports.[42] On the other hand, Darlan took all possible precautions to prevent a seizure. On 18 June the French Cabinet decided that the fleet would not be surrendered to Germany, and orders were issued for ships to sail from ports threatened by the advancing Germans. Even the unfinished battleships got to sea, the *Richelieu* bound for Dakar, the *Jean Bart* for Casablanca. On 20 June, Darlan signalled to his commanders that they were to obey no other government than the regular government of France, and that, whatever orders they received, they were never to hand over an intact warship to the enemy. On 22 June he ordered that a team should be ready aboard every ship to scuttle it if the enemy tried to lay hands on it. On 24 June, in the last signal he could send in code, Darlan emphasised that under the armistice warships would remain in French hands; if the enemy should decide otherwise, ships should without further orders be either sailed to the United States or sunk.[43] These signals all stressed that *no one* (including, by clear implication, the British) should be permitted to take over French warships.

It is not clear how far these orders to the French fleet were known to the British government.[44] However, the French certainly assured the British repeatedly that they would never allow their ships to fall into German hands or be used against Britain. On 19 June, Alexander (First Lord of the Admiralty), Admiral Pound (First Sea Lord) and Lord Lloyd (Colonial Secretary) visited Bordeaux and received Darlan's personal assurance on this.[45] On 23 and 24 June, separate messages were sent by Baudouin, Darlan, President Lebrun and even by Reynaud.[46] These assurances had no effect. The British emissaries to Bordeaux appeared to be satisfied at the time, but this was because they understood that a part of the French government was to go to Algiers, a decision which was later changed. News of the final negotiations by the French

H

with the German and Italian Armistice Commissions about
the stationing of warships in the Mediterranean did not reach
London in time to affect British policy, but in any case it is
unlikely to have had any influence. The British government's
mind was made up.

As early as 11 June the British chiefs of staff argued that
Britain could not afford to see the French fleet pass to the
enemy. The alternatives available were to persuade the French
to join with the British fleet, which they thought unlikely, or
to press the French to sink their own ships.[47] On 17 June,
Admiral Cunningham, commanding the Mediterranean fleet,
received a signal which he summarises thus: 'If France made
a separate peace, every endeavour would be made to obtain
control of the French Fleet beforehand, or failing that, to
have it sunk.'[48] At no point, on the evidence so far available,
does it appear that the British government would accept any
arrangement which placed French warships, even for a time,
within reach of the Germans and Italians. The terms of the
armistice seemed full of menace. Churchill said of article 8
on 26 June:

> From this text it is clear that the French war vessels under this
> armistice pass into German and Italian control while fully armed.
> We note of course in the same article the solemn declaration of the
> German government that they have no intention of using them for
> their own purposes during the war. What is the value of that?
> Ask half a dozen countries what is the value of such an assurance.[49]

The Cabinet considered that even North African ports were
not secure from a German airborne operation.

Impelled by these fears, the British government moved
rapidly towards its final decision. As early as 21 June, French
warships in British ports were prevented from leaving. On
27 June the use of force if necessary to prevent French warships from returning to their home ports was decided upon,
and the delivery of an ultimatum to the squadron at Mers-el-
Kebir was agreed in principle. By 29 June preparations were
well under way, and on 1 July the Cabinet took the final
decision. The unanimous opinion of the chiefs of staff was that
French assurances could not be relied upon; that, given the
necessity to concentrate British warships in home waters,
none could be spared to watch the scattered French ships;

and that action against the French fleet should be taken as soon as possible. During this time, protests and advice against the use of force from Admiral Cunningham at Alexandria and Admiral Somerville, commanding the squadron being sent to Mers-el-Kebir, were firmly rejected by the British government.[50]

On 3 July, then, operation CATAPULT against the French fleet was launched.[51] The ships in British ports were seized by surprise in the early hours. (Darlan's orders for scuttling proved of no avail against this British *coup de main*.) At Alexandria, the British and French admirals, Cunningham and Godfroy, both disregarded orders from home which would have caused fighting, and came to an agreement for the immobilisation and disarmament of the French ships without their seizure by the British. The courtesy and trust shown by these two commanders mark this episode out among the suspicion and recrimination clouding Anglo-French relations at this time. The warships outside British-controlled ports presented greater difficulties. At Mers-el-Kebir, the French commander, Admiral Gensoul, rejected an ultimatum offering various alternatives, including sailing to British ports or to Martinique. Somerville's squadron then opened fire on the French ships in harbour. The *Bretagne* was sunk, the *Provence* and *Dunkerque* badly damaged. The *Strasbourg*, five of the six destroyers, and the six cruisers at Algiers escaped to Toulon. The French casualties were 1,297 dead and 351 wounded. On 6 July, British naval aircraft again attacked the *Dunkerque*, hitting her with a torpedo. On 8 July, again after an ultimatum, the *Richelieu* was attacked by naval aircraft in harbour at Dakar, and damaged. Of the eight effective French capital ships (the ninth, the *Jean Bart*, was unarmed), seven were seized or disabled. Against this, at Toulon there was a concentration of the *Strasbourg*, ten cruisers, and several destroyers, which were in greater danger of capture than when in North African ports.

The main outlines of this tragic affair stand out clearly. The French were determined to preserve their fleet against all comers, and believed that their precautions were sufficient to attain this end. The British had little confidence in the good faith of Pétain's government and none in French capacity to safeguard their warships. On both sides, vital issues were at stake: for Britain, control of the sea and the possibility of invasion; for France, her only intact armed force and a decisive element in her relations with Germany. The alliance between Britain and France had rested on the assumption that their interests were the same. By 3 July 1940 their interests were diametrically opposed and the two countries were brought inexorably into conflict with one another. It is possible to look back and argue that events might or should have been different – that the British should have showed more restraint, that Gensoul should have agreed to sail to Martinique. But in the pressures and dangers of the time these would have been perilous choices, and such arguments carry little conviction.

Darlan's immediate instinct after Mers-el-Kebir was to launch a counter-attack on Somerville's force. This plan was abandoned, but French aircraft bombed Gibraltar on 5 July. An expedition against Sierra Leone or the Gambia was contemplated. General Huntziger wrote a memorandum on a possible attack on the oilfields of northern Iraq, '*pour le compte commun de la France, de l'Allemagne, et de l'Italie.*'[52] The crisis of Mers-el-Kebir thus passed without war being declared between France and Britain, but it gave a further impulse to the policy of collaboration between France and Germany. Laval, who entered Pétain's cabinet on 23 June, was able to exploit the emotion roused by the British attacks, which remained a theme of anti-British propaganda throughout the war.

The British, for their part, made no further attacks on the French fleet after 8 July, but they maintained their other activities directed against the French government. In August they supported General de Gaulle and the Free French movement in winning over French Equatorial Africa to continue the war. In September an Anglo-Gaullist expedition made an abortive attack on Dakar.

It is true that shadowy contacts were kept up between the two governments, through their embassies in Madrid, through the American and Canadian representatives at Vichy and through the dubious activities of Professor Rougier.[53] They still had something to hope for from one another: the Vichy government wanted freedom from blockade by sea; the British wanted to make sure that French warships and colonies were kept out of German hands. These matters provided scope for tentative negotiations, but for both countries they were of minor significance. In the great issues, the two countries were poles apart. Nothing could symbolise this better than the decree issued by the Vichy government on 1 August 1940, convoking the newly created *Cour suprême de justice* 'in order to seek out and pass judgement on all those who betrayed the duties entrusted to them by actions which were connected with the change from a state of peace to a state of war by 4 September 1939'. Thus did France accuse herself of war guilt, and set out to try those responsible for entering the war – the same war which Britain was still waging and was determined to continue.[54] Only a few lonely Frenchmen believed, as Jean Texcier wrote in September 1940: 'The struggle maintained by Britain against Germany is our struggle. It is still, and always will be, the same as that for which we stood side by side with her in September 1939.'[55]

The alliance was broken. Britain and France had become enemies, pursuing contrary objectives. Nor was this breach only one between governments and leaders. In 1940 the people of each country underwent a totally different experience. The French suffered defeat, the massive flight of the refugees, occupation, the division of their country. The British, protected by the Channel, were not subjected to the ordeal of invasion; they showed unity in the face of imminent danger; and they looked back on the experience as their finest hour. In the long run, it may be that the widely differing folk-memories of 1940 will be as important for relations between the two peoples as the military and political events discussed in these pages.

Notes

1 Hansard, *Parliamentary Debates*, Commons, ser. 5, vol. 359, cols. 40–41 (to be cited hereafter as *HC Deb*).

2 *Journal Officiel de la République Française, numéro spécial*, 7 April 1948, printing the debate of the Chamber of Deputies in secret session, 19 April 1940, pp. 115–16.

3 For a discussion of these problems, see J. C. Cairns, 'Great Britain and the Fall of France: a study in allied disunity,' *Journal of Modern History*, December 1955.

4 Henri Michel, *La Seconde Guerre Mondiale*, vol. I, *Les Succès de l'Axe* (Paris, 1968), pp. 132–3.

5 R. Macleod and D. Kelly (eds.), *The Ironside Diaries, 1937–1940* (London, 1962), p. 332.

6 L. F. Ellis, *The War in France and Flanders, 1939–1940* (London, 1953), pp. 246–8. The figures for 29 May – 4 June were: 139,732 British, 139,097 Allied, mostly French. There were a few Belgians in the evacuation. The total of 366,162 includes the whole period from 20 May onwards.

7 W. S. Churchill, *The Second World War*, vol. II, *Their Finest Hour* (London, 1949), pp. 38–9.

8 P. Dhers, 'Le Comité de Guerre du 25 mai 1940', *Revue d'Histoire de la deuxième Guerre mondiale*, May-July 1953, pp. 129–35, prints the different records of this meeting.

9 M. Weygand, *Rappelé au Service* (Paris, 1950), pp. 149–51.

10 Churchill, *Second World War*, vol. II, pp. 108–9.

11 Churchill, *Second World War*, vol. II, pp. 45–6.

12 Churchill, *Second World War*, vol. II, pp. 48–9.

13 Churchill, *Second World War*, vol. II, pp. 78–9; J. R. M. Butler, *Grand Strategy*, vol. II (London, 1957), pp. 209–17.

14 B. Collier, *Leader of the Few* (London, 1957), pp. 192–4.

15 Churchill, *Second World War*, vol. II, p. 137.

16 *Ironside Diaries*, p. 317.

17 E. Bauer, *La Guerre des Blindés*, vol. I (Paris, 1962), p. 113. Cf. the similar view in A. Goutard, *The Battle of France, 1940* (London, 1958), p. 33.

18 Churchill, *Second World War*, vol. II, p. 137.

19 Collier, *Leader of the Few*, pp. 189–90, 199.

20 On 15 May, after hearing Dowding in person, the War Cabinet decided not to send to France ten fighter squadrons requested by Reynaud. But on 16 May, eight half-squadrons were sent, and then Churchill telegraphed from Paris for six more: 'not for any local purpose, but to give the last chance to the French Army to rally its bravery and strength. It would not be good historically if their requests were denied and their ruin resulted.' The Cabinet agreed. The squadrons could not be found airfields in France, and operated from Kent over France. (Churchill, *Second World War*, vol. II, pp. 45–6.)

21 P. Reynaud, *La France a sauvé l'Europe*, vol. II (Paris, 1947), p. 271.

22 It may be worth emphasising to British readers how severe a fight the remaining French armies made on the line of the Somme and the Aisne. Using German figures published on 24 June 1940, which were certainly not too high, Bauer calculated an average of 4,762 casualties per day between 5 and 24 June. This may be compared with an average (again on published figures) of 4,506 German casualties per day in Russia between 22 June and 10 December 1941. (Bauer, *Guerre des Blindés*, vol. I, pp. 123–4.)

23 The French record of this meeting is printed in Reynaud, *La France a sauvé l'Europe*, vol. II, pp. 304–11. Cf. Churchill, *Second*

World War, vol. II, pp. 136–8; E. L. Spears, *Assignment to Catastrophe* (London, 1954), pp. 138–59.

24 The question of the balance of opinion in Reynaud's Cabinet on the question of an armistice has been much discussed. H. Amouroux, *Le 18 Juin 1940* (Paris, 1964), p. 69, n.l., and A. D. Hytier, *Two Years of French Foreign Policy: Vichy, 1940–1942* (Paris and Geneva, 1958), pp. 361–2, give analyses of the different accounts.

25 Reynaud used the phrases quoted here during the Cabinet meeting of 12 June: Reynaud, *La France a sauvé l'Europe*, vol. II, pp. 313–16; Y. Bouthillier, *Le Drame de Vichy*, vol. I, *Face à l'ennemi, face à l'allié* (Paris, 1950), p. 57.

26 Quoted in Churchill, *Second World War*, vol. II, p. 161. In the French record kept by de Margerie this appears as:

Dans tous les cas, nous ne gaspillerons pas nos forces en reproches et récriminations. Mais c'est là une chose différente que de devenir partie consentante à une paix séparée, conclue contrairement aux engagements conclus. Nous pensons que la première chose à faire est d'exposer au président Roosevelt la situation telle qu'elle est actuellement, et de voir, ensuite, quelle sera sa réponse. . . . J'ai déjà répondu que nous nous abstiendrons de reproches et de récriminations. La cause le la France nous restera toujours chère et nous la restaurerons 'in all her power and dignity' (dans toute sa puissance et sa dignité) si nous triomphons. Mais c'est une chose différente que de nous demander actuellement notre consentement, avant consultation avec le président Roosevelt.

De Margerie's record is printed in P. Reynaud, *Au Coeur de la Mêlée* (Paris, 1951), pp. 770–4. Paul Baudouin, *Neuf Mois au Gouvernement* (Paris, 1948), pp. 154–9, prints his own record, which puts even greater emphasis on Churchill's generous assurances and omits his refusal of consent to a separate peace.

27 Camille Chautemps, *Cahiers secrets de l'armistice* (Paris, 1963), pp. 141–2, 154–7, insists that this proposition, which has become attached to his name, was made on 16 June, but it is impossible to reconcile this with the other evidence.

28 Spears, *Assignment to Catastrophe*, vol. II, pp. 265–7.

29 Churchill, *Second World War*, vol. II, p. 181.

30 This account of this crucial episode rests on Churchill, *Second World War*, vol. II, pp. 184–7; Spears, *Assignment to Catastrophe*, vol. II, pp. 293–4; Reynaud, *La France a sauvé l'Europe*, vol. II, pp. 348–9, *Au Coeur de la Mêlée*, pp. 825–7; Baudouin, *Neuf Mois au Gouvernement*, p. 183; F. Charles-Roux, *Cinq Mois tragiques aux Affaires Étrangères* (Paris, 1949), pp. 57–8. (Charles-Roux was secretary-general at the French foreign ministry at the time.)

31 The text of Pétain's broadcast is printed in *Rapport fait au nom de la Commission chargée d'enquêter sur les événements survenus en France de 1933 à 1945* (Paris, ND), *Rapport*, p. 385 (to be cited as *Événements, Rapport*). A contemporary English translation, with the crucial phrase left in French, is in the BBC *Daily Digest of*

Foreign Broadcasts, No. 335, 18 June 1940, Part II, 2A, i. Cf. *Le Temps*, composite issue for 19, 20, 21 June 1940.

32 Henri Michel, *Vichy Année 40* (Paris, 1966), p. 224.

33 Amouroux, *Le 18 juin 1940*, p. 65.

34 This is a point which is still not widely grasped in Britain. It seems to be taken for granted that the British had some sort of divine right to do without a large army and conscription in peacetime, and still expect the French to bear the burden of war on land until the British made their leisurely preparations and, perhaps two years after the outbreak of war, contributed an army of continental proportions. General Ironside wrote in his diary on 17 May 1940: 'I found that Greenwood [a member of the War Cabinet] was inclined to say "these bloody gallant Allies". I told him that we had depended upon the French army. That we had made no army and that therefore it was not right to say "these bloody Allies". It was for them to say that of us.' (*Ironside Diaries*, p. 313.)

35 Speeches by Baudouin, 17 June (Baudouin, *Neuf Mois en Gouvernement*, pp. 179–81) and Prouvost, 24 June (*The Times*, 26 June 1940). In general, see the evidence set out in Michel, *Vichy Année 40*, pp. 53–4, 224–6.

36 Viscount Dillon, *Memories of Three Wars* (London, 1951), pp. 138–9; telegram from Noguès to Weygand, 18 June 1940, *Événements, Rapport*, p. 417; G. Puaux, *Deux Années au Levant, 1939–1940* (Paris, 1952), pp. 200–1; I. S. O. Playfair, *The Mediterranean and the Middle East*, vol. I (London, 1954), p. 123.

37 Charles de Gaulle, *Mémoires de Guerre*, vol. I, *L'appel, 1940–1942*, pp. 267–8, prints the official text. Amouroux, *Le 18 juin 1940*, pp. 367–8, notes some minor variations between this text and that published in *Le Petit Provençal*, 19 June 1940, presumably taken down from the radio broadcast.

38 De Gaulle, *Mémoires de Guerre*, vol. I, pp. 268–9.

39 De Gaulle, *Mémoires de Guerre*, vol. I, pp. 270, 274.

40 *The Times*, 24 June 1940.

41 Text of the armistice in *Documents on German Foreign Policy*, series D, vol. IX (London, 1956), No. 523; French text in *La Délégation française auprès de la Commission allemande d'Armistice*, vol. I (Paris, 1947), pp. 1–8.

42 For details of this negotiation, see Michel, *Vichy Année 40*, pp. 231–3; P. M. H. Bell, 'Prologue de Mers-el-Kebir', *Revue d'Histoire de la deuxième Guerre mondiale*, January 1959, pp. 28–9, 32–3.

43 Texts of the signals of 18, 20, 22 and 24 June in *Événements, Rapport*, pp. 443, 446, 454, 459, 466.

44 Albert Kammerer writes that the signal of 24 June was communicated to the British Admiralty by Admiral Odend'hal, the head of the French Naval Mission in London, on 25 June. The British official historians write that it was not known by the cabinet. See A. Kammerer, *La Passion de la Flotte française* (Paris, 1951), p. 119; Butler, *Grand Strategy*, vol. II, p. 220; Playfair, *Mediterranean and the Middle East*, vol. I, pp. 137–8.

45 Amouroux, *Le 18 juin 1940*, pp. 238–9, places this visit on 18 June.
46 *Événements, Rapport*, pp. 434–5, 466; *Événements, Témoignages*, p. 1029; Reynaud, *La France a sauvé l'Europe*, vol. II, p. 394.
47 Butler, *Grand Strategy*, vol. II, p. 218.
48 Lord Cunningham of Hyndhope, *A Sailor's Odyssey* (London, 1951), p. 240.
49 *HC Deb.*, ser. 5, vol. 362, cols. 304–5.
50 Butler, *Grand Strategy*, vol. II, pp. 221–3; Churchill, *Second World War*, vol. II, pp. 205–8; Cunningham, *Sailor's Odyssey*, pp. 243–6; W. M. James, *The Portsmouth Letters* (London, 1946), p. 65.
51 The dispositions of the French fleet on 3 July were as follows. In British ports, chiefly Plymouth and Portsmouth: the old battle-ships *Courbet* and *Paris*, four destroyers, some submarines and light craft. At Alexandria: the old battleship *Lorraine*, four cruisers, light craft. At Mers-el-Kebir: the new battle-cruisers *Dunkerque* and *Strasbourg*; the old battleships *Bretagne* and *Provence;* six destroy-ers, a seaplane carrier. At Oran, next to Mers-el-Kébir: seven des-troyers, some submarines. At Algiers: six cruisers. At Dakar: the battleship *Richelieu*, unfinished but armed. At Casablanca: the battleship *Jean Bart*, without her guns. At Toulon: four cruisers. In the West Indies there were an aircraft-carrier and two cruisers; in the Far East some cruisers and light craft. (S. W. Roskill, *The War at Sea*, vol. I (London, 1954), pp. 240–1.)
52 Quoted in A. Schérer, 'La Collaboration', in P. Arnoult *et al.*, *La France sous l'occupation* (Paris, 1959), p. 19.
53 For accounts of these contacts, see M. C. G. Schmitt, *Les accords secrets franco-britanniques: histoire ou mystification* (Paris, 1957); Hytier, *Two Years of French Foreign Policy*, pp. 90–107.
54 The decree is quoted in Michel, *Vichy Année 40*, p. 146; cf. P. Dhers, *Regards nouveaux sur les années 40* (Paris, 1958), p. 69.
55 Jean Texcier, *Notre Combat*, a clandestine pamphlet of September 1940, quoted in C. Bellanger, *Presse Clandestine, 1940–1944* (Paris, 1961), p. 27. Cf. *Pantagruel*, No. 1, October 1940, calling on the French to support de Gaulle: 'Soutenu par le peuple anglais dont le phlègme et les résolutions inébranlables sont légendaires IL VAINCRA' (quoted in Bellanger, *Presse Clandestine*, p. 36).

Bibliography

The literature of this subject is already very large. Excellent guides will be found in the following, which also provide good general accounts:

G. Chapman, *Why France Collapsed* (London, 1968).
H. Michel, *Vichy Année 40* (Paris, 1966).
G. Warner, *Pierre Laval and the eclipse of France* (London, 1968).

Any scholarly study of the subject must depend largely on the *Revue d'Histoire de la deuxième Guerre mondiale* (Paris, quarterly), edited by Henri Michel. As well as articles and reviews, this journal publishes regular bibliographies.

Valuable documentary material is in:
La Délégation française auprès de la Commission allemande d'Armistice (Paris, 1947 onwards).
Documents on German Foreign Policy, ser. D, vols. IX and X (London, 1956–57).
Foreign Relations of the United States, 1940, vols. I and II (Washington, 1957).

The French government published vast quantities of testimony by many participants, and some documents, in *Rapport fait au nom de la Commission chargée d'enquêter sur les événements survenus en France de 1933 à 1945* (Paris, ND). This consists of (a) *Rapport*, and (b) *Témoignages* (9 vols.).

The British government have published a series of official histories of the war, of which the following are particularly relevant:

J. R. M. Butler, *Grand Strategy*, vol. II (London, 1957).
B. Collier, *The Defence of the United Kingdom*.
L. F. Ellis, *The War in France and Flanders, 1939–1940* (London, 1953).
S. W. Roskill, *The War at Sea*, vol. I (London, 1954).
E. L. Woodward, *British Foreign Policy in the Second World War* (London, 1962).

Of the many memoirs, the following are particularly important:

P. Baudouin, *Neuf Mois au Gouvernement* (Paris, 1948).
Y. Bouthillier, *Le Drame de Vichy*, vol. I, *Face à l'ennemi, face à l'allié* (Paris, 1950).
F. Charles-Roux, *Cinq Mois tragiques aux Affaires Etrangères* (Paris, 1949).
C. Chautemps, *Cahiers secrets de l'armistice* (Paris, 1963).
W. S. Churchill, *The Second World War*, vol. II, *Their Finest Hour* (London, 1949).
Viscount Cunningham of Hyndhope, *A Sailor's Odyssey* (London, 1951).
C. de Gaulle, *Mémoires de Guerre*, vol. I, *L'appel* (Paris, 1954).
R. E. Godfroy, *L'aventure de la Force X à Alexandrie, 1940–1943* (Paris, 1953).

P. Reynaud, *La France a sauvé l'Europe*, 2 vols. (Paris, 1947).
P. Reynaud, *Au Coeur de la Mêlée* (Paris, 1951).
E. L. Spears, *Assignment to Catastrophe*, 2 vols. (London, 1954).
M. Weygand, *Rappelé au Service* (Paris, 1950).

In addition to the studies mentioned at the beginning of this list, the following should be noted:

H. Amouroux, *Le 18 juin 1940* (Paris, 1964).
Robert Aron, *Histoire de Vichy* (Paris, 1954).
E. Bauer, *La guerre des blindés*, vol. I (Paris, 1962).
J. Benoist-Méchin, *Soixante Jours qui ébranlèrent l'Occident*, 3 vols. (Paris, 1956) – very pro-armistice and anti-British, and sometimes inaccurate on important points; best read along with:
P. Dhers, *Regards nouveaux sur les années 40* (Paris, 1958), which combines a discussion of Benoist-Méchin's book with an analysis of the events of 1940.
A. Horne, *To Lose a Battle* (London, 1969).
A. D. Hytier, *Two Years of French Foreign Policy: Vichy 1940– 1942* (Geneva and Paris, 1958).
E. Jäckel, *La France dans l'Europe d'Hitler* (Paris, 1968).
A. Kammerer, *La Passion de la Flotte française de Mers-el- Kebir à Toulon* (Paris, 1951).
L. Noguères, *Le véritable procès du maréchal Pétain* (Paris, 1955).
A. Truchet, *L'armistice de 1940 et l'Afrique du Nord* (Paris, 1955).
P. Varillon, *Mers-el-Kebir* (Paris, 1950).

An article by J. C. Cairns, 'Great Britain and the Fall of France: a study in Allied disunity', *Journal of Modern History*, December 1955, provides a lucid and profound analysis of its subject up to the armistice.

9 The Second Wartime Alliance

Keith Sainsbury

Never will I believe that the soul of France is dead. Never will I believe that her place among the greatest nations of the world has been lost for ever. (Winston Churchill, 21 October 1940.)

Our greatness and strength consists solely in intransigence concerning the rights of France. We shall have need of this intransigence up to the Rhine, inclusive. (General de Gaulle, August 1941.)

On 16 June 1940, Paul Reynaud, prime minister of France, handed his resignation to president Lebrun and on the same day was succeeded by the elderly war-hero Marshal Philipe Pétain. Later that evening Pétain's government applied to Germany for an armistice and peace talks. The request was granted, and armistice terms agreed on 22 June. Under these terms, two-thirds of metropolitan France was occupied by the German army, and the Pétain government took up residence at Vichy, in unoccupied France, a week later. From this small spa town it continued to govern what was left of France for four years, until the invading Anglo-American armies liberated both zones in 1944.

Just two weeks earlier, on 17 June, Major-General Charles de Gaulle, under-secretary for war in the Reynaud government, flew to London and reported to the British government that he at least was willing to continue the fight, and to take the lead in organising French volunteers. Only recently promoted from colonel, unknown to the vast majority of Frenchmen and Englishmen, de Gaulle attracted the support at first of virtually none of the leading French politicians and military figures. He had only a handful of followers. Nevertheless this unknown general confidently summoned all Frenchmen who wished to continue the fight to join him.

It was this series of events, occurring in a period of two

weeks between 16 June and 1 July 1940 which basically determined the character of Anglo-French relations for the next five years.

Britain and Free France: the struggle for equality

From many points of view the period of Anglo-French relations between 1940 and 1945 was unique in this century. It was the only period in which the power of one country so much exceeded that of the other; it was the only period in which there were two rival contenders for the privilege of representing France – a Pope in Avignon, as it were, as well as in Rome: and it was the only period of which one can say so categorically that the interests, the passions and the conflicting claims of the two states were embodied in, and voiced by two men so exclusively.

Each of these characteristics played its part in shaping those relations. The collapse of France in 1940 and the creation of the government at Vichy, resulting as it did not only in the withdrawal of mainland France from the conflict, with all its material and human resources, but also in the neutralisation of the powerful French navy and the enforced immobilisation of the greater part of the French empire, meant inevitably that France, in so far as she existed as a factor in the Allied camp, was destined to be for a long time a very junior partner – and liable to be treated as such. Again, the existence of two rival regimes, each claiming to be the legitimate representative of France – Vichy in the common or garden sense of the *de jure* government, exercising effective control over a part at least of mainland France, Free France in the more rarified sense of embodying the true spirit and soul of France – this dualism inevitably imposed a novel strain on the conduct of relations between the two countries. So far as Britain was concerned, it is true, the choice was quickly made, and effectively adhered to in spite of occasional attempts to open channels of communication to Vichy and tempt its leaders to rejoin the Allied cause. Anglo-French relations were therefore spared to some extent the damage done to Franco-American relations by the prolonged American flirtation with Vichy. None the less, the very fact of the division between Frenchmen was bound to constitute a poisonous element in French relations with other countries, leading each claimant to make jealous demands for the exclusive loyalty of its patron governments, and ensuring that the recognition of either group would be accompanied by the antagonism and hatred of its rival and those Frenchmen who supported it. Many of the wounds inflicted on Anglo-French relations during these years – at Mers-el-Kebir, Dakar, in Syria and Madagascar, in North Africa and France – would never have occurred, or not to the same degree, if the tragic division between Frenchmen had not made them necessary.

Equally, the humiliation of France, and the reduction of French power to a pitifully low level had its effect on the alliance. The exertions of de Gaulle and his adherents with the material and moral help of the Allies only slowly and painfully raised it to a position where an effective French contribution to the common effort could be made: and then, after all the effort, not to a position of equality with Britain.[1] A position of resentful inferiority on one side and sympathetic but at times patronising regard on the other is no suitable foundation for a harmonious relationship. It is not that men always seek consciously to take advantage of a weaker partner,[2] but that the very circumstance of his weakness often lead to this being so; and still more often to the accusation that it is so. Equally, it is not that most men are ungrateful for help in time of acute need, but that men of spirit resent enforced gratitude and inescapable dependence. As it happened the leadership of Free France[3] devolved on a man of exceptional pride and patriotism, for whom the disgrace and inferiority of his country and the initial dependence on British help for virtually every need was particularly wounding. De Gaulle chafed continually against this relationship like a hair shirt: his only recourse was to be uncompromising and unbending in his defence of French interests, to be as he himself put it 'troublesome and pressing' or 'spiked and touchy'. To Churchill, urging him to be more pliant in his attitude to Roosevelt, he replied on one occasion that the British Prime Minister, with his assured position and the support of a great Empire, could afford to bend and compromise: he, de Gaulle, with virtually nothing except his independence and integrity, could not. As Churchill put it, 'It was essential to his position before the French people that he should maintain a proud and haughty demeanour towards perfidious Albion in order to prove to French eyes that he was not a British puppet.'[4] The severe strains which sometimes arose between the two – the bitter arguments and recriminations – were no doubt inflamed by the pride and obduracy of one and the masterful and emotional temperament of the other, but they derived fundamentally from the disparity of the relationship, and must therefore have characterised Anglo-French relations to some degree in these years whatever the personalities involved.

It would be a mistake therefore to attribute too much in this relationship to the particular character of the two leaders. An Eden and a Catroux in these roles might have mitigated some of its asperity (and indeed in their secondary positions sometimes did so) but could not have altered its fundamental character. None the less, the personalities of the two men, and their particular outlooks and objectives did have their importance, and must be taken into account as a factor influencing the course and character of Anglo-French relations. The fact that two men of such different temperaments but equally masterful personalities and unique prestige should have directed the policies of Britain and France for virtually the whole of the wartime period inevitably set its stamp on Anglo-French dealings of the period, as well as having profound importance for the future. In particular, Churchill's judgement, prompted by both reason and emotion, that the maintenance of Anglo-American unity must have supreme priority over all other considerations, and his unequivocal statements to that effect in more than one conversation with de Gaulle[5] helped to imprint an indelible picture of British subservience to the United States in de Gaulle's mind. On the other side, de Gaulle's intense and at times unreasonable suspicion of British motives, in particular in the Middle East, his belief that Britain would inevitably take advantage of French weakness wherever and whenever she could, gave a more sombre and bitter tone to inter-allied disagreements than might have been the case with a leader less profoundly pessimistic about the nature of human motivation and the sources of national policy.[6] The British foreign secretary, Anthony Eden, rightly sums up de Gaulle's attitude in his memoirs: 'The fervour of his faith made him at times too suspicious of the intentions of others. The schemes and greed not infrequently attributed to Britain . . . were many of them insubstantial myths. We did not want Madagascar, nor Syria, nor Jibuti, nor to succeed to the French position there or elsewhere . . . but I doubt if General de Gaulle ever believed this.'[7]

To suggest that de Gaulle and Churchill alone determined the course of Anglo-French relations during this period would be not only to ignore the significant impact of other personalities – Catroux, Giraud, Monnet on the French side, Eden, Macmillan, Lyttleton, Duff Cooper on the British – but also to do fundamental violence to historical truth. In the long run it is the facts of history and geography, of relative power and resources, of longstanding national aspirations and objectives which determine the conduct of foreign policies and the inter-relationship of states. Nevertheless, the personalities of the two men, together with their long and unquestioned pre-eminence, helped to give this period the unique character which distinguishes it.

The crucial questions throughout the war years, arising from the fundamental facts of French division and defeat, were firstly the status of Free France in the Allied coalition; secondly, the methods to be adopted in the rallying of the French empire, its re-incorporation in the Allied war effort, and the arrangements to be made for its administration; thirdly, the gradual building up and organisation of the armed forces of Free France, as and when they became available, and the use to be made of them in allied campaigns; and, fourthly, the position of France in the political counsels and military planning of the alliance. As de Gaulle himself with characteristic realism always understood, the first and last of these inevitably depended largely on the course of events in relation to the other two. As Free France gained territory and resources, as its army, navy and air force increased in numbers, fighting power and efficiency and so could play a larger part in battle, in that proportion the Free French movement would be able to claim and would be more likely to get recognition as the representative of the French nation and French interests; and increasingly be able to claim an accepted place at the council table as an equal partner in both political and military matters.

All this was to be achieved at last, but only after long efforts, and not without much argument. De Gaulle's views on all these matters – and they would almost certainly have been the views of any other Frenchman in his position – were clearcut and uncompromising. The sovereignty and independence of France must be asserted and acknowledged from the beginning. This meant that as a logical consequence French armed units whenever and wherever formed must be distinct and separate and under French command; French territories in every part of the globe, as they returned to the Allied camp, must be maintained under French political and administrative authority; and both territories and armed forces must be united, acknowledging responsibility to one authority, not parcelled out in separate and conflicting units, some leaning to Vichy, some to de Gaulle, some sponsored by Britain, some by the United States. For only as a single and undivided entity could they worthily represent France and enable France to claim its rightful place with the Allies. He alone and the movement he led would provide the necessary focus for that unity. For he alone combined the abilities, the inflexible determination, and the untarnished reputation which would serve the purpose. It was an arrogant but justifiable view, for no alternative which was proposed, not Weygand, not Darlan, not Giraud nor any political leader, could claim the same assets.[8]

Therefore, from the moment when the first Free French units were assembled, and the first French territories won back in Equatorial Africa, de Gaulle insisted on their independence. Notwithstanding that he was almost alone, an outlaw, with few followers and exiguous resources, totally dependent at first on Britain to equip and sustain whatever forces he could gather, his attitude was to insist on the independence of all French units and their responsibility to him – as he put it, 'to obtain from the British what was indispensable while maintaining towards them a resolute independence'.[9] As more troops became available successively in Equatorial Africa, in Syria and in North Africa, enabling first divisions, then corps and finally an army to be formed, the claim was made more unequivocally for full consultation as to their use. In its turn, this right could be used as a lever to force the admission of France into the highest councils of the Allies. To achieve these ends, shock tactics could be used where necessary. Thus, in February 1942 de Gaulle threatened to send two divisions to fight in Russia if they were not employed by the British Middle East command as he desired:[10] and, in December 1943, he refused a division requested by Eisenhower for Italy, and used the ensuing controversy to exact future arrangements for full military co-operation and consultation in that theatre, as well as an Allied promise that a landing in the south of France should take place in 1944 and all the French troops in Italy should take part in it.[11]

For the independence and unity of the empire, de Gaulle was also prepared to battle unrelentingly, whether against what he regarded as the sinister designs of the British Foreign Office and Middle East staff in Syria, or Roosevelt's ambition, as he saw it, to impose the regime of his choice on North Africa; even more uncompromisingly when it came to France itself. Some painful and thorny passages in Anglo-French relations derived from these objectives, inflexibly pursued. But on them de Gaulle felt unable to compromise.

The British attitude to these problems and to Free France itself inevitably varied as the circumstances of the war, the nature of the Allied coalition and the strength of Free France altered. To begin with, as de Gaulle admits,[12] it would have been easier to incorporate the small and disparate units of Free France in British forces and services: and to some extent with naval units, merchant shipping and air squadrons this was done. Later, as Free France acquired territory and forces of its own, the British government, desperately short of troops and fighting very often four or five separate campaigns in different parts of the globe, usually hoped – not unnaturally – that these French units would be placed at the disposal of its various commands and commanders wherever its military advisers judged they were most needed; and French objections or reservations tended to be regarded as unreasonable and unco-operative. Particularly after the creation of combined Anglo-American commands in the Mediterranean and later in France itself, the British attitude was that Free France should show the same willingness to place its forces under Allied command and so limit its sovereignty in the military sphere as the British government itself was doing. This was not unreasonable, but it expected of Free France the same confidence and trust in American and British goodwill that Churchill felt for Roosevelt; and this, in de Gaulle's case and many of his followers', was lacking.

In fact, however, it was in Britain's interest, and recognised as such, that Free France should grow in importance and stature, in military power and political importance; and that it should serve as an effective alternative to Vichy, both so as to attract Frenchmen to its service in sufficient numbers to make an effective contribution to the Allied cause, and so as to offer the hope that more and more French territories would rally to it. For the future too, it was important for Britain, as both Churchill and Eden recognised, that Free France should form the foundation for the restoration of French power in Europe.[13] None of this was likely if the movement were wholly submerged, either militarily or politically, in a British or Anglo-American enterprise; and in that fact lay the best assurance that, whatever encroachments de Gaulle might have to complain of from time to time, Britain would always ultimately respect French sovereignty and independence. In saying as he does in one of his more ungenerous moments that 'deep down Churchill could not bring himself to admit the independence of Free France' de Gaulle almost certainly does the wartime prime minister an injustice.[14]

In all the circumstances, it was to be expected that the question of the exact status of the Free French movement and the rights it could claim in the Allied camp would be a matter of uncertainty for a considerable period and consequently a cause of contention between Britain and France. For de Gaulle and his followers the position was simple: Vichy did not have, and never had possessed any true legality. Free France alone represented in any true sense the French people: it claimed the right, and desired the Allies to recognise that right, to be recognised as speaking for France. In that capacity it expected to take an equal part at the council table with Britain and other Allies, to share in Allied planning and to be consulted on all important political and military decisions. This recognition was slow in coming. As late as the beginning of 1944 de Gaulle was complaining that 'the Anglo-American powers never consented to deal with us as genuine allies'.[15] In the early stages the problem was not so acute. In the critical days of 1940–1 Free France had overwhelming need of Britain, and Britain, fighting alone, had need of Free France. Where French interests were involved – in relation to Equatorial Africa, for example, or the Dakar expedition, or the Syrian campaign of 1941, it was normally the case that Free France played a vital part and was necessarily involved in planning and decisions. British relations with Vichy having been severed after the attack on French naval units at Mersel-Kebir, there was little temptation for the British government either to ignore Free France, or to extend its patronage to any rival group. Later, however, after the shadow of American hostility to Free France had fallen on Anglo-French relations, the situation became more difficult and French complaints more numerous, particularly as the power of Free France grew in territory and military resources and its military contribution increased accordingly. Exclusion from Allied military planning in relation to Madagascar, North Africa and, in the early stages, in relation to Southern and Western Europe was bitterly resented. No less so the exclusion of French representatives from important political discussions – from the various top-level Anglo-American meetings in Washington, Quebec, Cairo and Malta and the tripartite meetings at Teheran, Yalta and Potsdam.

That this was more often due to American pressures than to British initiatives was fully appreciated by Free France and its leader. That for much of the time Churchill, Eden and his colleagues loyally fought to establish the claims of Free France and to break down Roosevelt's prejudices was less often appreciated and seldom generously acknowledged.[16]

To begin with, recognition of the Free French committee as a provisional or alternative government was not an issue. The British government regarded de Gaulle and his few followers as useful auxiliaries, but had not yet given up hope of weaning the Vichy regime away from its Axis allegiance, or at least tempting some of its more prominent personages – Weygand perhaps – into rallying French North Africa to the Allies. There could be no question therefore of recognising the Gaullists as an alternative French government.[17] De Gaulle himself accepted this view.[18] Britain recognised de Gaulle and his National Committee as representative of all Frenchmen and French territories which wished to carry on the fight: *ad hoc* agreements were signed between the British government and the committee for military, administrative and financial co-operation during the first nine months after the collapse of France. These sufficed for the time being. De Gaulle was concerned with the substance of effective consultation and participation in decision making rather than the shadow of recognition.

Later, the situation changed. Throughout much of the years 1942 and 1943 de Gaulle often felt that France was being denied both the shadow and the substance, as British policy towards Free France came to be more and more influenced by American prejudices. In June 1943 the merging of Free France with many of the elements which had formerly supported Vichy in the new Committee of National Liberation, controlling the whole of the French empire overseas and a growing resistance movement in occupied France, much enhanced the case for some form of Allied recognition of it as a provisional French government. The Nazi occupation of the whole of France six months earlier had already erased the case for regarding Vichy as an independent and sovereign government, and relations between the US and Vichy had been severed. From this time onwards, therefore, the Free French felt that they had a claim to such recognition, and this view was shared by Eden and many members of the British cabinet. But, at this period American hostility to de Gaulle was also at its height, all the more so since it became steadily more evident that the US protégé, Giraud, was no match for de Gaulle either in political capacity or in popular support. It took months of argument with Washington and much pressure by Eden and the British Cabinet on Churchill, and by Churchill on Roosevelt, before the Allies formally recognised the committee; and then only as the legitimate authority in French overseas territories.[19] Thereafter Free France continued to be excluded from top-level Allied discussions, though a French representative was admitted to the Italian Advisory Commission in November 1943 and the European Advisory Commission a year later.[20]

Undoubtedly, the French leaders felt that Britain was unduly subservient to the United States in these matters and had fought its battles with Washington less ardently than obligation and interest demanded. The difficulties of Churchill's position and the efforts of Eden, Macmillan and others on France's behalf were not as much appreciated as they might have been. Nevertheless, the controversy undoubtedly caused Anglo-French relations to deteriorate. De Gaulle himself affects to have come by this time (i.e. late 1943) to regard the question as of minor importance: 'I must confess,' he writes, 'that it was of little concern to me whether the diplomatic status of the Algiers government was regularised or remained indefinite. Looking back, I sensed that the worst was over, and that, if we persevered, the formalities would be solemnized sooner or later.'[21] Nevertheless, the tardy recognition of the national committee in the full sense of the word was felt as an affront, linked as it was to a clear unwillingness, on the part of the United States particularly, to contemplate the handing over of liberated France to its authority. In June 1944, on the eve of the Normandy landings, the committee itself took the step of proclaiming its status as the Provisional Government of the French Republic. It was not until over four months later that Roosevelt, influenced by de Gaulle's reception in liberated France and the clear evidence of French support for the committee, agreed to British importunities, and in recognising the de Gaulle government as the provisional government of France, also recognised the inevitable. But in the meantime Eden's fears that American policies towards France might jeopardise Anglo-French relations for years to come had been fulfilled, though the full consequences were not to be felt till many years later.[22]

The uneasy partnership

Mr Eden good-humouredly asked 'Do you know that you have caused us more difficulties than all our other European allies put together?' 'I don't doubt it,' I replied, 'France is a great power.' (De Gaulle, *Memoirs*.)

Just as to the newspaper reporter good news is no news, so the historian tends to focus his attention on the more troubled and therefore dramatic passages in diplomatic relations of two countries and to pay less attention to the steady processes of day-to-day co-operation at other times, which may, in fact, be the norm of those relations. In acknowledging the acerbic quality which all too often characterised Anglo-French relations during the Second World War it is easy to forget that in these years Britain and Free France together regained control of the French empire for the Allied cause: and ultimately together played their full part in liberating France from German occupation, restoring a French government to the French people and destroying the Third Reich.

Nevertheless, it cannot be denied that to follow the progress of Anglo-French relations during this period is somewhat akin to following the course of a fever-chart. At times the patient seems to be doing well, and the prognosis appears favourable: but every so often the temperature rises alarmingly; and there are critical moments when an early demise is predicted and the obsequies are already being pronounced. So it was with Anglo-French relations. During the first year after de Gaulle had come to London and formed the Free French committee[23] there were some difficult moments, but initial goodwill and the critical nature of the times enabled them to be surmounted. Thus the tragedy of Mers-el-Kebir,[24] much though it was deplored by the Free French as unnecessary and gravely damaging to Anglo-French relations, produced no public outburst of resentment, de Gaulle's broadcast on the subject being couched in restrained terms. This restraint and magnanimity was matched by that of the British government after the failure of the Dakar operation, aimed at rallying French West Africa, in September 1940. In the face of much criticism of the Free French part in the affair in the British Press and in parliamentary and governmental circles Churchill declared in the House of Commons, 'All that had happened had only strengthened His Majesty's Government in the confidence they extended to General de Gaulle.'[25] Such minor vexations as the unfortunate Muselier affair,[26] when the Free French naval chief was wrongfully accused by British Intelligence of counter-allied espionage, were also negotiated without too much difficulty, and indeed produced an improvement in the treatment of the committee by the British government and in co-operation between the two. Much was, in fact, jointly achieved during the twelve

months from June 1940 to June 1941. French Equatorial
Africa and French Oceania were rallied to the Allies: the
foundations of an effective French military contribution were
laid in London, French Africa and the Middle East; and the
first faint beginnings of a resistance movement in Occupied
France were encouraged.

Untoward events, however, had left their mark on the relationship. In British governmental and military circles there
were those who drew from the Dakar fiasco the conclusion that
the Free French and their leader were rash, imprudent and
inefficient, that their intelligence was as faulty as their
security was unreliable. It would be better not to have too
much to do with them or rely on them very much in the
future. (This view was, of course, shared by the American
government, fortified by the continuous stream of anti-
Gaullist propaganda, relayed via its special envoy to Vichy,
Admiral Leahy.)[27] On de Gaulle himself, the effect of Mers-
el-Kebir, Dakar and the Muselier affair was to rouse his latent
suspicion of the motives and attitudes to France of powerful
elements in British ruling circles, and to confirm his reluctance
to trust too much even in the goodwill of the British government.[28] In Syria and the Lebanon these mutual misgivings
were soon to rise to the surface. The Free French were to
encounter there a less cordial and co-operative attitude from
many elements in the British Middle East Command,[29] than
they had previously known; and the French for their part
showed little inclination to make allowances for either the
difficulties of an overstrained British military command or
the problems of a hard-pressed British diplomacy in the
complex and difficult situation which arose.

From the military point of view the 1941 campaign to take
Syria and the Lebanon from the control of the Vichy regime
was a competent and workmanlike job; with a British and
Free French force just adequate to the task, but no more than
adequate, the business was done in five weeks, in spite of
fierce resistance. From the point of view of Anglo-French
relations, however, the Syrian campaign and its aftermath
were disastrous. Both Britain and Free France had agreed

from the outset that a promise should be given to the two Arab states of eventual independence after the war, and a guarantee to that effect was made by the Free French at the outset of the campaign; but the French resented the fact that the British government had wished to be associated with the French guarantee, and when this was refused, had issued a separate statement to that effect. To de Gaulle France alone as the mandatory power was qualified to give these assurances, and furthermore as he put it, 'the word of France had no need of a foreign guarantee!'[30] It seemed evident to the French that Britain was seeking to curry favour with the Arabs at the expense of France, by making it seem that the promise of Syrian and Lebanese independence was due to British pressure: the long-range objective must be for British influence to supplant that of France in the Levant. The pages of de Gaulle's memoirs which deal with this incident are indeed, more than any other, bespattered with recriminations, accusations and innuendoes on the subject of the sinister designs of British diplomacy: Churchill himself is accused of aiming at 'establishing British leadership in the whole Middle East' and endeavouring 'to replace France at Damascus and Beirut'.[31] The repeated assurances given to de Gaulle by Churchill, Eden and Lyttleton (British minister at Cairo) that Britain sought no special advantages in Syria and the Lebanon were simply not believed.[32]

The conduct of the armistice negotiations with the Vichy authorities at the end of hostilities unfortunately added to these suspicions and gave the Free French genuine cause to feel affronted. Free France was not even mentioned in the agreement signed at St Jean d'Acre by the British and Vichy authorities on 14 July 1941, and moreover the Free French were at first debarred from making contact with the Vichy troops and trying to win them over; in both these respects contrary to assurances given to de Gaulle a few days earlier.[33] These, and other grievances were, for the most part, very soon rectified by Lyttleton in agreement with de Gaulle, and Free French authority was soon established in both states, with British co-operation. But the legacy of suspicion remained, and was to be revived two years later when the British government and Middle East command again felt obliged to intervene when trouble developed between the

Free French authorities and the political leaders of the Levant States. There was a (perhaps pardonable) tendency to attribute Free French difficulties with Arab nationalism exclusively to British meddling and encouragement – which was not the case.[34]

From London, of course, it all looked different. The British government, its resources severely overstrained, had had no desire to initiate the Syrian campaign in the first place: having judged it necessary, it was expedient to bring it to an end as soon as possible and therefore to give the Vichy French every incentive to come to terms and to keep them. This might seem to justify handling the Vichy commanders and troops with silk gloves. Equally it was desirable that Syrian and Lebanese nationalism should be firmly wedded to the Allied cause: Britain had enough thorny problems of this kind on her hands already, in Palestine, Egypt and Iraq, without adding to them. Moreover, since British arms had been invoked in Syria, Britain now had some responsibility for the consequences of that action to the people of these areas and could not simply wash its hands of the matter. To the British government the Free French attitude often appeared unco-operative, unreasonably suspicious and needlessly demanding. On all counts, the desirability of associating Free France with further efforts directed to rallying overseas French territories appeared more questionable, particularly since experience at both Syria and Dakar suggested that Vichy troops would fight equally hard (perhaps even harder) against Free French as against British troops. It might also be simpler in view of their demanding attitude, to keep them at a distance from forward planning of such operations. The consequences of this new attitude, noted by de Gaulle in his memoirs,[35] were soon to be apparent in relation to the island of Madagascar where both sides agreed that action would be necessary to forestall Japanese occupation.[36] Ultimately, however, British troops were landed in May 1942 with virtually no prior consultation or notice to the Free French, and without participation by Free French troops. This exclusion from an operation directed at French territory aroused the bitter resentment of de Gaulle and his associates, even though the assurances that French sovereignty would be respected were faithfully carried out, and the Free French representatives, Legentilhomme and Saint-Mart, duly installed in November 1942. Worse still however was shortly to follow in North Africa.

By June 1942 much of the initial goodwill and mutual confidence had departed from the relations between Britain and Free France; in their place were mutual suspicion, reserve and wounded feelings. A series of events had occurred in which not so much ill-will or sinister designs but tactlessness and maladroit handling had characterised British conduct of affairs; and exaggerated suspicion, over-sensitivity and on occasion unreasonable demands and unco-operative attitudes had too often been the contribution of Free France. A relationship already much frayed was now to be strained even more by a factor which had already begun to influence the situation – the distrust and in some cases bitter hostility towards de Gaulle of leading Americans, including president Roosevelt himself. From this time onwards, even where Britain most wished to accommodate Free France, she was often to be inhibited from doing so by the necessity of preserving the Anglo-American alliance.

This element was now to make itself heavily felt in the next major theatre of Allied operations – French North Africa. In the summer of 1942 the Anglo-American decision had been made for Operation 'Torch' (an Allied descent on North Africa) rather than a landing in France, and the American general Eisenhower appointed to command the operation. De Gaulle and the Free French were rigorously excluded from preliminary discussions and planning of this operation and no Free French troops were allowed to participate in it.[37] This exclusion was insisted on by the American government,[38] which distrusted and detested de Gaulle and his movement; believed that it had little or no support in North Africa; and was determined not to install the Free French in that area, but instead to set up some regime more congenial to it. It was hoped that either the Vichy minister Admiral François Darlan or General Henri Giraud, who had been brought out of unoccupied France, would serve as the focus for such a regime. The use of Free French troops was not only considered politically undesirable by the Americans, but also, so their representative Robert Murphy advised them, liable to strengthen the resistance of Vichy troops, and the hostility of the Vichy authorities.[39] So far as Free France indeed was concerned, the British were urged to sever their relations with that unco-operative and unreliable ally.[40]

Anxious, above all, to commit the Americans whole-heartedly to the North African enterprise,[41] and inclined to accept American assessments of opinion in North Africa, Churchill thus found himself committed to a policy which was bound, inevitably, to affront de Gaulle and the Free French more gravely than any previous action. Matters were made worse from this aspect by the American command's deal with Admiral Darlan, Vice-Premier in the Vichy regime, whom fate had decided to bring to Algiers at the precise moment of the Allied landings in November 1942. In assessing the rights and wrongs of the Darlan 'expedient' immediate military advantages, in terms of a cease-fire (and in effect acceptance of the Allied occupation throughout French North Africa),[42] had to be weighed against less easily assessable moral and political disadvantages. In the perspective of twenty-five years it is easier now to give due weight to Eisenhower's desire to secure his army's rear, and to Roosevelt's desire to save needless loss of American (and French) lives, than was possible for many people at the time. Certainly the British government had its doubts, and British public opinion reacted on the whole unfavourably to what seemed a squalid bargain. From the point of view of Free France this bargain with a leading member of the Vichy regime was morally unjustifiable and unacceptable;[43] it was prompted, they felt, not so much by a desire to save lives as a desire to achieve American political objectives in North Africa, to the disadvantage of Free France.

As so often, Eden pressed the Free French case on Churchill and to a lesser extent Churchill pressed it on Roosevelt.[44] The unexpected and, from the point of view of the Allies, highly fortunate removal of Darlan from the scene by assassination in December 1942 eased the situation somewhat, but not much. The Allied Supreme Command in Algiers, supported by the US government and, more hesitantly, by the British, now turned to the Roosevelt–Murphy protégé, Giraud, who was reluctantly accepted by the Vichy-ites in North Africa. Giraud's record was less tarnished than Darlan's but his claims to be either the legitimate head of a French government or the most plausible representative of French domestic opinion were certainly open to question. For de Gaulle this was a man with whom he could at least negotiate, but he saw no reason to throw himself into his arms, still less to let him take over Free France. A merger of the various French elements must certainly be achieved, but one which would restore Republican legality in North Africa, as elsewhere, which would have no sordid lingering ties with Vichy and which would unify French territory and the French military effort in such a way as to command the respect and support of the French people and particularly the growing French resistance movement. However ungraciously and intractably it was expressed, it is difficult now to deny the validity and indeed necessity of this attitude.

Six months of long negotiations were required to bring about this unity on terms which were acceptable to Free France: the tension created was certainly not helpful to Anglo-French relations. Under constant pressure from Washington, assailed by all the cares and anxieties of global war, Churchill grew impatient. Was this obstinate and recalcitrant man never to be satisfied? At the beginning of this period, in January 1943, and again towards the end, he even considered breaking off relations with de Gaulle.[45] On the latter occasion, Churchill proposed this to the British Cabinet from Washington, where he was under unusually heavy pressure from the Americans; but was met by united opposition from his Cabinet colleagues, led by Eden. It is possible indeed that Churchill made this proposal mainly for the benefit of the Americans, and both expected and desired the Cabinet's negative reaction. But there can be no doubt about his growing irritation and resentment at what seemed to him undue obstinacy on the part of Free France and its leader. At last, however, the desired merger was effected. At Algiers on 4 June 1943, the French Committee of National Liberation came into being under the joint presidency of de Gaulle and Giraud.[46]

For the next year or so the question which dominated Anglo-French relations was that of the status of the newly-formed committee. To the majority of the British Cabinet it seemed logical that the body which now clearly represented all shades of French opinion opposed to the Axis, should be recognised as in effect the provisional government in exile of France. Particularly was this so, as the resistance movement in France grew in strength and became steadily unified in its allegiance to the committee, and the French contribution to Allied military operations in Italy increased in importance. Churchill probably shared this view, but was determined not to move too far ahead of Washington, and no doubt from this point of view judged it expedient neither to seem to be pressing de Gaulle's claims too strongly nor to develop very close relations with the Committee. Thus, as so often during the war, Anglo-French relations continued to suffer because of the necessity of conciliating Washington. Churchill's position, indeed, seeking to reconcile two proud and difficult men, was not an easy one. His task was not made any easier by the fact that de Gaulle and Giraud found it difficult to co-operate. Giraud, vain, obstinate and politically inept, claiming to combine political and military power in a way which was neither constitutionally desirable nor administratively practicable, steadily lost ground to the more capable and masterful personality.[47] In November 1943, he was forced to resign from the committee.

The eclipse of Roosevelt's protégé, desirable as it undoubtedly was, did not of course serve to endear de Gaulle or the committee to the US president. However, Churchill continued to press the British Cabinet's view in favour of some form of recognition on Washington, in the end going so far as to make it clear that Britain would promulgate its own formula of recognition if necessary.[48] This brought the desired result, though the Anglo-American declarations in August 1943 limited their recognition of the committee to that of 'the body administering French overseas territories' and in effect representing French interests. These limitations, together with the recrudescence of political troubles in the Levant accompanied by the old mutual suspicions, continued to cast a cloud over Anglo-French relations. They were further exacerbated by the exclusion of French representatives from the Italian armistice negotiations in September 1943 and the lack of French participation in the Teheran conference between Britain, the United States and the Soviet Union in November. As was usually the case, both parties were to some degree at fault. Churchill was ready to tax the French with undemocratic behaviour in Syria,[49] though the French action differed little from that which Britain had itself taken earlier in Egypt and Iraq. De Gaulle made little allowance for the intricacies of the Italian negotiations, involving a pressing need for haste and secrecy, and equally took little account of the impossibility of Britain securing great-power status for France against the equally firm opposition of the United States and the Soviet Union. Nevertheless, the admission of a French representative to the Italian advisory commission in November 1943 and improved military co-operation with the Allies in Italy helped to ease matters: and from the turn of the year Anglo-French relations began to improve somewhat.

A permanent improvement of these relations, however, depended on the British government's ability to persuade Washington that the national liberation committee was now the only credible body which could be regarded as representing French interests; that no other body would be likely to emerge with whom the Allies could do business in liberated France; and that it therefore made sense for the Allies to accept the committee without reservations in this capacity. This Roosevelt refused to do: he ignored the committee's proposals for agreement on administrative co-operation in liberated France and finally, in April 1944, instructed Eisenhower that after the landings in Normandy he was to choose which French authorities he would work with. In earlier days there had been in the American attitude a genuine element of doubt about the representative quality of the Free French, and a genuine desire not to force any particular regime on liberated France; but by this stage these arguments had ceased to have much validity, as not only the British government but many Americans, including Eisenhower himself, also felt.

The French leaders, for their part, recognised that the British attitude was far more helpful and co-operative than the American; that Eden in particular was doing all he could.[50] Yet there remained a lingering resentment that, in the last resort, American goodwill was at this juncture of more importance to Britain than French goodwill; realistic though this attitude was in relation to the respective contributions of France and the United States to the war effort. Indeed, the very realism of the judgement deepened the wound in French feelings.

With the ready co-operation of Eisenhower, the British government had in fact assisted in the achievement of important French objectives in relation to the coming invasion of Europe, including the participation of Leclerc's French armoured division, with the promise that it would have the honour of liberating Paris, and the establishment of liaison between Eisenhower's command and the committee's resistance chief, general Koenig. The fact remained that Washington's insistence ensured that the committee should be largely kept in the dark about the planning for the invasion, this calculated isolation even going so far as to involve the suspension of transmission of coded telegrams between Algiers and London six weeks before D-day.[51]

Not surprisingly de Gaulle showed little enthusiasm for the British invitation to visit London on the eve of D-day and his first meeting with Churchill, on 4 June 1944, was acrimonious in the extreme.[52] However, things now began to improve. Notwithstanding Roosevelt's opposition, a visit to Normandy was arranged for de Gaulle and shortly thereafter the most positive proof arrived that British pressures, Eisenhower's representations and the inexorable pressure of events had at last overcome Roosevelt's obstinacy; namely an invitation to de Gaulle to visit the United States. Within a short while after this the necessary agreements for civil administration in France had at last been signed; by the end of August, de Gaulle was in liberated Paris, setting up the new French government, and clearly accepted by the vast majority of Frenchmen. This general acceptance, together with the firm manner in which de Gaulle brought the more radical elements of the Resistance under control, removed the last hesitations in Washington; and on 23 October the de Gaulle administration received Anglo-American recognition as the provisional government of France.

Thus, the greatest single cause of Anglo-French acrimony
was finally removed – but only after fifteen long months of
negotiation and bitter argument; and at great cost to Anglo-
French as well as Franco-American relations. The difficulties
for Britain and France caused by American attitudes were
not yet over. The French government naturally wished for
France to resume its place as a major European power and
to play a part in shaping the peace. The British government,
with an eye not only to the problems of occupying Germany
but also to the necessity of counterbalancing the Soviet
Union, also wished to restore France to its prewar role and
status.[53] With this in mind Churchill urged upon Roosevelt
the desirability of strengthening the French army, allotting a
zone of occupation in Germany to the French and admitting
a French representative to the forthcoming meeting with
Stalin at Yalta. But Roosevelt's prejudices were not only
personal but political; he believed that France had been
permanently reduced in status by its defeat in 1940 and had
no claim to equal representation with the big three: furthermore, a French presence at the council table would be 'a
complicating and undesirable factor'. Churchill was, however,
able to extort from Roosevelt agreement to the admission of
a French representative to the European advisory commission, which was making plans for the armistice terms and
occupation arrangements to be imposed on Germany and
other enemy states; and eventually to secure from Stalin
and Roosevelt agreement to a French occupation zone and
a seat on the Allied control commissions in Germany and
Austria. Moreover, Britain continued to provide arms for
newly-formed French divisions till the end of the war. With
full British support, a seat on the security council of the
newly-formed United Nations was allotted to France.

In all this, it is possible to see some justice in two different
but not necessarily conflicting points of view; in the British
view that France had some reason to be grateful for the
manner in which she had championed French interests against
Roosevelt and Stalin;[54] and in the French view that Britain
might have pressed the United States harder than she did on
behalf of France. The latter complaint certainly had less
justice at this time than on earlier occasions; and if Anglo-
French relations were not exceptionally close and amicable

I

as the war drew to a close, this was certainly due more to what had occurred earlier than to any British failure to offer support and recognition in the last crucial months.

The Alliance in Retrospect

An understanding with a powerful France ... will be indispensable for our security. ... We are likely to have to work more closely with France even than with the United States. (Anthony Eden, 12 July 1943.)[55]

The Almighty in his wisdom did not see fit to create Frenchmen in the image of Englishmen. (Winston Churchill, House of Commons, 10 December 1942.)

Britain is an island: France the cape of a continent: the United States another world. (General de Gaulle, *Memoirs*.)

In surveying this period of Anglo-French relations attention tends to focus at one level on the character and interrelationship of the two powerful personalities who dominated the policies of the two states; and at another level on the question of historical continuity and the long-term political aftermath. In what way did the events and the special character of these years influence future Anglo-French relations? Neither question is without its interest and significance, and the two are to some extent interrelated, since the personality and career of de Gaulle has made '*Gaullisme*' a continuing element in French politics which is certainly not yet exhausted.

These two men, Churchill and de Gaulle, could not certainly have been more different, either in personality or in outlook. The Frenchman was aloof, self-contained and inflexible; the Englishman gregarious, emotional, often overbearing but where necessary accommodating. The one realistic, even cynical, pessimistic in his assessment of human nature, allowing himself only a mordant wit; a patriot with lofty ideals, but at the same time an astute politician. The other romantic, humorous, trustful, occasionally petty, but in essence magnanimous and generous. Each was uniquely fitted to lead his country at a critical time: but neither was fitted by nature to co-operate with the other. They respected each other's qualities but they did not understand or fully trust each other.

Each too had peculiar qualities in his outlook which had a special and in some cases unfortunate effect on Anglo-French relations. Of Churchill it can be said that, just as his old-fashioned imperialism gave in some ways an unrepresentative picture of British political opinion to the Americans, so his extreme concern for American susceptibilities gave to the French a slightly distorted picture of British attitudes, since many of the British Cabinet were less inclined than he to pander to American prejudices. Judging rightly that Anglo-American co-operation was of pre-eminent and vital importance, not only to the winning of the war but to overcoming the dangers and uncertainties of the postwar world, Churchill determined never to get out of harmony with Washington, to carry Roosevelt with him every step of the way. At times he carried this too far and deferred too much to United States opinions. It was the judgement of Eden and others that this applied particularly to French policy, and certainly in regard to Anglo-French relations it did great harm,[56] notwithstanding Churchill's many battles with Washington on France's behalf.

Similarly de Gaulle's suspiciousness, sensitivity and inability to compromise were a source of damage to the Alliance, which with another man might have been avoided. The leadership of Free France might have fallen to someone more anglophil or more trusting – a Reynaud or a Blum. De Gaulle, however, was not an anglophil – no more so than Darlan or Laval or Weygand. On the contrary, he was deeply suspicious of British, as of American intentions towards France, especially in relation to the French Empire. Both would, he thought, take advantage of French weakness where they could, and show little regard for French interests; believing this, he naturally found evidence to justify his suspicions, often where little or none existed. The belief that France counted for little with the Allies, often justified in relation to the United States, was much less justified in relation to Britain, particularly in the later stages of the war. But it was always there, and made the difficult passages in Anglo-French relations which were bound to occur more painful than they need have been.

Inevitably these facets of the Anglo-French relationship were to have some effect on future relations between the two countries. So far as British policy was concerned the acrimonious passages and difficult controversies which occurred left comparatively little mark. It is both a strength and a weakness that British memories are short. Attlee and Bevin no less than Churchill and Eden, agreed on the necessity of military and political co-operation with France in postwar Europe, stopping short only at full economic or political integration. Both Labour and Conservative governments in turn pursued this policy without a backward glance at the difficulties of the wartime relationship.

With France it was different. De Gaulle's voluntary retirement from the scene, it is true, postponed the full effects for many years. None the less there was always an element of suspicion in the attitude of most French leaders towards British policy, a tendency to believe that Britain could not be completely relied upon as a friend of France. Many of the postwar leaders of France – Bidault, Pleven, Mendès-France, Queuille among others – had been associated with the de Gaulle regime. It would have been strange if they had not been in the least influenced by de Gaulle's ideas. Finally, in 1958, de Gaulle himself was to return to power, still sceptical of British goodwill, convinced that Britain valued its ties with the United States more than it could ever value those with France, and he was ready therefore to pronounce a veto on any future Anglo-French entente.

Notes

1 In 1940 Free France had only about 7,000 men at its disposal: in 1944 this had swollen to about 300,000 men constituting (1) an army of eight divisions, (2) a fleet of two battleships, twenty cruisers and frigates and a hundred smaller warships, and (3) an air force of 500 aircraft in thirty groups. But this compares with, for example, the four armies in the field and over a million men under arms of the British Commonwealth in the latter year. De Gaulle, *Memoirs*, vol. I, p. 93; vol. II, pp. 250–2 (Weidenfeld and Nicolson, 1971, English translation).

2 There is a perceptive comment on this difficult relationship by Oliver Lyttleton in his autobiography. (Viscount Chandos, *Memoirs*, London, 1962, p. 249.)

3 I have used the term 'Free France' for convenience throughout to denote the movement later known as 'Fighting France'.

4 W. S. Churchill, *The Second World War* (London 1948–54) vol. II, p. 451.

5 Cf. especially the well-known outburst at the time of the Normandy landings (6 June 1944), 'Each time I have to choose between you and Roosevelt I shall always choose Roosevelt' (de Gaulle, *Memoirs*, II, p. 227: A. Eden, *The Reckoning* (London, 1965), p. 453). Churchill (*Second World War*, vol. V, p. 556) describes this meeting as a 'rough interchange'. Cf. also Churchill, *Second World War*, vol. V, pp. 157–8. Cf. also de Gaulle, *Memoirs*, vol. I, p. 236.

6 Cf. de Gaulle, *Memoirs*, vol. I, pp. 88, 188, 235, 244–5.

7 Eden, *The Reckoning*, p. 250.

8 Equally de Gaulle had liabilities. He was disliked and distrusted by the majority of the French military hierarchy, who regarded him as a rebel and a traitor. French conservatives regarded him as a political revolutionary, and French radicals often suspected him of fascist, or at any rate authoritarian tendencies.

9 De Gaulle, *Memoirs*, vol. I, p. 150.

10 De Gaulle, *Memoirs*, vol. I, p. 231.

11 De Gaulle, *Memoirs*, vol. II, pp. 264ff.

12 De Gaulle, *Memoirs*, vol. I, p. 149.

13 Churchill, *Second World War*, vol. V, p. 159; Eden, *The Reckoning*, p. 398.

14 De Gaulle, *Memoirs*, vol. I, p. 235.

15 De Gaulle, *Memoirs*, vol. II, p. 262.

16 Churchill, *Second World War*, vol. IV, pp. 542–3; vol. V, pp. 157–9 and vol. VI, p. 215.

17 Churchill, *Second World War*, vol. II, p. 450.

18 De Gaulle, *Memoirs*, vol. I, p. 102.

19 Churchill, *Second World War*, vol. V, 157–9; Eden, *The Reckoning*, pp. 395–403.

20 Responsible for preparing armistice terms with the Axis and occupation arrangements. One of the most informative accounts of its work is given in Lord Strang, *Home and Abroad* (London, 1956), chapter 6.

21 de Gaulle, *Memoirs*, vol. II, p. 193.

22 Eden, *The Reckoning*, pp. 398, 467–9. Cf. also Churchill, *Second World War*, vol. VI, pp. 215–17; H. Macmillan, *The Blast of War* (London, 1967), Chs. XIV and XVI; and R. Murphy, *Diplomat Among Warriors* (London, 1964), p. 231.

23 The committee was not formally constituted until September 1941. It existed informally before that date.

24 When the British Mediterranean Fleet on 4 July 1940 attacked and crippled a substantial French naval force. Cf. Viscount Cunningham, *A Sailor's Odyssey* (London, 1951), pp. 243–5; de Gaulle, *Memoirs*, vol. I, p. 97.

25 De Gaulle, *Memoirs*, vol. I, pp. 134–5. Churchill, *Second World War*, vol. II, p. 437.

26 Admiral Muselier was later again to be the source of trouble in 1941 when he attempted to challenge de Gaulle's authority and was

temporarily supported by the British government. Both the two main protagonists have given their accounts of these matters, de Gaulle in his *Memoirs* (vol. I, pp. 150–3 and 258–61); and Muselier in his book *De Gaulle contre le Gaullisme* (Paris, 1946). Eden, in his memoirs, perhaps wisely, passes over these episodes in silence.

27 So far did these doubts go in Britain that Churchill found it necessary in February 1941 to circulate a memorandum to the Foreign Office, the ministry of information and the ministry of economic warfare instructing them to 'put an end to this cold-shouldering of de Gaulle and the Free French ... we should continue to give increasing support to de Gaulle' (Churchill, *Second World War*, vol. III, p. 653).

28 De Gaulle, *Memoirs*, vol. 1, pp. 96, 135, 153.

29 Wavell, the British C-in-C Middle East, complained that the Free French were 'ineffective and likely to aggravate the situation' and that 'their information was inaccurate'. At one point he asked to be relieved if the British Cabinet relied on Free French advice instead of his. (Churchill, *Second World War*, vol. III, pp. 288–94.)

30 De Gaulle, *Memoirs*, p. 188.

31 De Gaulle, *Memoirs*, p. 188.

32 Churchill, *Second World War*, vol. III, p. 294: Lyttleton (Chandos), *Memoirs*, pp. 246–50; Eden, *The Reckoning*, p. 249.

33 De Gaulle, *Memoirs*, vol. I, pp. 190–1; Chandos, *Memoirs*, pp. 246–7. Lyttleton (Chandos) concedes that British handling of Free French interests and susceptibilities in these matters was maladroit. Though, as he points out, the armistice agreement was approved by the Free French representative, General Catroux.

34 It has to be conceded that the somewhat elephantine approach of General Wilson (British C-in-C Palestine, and later C-in-C Middle East) and the ambiguous activities of the British representative at Beirut, General Spears, did not help matters. Moreover the French did not fail to notice that the British government was less tender to Arab nationalism in Cairo and Baghdad than in Damascus.

35 De Gaulle, *Memoirs*, vol. I, p. 236.

36 Cf. Churchill, *Second World War*, vol. IV, p. 198.

37 De Gaulle, *Memoirs*, vol. I, p. 244.

38 US accounts tend to attribute this policy equally to Britain and the US or even more to the wishes of the former (e.g. M. W. Clark, *Calculated Risk* (London, 1951), p. 38. Murphy, *Diplomat Among Warriors*, pp. 132–3, gives a rather different view but still regards it as a Roosevelt–Churchill policy. Churchill was certainly not in a friendly mood towards Free France at this time and appears in fact to have swallowed Washington's thesis about Free French untrustworthiness and poor security almost whole, while reserving the right to retain contacts with Free France, and refusing to disavow her (Churchill, *Second World War*, vol. IV, pp. 434, 542–3). Other members of the British government, notably Eden, were much less inclined to accept the American view (cf. Eden, *The Reckoning*, pp. 348, 351, 361). When later events showed US intelligence to be

at fault in its estimate of Gaullist support in North Africa, Churchill felt more willing to press Roosevelt in support of the claims of Free France (Churchill, *Second World War*, vol. IV, pp. 566–7).

39 Murphy, *Diplomat Among Warriors*, p. 134. The latter judgement may have been true. Experience at Dakar and Syria tended to suggest this.

40 C.f. Eden, *The Reckoning*, pp. 340–1.

41 General Marshall, US Army chief of staff, and many other leading Americans would have preferred to invade France in 1942. (Murphy, *Diplomat Among Warriors*, p. 131; General D. D. Eisenhower, *Crusade in Europe*, London, 1948, p. 79.)

42 Excluding Tunisia where the Resident-General Admiral d'Esteva, after much wavering, remained loyal to Pétain. (Eisenhower, *Crusade in Europe*, pp. 122–3.) The remaining political and military commanders in French North Africa obeyed Darlan's orders to cease fire, after the latter had concluded an agreement with the Americans.

43 De Gaulle, *Memoirs*, vol. II, pp. 56–8; Eden, *The Reckoning*, p. 349.

44 Eden, *The Reckoning*, pp. 349, 351. Churchill, *Second World War*, vol. IV, pp. 566–7, vol. V, p. 153.

45 Churchill, *Second World War*, vol. IV, pp. 609, 716; Eden, *The Reckoning*, p. 386; Macmillan, *Blast of War*, pp. 326–7.

46 Murphy's judgement (*Diplomat Among Warriors*, p. 225) that the terms accepted by de Gaulle were very similar to those proposed by himself five months earlier is an over-simplification. To mention only one point, the composition of the committee was of crucial importance. In June leading figures in the Vichy regime such as Noguès, Boisson and Peyrouton, who had earlier been proposed for admission, were excluded.

47 De Gaulle was already demonstrating his mastery of the political arts. Lord Attlee recalls (*A Prime Minister Remembers*, London, 1961, p. 56) that in reviewing de Gaulle's *Memoirs* he wrote that de Gaulle was 'a fine soldier but a bad politician'. This questionable judgement drew from de Gaulle the characteristic reply that 'he had concluded that politics were too dangerous a business to be left to the politicians'.

48 Churchill, *Second World War*, vol. V, p. 160. Macmillan, *Blast of War*, pp. 356–60.

49 Churchill, *Second World War*, vol. V, p. 165.

50 Cf. de Gaulle, *Memoirs*, vol. II, p. 192. Cf. also Eden, *The Reckoning*, pp. 446–7.

51 Cf. M. Viorst, *Hostile Allies* (New York, 1965), pp. 197–200.

52 Churchill, *Second World War*, vol. V, p. 556; de Gaulle, *Memoirs*, vol. II, p. 227. It was at this meeting that Churchill, provoked beyond endurance, made his famous remark about 'always siding with the Americans' – a remark from which his companions, Eden and Ernest Bevin, openly disassociated themselves (Eden, *The Reckoning*, p. 453). Churchill's account attributes this remark, or rather accusation, to de Gaulle. Eden's account however agrees with de Gaulle's.

53 Churchill, *Second World War*, vol. VI, p. 309; Eden, *The Reckoning*, p. 494.
54 Roosevelt's confidant, Hopkins, records of the Yalta meetings that 'Winston and Anthony fought like tigers for France.' R. S. Sherwood (ed.), *The White House Papers of Harry Hopkins*, 2nd ed. (London, 1948, 1949), vol. II, p. 849.
55 Eden, *The Reckoning*, p. 398.
56 Eden particularly feared the *long-term* effects on Anglo-French relations (Eden, *The Reckoning*, p. 398).

Bibliography

1 MEMOIRS

British

M. Borden, *Journey Down a Blind Alley* (London, Harper, 1948).

Viscount Chandos, *The Memoirs of Lord Chandos* (London, Bodley Head, 1962).

W. S. Churchill, *History of the Second World War* (London, Cassell, 6 vols. 1948–54).

Sir A. Eden (Earl of Avon), *The Reckoning* (London, Cassell, 1965).

H. Macmillan, *The Blast of War* (London, Macmillan, 1967).

Viscount Norwich, *Old Men Forget* (London, Hart-Davis, 1953).

Lord Strang, *Home and Abroad* (London, Deutsch, 1956).

French

G. Catroux, *Dans la bataille de la Méditerranée* (Paris, Julliard, 1949).

C. de Gaulle, *War Memoirs* (Paris, Plon; London, Weidenfeld, 3 vols., 1954–9).

H. Giraud, *Un seul but: la victoire* (Paris, Julliard, 1949).

E. Muselier, *De Gaulle contre le Gaullisme* (Paris, Editions de la Chine, 1946).

J. Soustelle, *Envers et contre tout* (Paris, R. Laffont, 2 vols., 1950).

2 SECONDARY SOURCES

R. Aron, *Histoire de la Libération de la France* (Paris, Libraire Arthème-Fayard, 1954). English edition entitled *De Gaulle Before Paris* (London, Pitman, 1962).

A. L. Funk, *Charles de Gaulle: The Crucial Years 1943–44* (Norton, University of Oklahoma, 1959).

H. Michel, *Histoire de la France Libre* (Paris, 1964).

D. Thomson, *Two Frenchmen: Pierre Laval and Charles de Gaulle* (London, Cresset Press, 1951).

A. Werth, *De Gaulle* (London, Penguin, 1965).

D. S. White, *Seeds of Discord* (Syracuse, Syracuse University Press, 1964).

The memoirs of Churchill, de Gaulle and Eden are, of course, essential sources for this period. The first two are inevitably coloured by the strong personalities and views of the two men. But both are honest in their fashion and sometimes generous. De Gaulle's suspicion of British motives and policies emerges clearly, particularly in his account of Middle East episodes. Eden's account is less personal and more detached; on some episodes it seems to be more reliable than Churchill. Among other English memoirs, those of Borden, Chandos, Macmillan and Norwich, throw some light on successive stages of British relations with the Free French movement in the Middle East, North Africa and in liberated France. Of the French memoirs, Soustelle's provide one of the best 'inside' accounts of the Free French, and Catroux's are important, coming as they do from the most senior French soldier to join de Gaulle and remain with him at the centre of affairs throughout. Catroux was also the 'man on the spot' in a number of crucially difficult moments in Anglo-French relations. A different viewpoint is provided by Muselier and Giraud who are both extremely hostile to de Gaulle. The impact of US policy and Roosevelt's personal hostility to de Gaulle on Anglo-French relations is dealt with from the American side in Admiral W. Leahy's *I Was There* (London, Gollancz, 1950), R. Sherwood's *The White House Papers of Harry Hopkins* (London, Eyre and Spottiswoode, 2 vols., 1948, 1949), *The Memoirs of Cordell Hull* (London, Hodder and Stoughton, 1948), and R. Murphy, *Diplomat Among Warriors* (London, Collins, 1964).

There is no completely satisfactory biography of de Gaulle in English. Alexander Werth's is one of the most complete and detailed, and David Thomson's book paints a discerning portrait. Michel's is possibly the best summary of the Free French movement. White, Funk and Aron between them cover most of the period from different viewpoints, White's book being an American account of the early wartime years, Funk an important contribution to the crucial middle period, and Aron a study of the last year of liberation.

10 The Reconstruction and Defence of Western Europe after 1945

Geoffrey Warner

Relations between Britain and France in the years immediately following the end of the Second World War were not nearly as important to either country as they had been in the years immediately preceding its outbreak. The emergence of the two super-powers, the United States and the Soviet Union, coupled with the economic prostration of Europe, meant that neither Britain nor France could really begin to solve their own problems, even in co-operation with one another. Anglo-French relations from 1945 to 1951, in fact, have the appearance of a sub-plot in a much larger drama. They are nevertheless of considerable interest, for like all good sub-plots, they throw light on the motives and behaviour of the characters involved. It is imperative, however, never to lose sight of the main action, which is why the present essay attempts to examine Anglo-French relations during the years in question in the context of developments in western Europe as a whole, and particularly their bearing upon the salient feature of the international scene: the intensifying 'cold war' between east and west.

One of the main issues in Anglo-French relations during the early postwar period was whether the two countries should conclude some form of alliance. In March 1946, the British ambassador in Paris, Duff Cooper, expressed his belief 'that it was always the intention of the late secretary of state,[1] as it has always been the desire of the present French

Note: During the course of my research for this essay, I have had the benefit of conversations with several personalities, both British and French, who played an important part in the events I have tried to describe. While I would like to take this opportunity of thanking them in public for the invaluable help which they gave me, I also owe it to them to point out that they are in no way responsible for any errors of fact or interpretation contained in the essay. The responsibility for these is mine alone.

foreign minister,[2] to conclude eventually an Anglo-French alliance. Repeated postponements have, however, taken place and no progress has been made.' The ambassador believed that some former obstacles, such as the personality of General de Gaulle and differences over the Middle East, had either disappeared[3] or were on their way to removal. Admittedly, there remained the French claim to the Rhineland and the Ruhr, which was contested by Britain and the United States, but in the ambassador's view, 'some settlement ... of this all-important question cannot be much longer delayed, and it is my submission that advantage should be taken of it to conclude a firm and close alliance with France'.

Duff Cooper's main preoccupation was the growing threat from the Soviet Union.

> Today the mighty arm of Russia is paramount in the countries that are nearest to her borders and the muscular fingers of that arm are busy in the lands that lie beyond. . . . The time has come, I submit, to count our friends, to fortify them and to bind them closely to our side. Of purely European countries France remains, despite her failures and perplexities, potentially the strongest and the richest on the continent, provided the mistake of allowing Germany to become powerful again is not repeated. An Anglo-French alliance would form a potent magnet for others who are now looking around rather wildly in search of security and salvation.[4]

But an Anglo-French alliance directed against the Soviet Union was premature in March 1946. French domestic politics were still dominated by *tripartisme* – the coalition between Communists, Socialists and Catholic MRP – and the Communist members of the government were quick to oppose anything which savoured of anti-Russian intent. The government as a whole, moreover, was still hoping for Soviet support for its policy of dismembering Germany. It was only after the Moscow foreign ministers' conference of March–April 1947 showed that such support could only be had on unacceptable terms, and after the Communists themselves had been driven from the French government in May, that there was more room for manoeuvre.[5]

While sharing Duff Cooper's anxiety about the Russians, therefore, the British government was well aware of the constraints under which the French were operating and displayed no great haste to become involved. Duff Cooper himself recalled that whenever he 'pressed the claims of France to receive more consideration and confidence from Great Britain' during the years of *tripartisme*, he 'was met by the argument, difficult to answer, that the French government contained Communists, who were presumably the servants of Stalin, and would communicate to him any information they obtained.'[6]

It was not surprising, therefore, that when an Anglo-French treaty was eventually concluded at Dunkirk in March 1947, its provisions were more or less exclusively concerned with the threat of a renewal of German aggression.[7] The French government saw it as a complement to the Anglo-Soviet treaty of 1942 and the Franco-Soviet treaty of 1944 and at a cabinet meeting on 5 February 1947, the president of the Republic, Vincent Auriol, expressed the hope that it would prove possible to link the various bilateral agreements by means of a general declaration, which 'would be the first pillar of a European organisation which would thereby enable us to prevent the confrontation of the large continents, the Soviet Union and the United States.'[8] Any such prospect, alas, was soon to be dashed by the growing division of Europe, exemplified by the Truman doctrine and the Russian refusal to take part in the Marshall Aid programme.

To begin with at any rate, the British government seems to have regarded the Dunkirk Treaty as largely symbolic. It certainly showed no disposition to extend the scope of the treaty and refused French requests for staff talks even after the Communists had been expelled from the French government.[9] It was only at the very end of 1947, possibly as a result of the latter's successful handling of a wave of Communist inspired strikes, that the British changed their mind and began to view the Dunkirk Treaty as a possible nucleus of a wider European and indeed Atlantic grouping directed against the threat of Communist aggression. Thus, on 23 December, the British foreign secretary, Ernest Bevin, told the chief of the imperial general staff, Field-Marshal Montgomery, 'that he had suggested to the Foreign Minister of France . . . that the time had come to begin the formation of a Federation or Union in Western Europe, and if possible to bring the Americans into it. He added that Britain and France must first agree on the military strategy, and staff talks to that end should therefore take place.'[10] In a major speech to the House of Commons on 22 January 1948, Bevin expressed the belief that 'the time is ripe for a consolidation of Western Europe' and the hope 'that treaties will . . . be signed with our near neighbours, the Benelux countries, making with our treaty with France an important nucleus in Western Europe.'[11]

The outcome of this initiative was the Brussels Treaty, signed in the Belgian capital on 17 March 1948 by representatives of Britain, France, Belgium, the Netherlands and Luxembourg.[12] The treaty was concluded in an atmosphere of increasing international tension. The Czech coup had taken place in February and, on 5 March, the American commander in Germany, General Lucius Clay, had telegraphed the director of United States army intelligence: 'For many months, based on logical analysis, I have felt and held that war was unlikely for at least ten years. Within the last few weeks I have felt a subtle change in Soviet attitude which I cannot define but which now gives me a feeling that it may come with dramatic suddenness.'[13] This state of anxiety, bordering on panic, was shared by many of the Brussels Treaty powers. A senior British foreign office official, who accompanied Bevin to the signing ceremony, subsequently wrote that he 'was painfully impressed by the low state of morale in the Allied camp. Our new Allies were all more or less borne down by the weight of Russian pressure. One of the ministers said that the Russians would be in Paris by August, an opinion in which the French chiefs of staff concurred.'[14]

Such an atmosphere doubtless explains why the military aspect of the Brussels Treaty assumed an early prominence. While negotiations aimed at involving the United States in the defence of western Europe got under way,[15] the five signatories desperately sought to co-ordinate their own defence, spurred on by the Berlin blockade, which began in earnest in June. Unfortunately, their efforts were marred by some bitter disputes, especially between the British and the French. 'One paramount object of the British Chiefs of Staff', records the secretary of the military committee of the

Brussels Treaty, 'was to set up a Command organisation, Commanders-in-Chief and their Headquarters, to give practical point to all our paper plans. This led to argument and much mistrust. Who was to be the Supreme Commander? ... The French were not at all anxious to subordinate themselves to the British and the British continued to maintain that no French general, since the *débâcle* of 1940, had sufficient experience of modern war. Let there be, then, a committee of three Commanders-in-Chief, Land, Air and Sea, with an additional and independent Chairman. This compromise took a deal of hammering out and led in the result to many tears.' Indeed, the French only accepted it as a result of 'an ultimatum, roughly and rudely presented' by the British defence minister to the French military representative, General Ély.[16]

Some clues as to the reasons for French hesitancy can perhaps be found in a letter, dated 13 October 1948, from Marshal Alphonse Juin to the French defence minister, M. Paul Ramadier, in which the former explained his refusal to accept the post of land commander-in-chief in the Brussels Treaty organisation. He had retained the impression given him by former governments, Juin wrote, that the military contacts in London were to be limited to those necessary for drawing up a list of requirements which only the United States was in a position to provide. 'I hardly imagined, I must confess,' he continued, 'that one could establish an effective regional command organisation before any formal assurance had been given us concerning this aid, or before the foundations of defence, within the framework of the new world war which we fear, had been laid.' He felt that the establishment of a command organisation at a time when everyone knew Europe was disarmed and when France's domestic situation remained uncertain was 'purely artificial and devoid of substance'. Indeed, one could only conclude that the real object of the exercise was to provide 'a hasty cover for Great Britain. . . .' As for the United States, it provided a little more security for their most vulnerable air base[17] and enabled the administration to 'play along' public opinion in an election year. 'Nobody among the Anglo-Saxons', Juin opined, 'has really bothered about France.'[18]

Juin's complaints were not altogether without foundation, as can be seen from Field-Marshal Montgomery's account of his long, and only partially successful, struggle to persuade the British government to commit itself to fighting a land campaign in Europe in the event of war. After a disagreement in the chiefs-of-staff committee early in 1948, Montgomery took his case to the prime minister on 4 February. 'I said it would be mighty difficult to achieve an effective Western Union if we could not promise support on land in the event of war,' he wrote later. 'The Prime Minister then weighed in strongly against a commitment to send our Army to the Continent. I replied that we already had an army there, the British Army of the Rhine. Did he propose we should withdraw it (through Dunkirk!) if the Russians attacked? Such action was unthinkable.' Bevin and A. V. Alexander, the defence minister, both supported Montgomery and it was finally decided to examine the implications of the strategy he proposed. On 10 May, he 'got agreement "on the essential need of fighting a campaign in Western Europe", with all that that decision entailed.'[19]

Although he described this as 'a great triumph', Montgomery soon found that his battles were not yet over. In the autumn of 1948, he was appointed chairman of the Brussels Treaty commanders-in-chief committee and soon discovered that 'there was deep suspicion of the British in political and military circles in Continental Europe', especially in France, based on 'the impression . . . that the British were concerned with a battle in Western Europe only in so far as it would provide a cushion for the defence of Britain.' Indeed, he was so alarmed by the situation that he told the British chiefs-of-staff on 2 December 'that French morale would not recover unless that nation could be convinced that Britain would contribute a fair quota of land forces to the defences of Western Europe.' In view of the weakness of the British Army of the Rhine, he proposed the commitment of an additional infantry brigade group in the event of war. After some argument, the chiefs-of-staff eventually accepted this proposal, but when their recommendation went to the government on 10 January 1949, it was so hedged about with qualifications that the latter had no difficulty in rejecting it.[20] As we shall see, the question of the presence of British forces, and especially ground troops, on the mainland of Europe continued to bedevil Britain's relations with France for some years and was not really settled until the Paris Agreements of October 1954.

However, it would be a mistake to view the Brussels Treaty solely in military terms. The first three articles pledged the signatories to co-operation in the economic, social and cultural spheres, and although not a great deal was accomplished under any of these headings, their inclusion in the treaty was significant. It reflected the impact upon the governments concerned of a powerful current of informed opinion – the strength of which could be measured by the proliferation of organisations calling for various forms of European unity – which took the view that traditional military alliances were no longer enough in the changed circumstances of the post-war world and that the only hope for the salvation of Western Europe lay in the pooling of all national resources to an extent scarcely contemplated before 1939.

For those who shared this outlook, the Brussels Treaty was but the first step towards the realisation of their goal of a truly united Europe. Another step was The Hague Congress of May 1948, which brought together some 800 delegates from many walks of life from all over Western Europe and which passed a number of resolutions calling for closer co-operation between the countries of Western Europe in political, economic, social and cultural affairs. One of the specific measures proposed was the convocation of a European parliamentary assembly. In August, a similar proposal was taken up by the French government and, with Belgian support, placed upon the agenda of the Brussels Treaty Organisation on 2 September.[21]

The British government felt that to call a European parliamentary assembly was to put the cart before the horse. Bevin told the House of Commons on 15 September 1948:

I feel that the intricacies of Western Europe are such that we had better proceed ... on the same principle of association of nations that we have in the Commonwealth. ... I think that adopting the principle of an unwritten constitution, and the process of constant association step by step, by treaty and agreement and by taking on certain things collectively instead of by ourselves is the right way to approach this Western Union problem. When we have settled the matter of defence, economic co-operation and the necessary political developments which must follow, it may be possible, and I think it will be, to establish among us some kind of assembly to deal with the practical things we have accomplished as Governments, but I do not think it will work if we try to put the roof on before we have built the building.[22]

When the foreign ministers of the Brussels Treaty powers met in Paris on 25 and 26 October therefore they were confronted not only by 'the Franco-Belgian suggestion for the convening of a European assembly', but also by a 'British suggestion relating to the establishment of a European council appointed by and responsible to Governments for the purpose of dealing with matters of common concern.' It was decided to set up a committee to examine these and any other proposals, which would report to the next meeting of the foreign ministers.[23]

Bevin expounded his ideas concerning the proposed council on 17 November to Hugh Dalton, Chancellor of the Duchy of Lancaster and leader of the British delegation to the committee. He said that, although he felt that the council should be confined initially to the five Brussels Treaty powers, it might eventually include all sixteen members of the OEEC, the organisation which had been set up to administer Marshall Aid. Indeed, the OEEC might even be subordinated to the council after the completion of the European Recovery Programme in 1952. 'The Council should deal with matters of common concern to Europe', he said. 'What were these? Economic affairs, rationalised defence, etc.' But it was clear that all this was contingent upon the council being a body of inter-governmental co-operation. Bevin 'was against a meeting of parliamentarians at this stage,' Dalton recorded. 'General debates, followed by no action, and fruitless controversies about federal constitutions, would make the peoples lose heart. What we needed now was solidarity without a constitution. Decisions must be kept in the hands of governments and their representatives. ... There was a danger of a clash between a parliamentary Assembly and governments. Some governments might refuse to accept the recommendations of the Assembly, and what remedy could the Assembly have then? The only result would be embitterment and frustration. But, since governments would be represented on the Council of Europe, there would be no such danger of a clash between the governments and the Council.'[24]

Despite its sponsorship of the proposal for a parliamentary assembly, the French government seemed to share the British view on the need for executive control. 'Governments must keep this firmly in their hands,' the French foreign minister, Robert Schuman, told Dalton on 25 November. '. . . Governments must choose Parliamentarians if we had a parliamentary Assembly.'[25] Unfortunately, when the committee met, Dalton noted that 'the French seemed divided among themselves, and to have no instructions from, nor any contact with, their Government,'[26] and there was sharp disagreement between them and the British, particularly concerning the selection and independence of the parliamentary assembly.[27] Reading the account of this controversy, it is hard to avoid the conclusion that the heart of the problem lay in the totally different relationship between parliament and the executive in Britain and France. 'The whole mentality of the French, even the Socialists,' Dalton wrote on 25 January 1949, 'is to be against the Government and mistrustful of the Executive. . . . André Philip,[28] I hear, has been canvassing in London for the French view, on the ground that we want a body which can criticise both the British and the French Governments at the same time! Not much smell of "United Europe" here!'[29]

A compromise was eventually reached at governmental level involving the establishment of a Council of Europe consisting of both a ministerial committee and a consultative parliamentary assembly. In the words of Bonnefous, 'The French point of view carried the day in so far as the constitution of the "Consultative Assembly", the nomination of its members by the [national] parliaments, and the freedom of voting were concerned. But the British point of view on the decisive role of the "Committee of Ministers" had triumphed.'[30] The British government, however, was clearly so disillusioned as a result of the controversy described above that it was no longer greatly interested in the Council of Europe. The situation was not improved by the way in which the Conservative opposition made effective use of the consultative assembly as a sounding board for its own views and, in the light of what the government regarded as the continuing pretensions of that body, there was serious discussion in January 1951 as to whether Britain should leave the organisation altogether.[31]

Britain and France also disagreed over economic policy. In 1947, serious consideration had been given to the possibility of a customs union between the two countries,[32] but nothing had come of it. In a letter to Bevin on 16 October, Duff Cooper blamed the Treasury and the Board of Trade for the paucity of results. 'I think their motives may be traced to two main principles,' he wrote. 'They believe: First, while we are both very poor, Great Britain is still richer than France and therefore if we combine our resources, we shall be giving more than we get; secondly, they are convinced that nothing in the world matters except dollars, and that therefore no country counts except the United States.'[33]

By the end of 1948, far from talking of a customs union, the two countries were in open dispute over their respective commercial policies. The British recovery plan presented to the OEEC provided for an export surplus of £12·5 million to Western Europe, compared with a prewar import surplus of £125 million. The French representative claimed that this did not give France and the other continental countries 'enough consideration'.[34] Speaking in the House of Commons on 9 December, Bevin laid the blame squarely at the door of the French for failing to adapt their economy to changing conditions:

The fact is that there was a luxury market in this country in the nineteenth and early twentieth centuries. The French must appreciate that that luxury market has gone. It is no use trying to hang on to something which one cannot have in any event. Britain, with her new needs, with her greater equality of income, will for a long time be a necessity market. I, therefore, appeal to my friends in France to shape their economy to meet a necessity market, rather than a non-essential one.[35]

It was probably as a result of this dispute that a series of highly confidential conversations between two small teams of French and British officials, headed respectively by Jean Monnet, the head of the French planning office, and Sir Edwin Plowden, the chief planning officer of the British government, took place at the former's home near Paris, from 21 to 24 April 1949. The talks were proposed by the French and, to judge from the available accounts, the main topic of conversation was the possibility of harmonising the French and British economies by means of some form of joint economic planning. The chancellor of the exchequer, Sir Stafford Cripps, was apparently quite interested in examining the matter further, but he was overruled by prime minister Attlee and Bevin.[36]

Monnet and his collaborators at the French planning office were the leading advocates in France of progress towards a federal Europe.[37] Indeed, according to one of them, the real aim of the Anglo-French conversations described in the previous paragraph was 'to try and find the bases of an economic operation between France and Great Britain which could serve as a nucleus around which a European economic union would develop.'[38] After their failure, Monnet found it easier to explore alternative approaches, and it was thus that he eventually came up with the proposal for a coal and steel pool, based upon a Franco-German rather than a Franco-British axis.

Nothing could have been achieved in this direction, however, had not the political situation been particularly favourable for a new French initiative in the twin fields of German and European policy. The then French foreign minister, Robert Schuman, wrote in his posthumously published political testament:

At the beginning of 1950 we felt that we were approaching a double crisis, both political and economic. First of all, there was a political crisis in respect of our relations with the USSR. If the Palais Rose conference (June 1949) had put an end to the Berlin blockade, no agreement was possible to solve such current problems as Germany, Austria, Trieste, etc. In so far as Germany in particular was concerned, the new policy of political and economic restoration, inaugurated by the London agreements (June 1948) and continued by the setting up of the West German Federation (September 1949) and the Petersberg agreements (November 1949), allowed a growing malaise to persist. The new policy was applied with old methods. Bitterly bargained for concessions were extracted from reticent and mistrustful conquerors by humiliated vanquished, who were more and more conscious of their renascent strength. ... France was particularly hesitant, and weighed the risks of each new renunciation of a right, once considered as a guarantee.

In the economic sphere, Schuman referred to the way in which the allies had divided up Germany's coal production among importing countries without any consultation with the Germans, and added that, while they recognised the need to restore both Germany's economy and her political independence, they were anxious at the same time to impose lasting restrictions upon her productive potential, particularly in respect of output which could be adapted for military purposes. 'In order to meet this situation', Schuman wrote, 'we had to change the spirit and direction of our policy and substitute loyal co-operation on the basis of equal rights and obligations for the old antagonisms. Thus, relations between the two countries would finally be placed on a healthy footing and would be freed from the nightmare of a possible conflict.'

'Moreover', Schuman went on, 'this fundamental objective coincided with preoccupations of an economic nature which went beyond the confines of the Franco-German problem and concerned the future of Europe.' While the rest of the world was busy organising itself into 'huge economic blocs', Western Europe still indulged in senseless and divisive competition. 'In practice,' Schuman believed, 'the problem consisted of organising Europe in the direction of unification by the progressive abolition of the barriers which hindered the transit of goods, by the rational co-ordination of the various countries' production, investments and exports, and finally by the free movement of labour and capital.' While there was no need to begin with a European federation, the attainment of these economic objectives did require 'a new political structure' and 'the convergence of the two kinds of problem (Franco-German and European) led us to envisage a concrete solution which was capable of responding to both these preoccupations.'[39]

Just as important as the political and economic context was the support of a leading politician. Monnet and his collaborators had worked out the plan for a coal and steel pool 'without the knowledge of the public, and even the government', and 'it was up to the minister of foreign affairs to provide his support and guarantee, and to assume the political risks of the initiative.'[40] Thus Schuman justified history's attribution of his name to the plan which he unveiled to the world at a special press conference in Paris on 9 May 1950.[41]

Britain was invited to join the preliminary discussions on the Schuman Plan on the same terms as other countries in Europe: i.e. on condition that she publicly accepted, in advance, the principle of a supra-national authority over her coal and steel industry. In view of the British government's earlier opposition to any supra-national element in either the OEEC or the Council of Europe, the French must have known this condition was unacceptable. Indeed, at one stage, Schuman seems to have been prepared to accept a British compromise proposal to the effect that an addendum be added to the communiqué which the French government wanted all would-be participants in the preliminary discussions to sign, setting out Britain's reservations concerning supra-nationality.[42] But Monnet soon torpedoed this suggestion. 'Acceptance of British participation in the negotiations on the terms of the addendum to the communiqué proposed by the British Government,' he wrote in a memorandum on 31 May, 'would destroy all possibilities of implementing the Schuman Plan and would give the negotiations a direction in which France would lose everything which she could have expected from them.'[43] 'It is obvious', he explained in another memorandum written at about the same time, 'that if Great Britain takes part in the negotiations under conditions which will enable her not to propose but to discuss the principles themselves, the other countries, especially Germany, will act likewise.'[44] The French government therefore reverted to its earlier insistence that all countries wishing to participate in the preliminary discussions should subscribe to the same communiqué, accepting the supra-national principle, without reservation. On 2 June, the British government informed the French that this involved an unacceptable prior commitment and proposed a meeting of ministers instead, a suggestion which was rejected by the French government on the following day.[45]

It was not only in order to avoid complications abroad that Monnet had advocated standing firm, but also to counter opposition at home. Just how strong this was can be seen from an account of a conversation between Sir Stafford Cripps and his French opposite number, M.

Maurice Petsche, on 10 June 1950, i.e. one week after the breakdown of negotiations between Britain and France. Petsche 'took the opportunity of opening his heart about the Schuman Plan' to Cripps. 'He said that he had not been consulted before it had been launched, that he, as well as M. Bidault[46] and M. René Mayer,[47] had grave misgivings about placing French industry under a supra-national authority, and they were particularly anxious for contact to be preserved with His Majesty's Government so that more practical views could prevail.' Petsche even proposed, allegedly with Bidault's support, the despatch of a secret emissary to London to keep open a channel of communication between the two governments on the issue. Cripps replied that he would have to consult his cabinet colleagues about this and they seem to have accepted the wise advice of the British ambassador in Paris that the British government 'must scrupulously avoid any appearance of taking a hand in French internal affairs. ... We must not go behind M. Schuman's back even if M. Petsche and M. Bidault appear to encourage us to do so. French ministers must have the courage of their opinions and make them felt in their instructions to M. Schuman.'[48] At any rate, nothing came of Petsche's remarkable proposal.

Even some of those Frenchmen who supported the Schuman Plan and who deplored the British refusal to take part in the preliminary discussions felt that the whole issue had been badly managed from the French side. 'There is no doubt that there has been a blunder', President Auriol noted in his diary on 15 June. 'The [French] Socialists are emphatic about this and they are right. The blunder consisted of presenting the matter in the form of a Franco-German agreement. It should have been presented in a wider context, the English should have been informed in advance and, above all, there should have been a thoroughgoing top-level discussion on the subject. It should not have been dealt with by ambassadors.'[49]

As for the British government, while it was undoubtedly piqued at the way in which the French had acted, it was not greatly concerned at being excluded from the preliminary discussions of the Schuman Plan, for it thought that they would fail, an impression which can only have been reinforced by news of the division inside the French cabinet. One of the senior British foreign office officials charged with examining the plan believed 'that the Franco-German talks would inevitably break down sooner or later and that we would then have a chance of coming in as *deus ex machina* with a solution of our own,'[50] a view which was shared by the British ambassador in Paris.[51] The government did in fact work out an alternative plan for the occasion,[52] but with the success of the conference of the six powers who had accepted the French proposal and the eventual formation of the European Coal and Steel Community, it never saw the light of day. Thus Schuman's bold initiative, which was regarded by the French government with mixed feelings and by the British government as 'not really a serious proposal, but just one more desperate manoeuvre by the French to make up for their failure either to split Germany up or to get the Ruhr industries placed under an international authority,'[53] marked the first decisive stage towards the formation of the European Economic Community.

Before the year was out, the Schuman Plan was followed by yet another spectacular European initiative on the part of the French government: the proposal for a European army. In order to understand its origins, one must look at the situation of the western alliance in the summer of 1950. NATO had been formed in 1949, but it was still in an embryo stage. Moreover, there seemed to be a difference of approach towards the problems faced by the organisation between the Americans on the one hand and the French on the other, with the British tending to side with the former. After the Anglo-Franco-American discussions which preceded the NATO council meeting in May 1950, Kenneth Younger noted in his diary that:

the Americans are under a compulsion to hot up the cold war in every way on account of the state of American opinion, while the French for a similar domestic reason are above all anxious not to seem to close the door against agreement with the Russians. The difference is only one of emphasis but it is important. . . . We and the Americans want to start building up an Atlantic Community which includes and transcends Western Europe, while the French still hanker after a European solution in which the only American function is to produce military and other aid. This difference is important because it stems from two quite different conceptions. Ernie [Bevin] has no faith in the solidity or efficiency of France or Belgium [and] believes W[estern] Europe will be a broken reed, and will not even attract the loyalty of Europeans or impress the Russians unless it is very solidly linked to North America.[54]

The Schuman Plan itself was seen by some to fit into this pattern and Mr Younger records the opinion of one senior Foreign Office official to the effect that it was 'largely designed to get away from the "Atlantic" conception and revert to a "European third force neutral between [the] USSR and [the] USA".'[55]

In retrospect, these judgements seem more than a little hard on the French. While it is true that a Communist vote of almost five million – about one-fifth of the electorate[56] – undoubtedly influenced the French government in deprecating too rigid an attitude towards the Soviet Union, there was much more to the French attitude than that. Back in April 1948, President Auriol privately noted his own views, which seem to reflect a dominant theme of French policy since the war:

> The policy of two blocs is dangerous, and Europe as the satellite of America would lose its independence and its purpose. But it is also true that a neutral position is childish nonsense. Switzerland can be neutral. . . . But France! Europe! . . . What is true is that united Europe is a force which can impose itself on everyone and upon which equilibrium depends. Finally, and because of this, it can offer itself as a mediator, publicly, solemnly, appealing to public opinion, putting forward just solutions and bringing back into the fold nations which have been able to slip outside.[57]

Nor were such ideas confined exclusively to the French. One only has to recall British diplomacy during the Korean war, Mr Churchill's 'summitry' after the death of Stalin and Mr Macmillan's pursuit of the same policy in 1959–60, to realise that Britain, too, has often sought to play the role of mediator in the conflict between east and west. The main difference has been that, until comparatively recently at any rate, Britain, unlike France, did not perceive the necessity of a European base but felt that she could act alone.

At the same time, one of France's main preoccupations in 1950, just as in 1948, was uneasiness about the extent of both the American and British commitments to the defence of western Europe. This explains Schuman's outburst at the NATO council meeting in May 1950, when he declared that 'considered as a treaty contemplating the "liberation of Europe" the North Atlantic Treaty was of no use. None of the Europeans present would live for that event.'[58] The outbreak of the Korean war at the end of June, which seemed to herald a new readiness on the part of the Communist world to resort to force, exacerbated French fears. The defence minister, M. Jules Moch, told the Council of the Republic on 3 August 1950 that 'our allies must understand that if we have to make the maximum effort, they are not absolved from a parallel exertion. There must be no question of a French army, an English navy and an American air force. Each country must participate with each service. France must have a navy and an air force, and her allies must be at her sides.'[59] The French reply to the American request for information concerning each country's proposals for strengthening its own defence was, with its emphasis upon the complete integration of all NATO functions, clearly part and parcel of the same policy of trying to bind both Britain and the United States indissolubly to Western Europe.[60]

Britain's reluctance to commit more troops to the defence of Western Europe was considered particularly reprehensible. 'I am petrified by the attitude of the English,' President Auriol recorded in his diary on 5 August 1950. 'The British people really have no sense of international or European solidarity.' British commentators had emphasised that it would be impossible to increase the number of British troops on the Continent without lengthening the period of national service and that the latter, which stood at 18 months, was already proof that Britain had made the greatest efforts in the field of defence. Auriol agreed that if one merely looked at the length of national service, this was indeed the case, but he noted that the proportion of exemptions in Britain was no less than 40 per cent and maintained that, in these circumstances, 18 months' conscription was no better than a year. 'In any event,' he added, 'it is heartbreaking to see that, just as in 1914 and 1939, the English will only realise the needs of the situation when it is too late.'[61]

The British government was quite simply exasperated by the French criticisms. It must have been about this time that the following ministerial meeting, so vividly recorded by Sir George Mallaby, took place:

> The discussion was about the French, their political instability, the deficiencies of their armed forces, etc. Someone was suggesting that the French were very critical of us, that they expected us to do far more for the defence of Western Europe than we were doing, and so on. 'What the hell right have they got to criticise us?' [Attlee] shouted: 'Tell them to go and clear up their own bloody stable. They haven't any decent generals. They haven't had a good general since Prince Eugene and he served their enemies.'[62]

The legacy of 1940 certainly died hard.

In so far as French fears were rooted in the sheer lack of troops on the ground in Western Europe, there was one solution which had been advocated unofficially for some months: the rearmament of West Germany. But this was totally unacceptable to the French government. Defeat and occupation were still too recent for any Frenchman to contemplate what he could only see as the revival of the *Wehrmacht*. Under the impact of the Korean war, however, the United States government decided that West Germany must participate in the common defence. Moreover, it put the question to its allies in a particularly brutal form: either accept the principle of German rearmament or forgo the commitment of additional American troops to Europe and the appointment of a supreme commander for the alliance.[63] In view of what has been said about France's fears and preoccupations, it will be appreciated that her dilemma could hardly have been more painful.

A way out was provided by the ubiquitous Jean Monnet. In a memorandum to the French prime minister, M. René Pleven, on 18 September 1950, he emphasised the 'need for a fusion of German units with those of other countries so that they cannot be separated and used for purposes other than the security of Western Europe and the Atlantic community,' and he accordingly proposed 'the organisation of European defence along the lines of the supra-national formula of the Schuman Plan.'[64] M. Pleven and his colleagues accepted Monnet's suggestion and the prime minister unveiled the finished plan for a European army before the National

Assembly and the world on 24 October. The plan envisaged a single force, integrated at the level of the smallest possible unit, with a European minister of defence, appointed by the participating governments and responsible both to them and a European assembly.[65]

In a speech to the Council of Europe one month later, M. Schuman freely admitted that the French government would not itself have chosen to take the next step in European unification in the field of defence. 'We would have preferred to build up the economic and political foundations a little further first,' he said, 'before starting on the military structure. But we have no choice in the matter; our tasks have been imposed on us, and we have no choice but to carry them out as and when they arise in our path.'[66] There was certainly a world of difference between supra-nationality in a restricted economic field, however important, like coal and steel, and supra-nationality in an area as sensitive as national defence. Even if German rearmament had not been involved, the plan would have been hard to implement. Since it was, it became virtually impossible. The French sociologist and political commentator, Raymond Aron, has described the latter stages of the controversy as 'the greatest ideological and political debate France has known since the Dreyfus affair; its most visible stake was German rearmament, but its ultimate significance concerned the very existence of the French national state.'[67]

It is possible, though by no means likely, that the plan for a European army would have stood more chance of success if it had obtained British backing. Instead, it was the object of barely disguised hostility. 'His Majesty's Government do not favour this proposal,' Bevin told the House of Commons on 29 November 1950:

> To begin with, we fear that it will only delay the building up of Europe's defences. . . . We take the view that the proposal . . . is also too limited in scope. We cherish our special ties with our old European friends but, in our view, Europe is not enough; it is not big enough, it is not strong enough and it is not able to stand by itself. I understand the urge towards European unity and sympathise with it. . . . But I also understand the new paradox that European unity is no longer possible within Europe alone but only within the broader Atlantic community.[68]

There were also other objections. 'As originally put forward,' the prime minister told the same audience on 12 February 1951, 'there were a number of features of that plan which we could not accept. There was the linking of it with a political superstructure; a Minister of Defence for Europe, and even an Assembly. We also were not entirely agreed that this was a really possible plan.'[69]

The French deeply resented the attitude of the British, not only because the latter poured cold water on the EDC, but also because they appeared to line up wholeheartedly with the Americans in an attempt to bully France into an early acceptance of the principle of German rearmament without adequate safeguards. Their motives moreover, were thought to be of the worst. 'In my opinion, England pursued a triple policy,' wrote Jules Moch, the French defence minister: 'first of all, to play the part of the only great faithful ally in the eyes of the United States, always with nostalgia for the important bilateral military and economic committees of the last war; next, to torpedo the European idea while isolating us at the same time; and finally, to have German divisions available as quickly as possible in order to be able to reduce her own effort on land.'[70]

While there is no doubt that the British did attach considerable importance to what they believed to be their 'special relationship' with the United States,[71] Moch's other imputations are as unfair to them as their own suspicion of France's lack of commitment to the Atlantic concept had been to the French. There is, for example, no evidence to suggest that they were seeking to 'torpedo the European idea' as such. As we have seen, their attitude was that the EDC was both inadequate and unworkable, and so it was perfectly understandable that they should oppose it. Nor is it true that the British were anxious to see West Germany rearmed in order to shuffle off some of their own obligations. Indeed, the cabinet were by and large opposed to German rearmament. What seems to have happened is that the by now desperately ill Bevin, who, together with the defence minister, Emmanuel Shinwell, assumed the lion's share of browbeating the French, did not keep his colleagues adequately informed of the progress of the negotiations, with the result that, in February 1951, the cabinet were 'shocked to find how far they

had been committed'.[72] There were, in fact, many who agreed
with Dalton that, although the 'Americans had . . . bulldozed
us with acceptance of [the] "principle" [of German rearma-
ment] . . . there were some principles that were accepted but
never applied.'[73] Attlee presented the government's considered view to the House of Commons on 12 February. 'We
have accepted the need for a contribution from Germany,'
he said, 'but the time, method and conditions will require a
great deal of working out. There is, first of all, the provision
of arms. Obviously, the rearmament of the countries of the
Atlantic Treaty must precede that of Germany. Second, I
think the building up of Forces in the democratic States
should precede the creation of German forces. Third, the
arrangements must be such that German units are integrated
in the defence Forces in a way which would preclude the
emergence again of a German military menace. Fourth, there
must be agreement with the Germans themselves.'[74] There
was little in that statement of principles with which the French
government would have disagreed.

There still remained the problem of the EDC, however.
The initial reaction in the United States to the French proposal had been, if anything, even more hostile than that in
Britain. '. . . To me,' secretary of state Dean Acheson wrote
later, 'the plan was hopeless, a view confirmed by General
Marshall[75] and concurred in by the President, and protracted
discussion of it [was] dangerous.'[76] During the summer of
1951, however, the United States government came round to
the view that the EDC was the best available solution to the
problem of German rearmament. Pressure was put on the
British, and on 14 September 1951, Acheson, Morrison and
Schuman issued a declaration which recognised 'that the
initiative taken by the French Government concerning the
creation of the European Coal and Steel Community and a
European defence community is a major step towards
European unity. They welcome the Schuman Plan as a means
of strengthening the economy of Western Europe and look
forward to its early realisation. They also welcome the Paris
Plan [for the EDC] as a very important contribution to the
effective Defence of Europe, including Germany.' In addition, Morrison affirmed that 'the Government of the United
Kingdom desires to establish the closest possible association

with the European continental community at all stages in its development.'[77]

'The closest possible association' did not, however, mean the same thing as membership, and neither the Labour government, nor its Conservative successor, which was returned to power in the general election of October 1951, showed any disposition actually to join either the ECSC or the EDC.[78] In fact, the phrase 'the closest possible association' may be taken to sum up the trend of Britain's policy towards France and Western Europe from 1945 until the first application to join the Common Market in 1961, although Winston Churchill, as usual, put it more pithily when he told the House of Commons on 11 May 1953, 'We are with them but not of them.'[79]

Many of the proposals for European unity during this period were opposed by the British government on the grounds of their federalist implications. There seemed good reasons for this at the time. As Sir Stafford Cripps said in the House of Commons debate on the Schuman Plan on 26 June 1950, 'In our view, participation in a political federation, limited to Western Europe, is not compatible either with our Commonwealth ties, our obligations as a member of the wider Atlantic community, or as a world power.'[80] But a closer examination reveals that no real incompatibility existed. Federalism, after all, was never the issue at governmental level. Although some Western European leaders may have dreamed of a federation one day, there is no evidence to suggest that any of the hard-headed realists who wielded power in the post-war period thought of it as anything but a very long-term prospect.[81] What was being asked of Britain in 1950, for example, was not participation in a federation, but commitment to some degree of supra-national co-operation in Europe. If this was incompatible with membership of the Atlantic community, why was the United States government so enthusiastic about the Schuman Plan?[82] And if it was incompatible with an imperial and world role, how was it that the initiative came from France, with her extensive interests in Africa, the Middle East and South-East Asia?

Psychology was almost certainly a more important factor than Britain's external obligations. The British government and people simply did not consider themselves as 'Europeans' in the years immediately following the Second World War. The pamphlet on European unity issued by the Labour party in 1950 was much criticised for its allegedly doctrinaire socialist tone, but it contained at least one statement with which few Englishmen of any party would have disagreed: namely, that 'in every respect except distance we in Britain are closer to our kinsmen in Australia and New Zealand on the far side of the world, than we are to Europe.'[83] Britain too, unlike France and the other countries of Western Europe, had been a victor in the Second World War and this undoubtedly coloured her attitude towards European union in general and federalism in particular. 'No doubt ... the experiences of war,' Dalton wrote in August 1950, 'including the experience of being occupied by the enemy, has broken the back of nationalist pride in many of these [European] countries and this helps to popularise the Federalist myth.'[84] The implication clearly was that Britain, having successfully defied the enemy, still had some 'nationalist pride' left.

But so had France. If French governments proposed what looked like federalist solutions, it was not, except on the part of a few enthusiasts, because of an abstract belief in their efficacy, but because they seemed best suited to the problems which had to be solved. Even a Frenchman as committed to the idea of European unity as Robert Schuman did not regard the supra-national principle as an article of faith. Indeed, his *directeur de cabinet*, M. Bernard Clappier, tells us that, at the time of the Schuman Plan itself, 'he had some difficulty in conceding it, for he was as mindful as anyone else of French sovereignty. If he did concede it, it was because it was in a restricted sphere and precautions could be taken. It was also because, by binding Germany in the same way as France, the supra-national nature of the institution to be set up finally seemed to him to be the only solution capable of guaranteeing the security of our country in the long term.'[85] The day was to come when Britain, too, arrived at a similar conclusion.

Notes

1 Anthony Eden.
2 Georges Bidault.

K

3 General de Gaulle resigned as prime minister of the provisional government of the French Republic on 20 January 1946.
4 Duff Cooper to Ernest Bevin, 19 March 1946 (copy in the *Duff Cooper papers*). I am greatly indebted to Sir Rupert Hart-Davis for permission to see and quote from this document. It is summarised in Duff Cooper's memoirs, *Old Men Forget* (London, Rupert Hart-Davis 1953), pp. 366–7.
5 For French attempts to gain Russian support for their German policy and for the shift of March–April 1947, see General Georges Catroux, *J'ai vu tomber le rideau de fer* (Paris, Hachette, 1952) especially pp. 23–4. General Catroux was French ambassador in Moscow.
6 Duff Cooper, *Old Men Forget*, p. 374.
7 For the text of the Dunkirk Treaty, see Margaret Carlyle (ed.), *Documents on International Affairs 1947–1948* (London, Oxford University Press for the Royal Institute of International Affairs, 1952), pp. 194–7.
8 Vincent Auriol, *Journal du Septennat 1947–1954*, Volume I, *1947*, edited by Pierre Nora (Paris, Armand Colin, 1970) p. 57. Other interesting references to the Dunkirk treaty can be found in the same volume on pp. 80–81, 105–6.
9 Duff Cooper, *Old Men Forget*, pp. 378, 380.
10 Viscount Montgomery of Alamein, *The Memoirs of Field-Marshal Montgomery* (London, Collins, Fontana edition, 1960), p. 505.
11 For the text of Bevin's speech, see *Documents on International Affairs 1947–1948*, pp. 201–21. The quotations are from p. 211.
12 For the text of the Brussels Treaty, see *Documents on International Affairs 1947–1948*, pp. 225–9. The conclusion of a multilateral treaty rather than a series of bilateral treaties on the Dunkirk model, as originally proposed by the British and French, was due to the Benelux governments. See Paul-Henri Spaak, *Combats Inachevés*, Volume I, *De l'Indépendance à l'Alliance* (Paris, Fayard, 1969), pp. 56–7.
13 Walter Millis (ed.), *The Forrestal Diaries* (London, Cassell, 1952), p. 367.
14 Sir Ivone Kirkpatrick, *The Inner Circle* (London, Macmillan, 1959), p. 205.
15 For an authoritative account of these negotiations, which eventually led to the Atlantic Pact, see Harry S. Truman, *Memoirs*, Volume II, *Years of Trial and Hope* (Garden City, NY, Doubleday, 1956), pp. 243–51. The whole purpose of the Brussels Treaty was, of course, to pave the way for an American commitment to western Europe.
16 Sir George Mallaby, *From My Level* (London, Hutchinson, 1965), pp. 156–7.
17 i.e. Britain, where the United States had sent a few nuclear bombers during the Berlin crisis.
18 Marshal Alphonse Juin, *Mémoires* (Paris, Fayard, 1960), II, pp. 166–70. It is interesting to note that, in his reply (II, pp. 170–71),

Ramadier did not contest any of Juin's arguments, but merely stated that France had no choice but to agree to the setting up of a command structure.

19 Montgomery, *Memoirs*, pp. 506–7.

20 Montgomery, *Memoirs*, pp. 517–19.

21 For the developments outlined in the previous two paragraphs, see Édouard Bonnefous, *L'Idée Européenne et sa Réalisation* (Paris, Éditions du Grand Siècle, 1950), pp. 97–111. The texts of The Hague Congress resolutions can be found on pp. 275–81.

22 *House of Commons Debates*, ser. 5, vol. 456, col. 106.

23 See the communiqué of the Paris meeting in *Documents on International Affairs 1947–1948*, pp. 232–3.

24 Dalton Diary, 19 November 1948 (*Dalton Papers*). I am greatly indebted to the Librarian of the British Library of Political and Economic Science for permission to use and quote from the *Dalton Papers*.

25 Dalton Diary, 25 November 1948.

26 Hugh Dalton, *High Tide and After: Memoirs 1945–1960* (London, Frederick Muller 1962), p. 314.

27 Bonnefous, *L'Idée Européenne*, pp. 113–18.

28 A French Socialist deputy and ardent advocate of European unity.

29 Dalton, *High Tide and After*, p. 316. In his conversation with Dalton on 25 November 1948, Schuman said that Bevin 'had explained to him that [the] British parliament didn't on its own initiative, do anything. It was different in France.' It was indeed!

30 Bonnefous, *L'Idée Européenne*, pp. 118–19.

31 See Ernest Bevin to Herbert Morrison, 22 January 1951 (copy in *Dalton Papers*).

32 Duff Cooper, *Old Men Forget*, pp. 370, 376.

33 Duff Cooper, *Old Men Forget*, p. 379.

34 *Manchester Guardian*, 30 November 1948.

35 *Commons Debates*, ser. 5, vol. 459, Cols. 580–81.

36 Etienne Hirsch (who was present), 'L'Angleterre fera-t-elle anti-chambre?', *Les Cahiers de la République*, **51**, January 1963, p. 9; Nora Beloff, *The General Says No* (London, Penguin 1963), pp. 53–4; private information.

37 An excellent account of the role of Monnet and his office in formulating French European policy is contained in Chapter V of Erling Bjøl's *La France devant l'Europe: la politique européenne de la Quatrième République* (Copenhagen, Munksgaard, 1966).

38 Étienne Hirsch in *Cahiers de la République*. The British did not get the impression that this was the object of the exercise at all (private information), but even if they had, it would have made no difference to the government's reticence. Indeed, it would almost certainly have reinforced it.

39 Robert Schuman, *Pour l'Europe* (Paris, Les Éditions Nagel, 1963), pp. 153–7.

40 Schuman, *Pour l'Europe*, pp. 164–5.

41 For the text of Schuman's declaration of 9 May 1950, see Margaret

Carlyle (ed.), *Documents on International Affairs 1949–1950* (London, Oxford University Press for the Royal Institute of International Affairs, 1953), pp. 315–17.

42 Cmd. 7970: Miscellaneous No. 9 (1950), *Anglo-French Discussions regarding French proposals for the Western European Coal, Iron and Steel Industries May–June 1950* (London, HMSO, 1950) especially Documents 7, 8, 9 and 11.

43 Quoted in Ulrich Sahm, 'Britain and Europe, 1950', *International Affairs*, **43**, 1, January 1967, p. 18.

44 Sahm in *International Affairs*, p. 17.

45 Cmd. 7970, *Anglo-French Discussions, 1950*, Documents 12, 13 and 14.

46 The French prime minister!

47 The French minister of justice. In fact, it is doubtful whether M. Mayer did have 'grave misgivings' about the Schuman Plan. He was, after all, one of the few ministers who was consulted before the plan was presented to the cabinet on the morning of 9 May and seems to have been responsible for the inclusion in Schuman's declaration of the passage referring to the way in which a united Europe could help develop Africa. See Pierre Gerbet, 'La Genèse du Plan Schuman', *Revue Française de Science Politique*, VI, 3, July–September 1956, p. 545.

48 Sir Oliver Harvey to Ernest Bevin, 10 June 1950 (copy in *Dalton Papers*).

49 Vincent Auriol, *Mon Septennat 1947–1954*, edited by Pierre Nora and Jacques Ozouf (Paris, Gallimard, 1960), p. 268.

50 *Diary* of the Rt Hon. Kenneth Younger, 12 June 1950. I am greatly indebted to Mr Younger, who was minister of state at the Foreign Office in 1950–51, for permission to quote from this diary.

51 'If, as seems only too probable, these discussions get stuck, then will be His Majesty's government's opportunity.' Sir Oliver Harvey to Ernest Bevin, 10 June 1950 (*Dalton Papers*).

52 Sahm in *International Affairs*, p. 21.

53 'A Comment by Kenneth Younger,' (on Ulrich Sahm's article) *International Affairs*, **43**, January 1967, p. 24.

54 Younger, *Diary*, 14 May 1950.

55 Younger, *Diary*, 12 June 1950. This was the same man who felt that the Schuman Plan negotiations would break down enabling Britain to step in 'as *deus ex machina*'. See above, p. 273.

56 The figures refer to the general election of 1951.

57 Auriol, *Journal de mon Septennat*, p. 114.

58 Dean Acheson, *Present at the Creation: My Years in the State Department* (New York, Norton, 1969), p. 399.

59 *Le Monde*, 5 August 1950.

60 The text of the French government's reply, which is dated 5 August 1950, is printed in *L'Année Politique 1950* (Paris, Éditions du Grand Siècle/Presses Universitaires de France, 1951), pp. 364–5. See also Acheson, *Present at the Creation*, pp. 436–7.
An additional cause for French concern was that the Atlantic Pact,

unlike the Brussels Treaty, did not provide for an automatic response to enemy aggression. This, of course, was to safeguard the American Congress's constitutional prerogative in declaring war. In the circumstances, the presence of substantial American forces in Europe, who would be directly affected by any attack, was the best guarantee of a prompt American response.

61 Auriol, *Journal de mon Septennat*, pp. 282–3.
62 Mallaby, *From My Level*, p. 57.
63 For an account of American policy, see Acheson, *Present at the Creation*, pp. 435–40.
64 Quoted in Georgette Elgey, *Histoire de la IVe République*, Volume II, *La République des Contradictions 1951–1954* (Paris, Fayard, 1968), p. 234.
65 For the text of Pleven's speech to the National Assembly, see *Documents on International Affairs 1949–1950*, pp. 339–44. It should be noted that the plan contained one obvious measure of discrimination against West Germany. While countries which already possessed their own forces – e.g. France – could retain national control over those units which they did not contribute to the European army, countries which did not as yet possess such forces – i.e. West Germany – had to integrate completely into the European army.
66 Council of Europe, Consultative Assembly, Second Session, *Reports*, Part V, 24 November 1950, p. 1688.
67 Daniel Lerner and Raymond Aron (eds), *France Defeats EDC* (New York, Praeger, 1957), p. 10. The European Defence Community (EDC) was the title under which the organisation comprising the European army came to be known. As the title of the book indicates, the French National Assembly eventually rejected the treaty establishing the EDC in a debate on 30 August 1954.
68 *Commons Debates*, ser. 5, vol. 481, cols 1173–4.
69 Denise Folliot (ed.), *Documents on International Affairs 1951* (London, Oxford University Press for the Royal Institute of International Affairs, 1954), p. 104.
70 Jules Moch, *Histoire du Réarmement Allemand depuis 1950* (Paris, Robert Laffont, 1965) p. 208.
71 It is doubtful whether the Americans reciprocated to quite the same extent. See, for example, Dean Acheson's account of his reaction to an Anglo-American staff paper on the 'special relationship' written in May 1950 in Acheson, *Present at the Creation*, pp. 387–9.
72 Younger, *Diary*, 4 February 1951. Bevin was forced to resign on grounds of ill-health on 9 March. He died on 14 April. His successor as foreign secretary was Herbert Morrison.
73 Dalton Diary, Mid-February 1951 (*Dalton Papers*).
74 *Documents on International Affairs 1951*, pp. 105–6.
75 The United States secretary of defence.
76 Acheson, *Present at the Creation*, p. 459.
77 *Documents on International Affairs 1951*, p. 136. See also Acheson, *Present at the Creation*, pp. 557–9.

78 I do not propose to go into the controversy, recently reopened by the publication of the third volume of Mr Harold Macmillan's memoirs, *Tides of Fortune 1945–1955* (London, Macmillan, 1969), to the effect that there was some sort of split in the Conservative government between 'pro-' and 'anti-European' forces on the question of Britain's future relationship with the EDC. The issue would seem to have been settled in the sense of the above statement by the letter in *The Times* of 12 September 1969 from Lords Chandos and Salisbury, who were both members of the Churchill cabinet at the time.

79 *Commons Debates*, ser. 5, vol. 515, col. 891.

80 *Commons Debates*, ser. 5, vol. 476, col. 1948, quoted by Sahm in *International Affairs*, p. 23. Herr Sahm makes the important point that the leader of the opposition, Winston Churchill, expressed himself in almost identical terms later in the debate.

81 Even today, after more than a decade of the EEC, the member countries are a very long way from constituting a fully-fledged federation.

82 See Acheson, *Present at the Creation*, pp. 382–9, and especially pp. 388–9, where Acheson shows how the United States government discreetly intervened from time to time to prevent any watering down of the original proposals.

83 *European Unity: A Statement by the National Executive Committee of the British Labour Party* (London, 1950), p. 4.

84 Hugh Dalton to Ernest Bevin, 18 August 1950 (copy in *Dalton Papers*).

85 Robert Rochefort, *Robert Schuman* (Paris, Les Éditions du Cerf, 1968), p. 278.

Bibliography[1]

Academic research into the postwar period is, of course, severely handicapped by the non-availability of archival material. Even with the recent introduction of the 'thirty year rule' in the United Kingdom and France, official documents for the period covered by this essay will not begin to become available for research until 1976.

Private papers can to some extent compensate for the lack of access to official files. However, the practice on the part of leading politicians and officials of leaving their personal papers to academic institutions for the purposes of research

[1] This essay is not intended to be in any way exhaustive. It merely offers a brief, introductory guide to the literature on the subject with particular reference to works which I found of assistance in preparing the essay.

is not as widespread in Europe as it is in the United States, with the result that it is often difficult to discover what collections even exist, let alone the conditions of access. A favourable development as far as Britain is concerned is that the recently formed Association of Contemporary Historians is currently preparing an inventory of private paper collections in this country, which will be an enormous boon to all scholars working in the field of twentieth-century history.

One notable collection which is deposited in an academic institution is the papers and diaries of Hugh Dalton at the British Library of Political and Economic Science (the LSE). Although he was never a Foreign Office minister in the Labour government of 1945–51, Dalton's position in the cabinet and the party was such that he knew a great deal of what was going on, and his diaries and papers contain a wealth of information on the course of British foreign policy during the period. In addition of course, he was the minister in charge of the British delegation to the Council of Europe, and the material in the Dalton collection on the formation and early development of the council is particularly rich.

Another compensation for the lack of archival material is the interview, and as I stated at the beginning of the essay, I have had the benefit of conversations with several personalities, both British and French, who played an important part in the events I have tried to describe.

The bulk of the source material for any essay on comparatively recent history however, must, of necessity be of a published and freely available kind. It can be divided, for the sake of convenience, into four main categories: (a) Documents; (b) Memoirs; (c) The Press; and (d) Secondary Sources – this last being subdivided into general works and more specialised monographs.

DOCUMENTS

The official collections of parliamentary debates of both countries are of course invaluable for any study of Franco-British relations during this period. Official publications of diplomatic documents, on the other hand, have undergone a sad decline since the war, particularly in Britain. The only one of value for this essay was the British government's White

Paper on the Schuman Plan, Cmd. 7970: Miscellaneous No. 9 (1950), *Anglo-French Discussions regarding French proposals for the Western European Coal, Iron and Steel Industries May-June 1950* (London, HMSO, 1950). Unofficial collections of public documents can also be most helpful. Indeed, the chronological series of *Documents on International Affairs*, published under the auspices of the Royal Institute of International Affairs (Chatham House), is indispensable.

MEMOIRS

On the British side, Hugh Dalton's *High Tide and After: Memoirs 1945–1960* (London, Frederick Muller, 1962), which is based on his papers and diaries, is extremely valuable. *The Memoirs of Field-Marshal Montgomery* (London, Collins, 1958), are very full on the strategic discussions concerning the role of Europe in British defence policy during the years 1946–8. Duff Cooper's *Old Men Forget* (London, Rupert Hart-Davis, 1953), has three chapters on the period of the author's Paris embassy and they include copious quotations from his diary and papers. Sir George Mallaby was secretary of the military committee of the Brussels Treaty Organisation and subsequently served in the Cabinet Office, and while his *From My Level* (London, Hutchinson, 1965), does not contain startling revelations, it does provide some useful – and not infrequently colourful – insights into both the mood of the time and the personalities involved. Lord Strang's *Home and Abroad* (London, André Deutsch, 1956), does not deal in any great detail with Britain's relations with France and Europe in the postwar period, but it gives a useful picture of the overall framework of British foreign policy during the Bevin era, written by the man who was permanent under-secretary of state at the Foreign Office from 1949 to 1953. The third volume of Harold Macmillan's memoirs, *Tides of Fortune 1945–1955* (London, Macmillan, 1969), says a great deal about Europe from the point of view of a leading Conservative MP who was also sympathetic towards the movement for European unity, and one must bear this bias in mind.

On the French side, one must begin with the truly remarkable diary of the President of the Republic from 1947 to 1954, Vincent Auriol. An abridged version of the entire document has been published as Vincent Auriol, *Mon Septennat 1947–1954* (Paris, Gallimard, 1970). At the same time, publication has also begun of the full text in seven volumes, one for each year of his presidency. The first to appear is Vincent Auriol, *Journal du Septennat 1947–1954*, Volume I, *1947* (Paris, Armand Colin, 1970), which runs to more than 800 pages of text, appendices and notes. When completed, the whole set promises to be one of the most important sources for recent French history ever published. After this, anything is bound to be an anticlimax and this description certainly fits Georges Bidault's *D'une Résistance à l'Autre* (Paris, Presses du Siècle, 1965),[1] which is based mainly on memory and is thin and disappointing. The latter can also be said of the diary of the head of protocol at the French foreign ministry, Jacques Dumaine, *Quai d'Orsay* (Paris, Julliard, 1955),[2] which consists largely of social and personal gossip, although it does contain one or two useful passages on foreign policy. Much more interesting is Robert Schuman's political testament, *Pour l'Europe* (Paris, Les Editions Nagel, 1963), which contains a valuable chapter on the genesis of the Schuman Plan, while Jules Moch's *Histoire du Réarmement Allemand depuis 1950* (Paris, Robert Laffont, 1965), is not really a 'history' at all, but a very revealing inside account of French policy and NATO discussions by the man who was French defence minister in 1950–51.

Although not by a Frenchman, the French language memoirs of the Belgian statesman, Paul-Henri Spaak, *Combats Inachevés*, Volume I, *De l'Indépendance à l'Alliance*, and Volume II, *De l'Espoir aux Déceptions* (Paris, Fayard, 1969), throw a great deal of light on French and British policy, as does the first volume of Konrad Adenauer's memoirs, *Erinnerungen 1945–1953* (Stuttgart, Deutsche Verlags-Anstalt, 1965).[3]

As the essay tried to show, Anglo-French relations in this period were inextricably bound up with relations between the United States and Western Europe. It is not surprising, there-

[1] English translation: *Resistance* (London, Weidenfeld and Nicolson, 1967).
[2] Abridged English translation: *Quai d'Orsay 1945–51* (London, Chapman and Hall, 1958).
[3] English translation: *Memoirs 1945–53* (London, Weidenfeld and Nicolson, 1966).

fore, that American memoirs should be among the most useful
sources. Harry S. Truman's *Years of Trial and Hope* (Garden
City, Doubleday, 1956), has a valuable chapter on the origins
of NATO and the controversy over German rearmament,
while George Kennan's *Memoirs: 1925–1950* (Boston, Little,
Brown and Company, 1967), give the views and impressions
of a high state department official. But by far the most
important American contribution is Dean Acheson's *Present
at the Creation: My Years in the State Department* (New
York, Norton, 1969). This massive volume, covering almost
the entire Truman administration, will henceforth be indispensable for any study of the European situation during this
period.

NEWSPAPERS

Throughout the period covered by the essay, the leading daily
newspapers in Britain were *The Times*, the *Manchester
Guardian* and the *Daily Telegraph*, with the *Daily Herald*
having a special importance as the official voice of the Labour
party. In France, the two leading dailies were *Le Monde* and
Le Figaro. However, many other newspapers in both countries and elsewhere printed valuable material and, as with
almost any recent international question, by far the best way
to begin a detailed examination of press sources is to use the
superbly organised library of press cuttings at the Royal
Institute of International Affairs (Chatham House) in
London.

SECONDARY WORKS

Apart from such obvious annual or semi-annual publications
as the Royal Institute of International Affairs' *Survey of
International Affairs* and the French *L'Année Politique* (with
its valuable documentary appendices), there are a number of
general books on British and French politics and foreign policy
which contain useful information on the subject matter of this
essay. Among the best are (on Britain): M. A. Fitzsimons,
*The Foreign Policy of the British Labor Government 1945–
1951* (Notre Dame, University of Notre Dame Press, 1953);
F. S. Northedge, *British Foreign Policy: The Process of*

Readjustment 1945–1961 (London, Allen and Unwin, 1962); and C. M. Woodhouse, *British Foreign Policy since the Second World War* (London, Hutchinson, 1961); and (on France): G. de Carmoy, *Les Politiques Étrangères de la France 1944–1966* (Paris, La Table Ronde, 1967);[1] A. Grosser, *La IVe République et sa Politique Extérieure* (Paris, Armand Colin, 1961); D. M. Pickles, *French Politics: the first years of the Fourth Republic* (London, Oxford University Press for the Royal Institute of International Affairs, 1953); and, despite its obtrusive left-wing prejudices, A. Werth, *France 1940–1955* (London, Robert Hale, 1956).

In a class by itself, however, because of the amount of previously unpublished material which was made available to the author and which she often quotes at length, is Georgette Elgey's *Histoire de la IVe République*, Volume I, *La République des Illusions 1945–1951*, and Volume II, *La République des Contradictions 1951–1954* (Paris, Fayard, 1965, 1968).

There are countless books on European unity, but one of the most useful from the point of view of this essay, in that its author was a French participant in events (as chairman of the foreign affairs committee of the National Assembly), is Édouard Bonnefous, *L'Idée Européenne et sa Réalisation* (Paris, Editions du Grand Siècle, 1950), which also contains a valuable documentary appendix. An excellent study of French policy towards European unity during the Fourth Republic is the Danish doctoral thesis (fortunately published in French) of Erling Bjøl, *La France devant l'Europe: la Politique Européenne de la IVe République* (Copenhagen, Munksgaard, 1966). Serge and Merry Bromberger, *Les Coulisses de l'Europe* (Paris, Presses de la Cité, 1968),[2] is a hagiographical account of the activities of Jean Monnet by two French journalists who specialise in 'inside' stories. The symposium edited by Daniel Lerner and Raymond Aron, *France Defeats EDC* (New York, Praeger, 1957), is a useful collection, while additional light is thrown on Robert Schuman's European policy by Robert Rochefort's sympathetic biography, *Robert Schuman* (Paris, Les Éditions du Cerf, 1968), which was clearly

[1] Revised English translation: *Foreign Policies of France 1944–1968* (Chicago, Chicago University Press, 1969).
[2] English translation: *Jean Monnet and the United States of Europe* (New York, Coward-McCann, 1969).

written with the help of some of Schuman's friends and collaborators.

On the British side, much of the literature is too polemical to be of much value, but there is a good introductory chapter on the period 1946–1954 in Miriam Camps's standard *Britain and the European Community 1955–1963* (Princeton, Princeton University Press, 1964). Two good books on American attitudes towards European unity are Max Beloff, *The United States and the Unity of Europe* (London, Faber, 1963), and Ernst H. van der Beugel, *From Marshall Aid to Atlantic Partnership* (Amsterdam, Elsevier, 1966). The Marshall Plan and the OEEC are inadequately covered in the essay and those interested in exploring the subject in detail should consult William Diebold, Jr, *Trade and Payments in Western Europe* (New York, Harper and Brothers for the Council on Foreign Relations, 1952), and Harry B. Price, *The Marshall Plan and its Meaning* (Ithaca, Cornell University Press for the Governmental Affairs Institute, 1955).

Articles are even more copious than books and I shall confine myself to listing two, both on the Schuman Plan. Pierre Gerbet's 'La Genèse du Plan Schuman' in the *Revue Française de Science Politique*, **VI**, 3, July–September 1956, is, as the title implies, a study of the way in which the plan was formulated. Ulrich Sahm's 'Britain and Europe 1950', *International Affairs*, **43**, 1, January 1967, is a first-class account by a West German foreign office official of the British reaction to the plan. In addition to published sources, both authors have made good use of interviews.

11 Allies at Suez

Hugh Thomas

At some time in the future, the great Anglo-French entente in the twentieth century will no doubt be dismissed as a minor incident in Egyptian history. For that alliance sprang partly from the need to resolve Anglo-French rivalries in Egypt; and it certainly fought its last battle at Port Said, in 1956, the political defeat which followed therefrom contributing largely to the end of the special friendship between the two countries.

The defeat in 1956 occurred at the end of a political crisis of dramatic importance for both countries both at the time and since. During the course of the crisis, relations between Britain and France were so close that at one point the British prime minister, Sir Anthony Eden, suggested the revival of the scheme of political union between the two countries which had been proposed by Churchill in 1940;[1] but at the end of the crisis the French blamed their defeat on British hesitation, and regretted that they had agreed to serve under a British flag; while even British politicians who supported the idea of force against Egypt as a reasonable response to the nationalisation of the Suez Canal Company, were ready to accuse the French government of luring Sir Anthony Eden into what seemed a discreditable conspiracy.

The broad picture of what occurred in 1956 is now no longer a matter for dispute. The two great declining Western European empires separately reached the conclusion that the prime minister of Egypt, Nasser, was responsible for most of their difficulties in the Arab world. Nasser personified a form of Arab nationalism with which they had attempted to make compromises but failed. The nationalisation of the Suez Canal Company was the last straw. A military expedition was mounted. A series of diplomatic efforts were made to make Nasser back down, more or less half-heartedly, while the military preparations were under way. In the end, the expedition took place, but with a very complicated political and military scenario which implicated the state of Israel. The nature of the military expedition undertaken was very heavy-handed. It was further launched without effective diplomatic and political preparation. In consequence, though the Allies – as they were proud to regard themselves, harking back to more successful joint undertakings in earlier years – won a swift military victory when they actually landed in Egypt, they were prevailed on to cease fighting very quickly. These events gave their enemy, Nasser, a considerable propaganda victory, and hastened the further decline of their own empires, the British and French governments concerned falling within a matter of months.

Although the British and the French governments reached for a time a perfect identification of views at one time or another during the course of the Suez crisis, their friendship was far from perfect throughout; and it can be argued that the discrepancies between the attitudes of the two governments were responsible for the political failure.

The British and the French governments reached their joint decision to try and overthrow Nasser for different reasons. The British by 1956 saw Nasser as the architect of all their difficulties in the Middle East, at a time when their Middle East interests and responsibilities were still great. A street urchin in Bahrein had only to throw a stone at the British resident's car for the Foreign Office to suppose that it was the work of a conspiracy in Cairo. It seems also to have been supposed that Nasser's strength in Egypt itself depended primarily on force and that, once he was got rid of, a more amicable, tractable and conventional Egypt would re-emerge. The assumption was also that virulent Arab nationalism as expressed by Nasser was at most a passing phenomenon, being the work of a minority of obsessed troublemakers. After Nasser had been destroyed, and the bubble of Nasserism pricked, the British government believed that they would be able to shore up indefinitely bourgeois or traditional Arab governments such as that of their old friend Nuri es-Said. Many officers and civil servants actually serving the British government in 1956 had had personal experience during their working careers, in the war or the army, of the other Arab world, and many remembered that the British after all had really helped the Arabs out of their subjection to the Turkish empire.

The British, that is, had a 'total' view of the Middle East. This view was expressed in its most extreme form by Julian Amery who saw in Nasser's over-reaching policies a 'gleaming opportunity' to redeem Britain's lost position in the Middle East.[2]

But there were, of course, many differing shades of view within the British position, and there were many ways in which as it happens Amery, though one of the best informed British politicians so far as the Middle East was concerned, was quite untypical; this was in that, though traditional in his outlook towards the Arabs, he did allocate in his scheme of the Middle East a place to Israel. The government on the other hand – if by that was meant, as it usually did in this case, the senior advisers in the Foreign Office – did not. Many British officials in the mid 1950s, as I recall, rather hoped that Israel would in some silent way vanish from the map. British policy at the time of the end of the Mandate in Palestine had been evidently and strikingly hostile to the conception of a creation of an Israeli state, and it had remained so.

There were thus innumerable currents of opinion within the British government and 'government circles' towards the Middle East, most of them characterised by strong, well-informed but partial views. Personalities played a big part, as did the recollection of the past role of these personalities. Thus much of the lives of active politicians in the 1950s had been occupied with Middle Eastern concerns. Eden was not only the architect of the Arab League after the war, but had spoken of Nasser to the Conservative 1922 Committee, when he had first got into power, as a great improvement on the pashas of the past. Hurt pride must therefore have been a factor in Eden's attitude to Nasser. Further, as late as his Guildhall speech of 1955, Eden had been regarded by the Israelis as favouring boundary revision at their expense; yet it was in fact Eden who in the course of the Suez crisis would rail (to Nutting) of the 'anti-Jewish spleen of you people in the Foreign Office'.[3] Further, Eden had as foreign secretary in 1954 pressed for and secured the British withdrawal from their old base at Tel-el-Kebir, near Ismailia on the Suez Canal.

This move had been accomplished in the teeth of the opposition even of Churchill who at the time was still nominally prime minister.

French attitudes were different and in some ways actively hostile to those of their ally. Latent in the French subconscious was the knowledge that France had been supplanted in the course of the nineteenth century by Britain in an area, which France had herself really opened up. Nearer the surface was the recollection of the British role in the course of the Second World War in what had previously been a French mandate, namely Syria (in this respect the French were as sensitive to their traditional interests in the Levant, after they had lost it, as the English were to the route to India, after that too had gone).

Nearer still, in time, the French distrusted the various Anglo-American or merely British schemes for collective defence in the whole region, and their distrust of the Baghdad Pact,[4] in particular, had almost enabled them to see eye to eye with Nasser.

But in fact French policy towards Egypt was really determined by two main considerations: first and foremost France was in the middle of a colonial war in Algeria, whose political complication for France itself was great. The Algerian rebels received propaganda encouragement from Egypt and several of the political leaders of the rebellion either had been or were still in Egypt. France also suspected Nasser, falsely, of being the main source of weapons for the rebels. Nasser was at that time, as later, much the best-known champion of the Arab cause internationally. The consequence was that as the war continued, Nasser had begun to be regarded as nerve centre of the whole rebellion. Remove Nasser, and Algeria would be assured for future generations as an 'integral part of France'.

Thus, speaking of Nasser, before the nationalisation of the canal company, the French and the British governments were already moving close together. But there were differences: as was natural in respect of a country at war, French public opinion was already before July 1956 much more nervous, and emotional, than was British. There was also already existing in France, before July 1956, the 'Rhineland complex'. This was the identification of Nasser with a new Hitler and the view that what France had failed to do over the German reoccupation of the Rhineland in 1936 could not be allowed to be repeated, in respect of Nasser. It would seem that this exaggerated historical parallel was not used even by Eden before the events of July 1956, though later on he would use it over and over again.

Yet there were already some interesting institutional similarities within the British and French systems. The Quai d'Orsay and the Foreign Office, for example, had much in common. Both departments of state had, to begin with, attempted to treat Nasser with kid gloves and both by early 1956 admitted to failure. Yet both departments were regarded from outside, with some justice, as the centre of pro-Arab feeling in the government, and certainly in the French case were more so than the government. In the event, as will be seen, the treatment of both these institutions by their governments had much in common.

This was partly because the Algerian war was the responsibility not of the Foreign Office at all, but of the Ministry of the Interior and the Ministry of Defence. Not surprisingly, the strongest opponents of Nasser were to be found even within these departments, and though there had been changes of government since the beginning of the war, successive changes had affected the new ministers as they came in. In 1956, in particular, the French minister of defence, Maurice Bourgès Maunoury, used the much admired French private cabinet system to the exclusion of the regular secretariat. Thus Bourgès Maunoury relied much more on his two main collaborators, Abel Thomas and Colonel Louis Mangin, than on the permanent head of the ministry, Geoffroy de Courcel.

The Ministry of Defence in France was also the nerve centre of the second main French consideration in 1956; namely enthusiastic support for the state of Israel. This had no equivalent in the British administration. At that time, enthusiasm for Israel was almost confined to the Labour party, which of course was in opposition. Some maverick Conservatives, such as Amery and Boothby, had different views, as did many young men, among them indeed many younger members of the foreign service. But, on the whole, Arabism pervaded Whitehall.

It was a different matter in France. The Socialist prime minister Guy Mollet when he got into power in early 1956 had told the Israeli minister of defence, Shimon Peres, that he, Peres, would soon see that he was not a new Bevin;[5] and in the course of the events of 1956, Mollet often spoke as if the need to save Israel was a prior consideration for him, even more than the Algerian war. He would recall with melancholy how Léon Blum had abandoned the Spanish Republic to its fate in the 1930s and stated that a new Socialist government in France would not again abandon another Socialist democracy.

The Israeli entanglement in the Suez affair afterwards of course became in fact most important, and here no doubt it was Israel which was in fact the prime mover.

Israel had had little contact with France on a governmental level before 1954. True, prominent French Zionists such as the Rothschilds had done much to bring the state into being in the first place but there was little feeling for Israel one way or the other. But during the early 1950s Israel had been driven to seek arms from where she could. France admittedly was with Britain and the USA a cosignatory of the Tripartite Declaration which not only guaranteed the 1948 frontiers of Israel but was also supposed to bind the three biggest arms suppliers in the West to try and keep the weapons available to Israel and the Arab states as roughly balanced. Israel therefore had had to make various shifts outside these states, starting indeed with Czechoslovakia, in 1948, both at the time of that country's communisation and before.

Israel bought small arms between 1948 and 1955 from a variety of countries: old tanks from the Philippines, anti-aircraft guns from Italy, and so on. But a reliable and continuous source of arms was not secured. The British sold Israel destroyers but not tanks (because, Shimon Peres has recalled, 'the Kingdom of Jordan had no sea-coast, in Selwyn Lloyd's words').[6] The Canadians despatched artillery. The US sold anti-tank guns (being defensive weapons). In late 1954, Israeli arms buyers succeeded in buying a number of French fighters (Mystères II), by reason of the enthusiasm for Israel of the then French air minister, General Catroux. But the Mystère II turned out to be of second-rate quality. The Israelis wanted the Mystère IV. But that aircraft had been ordered by NATO, so that, for Israel to secure any of these, NATO would have to waive its priority. The support of another French minister, General Koenig, minister of defence under Edgar Faure, ensured to the Israelis the AMX-1 tank and a quantity of 155 mm guns. But the Mystère IV, of which Israel had asked for twenty-four, was more of a problem. The opposition of the Quai d'Orsay to this (which would have been a significant change in the balance of armaments in the Middle East before the Czech-Egyptian arms deal of 1955) prevented any action. Only in late 1955 did the Israelis enter into contact with Bourgès Maunoury at the Ministry of the Interior on an unofficial basis. But thereafter a Franco-Israeli love-affair began. Bourgès Maunoury became minister of defence in early 1956 under Mollet. His assistants opened every door to the Israelis. The new foreign minister, Christian Pineau, was also led to be favourable to Israel. From March 1956 Israel received the Mystères IV which she had desired and, by the end of June, France had promised to supply Israel with all the arms that she needed.[7]

In the course of this developing political alliance, one important crossroads was reached. Up till the end of March 1956, France kept both Britain and the USA officially informed about her arms-selling policies. The USA thus approved the French sale of twelve Mystères IV to Israel: Eisenhower in his memoirs says that he was pleased that he had been so openly consulted by the French, as was proper under the terms of the tripartite agreement.[8] But unknown to the USA, at least officially, these twelve aircraft had been increased to thirty-six, at least by June of 1956.

The fact was therefore that behind these two considerations which affect judgement of the French attitude to the crisis of Suez, deriving both from her Algerian and her Israeli policy, there was an increasing hostility, even in government circles, to the orthodox foreign policy as laid down by successive governments of the Fourth Republic since 1945. It was galling to have to secure NATO and United States agreement for sales of French arms. Yet this had been done by all French governments for ten years. These minor infidelities to the North American alliance practised by the government of Guy Mollet and Bourgès Maunoury were not only the expression of sympathy with an experimental and democratic Socialist country who happened to be at war with the friend of France's enemies; not only an act of solidarity between men who had fought the Germans with those who, in creating the state of Israel, were securing the integrity and the security of world jewry for ever; they were the first assertion of independence on the part of French political leaders who had been for too long, as they supposed, subservient to the patronising authority of the USA – the first whiff therefore of that French nationalism which was to be re-affirmed so vigorously by De Gaulle after the fall of the Fourth Republic in 1958. Of course, De Gaulle was a Viollet-le-Duc, not a Saint Louis or a Bonaparte; he was to rebuild the chateau in the old style and not construct a quite new fortress. But he undoubtedly expressed a desire for an independent foreign policy which was not adequately articulated, in any way, by the men of the early 1950s.

The sale of the Mystères had no British equivalent. It was true that the men of the Suez group in the Conservative party in the early 1950s, entertained enmities towards the USA for their encouragement of local nationalism where this assisted the decline of the British empire; and incidents such as the known American wish for the British to leave the Suez Canal base and American private support for the claims of Saudi Arabia against the Sultan of Muscat and the Sheikh of Abu Dhabi had expressed these concerns in the Middle East itself. There seems little doubt that Conservative politicians on the right of the party, ultimately joined by the prime minister, Eden, were in some ways resentful of the changed position of the British and American respective world authorities since 1945. At the same time, there was on the left, among for instance the Bevanite wing of the Labour party a bitter distrust of the cold war policies of the Eisenhower administration, particularly indeed of the secretary of state, John Foster Dulles. But as yet before the nationalisation of the Suez canal there had been no overt expression of anti-American feeling in England, either on the left or the right, private or public. Indeed, in most matters British and US foreign policy was intimately co-ordinated. In particular, their sharing of intelligence, and the persistent day-to-day contact between the two foreign services, made such a thing virtually unthinkable.

Some further points might be made: both Britain and France were undergoing that surrender of empire which in the course of the next ten years, would entirely alter their international authority and their view of themselves. But Britain, which still ran half Africa, was scarcely aware of this. The pro-British personal attitudes of Eisenhower had assisted this deception. France, on the other hand, had already suffered a major defeat in a colonial war, over Indo-China. In a sense indeed, despite Algeria, France was already attempting to rehabilitate her reputation after the humiliation of Dien Bien Phu. Britain did not realise that there was anything to rehabilitate.

Secondly, the two governments were differently constituted: that of Sir Anthony Eden was solidly constructed from out of the orthodox Conservative party and, being in power since the middle of 1955, might be expected to last till 1959 or so, and perhaps then, if all things went well – and why should they not? – be re-elected. The government of Guy Mollet was, on the other hand, an uneasy coalition in power since January; it was the first occasion since the late 1940s that the Socialist party had entered the government; it had already lost the support of Pierre Mendès-France, its best known supporter, after a few weeks of power. Entering office with the expectation of being able to reach a swift peace in Algeria, it had early become evident (particularly after Mollet's own traumatic visit to Algiers in January) that peace was far; it had also become clear that the protestations of a Socialist party for African nationalism were one thing when it was out of power and another when they were in. Most members of the government thought that there was no other viable combination of parties in the Fourth Republic. Action, if there was to be any, therefore had to be speedy.

Yet if the Conservatives in England were more sure of their electoral position than the Socialist-led coalition in France, the latter were none the less in a stronger position *vis-à-vis* the country than was Eden's government. When it came to the point, Britain turned out, in relation to the Middle East to be a divided country; the Labour opposition helped, despite their fewer supporters, to make the government's position untenable; whereas, Mollet, for all his slight hold on a permanent parliamentary majority, could count on even greater support than his parliamentary figures suggested. His only serious opponents were the Communists and as on so many issues they voted on an anti-patriotic cause with noticeable lack of relish. There was very little civil service hostility towards Mollet's policies over Suez, even though many of the normal channels of decision were by-passed, and no ministerial resignations. Dissident members of Mollet's own Socialist party, such as Daniel Mayer, were relatively quiet. One casualty of the Suez crisis no doubt was the great gap which grew between the British and French Socialist parties, both nominally members of the Second International.

A final major point distinguished British and French initial reactions to the Suez crisis. When the storm broke and a military expedition began to be mounted, the British chancellor of the exchequer Harold Macmillan appears to have been among those keenest for action. At a later stage he is even reputed to have threatened to resign unless force were used.[9] At the end of July, possibly speaking expansively and informally, he is even believed to have said that he thought that action was essential, despite the cost to the nation of £500 million (not £5 million as erroneously reported by Eisenhower's political adviser, Robert Murphy, the error being due to a printer's error).[10] But he seems nevertheless never to have made any estimate at all of the likely foreign exchange costs of military action. Yet these were in the end important and even perhaps decisive, as the French realised at the time or later. The whole affair of the ceasefire indeed, highlights the difficulty of undertaking questionable military action for a country which has also a reserve currency. The pound collapsed. The franc, then in theory a far weaker coin, held up throughout 1956 and was placed under little strain by the military action.

The consequence of all these different attitudes between the British and French caused persistent divergences of views throughout the crisis. This was specially expressed in two aspects of the matter: first, in respect of the military planning of the enterprise, secondly of the political planning, in particular relation to the preparation of the 'scenario', to use the word of General Maurice Challe, its chief planner, which led to the actual despatch of the expeditionary force.[11]

At the present time, authoritative information on the details of the military planning in this undertaking derives, on the one hand, from a series of articles written by General Sir

Hugh Stockwell, the British army commander at the time, in the *Sunday Telegraph* in 1966; and on two books published in France, one by the French chief-of-staff at the time, General Paul Ely, the other by the French army commander, General André Beaufre, who was, according to the way the command structure was arranged, Stockwell's subordinate.[12] No official history has apparently been written and certainly not published. Indeed, from the British point of view, it has been officially represented that the contingent military planning begun in July and August for possible use in respect of the Suez canal crisis had nothing whatever to do with the 'international police action' embarked upon in October and November in consequence of the Israeli attack on Egypt. The memoirs of Sir Anthony Eden for instance are entirely silent on these matters. Nor has any French politician (most of whom are still either active in politics or cherish the hope that they may one day be so again) written about the military side of the Suez crisis. From a great many sources, some published and some not, it is admittedly possible to fit the story together (as I have done) but nevertheless the account by these three military men is if somewhat personal, the best source. They admittedly disagree in some details but, in the main the story is clear, from them, even though it differs from what was published at the time. This is that immediately after the nationalisation of the canal company at the end of July 1956, an Allied expedition was got ready. By the time it was ready, however, the political circumstances had changed and so the proposed D-day for landing in Egypt was postponed. The political circumstances kept on changing but nevertheless in the end the same military plan as envisaged at the end of July, or rather a sophisticated and modified version of it, was put into action.

It is of interest that the French and the British commanders seem to have different views, some minor in themselves, on the nature of the timetable of these actions: but perhaps this is merely a matter of bad memories. The most important difference however without doubt relates to the different assumption which seems to have characterised the two countries on the political background to the military plans. Thus Stockwell tells us that the British military assumed ('point 8', in the plan presented to and accepted by the chiefs-of-staff on 8 August), 'We would not enter Cairo'. He adds 'our aim was consistent. We were not trying to capture Egypt or direct ourselves to the overthrow of Nasser or capture Cairo . . . any thought of occupying Egypt or taking over Cairo would have been out of the question.' The British assumed that they would have to fight and beat the Egyptians before occupying the Suez Canal zone and it is also left unsaid (at least by Stockwell in his articles) as to how the Allies envisaged that they would get across Egypt from the southbound desert road outside Alexandria to the canal, without needing to pass through Cairo. Of course there are many roads across the Nile delta, but it is difficult to imagine, with the best will in the world, that the allied army would have been able to get easily across such a densely populated area so as to be able, as Stockwell hoped, to be 'lining up along' the Suez Canal by day 8.

General Beaufre writes on the other hand – and this in relation to his first visit to London for planning purposes, on 10 August:

First what was the object of the operation? I had no directive on this subject but it was clear from the French point of view the target was Nasser; his was the revolution which was setting alight the unifying of the Arab world. We must therefore defeat the Egyptian army and *go to Cairo* [Beaufre's italics]. Any more limited operation would leave the dictator's government in being and allow him to rouse world opinion through the radio. Moreover, if we did not directly or indirectly take over the reins of government in Egypt, guerrilla warfare, similar to that which has just driven the British from the canal zone would soon make its appearance.[13]

Here then is an incredible discrepancy which affects every further aspect of planning. General Beaufre, from his knowledge of French general policies, and perhaps even because of his own hopes and ambitions, assumes that the government of Egypt is to be overthrown. General Stockwell, his commander, again because of his own background knowledge assumes quite the contrary. Further, it is quite clear that General Beaufre (according to his own well-written and vigorous account) went on pressing his point in subsequent meetings of the plans committees. Thus: 'at my urgent request the French would secure the western and south western exits from the town by a combined sea-borne and air-borne operation. *We would then push forwards to Cairo* [My italics, HT] where a modern version of the Battle of the Pyramids would be fought.'[14]

General Ely's version of these events, it should be said, supports General Beaufre. Thus, he tells us:

the aim of the operation is, both for the French and the British, to defeat Nasser, which – even if one accepts that his regime is fragile and is bound to collapse as soon as the slightest amount of Egyptian territory is forfeited – involves having the capability to defeat the Egyptian army and to advance if necessary to Cairo.

Here indeed lies part of the real secret of the Suez operation. The two allies, who were supposed to be tightly organised in a single command structure, had in fact quite different assumptions as to the political aims of the whole operation. This major discrepancy must be explained because the unspoken assumptions of the military leaders, always of the greatest importance in battles and political undertakings of high risk, were utterly different. 'In this day and age,' Stockwell no doubt assumed that it was absurd to think of occupying Egypt. There was no point in even raising the matter. But Beaufre, the highly articulate soldier of a France which wished to renew itself (and would do so under De Gaulle), took the other point of view for granted: France was holding down most of Algeria by military force; she had been fighting for years in Indo-China; there was nothing inherently improbable about the idea of an occupation of Egypt. And indeed, whereas the British attitude was well intentioned and muddy, the French one had complete internal consistency.

The endless arguments about the different plans for the Suez expedition which followed after this initial and fundamental difference in approach are a matter for farce. They are chronicled by General Beaufre with a shade too much scorn perhaps to be completely convincing throughout. ('So at this first stage, we embarked on the tedious process which the British call planning.') It is perfectly obvious from this and other accounts by now that the British chiefs-of-staff were hoping against hope all the time that the whole operation would be cancelled, and that these views were communicated in one form or another down through the whole military structure. The first minister of defence, Walter Monckton, was also extremely doubtful about the use of force but seems never to have said so outright. The consequence was the plan as it ultimately turned out was excessively cautious and insured against the most minor setback. 'We could not afford to lose' was, according to Stockwell, the first principle which he and his colleagues established in their planning on 6 August. The plan was also chopped and changed very often, as a result of political delays, which themselves enabled new changes to be suggested by sometimes new military commanders. On the other hand, considered simply as a technical operation, the absence of political forethought on the part of the British military advisers (because of their long abstinence from political activity on their own) in what was certain to be a political situation when it developed was equally balanced by the excessive private political ambitions of the French commanders.

The plan ultimately used was the bizarre one of ten days of aero-psychological warfare, consisting of bombing, the dropping of leaflets on the Egyptian population and propaganda broadcasts from Cyprus. This activity would in fact continue until the commanders could announce 'all opposition is crushed or can be ignored'. Then and only then would the Allied armies land, at Port Said, with the minimum of casualties. The caution of this plan (apparently the brain child of Air Marshal Sir William Dickson, then chairman of the British chiefs-of-staff) was apparent to all the French commanders. How was it possible to suppose, in modern conditions, that the world, the UN and the US would wait during ten days of bombing and radio attacks? How would it be known anyway whether there would be no opposition until a landing had been effected?

The French argued that the adoption of this plan in itself was not only a mistake (which is obvious), but also that it suggested a lack of will or failure of nerve on the part of their British ally. This would seem indeed to be true. On the other hand, why did the French accept it? The answer, seems to be that the French supreme commander, Admiral Barjot, not to speak of some of his subordinates, saw the plan as a means of using one of their long cherished schemes whereby the allied attack could be implicated with an Israeli seizure of the Sinai peninsula, at the same time. Indeed, as one reads General

Beaufre's account, imagination boggles at the extent to which political cleverness on the part of himself and his compatriots in the armed services kept devising one new plan after another to advance one interest or another.

In the end, the scheme which was used was of course the highly complicated one of a joint military operation with Israel, in which the fact of the Allied understandings with Israel were to be kept secret. This secret alliance is naturally one of the most interesting and the most discussed aspects of the whole Suez crisis. Indeed, the subject of the Suez operation would not have remained a subject of political controversy for so long had it not been for that side of it. Its interest as an incident in Anglo-French relations is that here was a matter over which, for the first time since the Rhineland crisis of 1936 – or rather since the end of an independent French policy towards Germany in the early 1930s – a French government took an initiative and persuaded the British over to their way of thinking.

The facts of this part of the Suez crisis are now fairly clear. Thus we gather from General Ely's memoirs that the French had considered acting in collaboration with Israel either in addition to Britain or without, as early as the beginning of the crisis, at the end of July.[15] It was natural that when this idea was put on one side for the time being, the French should keep the Israelis closely informed of their planning; at that time the Israeli and French ministries of defence were working so closely together that anything else would have been unthinkable. This is confirmed by the memoirs of General Dayan and of Shimon Peres.[16] It would be prudent to assume that directly or indirectly the British Government were perfectly aware of the character of the Franco-Israeli contacts. One French writer Henri Azeau, in a well-written book, suggested that the idea of a joint collaboration with Israel was put by Mollet to Eden in their first conversation after the nationalisation of the Canal Company in the night of 26–27 July.[17] No doubt the idea came up in a general way several times during the endless discussions in August and September between the British and French governments, being always rejected by the British on the ground that any formal Israeli contact would cause uproar in the Arab world – not to speak of the Foreign Office. But Israel was herself not inactive, and during the same month, was anxiously seeking a way of securing permanent free access to the straits of Tiran, at the foot of the Sinai peninsular, of ending the terrorist *fedayun* raids into Israel from the Gaza strip and of damaging the Egyptian military machine before the accretion of Russian arms made it too strong. These political motives had existed with the Israelis for about a year and the heightened political tension in the whole Middle East area had sharpened Israeli resolve.

From a careful reading of the memoirs of Ely, Beaufre, Peres and Dayan, it is clear that it was really the French and not the Israeli government which finally brought matters to a head. Responsibility for this lies fairly squarely with Guy Mollet, the prime minister, though the vigorous part played in securing this by the ministry of defence (that is, the trio of Bourgès Manoury, Abel Thomas and Louis Mangin) was very important. In great secrecy, the French government secured in early October the complete refurbishment of the Israeli army. They ascertained that in order to take military action in Sinai Israel required air cover for her infantry, fighter cover over Israeli cities and air action to destroy as much as possible of the Egyptian army. General Challe, of the French general staff, visited Israel, and worked out an exact list of other Israeli military needs.[18] Admiral Barjot worked on a scheme for a joint Israeli-French military action but the Israelis were reluctant to take action without at least certainty of British neutrality. Finally Challe went to England on October 14 and at a conference with Eden at Chequers (the description of which forms the central piece of Anthony Nutting's book *No End of a Lesson*, but is also mentioned by both Challe and Ely[19]) put forward what Challe himself describes as:

the pretext or rather the scenario that he [Eden] was waiting for. The Israelis would attack the Egyptians. They would reach the canal. . . . At that moment the Franco-British forces would descend on the canal in order to separate the adversaries, and they would take control of the whole length of the canal. After that, we would see. 'Good idea', Eden told me, 'I will go to Paris tomorrow to discuss it with Guy Mollet.'[20]

Nutting has testified that Eden was thrilled by this plan[21] and General Ely recalled that Challe when he got back to Paris had said he was 'astounded'. He had not thought for a second that the English would have been interested in the plan and indeed if Monsieur Albert Gazier, one of Mollet's ministers acting on behalf of Pineau the foreign minister had not been present he would have thought that Eden was making fun of him.[22] In the event, as is known, this scenario was put into practice.

No one appreciated this at the time and indeed as late as 1967 when I published a book describing this event in some detail on the evidence of less substantial sources than those quoted above, *The Times Literary Supplement* suggested that the Earl of Avon (as Sir Anthony Eden has since become) should send his seconds to me for a duel or at least sue me.[23] The secret leaked out in the course of 1966 to 1970 though it is appropriate to note that in what seemed a sensational book at the time, *Les Secrets de Suez* by Serge and Merry Bromberger, published in 1957, General Challe's visit to England was accurately described, even down to the morsel of conversation which Challe records with Eden: 'Good idea'.[24]

It must remain always a matter of mystery why it should be this very contorted scheme which should have been the one among the many ideas discussed by the British and French that should ultimately have been employed. When it came to the point, it was not only very cumbersome and complicated but it was a piece of theatre so unusual that it was as if the scenery took over, at a certain point, from the players; for in the course of the inevitable crisis which followed the British government stuck firmly to the scenario and, though it had indeed been invented as a pretext for action, they treated it with all seriousness. Some ministers, though fully in the secret of what had transpired, argued that once the combatants had indeed been separated, and the fighting between Israel and Egypt had indeed ceased then the Anglo-French forces should abstain from further action themselves.[25] Thus in this last great Anglo-French enterprise, Albion showed herself in the French mind as now too feeble to be even perfidious. Challe in his book comments on this 'strange destiny of this old, solid people, of this old commercial people which hoped by yielding, to keep their markets . . .'[26] and adds how hypocritical it seemed even to him that the main preoccupation of Sir Anthony Eden was to avoid seeming to be the aggressor: 'the all-pervading hypocrisy made us prepare more or less murky pretexts'. Hypocritical and indecisive: unattractive adjectives to be applied to our country, regardless of our views of the policy concerned. But they are adjectives which are hard to avoid on this occasion.

The general morals of the Suez crisis have been discussed endlessly in a large bibliography of books and articles. For Anglo-French relations, the consequences were clear. In the event (in particular in the manner in which ultimately Eden insisted on the end of the operation) Britain showed herself an unreliable ally for the French, partly because of her desire to seem virtuous, partly because of her weak international currency, partly because of her sensitivity to American feelings. The French drew the inevitable conclusions, and in the course of the next decade ventured on the policy of *France seule*, which still, so far as allies are concerned, survived, even under Pompidou. It is ironic that the architect of this disaster should have been so great a francophile as Eden, a man who when breaking with one of his best friends and protégés, Anthony Nutting, should have dropped easily into French: '*Tout casse sauf l'amitié*'.[27] But Eden never met Nutting again, and Britain never met France again in quite the same way either – despite the Order of the Bath sent by the Queen to General Beaufre.

Notes

1 See Anthony Nutting, *No End of a Lesson* (London, 1967), p. 67.
2 Quoted in Hugh Thomas, *The Suez Affair* (London, Penguin, 1970), p. 65.
3 Nutting, *No End of a Lesson*, p. 89.
4 This had been founded in 1955 as a basically anti-Russian alliance. In 1956 it included Iraq, Turkey, Iran, Pakistan and Britain, but not Jordan and not Egypt.
5 Shimon Peres, *David's Sling* (London, 1970), p. 104.
6 Peres, *David's Sling*, p. 40.
7 Jacob Tsur, *Prélude à Suez* (Paris, 1968), p. 32.
8 Eisenhower, *Waging Peace* (London 1966), p. 29.

9 Thomas, *The Suez Affair*, p. 103.
10 Murphy letter to Thomas, 17 August 1967, referred to in Thomas, *The Suez Affair*, p. 56, n. 12.
11 Maurice Challe, *Notre révolte* (Paris, 1969), p. 27.
12 General Sir Hugh Stockwell, *Sunday Telegraph*, 30 October, 6 November and 13 November 1966; Paul Ely, *Mémoires*, II, *Suez ... le 13 mai* (Paris, 1969) and André Beaufre, *L'expédition de Suez* (Paris 1967, English ed. London, 1969).
13 Beaufre, *L'expédition de Suez*, p. 34.
14 Beaufre, *L'expédition de Suez*, p. 35.
15 Ely, *Mémoires*, pp. 82, 83–4.
16 Moshe Dayan, *Diary of the Sinai campaign* (London, Weidenfeld and Nicolson), 1966, p. 20. Peres, *David's Sling*, p. 189.
17 Heini Azeau, *La piège de Suez*, Paris 1964, 124.
18 Challe, *Notre Révolte*, p. 25.
19 Nutting, *No End of a Lesson*, pp. 74–8; Ely, *Mémoires*, p. 108; Challe, *Notre Révolte*, p. 27.
20 Challe, *Notre Révolte*, pp. 27–8.
21 Nutting to the author, see Thomas, *The Suez Affair*, p. 111.
22 Ely, *Mémoires*, p. 137.
23 *Times Literary Supplement*.
24 Serge and Merry Bromberger, *Secrets de Suez* (Paris, 1957), p. 13.
25 See Thomas, *The Suez Affair*, pp. 161–2.
26 Challe, *Notre Révolte* p. 27.
27 Nutting, *No End of a Lesson*, p. 123.

Bibliography

Apart from the despatch by General Sir Charles Keightley (*Operations in Egypt*; a supplement to the *London Gazette*, 10 September 1957), there are no government papers generally available though, as has been seen, possibly the British papers will yield few secrets; they are bound to have some however and the French and Israeli documents may be more complete. US papers will become available in a few years: Dulles's are already; but it is doubtful whether the State Department papers at least will throw much new light on what has already become known.

As for memoirs, there are now, on the English side: Eden's (first) volume of memoirs *Full Circle* (London, Cassell, 1960), naturally of great interest, but an apologia and purely official and diplomatic. There is nothing about the Israeli friendship, but no denial of it. The only other cabinet minister of that time who has yet written a memoir is the Earl of Kilmuir, with his *Political Adventure* (London, Weidenfeld & Nicolson, 1964). Anthony Nutting's *No End of a Lesson* (London, Constable, 1967) is a study of great interest. Harold Macmillan's account of this crisis is awaited with keen interest. Mr Selwyn Lloyd's review of the first edition of my book *The Suez Affair* (London, 1967) (*Sunday Telegraph*, 30 April 1967) is of interest. Kirkpatrick wrote his memoirs, *Inner Circle* (London, Macmillan, 1959), but decided not to discuss Suez. Two British executants of policy have contributed some memories: Sir William Hayter, the ambassador in Moscow, in Chapter 2 of his *The Kremlin and the Embassy* (London, Hodder, 1966), and General Sir Hugh Stockwell has written an honest account from his point of view in the *Sunday Telegraph*, 30 October, 6 November and 13 November 1966. The relations between government and press during the Suez crisis are discussed in Harman Grisewood's *One Thing at a Time* (London, Hutchinson, 1968).

On the French side, Pineau, Mollet and Bourgès Maunoury have given some sort of account to Terence Robertson (see below) and Pineau also spoke to Peter Calvocoressi on the BBC (19 July 1966). Pineau wrote an article about his part in the affair in *Le Monde* (4 November 1966) and again contributed some interesting views in the *Daily Telegraph*, 6 June 1967. General Beaufre wrote first an article in *Le Figaro* (8 November 1966) and then a brilliant military study, *L'Expédition de Suez* (Paris, Grasset, 1967). There is, as this essay suggests, a short but revealing passage about Suez in the memoirs of General Maurice Challe (*Notre Révolte*, Paris, Presses de la Cité, 1968) and a long and even more interesting one in Volume II of the memoirs of General Paul Ely, *Mémoires*, II, *Suez . . . le 13 mai* (Paris, Pion, 1969).

The Israelis are represented by General Moshe Dayan with *Diary of the Sinai Campaign* (London, Weidenfeld & Nicolson, 1966), and *David's Sling* by Shimon Peres (London, Weidenfeld & Nicolson, 1970). The diaries of Tsur (*Prélude à Suez*, Paris, Presses de la Cité, 1968) are of interest. Iraqi policy is illuminated by Waldemar Gallman, *Iraq under General Nuri: my recollections of Nuri al-Said* (Baltimore, 1964).

The U S have now Eisenhower's second volume of memoirs, *Waging Peace* (London, Heinemann, 1966), of considerable interest (the appendices especially), and Robert Murphy's *Diplomat Among Warriors* (London, Collins, 1964). Memoirs by Emmett Hughes (*Ordeal of Power*, London, 1963) and Sherman Adams (*First Hand Report*, London, 1963) have some relevant passages. See also the article by W. Aldrich, the then U S ambassador, in *Foreign Affairs*, April 1967, and Cary Joynt, *John Foster Dulles and the Suez Crisis*, which makes use of the Dulles papers, in Gerald N. Greb (ed.), *Statesmen and State-craft of the Modern West: Essays in Honour of Dwight E. Lee and H. Donaldson Jordan* (Barre, Mass., 1967). For Egypt, Nasser has given occasionally interesting interviews (e.g. *Sunday Times*, 17 June, 24 June and 1 July 1962).

The most useful secondary books are: Henri Azeau, *La Piège de Suez* (Paris, Laffont, 1964), a brilliant book written from the French point of view, very suggestive but not always fair or accurate where the British are concerned; Michal Bar Zohar, *Suez: ultra-secret* (Paris, Fayard, 1965), is a somewhat sensationalised account of Franco-Israeli friendships though based on good evidence from the Israeli side. Terence Robertson, *Crisis* (London, Hutchinson, 1965), is a book of great interest but open to doubt as to the exact accuracy of some of the conversations. He is most reliable where Canadians are concerned. Herman Finer's *Dulles over Suez* (London, 1964) is a passionate attack on Dulles, with the accusation that Dulles acted out of fear of Russia and against Eisenhower, who is accused of panic. Leon David Epstein's *British Politics in the Suez Crisis* (London, 1964) is a scholarly treatment of internal party politics and public opinion. The various pieces of testimony by actors of the time to the B BC programmes in 1966 were brought together by the B BC in *Suez Ten Years After* edited by Anthony Moncrieff (BBC, 1967). My own *The Suez Affair* (Weidenfeld, 1967) has recently been re-issued in a revised form (Penguin, 1970).

On special subjects, there is A. J. Barker's excellent account of the military operations, *Suez: The Six Days War* (London, Faber, 1964), and Edgar O'Ballance's *The Sinai Campaign* (London, Faber, 1959), written from the Israeli viewpoint. There is also S. L. A. Marshall's *Sinai Victory* and Sholmo

Bauer's *The Weekend War*. A contrast is Erskine Childers' apologia for Egyptian nationalism, *The Road to Suez* (London, MacGibbon & Kee, 1960). Sir Anthony Eden emerges much the worse for wear from Randolph Churchill's *The Rise and Fall of Sir Anthony Eden* (London, MacGibbon & Kee, 1959), which has new material in it. (See also the debates in the House of Commons in December 1958 deriving from a serialisation of it.) Merry and Serge Bromberger gave a famous account in *Les Secrets de Suez* (Paris, Editions des 4 fils Aymon, 1957), deriving from the French Ministry of Defence for whom it is an apologia; much of it is true, even the conversation. Paul Johnson's *The Suez War* (London, MacGibbon & Kee, 1957) is an exciting account of the background, though on the details events turned out to have been even more unusual than he thought. The two volumes of the *Survey of International Affairs* published by Chatham House (1955–6 and 1956–8) are as usual a useful general guide to both background and events. Patrick Seale's *The Struggle for Syria* (Oxford University Press, 1965) is most illuminating both for the general background and for Anglo-Iraqi activity against Syria. A recent general study is that by Kennett Love, *The Twice-Fought War* (New York, McGraw-Hill, 1969), a somewhat moralistic treatment though it is not always clear what moral is being drawn.

A novel, *No. 10* by William Clark, Eden's press officer, though not a *roman à clef*, provides some keys.

Addendum

Since this chapter was written, Mr Harold Macmillan has published a volume of memoirs which deals with the Suez crisis. It is melancholy to have to add that their contribution is perfunctory to an understanding of the matters discussed here.

12 Security and Settlement in the Mediterranean since 1914

Ann Williams

On the eve of the First World War, France and Britain stood as the major imperial powers, their influence felt in the Far East, on the African continent and in the Mediterranean. In the last area British and French imperial roles were made more complex by the closeness of Europe with its own problems of alliance and strategy. For France, indeed, the Mediterranean was one of its frontiers. Britain, and in particular France, had traditional interests which were expanded by nineteenth-century ambitions. Their pre-eminence in the area in its turn made them the obvious choice for mandatory guardians when the system was established in 1920. In the Second World War their relations with one another and with the countries of the area again played an important part in international events. Finally, the trauma of the end of the empire left both powers uncertain of their role in the Mediterranean at a time when economic backwardness and political instability still exposed it to outside interference.

In this essay three major aspects of French contact with Britain and with the Mediterranean countries will be examined. The First World War which brought about the final collapse of the Ottoman Empire, laying its provinces open to the surgery of the European peace makers, and the establishment of French and British Mandates, faced the two powers with similar problems which they met in different ways. This provides the only direct comparison of their aims and achievements in the Mediterranean sphere, for France's considerable settlement in North Africa cannot be paralleled in British experience. Britain was content to maintain only the amount of control needed to preserve strategic interests in the area. Secondly the diplomatic negotiations leading up to the Second World War brought France and Britain together to guard their complementary interests in the Mediterranean, while the collapse of France placed a heavy burden of territorial commitment on Britain which in its turn led to hostility between the Allies. Thirdly, Britain and France in the post-imperial period have found themselves in the difficult position of being neither friends nor complete strangers in the Mediterranean and in their efforts to cope with the new situation have joined international groupings and offered programmes of military, economic and technological aid.

Imperial involvement before World War II

French interests in the Mediterranean stretched back to the middle ages.[1] The demands of European aggrandisement had masked the fact that she had a wide Mediterranean-facing shore with economic and cultural tentacles reaching out to the Levant. These increased their hold in the nineteenth century. Napoleon's expedition brought to Egypt a non-Christian message, acceptable to the Muslims, and an interest in French culture and education which strengthened when the dual control of France and England, over the shaky regime of the country, was established in 1876.[2] Her protection of Catholicism was reinforced by the work of the religious orders, particularly the Jesuits. The University of St Joseph in Beirut was founded in 1875, and its Catholic printing press was important in disseminating ideas. The French language became the common intellectual currency from Istanbul to Cairo. France was also investing extensively in enterprises within the Ottoman Empire, for example road and rail communications in Syria, and taking a controlling share in the Ottoman Bank. It was estimated that in 1914, France held 60 per cent of the Ottoman Empire's national debt compared with the 21 per cent held by Germany and 14 per cent by Britain.[3]

In British policy the Mediterranean was from the first part of a larger scheme of imperial defence and the protection of the route to India.[4] Napoleon's plans which began with the invasion of Egypt in 1798 were to extend French control eastwards to threaten the whole of England's eastern trade. The latter part of the scheme was never carried out, but it proved to Britain that she had to safeguard her possessions. Beyond the Mediterranean, the treaties with the Arabian rulers and occupation of Aden in 1839 were part of the policy. Within the Mediterranean, the occupation of Malta in 1800 and the creation of an important naval base there and the increasing interest in Egypt provided the support for her maritime interests. Cyprus was acquired in 1878 to counter Russian ambitions.

The international importance of the Mediterranean also increased in the nineteenth century. The Ottoman Empire which had stretched half way round the Mediterranean was falling apart and the diplomatic problems of the 'eastern question' absorbed the powers of Europe; in particular Russian ambitions in the Mediterranean led to co-operation between France and Britain to preserve the Sultan's rule. They united in their opposition to Muhammed Ali's territorial ambitions. Later in the century they co-operated over the project to build the Suez Canal. The Canal was opened in 1869, and seven years later the two powers were forced to take joint control of the country to prevent the collapse of the Egyptian economy, and to keep the Canal open. There was no enthusiasm for direct colonial control by either power in Egypt because of the poverty of the country.

This early co-operation in the area was strained by the scramble for Africa. The Fashoda incident in 1898 marked the lowest point in their relations. But Britain's African interests lay mainly south of the Sahara (apart from her strategic concern with Egypt), while France, on the other hand, built up an extensive commitment in North Africa for reasons of prestige and strategy.[5] The invasion of Algeria in 1830 led to a hard-fought struggle for its acquisition, and the close assimilation of the country to France under the aegis of the Ministry of the Interior. Protectorates were acquired over Tunisia in 1881 and over Morocco in 1912.

By the end of the century there was the quarrel over France's position in her North African territories, and she herself, now that she had her feet on two shores of the Mediterranean, was quite happy to relinquish the unenviable control of Egypt to the British. The entente embodied the agreement.[6]

The campaigns and diplomacy of the First World War

consolidated the position of France and Britain in the Middle East, and also brought them into closer contact with one another in an area where each had vital interests to maintain. Militarily, the region had become important when the Allies found that they could no longer hope for the neutrality of the Ottoman Empire and declared war on her.The alliance meant a reversal of British and French nineteenth-century policy towards Russia's Mediterranean ambitions which threatened to alter the balance of power in the area.

Britain, anxious for the safety of the route to India, for the oil they hoped would flow from the oilfields of Southern Persia, and for the loyalty of the Muslim population of India, declared a protectorate over Egypt and used the country as a military base. She bore the brunt of the war in this area, and in the first two years it was a disheartening experience. The failure of the Gallipoli campaign meant that the Ottoman Empire could not be defeated quickly. German officers organised the Turkish army to fight on two fronts, in Mesopotamia and the Levantine provinces where the British were driven back to the Suez Canal. Fortunes were not reversed until the appointment of General Allenby as commander-in-chief of the Egyptian expeditionary force in June 1917. His success in winning back Palestine and Syria meant that British troops were in possession of all the areas in which France was interested at the time the fighting stopped. France felt that she must have some territorial footing in the eastern Mediterranean to balance British control of both sides of the Canal. The signing of the armistice with the Turks at Mudros brought feelings of tension into the open, and Lloyd George wrote to Clemenceau expressing the emotional involvement felt by the British people in this front and his reluctance to hand over to the French.[7] The campaigns of the war and the way in which the Turkish army had threatened Egypt and the Canal had also made a deep imprint on the mind of the British. They were sure they must have Palestine for the greater protection of their interests.

Such was the background to the diplomacy of the war years. The Allies were confident of their ultimate success, and that the Ottoman Empire would be theirs to dismember. In the early part of the war, Russia's desire for an outlet for her Black Sea fleet and for the city of Constantinople itself, drove Poincaré and Grey into the amity of common concern.[8] It was apparent even at this stage, however, that France wanted Syria, a greater Syria that included Palestine and Cilicia.[9] She felt this would counterbalance Britain's increased control of Egypt. As the war progressed, Britain's anxiety for practical help in the area led her to support the Arabs, particularly the Amir Hussein, the Sharif of Mecca, to whom certain promises were made.[10] Britain recognised Arab independence and the Arab claim to much of Syria; the largely Christian areas west of Damascus, Homs, Hama and Aleppo were excluded from the agreement, a clause which was to cause great difficulty later on because no mention was made of Palestine.

Negotiations were going on at the same time between Britain and France on the future of the Arab provinces. Britain wanted a clear statement of what France's demands were. In November 1915 Sir Mark Sykes met M. Georges Picot to sort out spheres of influence. Sir Mark had almost certainly seen the Hussein–MacMahon correspondence in Cairo, but appeared not to have considered it binding, because the Sykes–Picot agreement differed from it in several respects.[11] France was to have an area from Damascus to Mosul. Great Britain was to administer the area from Gaza to Kirkuk, regions where they could establish 'such direct or indirect administration or control as they desire and as they may think fit to arrange with the Arab State, or Confederation of Arab States'. A 'brown' area of the map, Palestine was to be administered internationally, 'the form of which is to be decided upon after consultation with Russia, and subsequently with the other Allies, and the representative of the Shereef of Mecca'. The confusion of the two documents' ambiguities did not become apparent until the influence of Jewish immigrants in the nineteen twenties.

As the war progressed more promises were made. In November 1917 the British government published the Balfour Declaration, and committed themselves to allow the Jews to set up a national home in Palestine. The promise exacted was a triumph for the Zionist movement which had arisen out of the pogroms of Russia and Eastern Europe in the nineteenth century. The influence of Theodore Herzl and his book *The Jewish State* had brought an international following for the Zionists and their ideas had been received with sympathy in Britain from the first. In 1902 Joseph Chamberlain suggested that the Zionists should accept land for the Jewish Settlement in the East African Protectorate as an alternative to Palestine, an offer which was unacceptable to the Jews because of the importance they attached to the City of David, Jerusalem.[12] The second stage of British political involvement with Zionism came as a result of Chaim Weizmann's persuasive arguments for the Palestine home which were brought to the attention of the British Cabinet.[13] The Bolshevik revolution removed Russia as a threat in the Mediterranean but the entry of the United States into the war added another complication to international diplomacy. President Wilson's Fourteen Points led the Arabs to hope for recognition of their independence and to resent the imposition of another outside government over there. However, the Mediterranean had been a 'sideshow' in the war, and so it was at the Peace Conference. Clemenceau had promised Mosul and Palestine to Lloyd George before the conference opened and the guarantee was kept.[14] But the two remaining problems, the conclusion of a peace treaty with Turkey and the question of Arab independence, led to increasing tension between France and Britain.

In the first case the Allies could not agree about the terms to be offered to Turkey; the problems of winding up the vast Ottoman Empire together with the question of international access to the Straits prolonged the haggling. The situation was made more difficult by civil war within Turkey; the Turkish nationalist movement under the army officer Mustafa Kemal provided a focus for discontent against the corrupt regime which it was felt was selling out Turkish interests. Greece took the opportunity to push her claims to Smyrna and Thrace by force, and traditional British sympathy with Greek enterprises led Lloyd George to make an agreement with Venizelos to support Greece in her attack on Smyrna. So far the British and the French were together; a combined naval force with American support protected the landing. They were still together when the Sultan agreed to the Treaty of Sèvres in May 1920.[15] The harsh terms of the treaty provoked the Turkish nationalists to greater efforts, and France, seeing the straws in the wind, made terms with them in

October 1920 and agreed to evacuate Cilicia.[16] Britain clung to her romantic loyalty to the Greeks, but eventually accepted the new regime and joined the Allies in concluding the Treaty of Lausanne in 1923.[17]

On the second question of the Arab provinces the peace makers felt that they still needed paternal guidance and might well come within the new system of Mandatory administration. The San Remo conference met in 1920 to continue discussions on the settlement of the Arab problem and to apportion the Mandates. 'Certain communities formerly belonging to the Turkish Empire' were said to have 'reached a stage of development where their existence as independent nations could be provisionally recognised subject to the rendering of administrative advice and assistance by a Mandatory until such time as they are able to stand alone'. A Permanent Mandates Commission was set up consisting of independent experts, to whom the Mandatory was to report, and who in its turn could report to the Council of the League of Nations. The day-to-day administration of the areas was not dictated from above, and the Mandatory powers were given a free hand in interpreting the vague clauses of their concession.

France was given Mandatory control over Syria and Lebanon; Britain was given Palestine.[18] It might have been supposed that the common problems of working out this new mandatory system might have led to fruitful discussion between the two powers, but the suspicions which had arisen in peacemaking were too strong to allow such co-operation, or even in most cases to allow either power to take advantage of observed practice. The political problems, although they had a common base of growing nationalism, were different in each area. Britain had complicated her administration from the start by the acceptance of a national home for the Jews in Palestine, and it was increasing hostility between Arab and Jew which bedevilled her control of Palestine and led to the near anarchy of the later thirties. There had been outbursts of violence between the two countries before the Mandate was established, but in September 1928 a serious incident took place at the Wailing Wall in Jerusalem, in the Temple area that is sacred to both Jews and Arabs. In the following year, there were further clashes, and 133 Jews and

116 Arabs were killed. Demands of both sides for a clear statement of British policy in Palestine were not met either by the Shaw Report of 1930 or by the open letter from the prime minister Ramsay MacDonald to Dr Weizmann in February 1931. France took on a region in part of which autonomy had already been enjoyed; Lebanon had been granted self-government within the Ottoman Empire in 1860, and its trading contacts and the investment of foreign capital had led to the development of a more sophisticated economy than elsewhere in the Middle East.

The balance of religious groups, Christians and Muslims, was made more precarious by the redrawing of frontiers between Lebanon and Syria, but France could rely on support from the Christians. In Syria Arab nationalism had its strongest roots, and France's first task was to regain Damascus from the Amir Feisal. The Syrians never forgave the French for the damage they did to the Arab cause.[19] The area took some years to bring under control, and the presence of French armies did not improve relationships with the native population.

France and Britain approached their administrative problems differently. The need to subdue their provinces led the French to employ a succession of generals, Gouraud, Weygand and Sarrail. Their harshly military methods contrasted notably with the diplomacy of Lord Plumer's administration in Palestine.[20] He cut down the security forces and built a police force to replace them, although this was done against the advice of the Mandates Commission. The French were determined to divide and rule their Mandates. Greater Lebanon, established in August 1920, was put under a French official, and an advisory council, representative of the Lebanese, but nominated by the high commissioner. Syria was declared a state with a representative council in December 1924, and here again strict supervision was exercised by the French. The area of Latakia, populated by a Muslim minority group, the Alawis, was ruled directly by the French administration.

Robert de Caix, at a meeting of the Permanent Mandates Commission had spoken of the provisional nature of the system, maintaining 'consequently, the Mandate system calls for a complete native organisation, but side by side with it an organisation of a tutelary nature, possessing the necessary authority to ensure the good government and progress of the country'.[21] This 'tutelary' institution was developed into a highly organised bureaucracy. The high commissioner, appointed by and responsible to the Ministry of Foreign Affairs in Paris, was flanked by a number of departments within the mandated territories, and by a network of local officials in the districts, the *Services Spéciaux*, who were widely disliked and accused of too much interference in local affairs.[22]

If the Mandatory powers learnt little from one another, the nationalists were quick to profit from other people's experience. The granting of the Anglo-Iraqi Treaty in October 1922 was the signal for similar demands in the French territories. The French were prepared to negotiate with the Syrians, but the two parties could not come to an agreement, and the high commissioner dissolved the constituent assembly and imposed his own constitution. In June 1936 Léon Blum's Popular Front government came to power, and for the first (and last) time initiative for reform came from Paris. Twenty-five year treaties were negotiated with both Syria and Lebanon, promising the independence of the countries after a three-year probationary period. The Popular Front government fell before the treaties were signed and the local administration returned to repressive measures, fearing that the example of Palestine might spread to Syria and Lebanon. The increasingly grave international situation was also used as an argument for retaining a strong hold over the Mandates. Nationalist movements were disunited in Syria and Lebanon in the inter-war years; small groups gathered round individual personalities rather than uniting on a common programme, and the weak French governments of the period were content to let matters drift when there was no open hostility.

Britain's position in the Middle East on the eve of the Second World War was an equally precarious one. The situation in Palestine after 1936 became almost unmanageable for the British authorities. Hitler's persecution of the Jews in Germany ended all hope of setting limits to Jewish immigration into Palestine. In 1936 the Arabs tried to organise a general strike in protest. It was not successful but it was a signal for Arab revolt, and although the British forces in Palestine were increased threefold to nearly 30,000 men they

324 *Troubled Neighbours*

could not suppress the guerrillas. Lord Peel was sent out with a commission in November 1937 to report on the situation. His recommendation was a new partition. 'Partition seems to offer at least a chance of ultimate peace. We can see none in any other plan.'[23] The solution appealed to no one, Permanent Mandates Commission, Arabs or Jews. Discussion continued until the outbreak of war when the Jews declared their loyalty to Britain and the Arabs opted for neutrality.

Palestinian troubles and the illustration they gave of British vulnerability affected the British position in Egypt as well. There was strong nationalist opposition to Britain's presence and in 1936 a treaty was signed announcing the end of British military occupation, but because the Suez Canal was vital as a means of communication, Britain was authorised 'to station forces in Egyptian territory in the vicinity of the Canal in the zone specified with a view to ensuring in co-operation with Egyptian forces the defence of the Canal'.[24] The only factor which saved Britain's position in Egypt was the common fear of Italian aggression.[25]

Co-operation followed by Hostility in World War II

The rise of fascist Italy also had its effect in bringing about closer co-operation between Britain and France in their Mediterranean policies. In reaction to Mussolini's invasion of Abyssinia, a member of the League of Nations in 1936, Britain was prepared to impose economic sanctions. France was less sure; the question for her was connected with the security of her own territorial frontiers (Germany re-militarised the Rhineland in March 1936), and she had been attempting to keep peace with Italy to remove anxiety in this quarter.

Britain and France were uncertain about Italy's ambitions and how far she was prepared to maintain a friendly attitude towards them in spite of her alliance with Germany. Anxiety was increased by German and Italian recognition of Franco's regime in Spain. In January 1937 an Anglo-Italian Joint Declaration (often referred to as the Gentleman's Agreement) was signed, in which their common interests in the Mediterranean were stressed and both agreed on their determination to maintain the political status quo in the area. The agreement, however, did not remove tension. The attacking of neutral shipping in Spanish waters in the Civil War and the torpedo attacks on merchant ships on their way to Spain produced an inflammable situation, especially as the submarine activity was presumed to be Italian. The British and French immediately co-operated at a conference at Nyon on 10 September 1937 to protect their vessels with a joint naval and air cover. (Italy refused to attend and it seemed to Britain and France that their suspicion of her had been justified.)

But it was clear to both Britain and France, particularly after the Rome–Berlin axis was announced in November 1936, that Italy was still an uncertain quantity and that they must share the responsibility of protecting their interests in the Mediterranean. By the late thirties oil production in the Middle East was increasing in importance.[26] For both economic and strategic reasons it was necessary to keep the seaway open. France had no naval base east of Bizerta. At the beginning of January 1939 when the new base at Mers-el-Kebir was begun, the French planned to base their Mediterranean strategy on the triangle Toulouse, Bizerta, Mers-el-Kebir. (The last was necessary because the new threat from Franco's revolution in Spain left this flank uncovered.) Britain had a line Gibraltar, Malta, Alexandria, Cyprus and Palestine, although in the last three they were by no means a welcome occupying force.[27]

As events moved towards war France and Britain continued this co-operation. It seemed clear that the Mediterranean and North Africa (the Italians would not attempt a crossing of the Alps) would be important if Italy could not be persuaded to remain neutral. At the other end of the Mediterranean it was hoped that Turkey would remain friendly and unengaged. (The Italian invasion of Albania persuaded her to sign a tripartite treaty with France and Britain in September 1939.) As a contingency plan it was agreed to divide the Mediterranean into eastern and western spheres divided by the Straits of Messina, the British taking care of the former, including Malta, and the French the latter, including Tripoli.[28] In the event, the collapse of France put the whole onus on Britain. Vichy governments were set up in North Africa and in the Levantine provinces. The immediate problem was the French fleet, possession of which by the Germans would completely thwart Britain's attempts to keep open the Mediterranean. Britain decided with reluctance that the only course was to scuttle the French ships and this was carried out in July 1940.[29]

Politically the British had difficulty in deciding what really constituted the French government. Pétain's regime commanded little support, and Britain hoped that the French colonies would continue to fight against the Germans, or at least maintain neutrality. The establishment of General de Gaulle's Free French movement did not immediately provide a solution for the British. In June 1940 he was given limited recognition 'as the leader of all Free Frenchmen, wherever they may be, who rally to him in support of the Allied cause,' not as the head of government.[30] In the French mandated territories this caused great ill-feeling. Britain and the Free French invaded the area in order to prevent the German use of Syrian air bases in June 1941. Britain assured General de Gaulle in an exchange of letters that:

> We have no desire to encroach in any way upon the position of France. Both Free France and Great Britain are pledged to the independence of Syria and Lebanon. When this essential step has been taken, and without prejudice to it, we freely admit that France should have the predominant position in Syria and Lebanon over any other European power.[31]

These words were rendered meaningless however by the high-handed actions of the British political mission under Sir Edward Spears.[32] His support of the Arabs and his anti-French attitude had a permanent effect on General de Gaulle's opinion of the British.[33]

Militarily North Africa was important in two phases of the Second World War. The initial Italian offensive in 1940 against Egypt was not conclusive, and in the spring of 1941 Rommel's Deutsche Afrika Korps came to their aid. The Germans had also invaded Greece and Yugoslavia in 1941. The lowest ebb of British fortunes in the Mediterranean was reached in 1942 when Malta lay under siege and Tobruk had fallen. In November 1941 an Allied force, British and American, invaded North Africa (General de Gaulle was not informed until the landings had taken place). The Allied conquest of North Africa gave a base for the counter offensive against the fascists in the invasion of Italy. In the course of the war Britain had changed her role in the Mediterranean; from relying on sea power to control her interests she had become extensively involved on land. In the Arab lands her presence was tolerated during the war, although the restrictions imposed by the Middle East Supply Centre[34] established by the British caused discontent among the population.

The End of Empire

The end of the war saw France and Britain in a changed world in the Mediterranean as elsewhere. France had been more noticeably hit by the fortunes of war, by her collapse and by her obvious decline in prestige. Britain's role had also changed although this became apparent more slowly. On the other side of the coin, the Arab countries of the Middle East and North Africa had gained confidence as they saw their old masters' discomfort and, encouraged by the terms of the Atlantic Charter and the newly founded United Nations Organisation, became more vociferous in their demands for independence. It was at first most evident in the Mandated territories. Even before the war ended the French authorities had been forced to allow local governments to be established in both Syria and Lebanon. In January 1946, after a United Nations debate on the French Mandates, British and French troops were asked to leave the area and independence was granted. In Syria it meant an increasing Arabisation of the country and rejection of French education, but in Lebanon the cultural ties were stronger and remained in evidence after the abolition of the Mandate. France kept in mind the actions of the British in causing her embarrassment in the area.

In the British Mediterranean Mandate, Palestine, the unwritten truce of the war years was quickly broken. The situation had been exacerbated by the increased persecution of the Jews in Hitler's Germany. In May 1942 David Ben Gurion, the new militant leader of the Zionist movement, had presided over a Zionist conference at the Biltmore Hotel in New York. The Biltmore Program rejected British rule and demanded Palestine as a Jewish State, 'a Jewish

Commonwealth integrated in the structure of the new democratic world'.[35] Increased violence by the Stern Group in Palestine, from the murder of Lord Moyne in November 1944 to the blowing up of the King David Hotel which housed the British administration in July 1946, did not speed up the withdrawal of Britain. Britain asked the United States for help in settling the problem and finally in April 1947 put the matter before the United Nations. A special committee, the United Nations Special Commission on Palestine (UNSCOP), was established to report on the situation. Their recommendations were that the area should be divided into a Jewish and an Arab State. On 29 November 1947 the resolution was adopted by the General Assembly of the United Nations.[36] The British Mandate was to end 'as soon as possible but in any case not later than August 1948' and troops were to be withdrawn gradually.

Even before the evacuation began violence had broken out between Arab and Jew. The Arabs able to draw on the trained soldiers of the Arab Legion looked more likely victors, but the Jews took over positions left by the British and were able to put the Arabs on the defensive. In May 1948 Ben Gurion announced the new State of Israel which was recognised by the United States and the European powers, and a year later became a member of the United Nations. When the ceasefire was signed between Arab and Israeli in February 1949, Jerusalem was a divided city, the Israeli-Syrian border was not firmly delineated and the large number of Arab refugees in the Gaza strip were a perpetual reminder of Arab humiliation. The Arabs would not, and still do not, recognise the Jewish state. Britain had come out of the affair badly; her muddled actions and apparently partisan behaviour in the United Nations had lost her the respect of both Arab and Jew.

In Egypt her reputation was not much better. The Egyptians had remained neutral during the war, but there was a strong current of pro-German feeling, intensified by the high-handed actions of Lord Killearn in threatening the king and the politicians. The Egyptian nationalist movement increased in strength in the closing years of the war and linked itself for the first time with the general aspirations of the Arab nationalists. When the Arab League was founded in

1945 it had its headquarters in Cairo and its secretary-general was an Egyptian, Abdel Rahman Azzam. The debate over the British bases was revived in the postwar years. The Egyptians hoped that the British labour government in 1945 would prove more tractable than its predecessors, but there was little room even for Ernest Bevin to manoeuvre.[37] On both the questions of retaining control of the Canal Zone and of the Sudan, no agreement could be reached, and by the early fifties Britain had added the argument of international obligations to her previous justifications for staying in Egypt. In 1950 Herbert Morrison said in a Commons debate: 'The problem of the presence of British troops in Egypt is not now a purely Anglo-Egyptian problem. We are a Power bearing responsibilities in the Middle East on behalf of the rest of the Commonwealth and the Western Allies as a whole.' The Egyptians renounced the 1936 treaty unilaterally, an act which the British government denied its right to do. There seemed to be no solution to the problem.

In the postwar Mediterranean France, having withdrawn from the Levant, remained preoccupied with the problems of her own North African empire, thus leaving Britain alone in the area. This drew upon the latter the whole barrage of nationalist feeling from the Arabs to the Cypriots in the fifties and even loyal Malta in the same period. This area was still one of importance to her even after the loss of India in 1947, for the route was now important for the preservation of Commonwealth links in both directions and for the passage of oil tankers. The war had increased the demand for Middle Eastern oil, and in the postwar years this demand increased still further when it was important for Europe to avoid the dollar demanding supplies of America. In 1948 the Middle East was producing one eighth of the world's total production, by 1960 a quarter, for Iraqi and Iranian supplies were augmented by rich Kuwaiti supplies from 1949.[38] Although Britain was by no means the sole purchaser of Middle Eastern oil, its safety gave her an additional reason for wanting political stability within the area.

The Mediterranean region was also of importance in the 'cold war'. The emergence of the United States and the Soviet Union as the two super-powers in the postwar period led to a build up of international tension which was reflected in the treaties of co-operation drawn up among the Western powers. Britain's financial difficulties convinced the United States of the need to support her ally. The Truman doctrine, published on 12 March 1947, stressed the importance of propping up Turkey and Greece, two countries where Communism might take hold.[39] Two years later the North Atlantic Treaty Organisation was formed in which these two countries were included. It also saw the co-operation of Britain and France within the framework of an international organisation. Both contributed military resources and personnel to the enterprise. France did not join the countries who signed the Baghdad Pact in February 1955.[40] In fact it was her hostility to the arrangement that led her in the spring of 1956 to a period of rapprochement with Nasser.

But France's natural ally in the eastern Mediterranean was Israel. The opposition of the Arab bloc to her policy in North Africa made her anxious to have some local support in the area. Some French arms had found their way to help the Israelis in the 1948–9 Arab-Israeli war, but France was not anxious to declare herself too strongly for the new state, again because of antagonising Arab opinion. In 1953 however the ties became stronger. Israel was able to offer a cheaper process for producing heavy water for France's nuclear programme, in return for the delivery of arms and Ouragan fighters. These arrangements were made in spite of the May 1950 Tripartite Declaration signed by Britain, France and the United States to try to prevent the Arab-Israeli arms build-up.[41]

The immediate events leading up to the Suez affair, the rise of Nasser, and the co-operation of France and Britain in this enterprise, are dealt with in an earlier chapter. France, although annoyed at the quick collapse of her British ally, recovered quickly from the adventure for she had less to lose in the eastern Mediterranean and her primary concern was with North Africa. But for Britain the blow was a heavy one. Her prestige in the Arab world, which even as late as 1956 had been considerable, was shattered. Practically it reduced her power in Aden and the Gulf, and in the former the signs already were that her presence was not welcome. At home the policy of the new prime minister, Harold Macmillan, was one of closer links with the United States which led Britain further away from the French. The United States, worried at the activities of Britain and France in the Middle East, stepped in with the Eisenhower Doctrine in December 1956.[42] It declared that any Russian intervention in the area would be met by the United States with force if all else failed. Between 400 and 500 million dollars were to be given in aid. At the time of the 1958 'troubles' in Iraq, Jordan and Lebanon, it was Britain and the United States who stood by; France took no part.[43] In the sixties, as she was drawn further and further into the Vietnam conflict, the United States gave less aid to Egypt; Nasser's involvement in the Yemeni war made him less acceptable as a recipient of loans. But the United States continued to sell arms to Israel which in its turn led to the Russian support of the United Arab Republic in their arms race against the Israelis.

Meanwhile the French were occupied with the problems of North Africa. The slow growth of Arab nationalism in the area in the inter-war years, retarded largely because French educational and cultural policy had cut the Arabs off from their own civilisation, was speeded up by the promises of the Free French administration, and by expectations of the new policy of the United Nations. Anti-colonial views were being voiced on every continent and they were assimilated by nationalist groups everywhere, even if their strength sometimes remained unappreciated by colonial rulers. The nationalists were able to adapt their ideas more quickly because they had nothing to lose and they saw politics as a simple matter of independence. For the colonial powers, each case was an individual one with problems of its own and their concern with the difficulties of handing over administration to inexperienced men, or choosing an appropriate moment to do so, led them to hold on to power too long on occasion after occasion.

Britain, with a differing, and perhaps a greater range of problems within her empire, had evolved a system which allowed for a variety of relationship under the headship of the monarch. The idea of Commonwealth could be modified to meet the demands of the states gaining their independence, dominion, colony or protectorate.[44] The independence of India and the newly created Pakistan in 1947 had not altered the importance of the sea route in her policy.[45] But she could not parallel French colonial experience in the Mediterranean. In comparison with the idea of Commonwealth, the Union Française, even as re-interpreted by de Gaulle, was much less flexible. At the Brazzaville conference of 1944 France could envisage no existence for her colonies outside the French sphere, and as she made no provision for weakening or changing colonial ties each new demand met her unprepared. In 1945, Vietnam broke away, a year later Laos and in 1947 French Indochina, but war continued in the areas because of Communist infiltration. The demands for independence of the African colonies of both Britain and France, and the gradual granting of their requests form a background to the Mediterranean policy of the fifties.

In North Africa, the two Protectorates, Morocco and Tunisia, were the first to react against French rule. In the former, the nationalist Istiqlal (Independence) party had the support of the Sultan Mohammad V. His deposition by the French led to terrorism which forced a reversal of French policy. Complete independence was granted in 1956. In Tunisia the nationalist movement under Habib Bourguiba, again after violent exchanges between the French and the Arabs, obtained self-rule in July 1954. But France's close links with Algeria produced the most bitter struggle for independence. The physical closeness of the country – Algiers is only 400 miles from Marseilles – and its integration within France itself, led the French to feel that its loss would be much the same as the loss of Brittany or Provence.[46] The Statute of Algeria granted in 1947, which merely offered much the same concessions that had failed to get through when the Blum Government fell in 1937, was a milestone on the road to nationalist organisation. Violence did not break out until All Saints' Night 1954, but when it did it found successive French governments undecided about how to meet the situation, but only sure that it could not be met by complete independence for the Arabs, and that the solution lay in a compromise that would preserve the basic structure of the French colony. The issue, and the fierce debate it caused within France, summarised the feelings of uncertainty and hostility felt by many groups in society towards the loss of empire and France's changed international role. The army, in particular, humiliated in the war and by the loss of Indochina, joined the *colons* to set up their own government in Algiers.[47] The generals' demand that General de Gaulle should return to power showed that they had the ability to overthrow the Republic. In Britain no such political soul-searching took place at the loss of empire, even at the time of the renunciation of India. As has been suggested the high proportion of metropolitan settlers in the North African colonies (and the large colonial armies) could not be matched in any British colony. The *colons* formed a powerful lobby of opinion which met discontented groups at home who were completely disillusioned with democratic government, again feelings which were not matched in Britain.

Although the problem for the French remained as before, the changed regime made it seem that new solutions could be found. General de Gaulle showed a kind of 'style' that had been absent in the politicians of the Fourth Republic. This, together with his ability to keep people guessing about his proposed policy for Algeria, saw him through the first difficult period of establishing his rule. He obviously intended some form of emancipation from the first.[48] The year's pause before the referendum enabled him to get certain economic schemes under way. In the autumn of 1958 he proposed the Constantine Plan, a foretaste of French policy in the post-independence era of its relations with North Africa. It was stated that the scheme '. . . departed from the classic concept of technical assistance by bits and pieces, doled out according to political considerations, and substitutes for it an all-inclusive programme balancing the human and national development of Algeria'.[49] The programme provided for economic aid for two periods of five years which it was hoped would lead to the doubling of Algerian per capita income and a 20 per cent surplus of national income for investment resulting in economic 'take off'.

France's relations with independent North Africa have been summed up as combining 'a sense of *noblesse oblige* and *mission civilisatrice* rolled together'.[50] She signed agreements with all three countries after independence to provide teachers and technologists. Uncertain of its attitude to the Arab world and to the rest of Africa, North Africa's aim has been to finance projects for economic development; and, although the three countries have looked throughout the world for assistance and accepted it from as far afield as Sweden, the Eastern Bloc and Communist China, those new sources have not replaced France. Only in their attempts to retain military and political control have they been rejected. The French had to withdraw from Bizerta in 1961–3, and similarly in Morocco all forces were removed by 1963. Attempts to keep political control over the Sahara, which France wanted for atomic tests and because of natural gas deposits, led to disputes between France and Algeria in 1963.

General de Gaulle's overall policy was one of prestige for France, and for France alone, as a traditional nation state. He withdrew French troops from NATO in 1966 and refused to allow the Organisation to retain its bases in France in the following year. He announced in a press conference, in January 1968, that French 'strategy must be *tous azimuts*'. The Mediterranean was, of course, one point of the compass, and French policy took the form of rapprochements with the Arab states. In 1967 an arms agreement was announced with the UAR, and in the following year visits were received from the president of Iraq and the prime ministers of Syria and Lebanon. The simple anxiety to sell arms to help the French economy cannot be discounted as a motive behind French policy. But it was a policy of trying to exact as much influence as possible without any involvement, as was clear in the Arab-Israeli War of 1967. General de Gaulle attempted to act as a mediator, but continually stressed that the Western Powers should not concern themselves actively in the fight.

In the sixties Britain reviewed her policy in the Mediterranean as part of a larger scheme of retrenchment. The 1966 Defence White Paper announced withdrawal from Aden, but stressed Britain's international obligations in NATO and CENTO.[51] In 1967 the run down of the naval base at Malta (bases at Simonstown and in the West Indies were also reduced) caused anxiety in Malta and led to financial disagreements which still have not been settled. In 1968 renunciation of Britain's commitment east of Suez further reduced the importance of the Mediterranean for her in national terms. Like France, Britain stood aloof from any active part in the 1967 Arab-Israeli War. For both powers the closing of the Suez Canal since this war has reduced the value of the Mediterranean as a through seaway. France has looked to North Africa for her oil. Britain has developed larger tankers for the Cape route. Both powers are conscious of the need to reduce tension between the Arabs and Israelis and have joined four-power talks with the United States and the Soviet Union to try and reach a settlement (a hope as yet unfulfilled) in the area.

As the world moves into the seventies the Mediterranean, and particularly the eastern part of it, is still an area of international concern. What roles are left for Britain and France? Memories of British imperialism in the Middle East and Aden die hard. Libya was quick to break British contracts after her revolutionary coup in 1969. Britain, therefore, has to tread carefully. France, because of her complete defeat in the Second World War, and by the creation of the Fifth Republic, appeared to have made a complete break with the past and was therefore able to create a new relationship with her former colonies and with the Arab states of the Middle East. The anti-American attitude of General de Gaulle inspired admiration in the area. Although the Mediterranean policy of M. Pompidou is not yet clear, the selling of ships to Israel and the hasty picking up of the Libyan arms contract in 1969, suggest that France is still anxious to gain quick prestige on any occasion. At present there appears to be no role that France and Britain can, or want to play jointly in the Mediterranean, except in the limited theatre of the conference room where their past experiences of the area still make them welcome as participants.

Notes

1 René Ristelhueber, *Les traditions françaises au Liban* (Paris, 1918).
2 See A. H. Hourani, *Arabic Thought in the Liberal Age* (London, 1962), for a full discussion of the impact of French ideas on Arabic thought.

3 Z. Y. Herschlag, *Introduction to the Modern Economic History of the Middle East* (Leiden, 1964), pp. 89–90.

4 H. L. Hoskins, *British Routes to India* (London, 1928), discusses the importance of the eastern Mediterranean to Britain before and after the building of the Suez Canal.

5 J. Ganiage, *Les Origines du Protectorat français en Tunisie 1861–1881* (Paris, 1959), has an interesting analysis of French reasons for wanting North African colonies. He refutes the idea that economic incentives were important in the early stage.

6 J. J. Mathews, *Egypt and the Formation of the Anglo-French Entente, 1904* (an unpublished thesis, Philadelphia, 1939) provides an interesting analysis of the subject.

7 H. H. Cumming, *Franco-British Rivalry in the Post-War Near East* (London, 1938), p. 55.

8 *Documents on British Foreign Policy*, ser. I, vol. IV, p. 635.

9 J. C. Hurewitz, *Diplomacy in the Near and Middle East*. vol. II, 1914–56 (Princeton, 1956), pp. 9–10.

10 Correspondence between Sir Henry MacMahon and the Sharif of Mecca. *British Government Papers*. Cmd. 5957 (London, 1939).

11 *Documents on British Foreign Policy*, ser. I, vol. IV, pp. 245–7.

12 Leonard Stein, *The Balfour Declaration* (London, 1961), pp. 3–4.

13 *ibid.*, pp. 119–20.

14 *Documents on British Foreign Policy*, ser. I, vol. IV, pp. 340–1.

15 As well as losing the Arab provinces which the Turks had accepted, they also lost eastern Thrace, Gallipoli and Smyrna to the Greeks, with the probability that they would lose even more territory when the Kurdish and Armenian questions were settled. Britain agreed to French and Italian spheres of influence in Asia Minor with their exact nature unspecified.

16 Roderic H. Davidson, 'Turkish Diplomacy from Mudros to Lausanne', in Gordon A. Craig and Felix Gilbert (eds.), *The Diplomats, 1919–1939* (Atheneum and Princeton, N. York, 1963), Vol. II, p. 189.

17 The Straits Convention signed at the same time put this area under control of the League of Nations.

18 The term Syria as used at this period gives rise to confusion. Geographical Syria covered the whole area from Taurus to Sinai and from the Mediterranean to the Syrian desert. The creation of the Mandates divided it into two political regions, Palestine and Syria. The French divided the latter into smaller states of which political Syria was one. The term 'Syria' will be used in the last sense for the rest of the essay.

19 A. H. Hourani, *Syria and Lebanon; a political essay* (London, 1946), p. 176.

20 Christopher Sykes, *Crossroads to Israel* (London, 1965), p. 106.

21 Quoted in Hourani, *Syria and Lebanon; a political essay*, pp. 169–70.

22 S. A. Longrigg, *Syria and Lebanon under French Mandate* (London, 1958), p. 115, compares this system with 'the half-dozen British

officials, who from the winter of 1920–1 onwards formed in Baghdad the office of high commissioner in Iraq'.

23 *Palestine Royal Commission.* (The Peel Commission Report.) Cmd. 5479 (London, 1937).

24 *Documents in International Affairs, 1936,* Royal Institute for International Affairs (London, 1937), pp. 478–503.

25 Italy's nineteenth-century colonial ambitions had been to some extent satisfied by the acquisition of Libya and the Dodecanese in 1911–12, although Libya seemed a bleak economic prospect at the time. Although Italy had finished on the winning side in the First World War, Britain and France had trampled on a number of her aspirations in the peace treaties. Mussolini was determined to redress the balance.

26 See Elizabeth Monroe, *Britain's Moment in the Middle East, 1914–1956* (London, 1963), p. 95. In 1938, its oil production was less than one twentieth of the world's total, but its loss would have been significant.

27 Cyprus was leased from the Turks in 1878. Problems over the Turkish tribute money allegedly (but not satisfactorily) settled in 1927 together with the Greek community's desire for union with Greece, led to outbreaks of violence in 1931. In the late thirties fear of Italy kept Cyprus moderately content with British rule.

28 I. S. O. Playfair, *The Mediterranean and the Middle East,* 'History of the Second World War', vol. I (London, 1954), p. 28.

29 Playfair, *Mediterranean and the Middle East,* pp. 131–8.

30 Sir Llewellyn Woodward, *British Foreign Policy in the Second World War* (London, 1962), p. 77.

31 Hourani, *Syria and Lebanon: A Political Essay,* gives the text of the letters, pp. 371–2.

32 Hurewitz, *Diplomacy in the Near and Middle East,* vol. II, 1914–56, p. 232.

33 General Charles de Gaulle, *Mémoires de Guerre, vol. I, L'Appel, 1940–42* (Paris, 1954. English translation, Weidenfeld and Nicolson, 1971) traces the relation between the two countries in Syria and Lebanon in detail.

34 Monroe, *Britain's Moment in the Middle East,* p. 93. It was an attempt to regulate shipping and supplies for the area and to organise local production.

35 Hurewitz, *Diplomacy in the Near and Middle East,* vol. II, pp. 234–5.

36 Hurewitz, *Diplomacy in the Near and Midlde East,* vol. II, pp. 281–95.

37 Elizabeth Monroe, Mr Bevin's Arab Policy, in *St Antony's Papers; Middle Eastern Affairs,* 2 (London, 1961), pp. 9–48.

38 Elizabeth Monroe in *St Antony's Papers,* p. 95.

39 Hurewitz, *Diplomacy in the Near and Middle East,* vol. II, pp. 273–5.

40 Turkey and Iraq made a pact of mutual co-operation in February 1955 (the Baghdad Pact), which was joined later by Britain, Pakistan and Iran.

41 Hurewitz, *Diplomacy in the Near and Middle East*, vol. II, pp. 308–11.
42 Monroe in *St Antony's Papers*.
43 Pierre Rondot, 'July Days', in *Changing Patterns of the Middle East, 1919–1958* (London, 1961), pp. 13–22.
44 Nicholas Mansergh, *The Commonwealth Experience* (London, 1969), pp. 19–20, on the development of the idea of commonwealth.
45 See above, pp. 316–17.
46 The percentage of European settlers in the populations of the three North African countries was high; the figures for 1946–7 were 12·3 per cent in Algeria, 7·4 per cent in Tunisia and 3·4 per cent in Morocco. The European population of the British 'settled' colony of Kenya was only 1 per cent. The only comparable British figures would be for South Africa and Southern Rhodesia which opted out of the Commonwealth and have not yet coped with the problems of decolonisation.
47 For this paricular strand of opinion, see John S. Ambler, *The French Army in Politics, 1945–1962* (Columbus, Ohio, 1966), and Edgar Stephenson Furniss, *De Gaulle and the French Army; a crisis in civil–military relations* (New York, 1964).
48 *Le Monde*, 8–9 September, 1957.
49 A. S. Meyer in Carl Leon Brown (ed.), *State and Society in Independent North Africa* (Washington, 1966), p. 244.
50 William Zartman in Brown (ed.), *State and Society in Independent North Africa*, p. 61.
51 The newly reconstructed Baghdad Pact group; The Central Treaty Organisation.

Bibliography

There has been a spate of material on the Middle East and North Africa since the Second World War. Much of it is concerned with the growth of nationalism and with social and economic change in the area. Perhaps the most neglected aspect at the moment is the detailed study of colonial institutions and administration, particularly the French. The *Annuaire de l'Afrique du Nord*, published by the Centre de Recherches de l'Afrique musulmane at Aix-en-Provence since 1962, is valuable for its bibliography, for its comments on current events and for its articles on past history. Three bibliographical articles are worth consultation for the discussion of material up to their date of publication; B. Rivlin, 'A selective survey of the literature in the social sciences and related fields on modern North Africa' (*The American Politi-*

cal Science Review, **XLVIII**, 1954, pp. 826–48); M. Flory, R. Le Tourneau and J.-P. Trystram, 'L'Afrique du Nord; état des travaux' (*Revue française de Science politique*, **IX**, 1959, pp. 410–53); A. Martel, 'Le Maghreb' (*Revue française d'Histoire d'Outre-Mer*, **LV**, 1968, pp. 231–59).

It is not possible within this selective reading list to relate the problems experienced by France and Britain in the Mediterranean to the general picture of their colonial activities. The following books on imperial theory do, however, discuss global policy and its underlying assumptions. H. Brunschwig's *French Colonialism, 1871–1914; Myths and realities* (London, 1966), is an expansion of the author's French edition, and gives a background to the period discussed by the present article. Similarly Hubert Deschamps, *Les Méthodes et les Doctrines coloniales de la France du XVIe siècle à nos jours* (Paris, 1953) gives historical as well as world perspective. For Britain, H. L. Hoskins, *British routes to India* (London, 1928) and R. Robinson and J. Gallagher, *Africa and the Victorians; the official mind of imperialism* (London, 1961), bring out the importance of India and its demands on Whitehall. The practical applications of these general principles to the Mediterranean are less well treated. Elizabeth Monroe, *Britain's Moment in the Middle East, 1914–1956* (London, 1963) covers the aspect suggested by its title ably. There is no comparable attempt to discuss French policy in the area. Ann Williams, *Britain and France in the Middle East and North Africa, 1914–1967* (London, 1968) attempts a comparison of aims and achievements at an introductory level.[1]

France's traditional interests in the eastern Mediterranean and her increased commitment in the nineteenth century have not been treated thoroughly. René Ristelhueber, *Traditions françaises au Liban* (Paris, 1918) stresses French protection of Christian groups and her cultural ambitions. Vernon J. Puryear gives a more detailed economic and diplomatic analysis for a limited period of the nineteenth century in *France and the Levant; from the Bourbon restoration to the Peace of Kutiah* (Berkeley and Los Angeles, 1941). France's attitude to the 'eastern question' as a diplomatic

---

[1] She hopes to deal with French Mediterranean policy at greater depth in a future book.

problem, of course, finds its place in the general textbooks of European policy in the nineteenth century.

More detailed studies have appeared on the colonisation of North Africa. Ch.-André Julien is producing a large-scale history of the French occupation of Algeria of which Vol. I has appeared, *Histoire de l'Algérie contemporaine*, Vol. I, *Conquête et colonisation, 1827–1870* (Paris, 1964). E. F. Gautier, *L'évolution de l'Algérie de 1830 à 1930* (Algiers, 1931) is interesting as a statement of France's attitude to the country on the centenary of French occupation when she felt that all was going well. J. Ganiage, *Les origines du Protectorat français en Tunisie, 1861–1881* (Paris, 1959) is a critical analysis of the reasons for French intervention in Tunisia: J. Poncet, *La colonisation et l'agriculture européenne en Tunisie depuis 1861* (Paris, 1962) deals with further aspects of French rule. Morocco has been less well served with monographs, and much of the earlier history of French occupation is hung on biographies of the proconsul Maréchal Lyautey. The best life is that written by General Georges Catroux, *Lyautey le Marocain* (Paris, 1952). A general account of the French in Morocco is A. Ayache, *Le Maroc; bilan d'une colonisation* (Paris, 1956).

French military and diplomatic ambitions in the Mediterranean in the First World War are dealt with in M. Larcher, *La Guerre turque dans la Guerre mondiale* (Paris, 1926) and A. Pingaud, *Histoire diplomatique de la France pendant la Grande Guerre*, vols. I and III (Paris, 1940). Henry H. Cumming, *Franco-British rivalry in the post-war Near East* (London, 1928) is valuable for its quotations from documents and letters. Jukka Nevakivi, *Britain, France and the Arab Middle East, 1914–1920* (London, 1969) contains material from recently opened archives, but offers few new insights. Pierre Lyautey, *Le drame oriental et le rôle de France* (Paris, 1923) is a contemporary French assessment.

The best analysis of the French Mandate in the Levant is A. H. Hourani, *Syria and Lebanon; a political essay* (London, 1946). S. H. Longrigg, *Syria and Lebanon under the French Mandate* (London, 1958) provides a more detailed narrative of events. G. Henry-Haye and Pierre Viénot, *Les relations de la France et de la Syrie* (Paris, 1939), a critical account of French policy. General Charles de Gaulle, *Mémoires de guerre,* vol. I, *L'Appel, 1940–1942* (Paris, 1954) explains the hostility between France and Britain in Syria and Lebanon. Refer to C. Sykes, *Crossroads to Israel* (London, 1969) for the effect of the Palestine situation on the area. Jean Despois, *L'Afrique du Nord* (2nd ed., Paris, 1960) is a human geography of the area which sheds light on the problems of ruling the North African states. Nevill Barbour (ed.), *A survey of North West Africa* (2nd ed., London, 1962) is a convenient reference book. Two books about the growth of nationalist movements also contain comments on French policy; Ch.-A. Julien, *L'Afrique du Nord en marche* (2nd ed., Paris, 1959) is the work of a liberal French administrator. Roger le Tourneau, *Évolution politique de l'Afrique du Nord musulmane* (Paris, 1962) is one of the best and most balanced books on North Africa. On French administration in the area there are two books which, unfortunately, are not easily accessible. Georges Surdon, *La France en Afrique du Nord* (Algiers, 1945) only reaches the First World War. Herbert J. Liebesnes, *The Government of French North Africa* (Philadelphia, 1943) is a University of Pennsylvania short African handbook. Robert Montagne, *Les Berbères et le Makhzen dans le Sud* (Paris, 1930) deals perceptively with one problem of French administration in Morocco. There are several books by French administrators in the area; P. Boyer de Latour, *Vérités sur l'Afrique du Nord* (Paris, 1956); Gilbert Grandval, *Ma mission au Maroc* (Paris, 1956); General Juin, *Le Maghreb en feu* (Paris, 1958) and General H. L. (later Marshal) Lyautey, *Paroles d'action* (Paris, 1938).

G. E. Kirk, *The Middle East in the War, 1939–1946* (London, 1952), and the official British war history, I. S. O. Playfair, *The Mediterranean and the Middle East* (4 vols., in progress 1954–   ) give a detailed account of the course of the war and its implications for the area. A list of books on postwar diplomacy and the events leading to the Suez crisis will be found at the end of Professor Thomas' essay, but perhaps the following are worth mentioning here; G. E. Kirk, *The Middle East, 1945–1950* (London, 1954) is a good survey of the period. Royal Institute of International Affairs, *British interests in the Mediterranean and the Middle East* (London, 1958) is a debate on Britain's changing role, while Rosalyn Higgins, *United Nations Peace Keeping, 1946–1967; Documents and commentary*, vol. 1, *The Middle East* (London, 1968) shows the relationship of the two powers to the United Nations.

The independence of North Africa and particularly the Algerian War gave rise to extensive heart searching among French politicians and intellectuals which had its effect on the French government. The following are a representative selection; Georges Bidault, *L'Algérie; l'oiseau aux ailes coupées* (Paris, 1958); Jean Dresch and others, *La question algérienne* (Paris, 1958); La Nef, *Ou va l'union française? Du colonialisme à l'association* (Paris, 1955); François Mitterand, *Aux frontières de l'Union française; Indochine–Tunisie* (Paris, 1953); Paul Mus, *Le destin de l'union française de l'Indochine à l'Afrique* (Paris, 1954) and Alain Savary, *Nationalisme Calgérien et grandeur française* (Paris, 1960).

A comprehensive bibliography of the North African independence movements is given in Ann Williams, *Britain and France in the Middle East and North Africa*. The following books are general accounts of French withdrawal; Dorothy Pickles, *Algeria and France, from colonisation to co-operation* (London, 1963); Stephane Bernard, *Le conflit franco-marocain 1943–1956* (3 vols., Brussels, 1963, English translation now appearing); Lorna Hahn, *North Africa, Nationalism to Nationhood* (Washington, 1960). General de Gaulle's role in North African affairs still awaits a detailed analysis, but material will be found in Jean Ferniot, *De Gaulle et le 13 mai*, and in general accounts of the Fifth Republic, for example Philip Williams and Martin Harrison, *De Gaulle's Republic* (London, 1960); David C. Gordon, *North Africa's French Legacy; 1954–1962* (Cambridge, Mass., 1962) and Elizabeth Monroe, 'The colonial imprint' in Leon Carl Brown, *State and Society in Independent North Africa* (Washington, 1966) attempt to assess the enduring aspects of French rule.

The impact of French technological and economic aid to North Africa has to be traced in detail in the official publications of Tunisia, Algeria and Morocco, available at the School of Oriental and African Studies, in London University, and at the Middle East Centre, St Antony's College, Oxford. Samir Amin has attempted a two volume survey of *L'Économie du Maghreb,* vol. I, *La Colonisation et la décolonisation* and vol. II, *Les perspectives d'avenir* (Paris, 1966).

Finally in the present state of knowledge information and ideas must be gleaned in the files of newspapers, like *Le Monde.* Periodical publications like the surveys and documents published by the Royal Institute of International Affairs in London, and Keesings Contemporary Archives provide new material for discussion. Researches in other colonial fields may also be suggestive for Mediterranean policy, for example John D. Hargreaves, *West Africa; the former French States* (Englewood Cliffs, N. Jersey, 1967) and Guy de Lusignan, *French Speaking Africa since Independence* (London, 1969).

13 Defence and Unity of Western Europe since 1958

Guy de Carmoy

Political regimes and leaders

Relations between France and Britain during the Fourth Republic were those of two countries belonging to the same defence system, the Atlantic Alliance, and practising with different degrees of success the same type of political system, parliamentary democracy. There were rivalries within the Alliance, especially over the structure of Europe. While France tried increasingly to forge between the European states stronger links than those of mere co-operation and invited Britain to join her, Britain continually rejected such invitations, whether they were to join the European Coal and Steel Community, the European Defence Community or the European Economic Community.

Anglo-French relations during the Fifth Republic took a different turn. Similarities between the two political systems disappeared. France was no longer a parliamentary democracy. The 1958 constitution created an authoritarian regime which significantly reduced parliament's control over the executive and invested the president of the republic with extensive powers which were augmented in practice by General de Gaulle. As early as 1959, Jacques Chaban-Delmas, then President of the National Assembly, analysed 'the development of the constitutional role of the Head of State,' which he called the 'reserved sector'. This sector comprised Algeria, the Economic Community, foreign affairs, and defence.[1] On several occasions and notably during his press conference of 9 September 1965, de Gaulle expressly revindicated his responsibility for orientation, development and decision-making at the highest levels in relation to the problems affecting the nation's destiny. He alone directed foreign policy, his own foreign policy. Parliament no longer debated the major options. It debated in an academic manner the consequences of unilateral decisions made by the head of state. Radio and television reflected the views of the executive. The press enjoyed a greater degree of freedom, but, with one or two exceptions, exercised it with the greatest caution. The general public, exhausted by the many crises of the Fourth Republic, was relieved to accept an ordered continuity and put itself in the hands of the man who called himself '*le guide de la France*'[2] as far as foreign policy was concerned. His uncounterbalanced power as head of state, his 'gambler' temperament together with his imagination and courage, made General de Gaulle a master of the strategy of movement in foreign affairs. His principle of taking the offensive, his skill in moving step by step, his mastery with words all enabled him to create diplomatic situations and to exploit them to the surprise of his partners or opponents.

In Britain on the other hand, the rules of the game as set out in the unwritten constitution were still observed. Granted that the government enjoyed a certain freedom of action during a parliamentary recess, but it never failed to consult the House of Commons on the directions of foreign policy. The opinion of the press, more developed than in France, often paved the way for changes in policy and continually analysed, and if need be, criticised government action. However, changes in policy were made gradually and cautiously. Although the government carried out the political programme of the majority party in the House of Commons, until 1961 foreign policy was to a large extent bipartisan, whether it was a question of relations with the super powers, the Commonwealth or western Europe. The two men who came to power in Britain while de Gaulle ruled in France had to face serious difficulties at home and abroad. In 1961 Harold Macmillan had a large parliamentary majority, but it was quite obvious that the Conservative party, after ten years in office, was declining. Harold Wilson won the 1964 election by a very narrow majority but had to adjust Labour party policy to meet the requirements of the state of the balance of payments and of the currency. Both men witnessed the slow disintegration of the Commonwealth. Both men, not without regret or reservation, had to alter,

M

even reverse traditional British policy towards the European continent.

While Macmillan, and later on Wilson, acting out of necessity rather than conviction, brought about a profound change in British foreign policy towards Europe, de Gaulle, by desire and not out of necessity, boldly reversed the Fourth Republic's foreign policy affecting France's relations with the United States within the Atlantic Alliance and with her partners in the European Economic Community. Both changes affected France's relations with Britain.

A Three-Power Directorate within the Atlantic Alliance?

Although France and Britain belonged to the same Alliance, their ideas of how it should operate in peacetime were not the same. Both countries wished to build strategic nuclear forces, but each had different ideas as to how they should be used. The bilateral relations of the two countries with the United States and General de Gaulle's temperament account for these differences to a large extent.

One of the first things the General did after his return to office was to propose in a memorandum to President Eisenhower and Premier Macmillan dated 24 September 1958 'the creation of a tripartite organisation to take joint decisions on problems of global interest'. This was followed by the assurance that France would 'subordinate' her participation in NATO to the recognition of her 'world interests' and her 'equal participation' in global strategy.[3] This proposal implied a great deal: for France it meant having the power of veto over the American deterrent. The proposal was doubtless made with a view to provoking a negative response which in turn would justify France's gradually regaining her freedom of action. But in October 1959 de Gaulle published the third volume of his War Memoirs in which he described the 'vast plan' which he had conceived during the liberation: 'To collaborate with the West and with the East, to make such alliances as are necessary with one or the other, without ever accepting any kind of dependence.'[4] Surely the publication in 1959 of thoughts which the General ascribed to his first term of office should have acted as a warning to the 'Anglo-Saxons' who had paid no attention to his proposal for a Three-Power

Directorate for the West. The evidence of the *Mémoires d'Espoir*, published in October 1970, confirms this interpretation. 'As I expected,' wrote de Gaulle, 'the two recipients of my memorandum [Eisenhower and Macmillan] replied evasively. Nothing held us back, therefore, from taking action.' The action, as defined by de Gaulle later in the same passage, was 'to initiate with appropriate measures the process of Atlantic disengagement, while maintaining direct relations with the United States and Britain.'[4a] In fact, moves to withdraw from NATO increased and took the form of direct attacks on the organisation and rejection of any form of military integration within the Alliance. The correspondence between de Gaulle and Kennedy in 1961 was no more fruitful than the previous one between de Gaulle and Eisenhower.

Harold Macmillan kept out of this controversy. In effect he looked to the United States, the leading power in the Alliance, when it came to giving an opinion on the proposal for a Three-Power Directorate. Besides, the British government had less cause to criticise NATO's system of limited integration, especially as the American alliance was the foundation of British policy, and relations between the British and American nuclear forces had, since 1955 become very close.

British and French nuclear arms

Anglo-American nuclear collaboration, active during the war, but interrupted in 1946 by the MacMahon Act enforcing atomic isolation, had been partially re-established. In 1955 Rolls-Royce was authorised to manufacture the Blue Streak ballistic missile under licence. In 1957 a second agreement, authorising the communication of plans for nuclear powered submarines, was given congressional approval like the previous one. The amendment to the MacMahon Act specified that any state receiving United States assistance should have 'already made considerable progress in the development of atomic weapons'. France however was not given the same advantages as Britain when, in 1959, she reached the same stage of development. Congress did not have the same confidence in her and feared a leakage of military secrets to the Russians.[5] This situation inevitably made General de Gaulle angry with those whom he called the 'Anglo-Saxons'. Furthermore, the British White Papers on defence seemed to indicate that one overwhelming argument for nuclear armament was that it would increase Britain's standing in Washington's eyes.[6] The conditions of nuclear collaboration, including the use of Scottish ports for American nuclear submarines, were such that the use of the British nuclear force was inconceivable without US agreement. Nor did the British government raise any serious objections to the theory of graduated response formulated in 1962 by secretary of defence McNamara, a theory which presupposed a centralised – i.e. American – system of command and control.

The decision to make a plutonium bomb was taken in 1958 by the Gaillard government shortly before the fall of the Fourth Republic. The first French 'A' bomb was exploded in 1960 while Britain had had it since 1952 and the 'H' bomb since 1957.

As early as 1959 de Gaulle stressed the need for French autonomy in nuclear armament,[7] and in 1961 and 1962 he put forward two arguments in support of this claim. From a political point of view, he argued that a nation could not rank as a great power unless it had the ultimate weapon, and what was more, unless it had the power to decide when it should be used, a decision vitally affecting its destiny. On strategic grounds he argued that the United States had become vulnerable; Western Europe was more open to danger than its protector and the countries of the Atlantic Alliance were not at all sure in what circumstances the American deterrent would be used.[8]

However, if France could decide independently when to use her nuclear force, she would be compelled, by reason of the technical limits of such a force, to launch a first-strike counter-city attack. Unlike Britain, France refused to adopt McNamara's doctrine of graduated response since she rejected the American proposal of a unified command. Instead, she adopted the doctrine of 'proportionate deterrence', according to which a medium-sized power which possessed a nuclear weapon, would be likely to deter an attack from a greatly superior power.

The Nassau Agreements

Beginning in 1961, the countries of the West wove a complex web of negotiations touching on political, economic and military matters at various levels, which were to have a profound effect on Franco-British relations.

First of all, the Six, in view of their successful co-operation in the economic sphere, started in February 1961 on General de Gaulle's initiative to explore means of extending this co-operation into the field of politics, in the form of a Union of States exclusive of any kind of integration. The negotiations broke down on 17 April 1962 over the question of British participation. De Gaulle wanted to specify that membership of the Union of States would not follow automatically from membership of the other European Communities.

Besides, negotiations between Britain and the Six, following the British application for membership in August 1961, were making slow progress amid many technical and political difficulties. Since becoming president of the United States, Kennedy had strongly encouraged British attempts to enter Europe. He did more than this: on 4 July 1962 he made a statement on the interdependence of the United States and a united Europe saying that they could be the two pillars of an Atlantic Community. He was implying that the United States would regard an integrated Europe as responsible – something it did not regard a coalition of states as. He would be prepared to grant to a united Europe the nuclear autonomy which he refused to give to national nuclear forces.

The geopolitical ideas of Kennedy and de Gaulle were diametrically opposed, and Kennedy's enthusiasm for British admission into the EEC inevitably chilled relations with the French president, always distrustful of any Anglo-American collusion.[9]

On the other hand, relations between de Gaulle and Adenauer were close. At his press conference of 15 May 1962 the General presented Franco-German solidarity as the keystone of the foundations of Western Europe in the first place and of the whole of Europe in the long run. Following his visit to Germany in September when he was enthusiastically received everywhere, he and Adenauer prepared a bilateral Franco-German Treaty inspired by the vision of the

Union of Six States which he had not been able to realise. After the 1961 Berlin crisis, Adenauer wanted to guarantee the Federal Republic the moral support of a stronger partner.[10]

Franco-German negotiations had reached a fairly advanced stage when Macmillan undertook to redefine Anglo-American nuclear relations in terms of equipping British bombers with ballistic missiles. This had brought the first setback to Britain in 1957 when she had to abandon production of the Blue Streak rocket in favour of Skybolt, a ground-to-air missile which was to be made in the United States. Now McNamara considered that the American armed forces no longer needed Skybolt because they had the Minuteman, a long-range missile launched from underground. How was one to reconcile the myth of the independence of the British deterrent with America's desire to integrate all strategic forces within the Alliance?

Macmillan and Kennedy met in Nassau in the Bahamas on 19–21 December 1962. Macmillan asked for and was given Kennedy's word that the United States would supply Britain with Polaris missiles. Britain was to build the submarines, launchers, and nuclear warheads, with American technical assistance. The British submarines, equipped with Polaris missiles, were to be part of a multilateral NATO force to be set up by the United States and Britain and some of their allies. Britain undertook to use her nuclear force 'for the purposes of international defence of the Western Alliance', but would resume freedom of action in the event of her government deciding that 'supreme national interests are at stake'. Macmillan insisted that this clause was essential to the continued existence of the Conservative government.[11] It was interpreted by the Labour party as proof that British independence was non-existent.

Before the Nassau meeting on 15–16 December Macmillan had discussions with de Gaulle in Rambouillet. Apparently Macmillan informed de Gaulle of the probable substitution of Polaris for Skybolt, but neither party made any suggestion as to pooling their nuclear power.[12] In his speech in Liverpool on 21 January, Macmillan, commenting on the Rambouillet discussions, said that he had emphasised to de Gaulle that interdependence was essential in a modern defence system.

Kennedy wrote a personal letter to de Gaulle from Nassau,

offering France Polaris rockets under the same conditions as England. In his reply of 21 December, de Gaulle did not commit himself, but his hesitation did not last long. At the very beginning of 1963 the French press interpreted the Nassau agreements as British capitulation to the United States. An article by André Fontaine insinuated that British entry into the Common Market was a way of increasing American military and economic influence in Europe.[13] De Gaulle used this argument at his press conference of 14 January 1963 to justify his vetoing British entry into the Common Market. Supposing that Britain, followed by other countries, were admitted, he predicted 'that no doubt an enormous Atlantic Community would emerge, dependent upon and directed by America, into which the European Community would soon be absorbed.' After having stressed his doubts about American nuclear intervention to defend Europe, de Gaulle rejected the multilateral force for two reasons. Above all, it was a question of who held the command: the greater part of American nuclear capacity would remain under the US president's orders. Then there was a technical reason: Polaris missiles would be quite useless to France who had neither the submarines to launch them nor thermonuclear warheads to arm them.

There was a striking contrast between Britain's doggedness in discussing the economic conditions of her entry into the Common Market and the alacrity with which she decided upon her nuclear future with the United States. As Kissinger observed: 'The British request necessarily raised the question of whether it was compatible with the aspirations of a *united* Europe for one of its members to have exclusive relations with the United States on such a vitally important issue as nuclear strategy.'[14] De Gaulle's declaration of hostility to the projected multilateral force pushed the Americans into action. The multilateral force was intended both as a reply to the autonomous French force and as a means of making America's most committed European ally, West Germany, a party to the Alliance's deterrent policy. The matter was given much thought. Washington banked on London being unable to refuse, on the smaller countries following suit, and on France finding herself isolated. These plans were frustrated by the British general election of October 1964. The Labour party was opposed to the multilateral force. On 23 November Harold Wilson stated that the American proposals 'would in no way increase Western power' and that at all events America was to have the absolute veto on the use of nuclear power. On 16 December Wilson confirmed to the House of Commons that Britain's nuclear capacity, both aerial and submarine, with the exception of some bombers which would be kept for strategic missions east of Suez, would be assigned to NATO. Under the name of the Atlantic Nuclear Force he presented a variation on the multilateral force, which – unlike the MLF – contained no 'European clause', and which gave Britain a privileged role compared with her European partners. West Germany did not find this proposition attractive. The United States then ceased to press for the formation of a multilateral force. The only effect the American proposal had was to heighten British suspicions of West Germany and give birth in France to fears of 'some kind of American-German alliance'.[15]

France's relations with West Germany, and more generally with her NATO partners, were already strained when, in July 1963, she was the only member of the Atlantic Alliance to refuse to sign the Moscow Treaty banning nuclear tests, a treaty which Britain had worked hard to bring about since 1958.

French withdrawal from NATO

While he concentrated on building up a national deterrent and thwarted the establishment of a multilateral force, General de Gaulle became more and more critical of the Alliance. He opposed Robert McNamara's proposal in November 1965 to set up a special nuclear committee with a view to bringing in countries, even non-nuclear ones such as Germany, for the working out of Alliance strategy. Vestiges of French isolationism could be discerned in his address of 27 April which acclaimed 'the re-emergence of a nation whose hands are free', and in his television interview of 14 December 1965 when he proclaimed that 'France need not rule out any possibility for herself'. At the same time he disassociated France from the United States with regard to their military intervention in Vietnam. Finally, he actively pursued a rapprochement with the Soviet Union.

On 9 September 1965 de Gaulle indicated that France would withdraw from NATO before 1969, and speeded up the process bringing this about after he was re-elected president in December. The decision was announced during a press conference on 21 February 1966. De Gaulle distinguished between the Alliance Treaty, which in his eyes was still valid, and the integrated organisation of the general staffs which he could not accept. He pointed out the risk of France's being drawn into a war provoked by or forced upon the United States.

On 18 March France's fourteen allies within the Atlantic Pact published a statement affirming their adherence to the principle of NATO integration and their intention of strengthening the existing organisation. Perhaps a British initiative in favour of a European Defence Community would have removed certain criticisms of a lack of balance within NATO and served as the first step towards countering France's challenge. But the Labour government was not ready to take such an initiative.[16]

On 21 June General de Gaulle went to Moscow. His Kremlin speech confirmed his intention of establishing a new order in Europe based on Franco-Soviet co-operation. A joint declaration paved the way for regular consultations between the two governments on matters of foreign policy and defence. France found herself in the ambiguous position of being a member of the Atlantic Pact and protected by the United States, but able to adopt a neutral position in the event of a crisis between the United States and the Soviet Union – a position of 'national neutralism' in the words of Lord Gladwyn.[17]

Britain had also wished for a long time to improve relations with the Soviet Union and on several occasions had endeavoured to act 'if not as a mediator, at least as a moderating influence in any Soviet-American confrontation'.[18] But her support, by and large, for American policy in Vietnam prevented her from offering help in the Far East and from playing an active role in the Middle East, where General de Gaulle, immediately after the Six Day War, came out in support of Soviet policy. The gap between the French and

British positions became still more obvious on 1 July 1968 when France refused to sign the nuclear non-proliferation treaty of which England had been one of the most active protagonists.

However, the two minor nuclear powers suffered under the impact of technical progress in the strategic arms race. The decision of the two super powers in 1967 to equip themselves with light anti-missile missiles seemed aimed against China and not against each other. But it had the immediate effect of rendering the British and French deterrents obsolete.

Although the two super powers were on opposite sides in the Far East and the Middle East, in Europe they pursued a quite remarkable policy of peaceful co-existence after the settlement of the Cuban affair in 1962 until the invasion of Czechoslovakia in August 1968. This improvement in relations, evinced by the signing of the two nuclear treaties of 1963 and 1968, had repercussions on the work of the Atlantic Alliance. In December 1967 the NATO Council accepted the Harmel report which said that the Alliance's two functions, to promote military security and the East-West detente, were not contradictory but complementary. France, who had a say in the Alliance's political decisions (but not its military decisions) found herself beside Britain in approving the new line of policy.

British withdrawal from east of Suez

While France was withdrawing from the Atlantic Alliance, Britain was questioning the merits of her military commitments outside the Alliance, contracted for the good of the Commonwealth. Centrifugal forces were continuing to break up the Commonwealth: the dissolution of the Federation of Malaysia in 1966, the war between India and Pakistan settled by Soviet mediation in 1966, the series of *coups d'état* in Nigeria, the conflict between Britain and Rhodesia – these were all equally signs of Britain's inability to co-ordinate the policies of dispersed and disparate countries. In these circumstances should Britain continue to bear her heavy military burden 'East of Suez'?

When Harold Wilson came to power it was his intention to strengthen the Commonwealth. But in February 1966 the

White Paper on defence revealed for the first time that Britain could never fight a war in the Indian Ocean on her own.[19] This did not go far enough for Christopher Mayhew, minister for the Navy, who resigned, contending that Britain should concentrate on two objectives: withdrawal from East of Suez and European leadership.[20] Nevertheless, on 16 June 1966, Harold Wilson again defended before the parliamentary Labour party the view that Britain was more than a European power. Among the arguments he put forward were that a withdrawal of British forces could incite a state such as India to turn to one of the two super powers for nuclear protection, and that Britain's presence could prevent a dangerous confrontation between the United States and China.[21] The balance of payments crisis in the summer of 1966 led to a reduction of British troops in Malaysia after the end of the confrontation with Indonesia. The Defence White Paper of July 1967 openly advocated withdrawal from east of Suez and drew up plans for the complete evacuation of British troops from Singapore and Malaysia by 1975. Britain's contribution to NATO was maintained: the choice had been made. The devaluation of the pound in November 1967 led to a further reduction in overseas military expenditure, and notably in January 1968 to the cancellation of the order for fifty American F111 bombers no longer required now that the government had abandoned its east of Suez policy. In spring 1968 Britain increased her sea and air strength in the Mediterranean within NATO's sphere of influence. Thus the defence of Europe became Britain's major preoccupation.

The Soviet invasion of Czechoslovakia in August 1968 justified the British government's choice and led the French government to reconsider its position *vis-à-vis* the Alliance. In November 1968 France endorsed the North Atlantic Council's communiqué warning the Soviet Union, in forcible terms, against further intervention in Europe or the Mediterranean. In December Pierre Messmer, the minister of defence, announced to the national assembly, 'we are in the Atlantic Alliance and we will stay there'. In April 1969 General Fourquet, chief of the defence staff, spoke out against the principle of '*défense tous azimuts*' (an omni-directional defence system), put forward in December 1967 by his predecessor, General Ailleret, and declared his support for the doctrine of graduated response that France had hitherto opposed within the Alliance. This change of position seemed to indicate that France no longer envisaged using her nuclear striking force on her own. Were conditions becoming favourable for closer military co-operation between France and Britain, now that the United States was talking of reducing her troops in Europe?

The British and the French have only recently pooled their resources in aerospace manufacture: in the production of the military aeroplane the Jaguar, the first flight of which took place in 1968, and the ground-to-air missile Martel, which began to be mass-produced in 1969. Is wider co-operation possible in the field of nuclear armaments, even in that of strategy? The industries of the two countries are complementary. British superiority in the field of aircraft engines is indisputable as is French superiority in the field of airframes. France is in the lead as regards solid-fuel missiles, while Britain is very much in the lead as regards thermonuclear bombs. There are certain politicians who support the idea of pooling the strategic power of the two countries: Edward Heath in Britain and Jean Lecanuet in France. A European Community for Nuclear Defence is not possible while Western Europe has no federal-type institutions. A less ambitious type of co-operation within the Western European Union, an institution with military responsibilities common both to Britain and to the Six, remains improbable so long as Britain remains outside the EEC.

Britain turns toward Europe

After being invited to take part in the Brussels negotiations of 1955 which led to the signing of the Treaty of Rome, Britain soon withdrew her representative. Once the Treaty was ratified, the British government joined diplomatic battle to minimise the scope and influence of the new institution.

At the end of 1957 it suggested that a free-trade area be created within the OEEC, embracing all OEEC member states apart from the EEC countries. Since Britain was not within a customs union and therefore not subject to a common external tariff, she would keep her preferential links with the Commonwealth and her system of agricultural protection, while at the same time her industry would benefit from the large Continental market. Discussions within the OEEC inter-ministerial committee, suspended during the French political crisis of May 1958, were resumed in the autumn. However, following General de Gaulle's talks with Chancellor Adenauer in Bad-Kreuznach in November, the two governments got their EEC partners to accept proposals concerning the abolition of quotas and the reduction of customs duties, which were certainly liberal, but in the main reserved for members of the Community. At the OEEC committee meeting on 15 December over which Mr Reginald Maudling presided, the disagreement between the Six and Britain was quite evident. The devaluation of the franc brought into effect on 28 December, enabled France to meet her tariff and quota obligations to the EEC and OEEC.

Consequently, the chances of setting up a multilateral system for commercial relations between the European states faded. Maudling then explored the possibility of creating a small free-trade area centred around Britain and comprising most of the Western European peripheral states, i.e. Sweden, Norway, Denmark, Austria, Switzerland and Portugal. The Treaty setting up EFTA (European Free Trade Area) was signed by the seven states in Stockholm in November 1959. To the United States the agreement seemed a defensive move on Britain's part, a measure taken in the face of the Common Market, and a commercial arrangement devoid of any long-term political significance.[22] Its signature in fact coincided with a thorough re-examination of Britain's position with regard to Europe.

As early as the beginning of 1959 the *Economist* examined the question of whether Britain should join the Common Market. A committee of high officials under the chairmanship of the secretary of the treasury, decided early in 1960 that Britain should join the EEC, mainly for political reasons: if she did not join, she would be bound to lose relative power and influence with regard to the United States and the Commonwealth.[23] General de Gaulle's observation during his press conference of 31 May 1960 that the Common Market had become a practical reality seemed to consecrate the institution.

Harold Macmillan, who had sounded out Adenauer on the subject of Britain's entry into the EEC in August 1960, and had made the basic decision at Christmas,[24] visited General de Gaulle in Rambouillet in January 1961 and in April received strong encouragement from President Kennedy. He decided to draw up a qualified acceptance of the Treaty of Rome principles in his speech of 31 July 1961 to the House of Commons. After having stressed the political finality of the Treaty, he declared that 'if a closer relationship between the United Kingdom and the EEC countries were to disrupt the long-standing and historic ties between the United Kingdom and the other Commonwealth nations, the loss would be greater then the gain.'

The government continually asserted that there was no question of choosing between the Commonwealth and Europe. This ambiguity, unconvincing to the Labour party which abstained from voting on 3 August, was to hang over the negotiations.

First application for membership and first veto

General de Gaulle received the British application with cautious good-will at his press conference of 5 September. But this good-will was only apparent. De Gaulle explained clearly his attitude towards the British application in his *Mémoires d'Espoir*. He recalled that on 29 June 1958 Harold Macmillan had visited him in Paris and had exclaimed: 'The Common Market is the Continental System [a reference to Napoleon's anti-British organisation]. It is unacceptable to Britain; I appeal to you to give it up!' De Gaulle went on to describe how, towards the middle of 1961, the British renewed their offensive, and he commented that 'as they were unable from the outside to prevent the European Community from being born, they now intended to paralyse it from within.'[24a]

After delays both on the part of the French, who wished to consolidate their common agricultural policy before discussing it with the British, and on the part of the British, who hesitated too long before proposing a compromise on their original position, it was not until the beginning of May 1962 that the negotiations, led by Edward Heath for Britain, reached an active stage.

Meanwhile, de Gaulle met Macmillan on a number of occasions to discuss the *'grand sujet'* of the British application; but, he recalled in *Mémoires d'Espoir*, 'I could not believe, although I wished it were so, that his country was ready to become the new Britain who would attach herself to the Continent.' De Gaulle added that subsequently the Nassau agreement on the supplying of American rockets to Britain 'was to justify my circumspection'.[24b]

The problems of the Commonwealth and of British agriculture were the only topics to be discussed. Monetary questions were not touched upon. Defence questions were in the back of the negotiators' minds, but were taken no further, not being within the terms of reference of the Treaty of Rome.

However, the debate among the Six, or rather between General de Gaulle and his Common Market partners, on the structure and political orientation of Europe was in turn to influence events following the British application for membership.

At his press conference of 5 September 1960 de Gaulle compared 'a real Europe' – one made up of states – to 'a dream Europe' – one comprised of 'certain more or less extra-national bodies'. During the discussions on the creation of a union of states – a kind of political confederation with extensive powers and organically separate from the existing communities – de Gaulle showed himself concerned with three basic considerations: the substitution of inter-governmental collaboration for the dialogue between a Community executive and a council of ministers representing member nations, the withdrawal of all reference to the Atlantic Alliance, and the obstruction of Britain's admission into the new institution. To which the Dutch replied with the slogan: 'No Europe *à l'anglaise* without the English'. The Germans and the Italians were prepared to compromise on the inter-governmental nature of the institution. But the Dutch and the Belgians feared that such a system would lead to a Franco-German *entente*. Britain's entry into a political union guarded simultaneously against the risk of this happening and against that of a Western Europe disassociated from the

United States. Such were the reasons for the break on 17 April 1962 provoked by Spaak and Luns. A few days before, in a speech in London to the council of the Western European Union, Edward Heath had asked that Britain be allowed without delay to take part in the negotiations on the political structure of Europe. He accepted that the union of states 'would have a common attitude towards defence,' but he considered it essential that 'any European defence policy be directly linked to the Atlantic Alliance'. This speech underlined General de Gaulle's conviction that Britain only intended to become part of a Europe closely associated with the United States. In his press conference of 15 May he affirmed that political integration would lead to subjection to the United States: 'Perhaps there would be a federator but he would not be a European'. This statement provoked a minor political crisis in France resulting in some ministers belonging to the MRP (*Mouvement Républicain Populaire*) leaving the government.

Such was the political climate when Macmillan visited de Gaulle at Champs on June 1 and 2. The General was astonished to learn that Macmillan intended henceforward to give priority to Britain's European role and to take the consequences this would have on her relations with the Commonwealth. Macmillan might have underlined his desire for a Europe run on confederal lines, with its own defence system. But it seems that the subject of Franco-British co-operation in the sphere of nuclear armaments was not broached.[25]

However, negotiations concerning Britain's request to join the EEC were continued on a technical level. The commercial problems of the Commonwealth were examined in detail, product by product and country by country. France was prepared to open up new markets for manufactured goods from India, Pakistan and Ceylon. She suggested extending associate membership, by which French-speaking African countries benefited, to the independent Commonwealth countries and to British colonies which found themselves in a comparable situation, notably in Africa and the Caribbean. On the other hand, France was particularly demanding with respect to products coming from the temperate zone – cereals, meat and dairy produce – from Canada,

Australia and New Zealand. She intended to maintain the principle of agricultural preference within the Community which she had recently got her partners to accept and made any agreement with Britain on agricultural exports from the white Commonwealth subordinate to an agreement among the Six on financial control of agriculture. The privileges accorded to French food products on the German market were considered a compensation for opening the French market to German industrial products.

Negotiations were suspended at the beginning of August, a month before the Commonwealth Prime Ministers conference opened in London, which took place in an atmosphere heavy with the sounds of the electoral battle already under way between the Conservative and Labour parties. The conference did not reject results already achieved in the course of the negotiations. The final communiqué recognised that the decision rested with the British government alone. The Commonwealth countries were not in a position to offer Britain an alternative solution. The Labour party conference took place shortly afterwards. Hugh Gaitskell, who had fought incessantly and passionately against British membership of the Common Market, drew up demands over and above those of the negotiators: he demanded freedom for Britain to pursue independent planning and foreign policies. The Conservative party conference was accompanied by an energetic campaign seeking the support of public opinion. The conference indicated its confidence in Harold Macmillan by a very large majority.

The discussions between Britain and the Six then concentrated on problems connected with British agriculture. Within the Common Market external protection, by means of a system of variable import duties (*prélèvement*), guaranteed remunerative prices to farmers; while within the British system the consumer benefited from world market prices and the farmers benefited from prices guaranteed by budgetary subsidies. The British delegation asked that this system be continued during the transitional period, but the Six insisted on the immediate application of the Community system after entry. By mid-December negotiations had ground to a halt.

Was France's more intransigent attitude during the

N

preceding months due to General de Gaulle's deeply hostile reaction to President Kennedy's declaration of 4 July on the interdependence of the United States and a united Europe? As Kennedy saw it, both should follow a common foreign policy; while in de Gaulle's view, Europe should pursue its own foreign policy. The fact was that de Gaulle was breaking away from the 'Anglo-Saxons' and drawing closer to Germany. After his triumphant visit to Germany in September, the preparation of the Franco-German Treaty of Co-operation was actively hurried up.

However, defence problems were once again to interfere with the plans concerning Europe's structure. On his way to Nassau to discuss with Kennedy the possibility of substituting Polaris for Skybolt missiles, Macmillan stopped off at Rambouillet on 15 December. De Gaulle expressed his doubts about Britain's ability to make the political adjustments necessary to enter the Common Market. Macmillan informed de Gaulle of the object of his talks with Kennedy. It seems that neither party made any suggestion of co-ordinating French and British nuclear research and production.[26] The two questions of Britain's entry into the Common Market and British arms were discussed in Nassau. According to Nora Beloff, originally the Americans did not wish to conclude a nuclear agreement with the British until the Brussels negotiations had ended. Kennedy was mistaken at Nassau about Macmillan's chances of bringing the negotiations to a successful conclusion.[27]

Without consulting his EEC partners, de Gaulle, in a press conference on 14 January 1963, announced his decision to say 'no' to two closely-related questions; one to Kennedy's offer to supply France with Polaris missiles, and the second to Britain's entry into the Common Market. On the 'really important' subject of Britain, de Gaulle laid bare the 'real facts of the problem'. The Treaty of Rome was concluded between interdependent states of a similar type. It had first been applied in the field of agriculture. Britain would hinder the working of the Community by submitting an application 'on her own terms'. From these facts arose the question of whether Britain could accept a common tariff and renounce all Commonwealth preference, a question which remained unresolved and which Britain alone could answer. Moreover, an enlarged Common Market including Britain and other states would be 'under the direction of and dependent upon America', while France wished to set up a 'purely European body'.

It was his awareness of the interdependence between America and Britain that decided General de Gaulle to break off negotiations. His decision involved risks in international relations only to a very limited extent because of the personal agreement between de Gaulle and Adenauer and the imminent signing of the Treaty of Franco-German Co-operation. There was hardly any risk of its affecting French domestic politics. As Dorothy Pickles observed: 'France had learned to live with Germany and like it, and without Britain without minding it'.[28] In the economic world no one wanted the competition of British industry in addition to that of German industry. De Gaulle reaped his reward for bringing about peace in Algeria by winning a workable majority in the National Assembly in November 1962.

Had the British government made the most of its opportunities? Because of her attitude in the past towards the structure of Europe, 'Great Britain could not be in any doubt that her belated action would be met with a certain amount of suspicion.'[29] In Nora Beloff's opinion, 'history will surely decide that Macmillan also had his part in the final rupture. The long delay in starting the negotiations; the even longer delay in building up British confidence in the European venture; the absence of any firm political commitment until the Government seemed to face imminent electoral defeat – all these prepared the setting for the final disaster.'[30]

British public opinion between 1963–7

The French veto deprived the Conservative party of its slim chance of victory. In its 1964 election campaign the Labour party concentrated on domestic issues and commercial relations with the Commonwealth. However, British industry continued investing on the Continent, assured in all eventualities of being well placed in an expanding market.

The Labour Government that was formed in October 1964 was made up of anti-Common Marketeers. One of its first actions was to impose a surtax of 15 per cent on imports from the free trade area, which antagonised the EFTA countries.

The monetary crisis of autumn 1964 forced the government to raise massive loans from the central banks of the leading industrial nations and to restrict capital investment in the sterling area. It showed the prime minister painfully to what degree the future of the pound depended upon the co-operation of the United States and of the countries of Europe, and that the Commonwealth had become an economic and financial liability.

People in leading circles began to ask what Britain's world role was – a question which led to a certain degree of self-criticism. 'There was a growing feeling that the United Kingdom was over-extended politically as well as economically,' wrote Miriam Camps.[31]

Harold Wilson observed that the scientific industries – the aircraft industry, nuclear energy, computers – were not profitable except on a European scale, a belief which led him to undertake with France the Concorde project for a supersonic airliner. The silence he had to observe on the Vietnam war so as not to displease the United States weighed heavily on him. He was concerned by the political division in the Commonwealth with regard to the United Nations decision on economic sanctions against Rhodesia.

Harold Wilson changed his attitude towards Europe during the summer or autumn of 1965.[32] As Anthony Sampson remarked: 'Mr Wilson's volte face was even more surprising than Macmillan's ... but it was also more complete.'[33] The prime minister took care not to intervene in the quarrel between France and her EEC partners in 1965 over the method of financing their common agricultural policy, although Britain was a factor in the crisis, a fact of which everyone was aware. He did not commit himself on the subject during the March 1966 election campaign, while the Conservatives announced their intention of seizing the first favourable opportunity to enter the EEC and the Liberals remained convinced that this was the right thing to do. In any case, the new Labour Cabinet was much more pro-European. George Brown was the minister responsible for economic negotiations with Europe, and in July he became foreign secretary. Within the Cabinet, a re-examination of Britain's world role and her defence policy led ministers to concentrate their attention and ambitions on Europe. The visit of Georges Pompidou and Maurice Couve de Murville to London in July 1966 was however not at all encouraging. The French ministers gave their opposite numbers advice on a policy of economic austerity, similar in tone to the more pressing advice given by the Americans.

On 23 January 1967 Harold Wilson affirmed his conviction that Britain should enter Europe before the Council of Europe in Strasbourg, and took a stand against 'an industrial helotry' for Europe in relation to the United States. Accompanied by George Brown he made a European tour of the capitals of the Six and was supported in his actions by the Confederation of British Industry and by public opinion as a whole.

Second application and second veto

On 2 May 1967 Harold Wilson moved in the House of Commons that an application by Britain to join the EEC be approved. He declared that his government 'would be prepared to accept the Treaty of Rome subject to the necessary adjustments consequent upon the accession of a new member'. He recognised that 'the Community's agricultural policy is an integral part of the EEC'. He stated his conviction that 'Europe is now faced with the opportunity of a great move forward in political unity'. After a debate of high standard the government motion was carried on 10 May by the overwhelming majority of 488 votes to 62. Britain's application was followed on 11 May by those of Ireland and Denmark, and shortly afterwards by that of Norway.

General de Gaulle chose to reply to the British premier in his press conference of 16 May without previously consulting France's Common Market partners whom he was to meet on 29 May to commemorate the tenth anniversary of the Treaty of Rome. He vigorously repeated all his arguments of 1963 and added some new ones.

On the economic level, he once again stressed the fact that Britain would find it impossible to stand the price rises that would follow as a result of applying the common agricultural policy. For the first time he put forward the monetary argument. Britain was obliged to curb capital movements because her currency was over-valued. The position of the pound as a reserve currency and the handicap of the sterling balances were incompatible with 'monetary parity and solidarity' which 'are essential conditions of the Common Market'.

On the political level, the General once more called attention to Britain's close relations with the Commonwealth and the United States, a fact he alleged, which showed that British policies were incompatible with those of the Six 'unless the British resumed total control of their own defence system or the Continentals gave up the idea of ever creating a European Europe'. He was disturbed by the application to join of other EFTA countries, the effect of which would be to alter radically 'the inspiration, the dimensions and the decisions of what today is the organisation of the Six'. At the summit meeting in Rome de Gaulle admitted in the communiqué of 30 May that the question of British membership should be examined by the Community's Council of Ministers.

Despite the quasi-veto of 16 May, Harold Wilson accepted the General's invitation to visit him in the Grand Trianon on 19 June. Although received with pomp, the prime minister did not take away with him any promise of negotiation.

At the meeting of the Council of the Western European Union at The Hague on 4 July, George Brown declared – and this marked an important step – that Britain was ready to accept the external common tariff in the form it would take after the Kennedy Round reductions came into force. He also agreed to dissociate Britain's application from those of the other EFTA countries.

However, at the Council of Foreign Ministers of the Six, Maurice Couve de Murville raised a new objection based on political grounds: if the Common Market were expanded the eastern bloc might be encouraged to close its ranks. Thus British membership could be an obstacle to the achievement of a *détente* between the two blocs. The French minister persuaded his colleagues that the Brussels Commission should be consulted. Delaying tactics thus followed the use of the bludgeon on 16 May.

The Commission presented its report on 29 September. It

underlined the value for the Community of 'the membership
of states whose traditions of stability and democracy are so
ancient and deep-seated'. It explained precisely how the
Community's common agricultural policy would affect
Britain: she would suffer a slight rise in the cost of living and
would be bound to uphold agreements to purchase products
from the West Indies and New Zealand. But it was pessimistic about Britain's economic and financial situation. It
recommended covertly what General de Gaulle had called
for *urbi et orbi*, namely the devaluation of the pound and
abandonment of its role as a reserve currency.

The pro-European members of the British Cabinet were
in favour of devaluing the pound in July 1966 so that
Britain could submit her application to join the Common
Market in conditions of favourable economic competition.
Harold Wilson was opposed to this at the time, but had to
give in by November 1967 in face of the power of international
speculation. During the Basle discussions between representatives of the member states of the Group of Ten, France
insisted that the new massive loan granted to Britain be
subject to strict conditions and refused to have any part in
a loan made through the central banks. At the height of the
crisis, France announced that she had withdrawn from the
Gold Pool in June, thus intensifying monetary speculation.

This attitude presaged no change in France's rejection of
Britain's application. De Gaulle did not take into account
the decision to devalue the pound which opened up the way
to restoring equilibrium in the balance of payments. Quite
the contrary, in his press conference of 27 November he
referred to the report made by the EEC Commission prior
to devaluation 'which very clearly demonstrates that the
Common Market is incompatible with Britain's economy in
its present state'. He repeated his previous objections and
stated that France could not 'at present enter into negotiations with the British which would lead to the destruction of
the European pattern of which she was a part.'

In fact, de Gaulle acted out of other interests. It was
because Britain had been forced to accept the substance of
the economic and monetary conditions set by France that
de Gaulle vetoed, not her entry into the Common Market,
but the negotiations prior to entry. By refusing to negotiate,

he was able to avoid a discussion among the Six on his un-admitted political reason for rejecting the British candid-ature: Britain's presence would alter the balance of power within the enlarged Community. France would no longer have the freedom of action she enjoyed in an institution where she held the political reins and Germany was content to follow her lead.

On December 18 and 19 the Council of Ministers had to register disagreement between five member states and the Commission who wanted to open negotiations immediately on Britain's entry, and France who was opposed to such action. Germany, putting her agreement with France first, had to give in. At the beginning of 1968 Germany tried to give some body to the commercial 'arrangement' with Britain to which she had referred in her December press conference, but without success.

Towards a revision of the French position

General de Gaulle's refusal to negotiate did not diminish the determination of the British parties, all of which sub-scribed to the political objective defined by Lord Chalfont in his speech of 15 September 1967: 'We wish to exert what influence we can from a European base.' This objective was more within Britain's capacity, and was the reason for the decision of the three parties, announced on 24 October 1968, to join the Action Committee for the United States of Europe, founded by and presided over by Jean Monnet. The terms of the Labour party's letter of application, signed by Harold Wilson, were significant: 'Our party considers that the political, economic and technological integration of Europe is essential if Europe is to realise its great potential.'

This feeling was not shared by General de Gaulle who, at his press conference of 9 September 1968, his last one, de-clared: 'Although a member of the Common Market, we have never agreed to a so-called 'supranational' system for the Six which would submerge France in a stateless entity, and which would have no policy other than that of the overseas protector.' He followed this up immediately with: 'Our desire to avoid at all costs being absorbed into an Atlantic system is one of the reasons why, to our great regret, we have hitherto delayed Great Britain's entry into the present Community.'

These statements were made shortly after two major events which were to change the course of French foreign policy: the French economic and social crisis of May–June 1968 which forced her to appeal to the industrial countries of the West, and especially to the United States, for financial help; and the Soviet invasion of Czechoslovakia, which showed that the Warsaw Pact was still the tool of Russian imperialism.

The Prague coup led France publicly to affirm her solidarity with the other members of the Atlantic Pact. The decisions taken at the monetary conference of the members of the Group of Ten in Bonn in November 1968 demonstrated the disparity in purchasing power between the mark and the franc and consequently the imbalance between the French and German economies.

Returning to the fold of the Alliance, de Gaulle had to make his peace with the United States. President Nixon's visit to Paris in February 1969 presented the opportunity for such a reconciliation. The change in the balance of power within the Community, to France's disadvantage, led de Gaulle to put out new feelers towards Britain, while the British government for its part sought to establish political contacts with the Six through the Western European Union.

At the February 1969 session of the WEU in London, the British government intended to discuss the Middle East. France questioned the competence of the meeting, refused to attend and announced that she would no longer take part in the activities of the organisation's Council. The British government replied by publishing an interview between de Gaulle and Christopher Soames.

De Gaulle expounded to the ambassador his well-known theses on the necessity for a Europe independent of the United States, his aversion to the ideas on which the Treaty of Rome was based, and the structural changes which British membership of the Community would entail. He advocated the idea of a broad economic association incorporating a political council limited to four members (France, Great Britain, Germany and Italy) and wanted to be sure that France and Britain saw eye to eye on this idea. The British government, fearing that the interview concealed a trap, replied that Great Britain intended joining the Common Market in its present form, and it informed Kiesinger and the other governments of the Six about the exchange of views.

What did General de Gaulle really want? To stick to his idea of a European Europe or, on the contrary, to make new overtures to London? Michel Debré, then foreign minister, maintained the former opinion in an interview on 22 February, and the latter on 12 March before the national assembly's foreign affairs committee, i.e. that the British had not understood 'the considerable overtures made in their direction'. This explanation seems to be the correct one. On the one hand the General was agreeable to Britain's admittance into an organisation which was free of any trace of supra-nationality and thus fitted in with his slogan of a Europe of States; while on the other hand, within this organisation, Great Britain would be able to counterbalance West Germany whose economic potential could not fail to increase her political influence.

It would be going too far to say that de Gaulle reversed his policy towards Great Britain. He rather re-examined it at a time when there was a shift in the balance of power in Western Europe.

A negative balance-sheet

Franco-British relations between 1961 and 1970 fall within the period of bold diplomacy of the Fifth Republic. In 1961 de Gaulle resigned himself to Algerian independence. He knew that now offensive action had come to an end peace was only a matter of months. From 1962 onwards, he had complete freedom of action in foreign affairs.

In order to gain a true understanding of Franco-British relations it is necessary to consider the respective areas of application of the two foreign policies. Both France and Britain completed the process of decolonisation during the sixties. France had terminated the Algerian war and had granted independence to her Black African territories. British monetary and commercial links with countries already politically independent were strained. Although colonial rivalries had come between France and Britain in the past, the parallel processes of decolonisation did not involve clashes between the former mother countries.

France and Britain both belonged to the Atlantic Alliance, and although they saw the Alliance's peacetime role differently, this difference of opinion did not lead to direct confrontation. The Atlantic Alliance was indeed dominated by the United States. Its credibility rested on the deterrent power of American conventional and strategic forces. While Britain accepted this supremacy without question, France rejected it, at least verbally; and whereas British loyalty could not be doubted, French loyalty was questionable and in question, at least until the Prague coup of 1968. The two states had made considerable financial sacrifices to attain the rank of minor nuclear powers. But this 'status symbol' only deceived a small proportion of public opinion in the two countries and made no impression at all beyond their own frontiers. If Britain had fared better than France in being given certain American atomic secrets, both countries had suffered technical setbacks. The isolated use of the British deterrent was out of the question, and that of the French less and less likely. Faced with this anomalous situation, did France and Britain pool their efforts to play a larger part in developing American nuclear strategy within the framework of the Alliance? No such collaboration took place, principally because of France's withdrawal from NATO. Did France and Britain try to use the Western European Union, a political and military institution created shortly after West Germany joined the Alliance, to sketch the outline of an embryo European military organisation, if only one dealing with armaments and logistics? Britain blocked this institution in its first years of existence and France boycotted it when Britain, more for political than military reasons wanted to revive it. As a result, when American politicians called for the gradual withdrawal of troops stationed in Germany, the two Western European states who, together with the United States and the Soviet Union, were responsible for the status of Berlin, did not seem to have discussed joint action to meet an eventuality which was being freely talked about in the American press.

France and Britain are both part of Western Europe. The political and economic organisation of this corner of the continent is a field which offered the two countries, as a result of the defeat and division of Germany, wide scope for action, so long as they kept within the bounds set by the more or less peaceful co-existence of the United States and the Soviet Union. But they did not take advantage of this scope for action. During the sixties Britain only slowly revised the Churchillian doctrine of three circles: the Commonwealth, the special relationship with the United States, and Europe; and it was only about 1966 that the order of priority was reversed in Europe's favour. In 1962 Gaullist France openly rejected the idea of the gradual integration of states with a view to building up a federation. Prepared to accept nothing other than a Europe of States, de Gaulle obstructed all institutional progress within the EEC. First playing his card of Franco-German co-operation, then balancing this in 1966 by his moves on the side of the Soviet Union, he excluded Britain, because of her allegiance to the United States, from his dream of a Europe extending as far as Russia. With the result that by 1969 Western Europe had no responsible executive, no legislative assembly and no money, and as we have seen, not even the embryo of an army. In short, it lacked all the attributes of sovereignty which the two states, rivals although members of the same system of protection, wished to preserve.

Have these countries at least retained their own status and relative power during the last decade? The advances made in thermonuclear technique continually devalue the deterrents of minor powers. Japan's industrial output is greater than those of France, Britain and, since recently, of West Germany. Britain and France, at one time influential in the Middle East, are now onlookers at a confrontation there involving the Americans and the Russians. The West is losing control in the oil-producing countries at a time when its fuel economy is largely dependent on oil.

Does responsibility for the political confrontations of the sixties, certainly sterile if not exactly hostile, lie with the deep-seated feelings of the French and British peoples? The answer seems to be no. Personal relations are excellent; cultural exchanges are taking place. However, historical memories still haunt those politicians who did not feel in time the Wind of Change.

Notes

1 Assises nationales de l'UNR, Bordeaux, 13–15 September 1959.
2 Press conference of 20 September 1962.
3 David Schoenbrun, *Les trois vies de Charles de Gaulle* (Paris, Julliard, 1965), pp. 411, 413.
4 Charles de Gaulle, *Mémoires*, vol. III Paris, Plon, 1959, p. 179.
4a Charles de Gaulle, *Mémoires d'espoir: le Renouveau, 1958–1962* (Paris, Plon, 1970), pp. 214–15.
5 Leonard Beaton and John Maddox, *The Spread of Nuclear Weapons* (London, Chatto and Windus, 1962), pp. 54 *ff*.
6 Beaton and Maddox, *The Spread of Nuclear Weapons*, p. 74.
7 Speech to the Ecole de Guerre, 3 November 1959.
8 Speech in Strasbourg, 23 November 1961; Press conferences 11 April and 15 May 1962.
9 Nora Beloff, *The General Says No* (London, Penguin, 1963), p. 152.
10 Henry A. Kissinger, *Les malentendus transatlantiques* (Paris, Denoël, 1965), p. 87.
11 Beloff, *The General Says No*, p. 160. The text of the Nassau communiqué is in *Keesing's Contemporary Archives*, 5–12 Jan. 1963, pp. 19174–5.
12 Miriam Camps, *Britain and the European Community* (Princeton NJ, Princeton UP), p. 469.
13 *Le Monde*, 10 January 1963.
14 Kissinger, *Les malentendus translantiques*, pp. 106, 109.
15 Georges Pompidou to the National Assembly, 5 November 1964.
16 Miriam Camps, *European Unification in the Sixties* (New York, McGraw-Hill, 1966), p. 196.
17 Lord Gladwyn, Speech to the Congress of the North Atlantic Treaty Association, Munich, 29 September 1966.
18 F. S. Northedge, 'British Foreign Policy' in *The Foreign Policies of the Powers* (London, Faber, 1968), p. 151.
19 Pierre Uri (Ed.), *From Commonwealth to Common Market* (London, Penguin, 1968), p. 64.
20 Christopher Mayhew, *Britain's Role Tomorrow* (London, Hutchinson, 1967), p. 104.
21 Neville Brown, *Arms Without Empire* (London, Penguin, 1967), p. 39.
22 Camps, *Britain and the European Community*, p. 237.
23 Camps, *Britain and the European Community*, p. 237.
24 Beloff, *The General Says No*, p. 104.
24a De Gaulle, *Mémoires d'espoir: le Renouveau, 1958–1962*, pp. 199–200.
24b De Gaulle, *Mémoires d'espoir: Le Renouveau 1958–1962*, p. 232.
25 Camps, *Britain and the European Community*, pp. 428 *ff*.
26 Camps, *Britain and the European Community*, pp. 468 *ff*.

27 Beloff, *The General Says No*, p. 159.
28 Dorothy Pickles, *Uneasy Entente* (London, Oxford UP, 1966), p. 32.
29 Pierre Drouin, *L'Europe du Marché Commun* (Paris, Julliard, 1963), p. 248.
30 Beloff, *The General Says No*, p. 147.
31 Camps, *European Unification in the Sixties*, p. 160.
32 Uri (ed.), *From Commonwealth to Common Market*, p. 63.
33 *Le Monde*, 20 October 1967.

Bibliography

Leonard Beaton and John Maddox, *The Spread of Nuclear Weapons* (London, Chatto and Windus, 1962).

Nora Beloff, *The General Says No* (London, Penguin, 1963).

Neville Brown, *Arms without Empire* (London, Penguin, 1967).

Miriam Camps, *Britain and the European Community* (Princeton NJ, Princeton UP).

Miriam Camps, *European Unification in the Sixties* (New York, McGraw-Hill, 1966).

Guy de Carmoy, *The Foreign Policies of France 1944–1968* (Chicago, Chicago University Press, 1970).

Pierre Drouin, *L'Europe du Marché Commun* (Paris, Julliard, 1963).

Henry A. Kissinger, *The Troubled Partnership* (New York, McGraw-Hill, 1965).

Charles de Gaulle, *Mémoires* Vol. III (Paris, Plon, 1959).
Mémoires d'espoir: le Renouveau, 1958–1962 (Paris, Plon, 1970) (trans. London, Weidenfeld and Nicolson, 1971).

Christopher Mayhew, *Britain's Role Tomorrow* (London, Hutchinson, 1967).

Wolf Mendl, *Deterrence and Persuasion* (London, Faber, 1970).

F. S. Northedge, *The Foreign Policies of the Powers* (London, Faber, 1968).

André Passeron, *De Gaulle parle – 1958–1962* and *1962–1966* (Paris, Fayard, 1963 and 1966), 2 vols.

Dorothy Pickles, *Uneasy Entente* (London, OUP, 1966).

David Schoenbrun, *Les trois vies de Charles de Gaulle* (Paris, Juillard, 1965).

Pierre Uri, (ed.), *From Commonwealth to Common Market* (London, Penguin, 1968).

Index

Index

384 *Index*

386 *Index*